GILLES DELEUZE'S LUMINOUS PHILOSOPHY

Hanjo Berressem

EDINBURGH
University Press

Edinburgh University Press is one of the leading university presses in the UK. We publish academic books and journals in our selected subject areas across the humanities and social sciences, combining cutting-edge scholarship with high editorial and production values to produce academic works of lasting importance. For more information visit our website: edinburghuniversitypress.com

© Hanjo Berressem, 2020

Edinburgh University Press Ltd
The Tun – Holyrood Road, 12(2f) Jackson's Entry, Edinburgh EH8 8PJ

Typeset in Warnock by Biblichor Ltd, Edinburgh

A CIP record for this book is available from the British Library

ISBN 978 1 4744 5071 3 (hardback)
ISBN 978 1 4744 5073 7 (webready PDF)
ISBN 978 1 4744 5074 4 (epub)

The right of Hanjo Berressem to be identified as the author of this work has been asserted in accordance with the Copyright, Designs and Patents Act 1988, and the Copyright and Related Rights Regulations 2003 (SI No. 2498).

Contents

Overture	v
Acknowledgements	vii
Abbreviations	xi
INTRODUCTION: LIGHTNING AND CRYSTALS	1
1. THE BIRTH OF PHILOSOPHY	21
2. PHILOSOPHY'S JOY	49
3. PHILOSOPHICAL TIMES AND SPACES	115
4. LUMINOUS PHILOSOPHY	169
CONCLUSION: WHITE LIGHT, WHITE LIFE	217
Bibliography	223
Index	234

For my daughter, Dahlia
and my wife, Nadine

Overture

> Letizia Alvarez de Toledo has observed that the vast library is useless. Strictly speaking, *one single volume* should suffice: a single volume of ordinary format, printed in nine or ten type body, and consisting of an infinite number of infinitely thin pages. (At the beginning of the seventeenth century, Cavalieri said that any solid body is the superimposition of an infinite number of planes.) This silky vade mecum would scarcely be handy: each apparent leaf of the book would divide into other analogous leaves. The inconceivable central leaf would have no reverse.
>
> Jorge Luis Borges, *Ficciones* (88)

In 1984 the German avant-garde rock band Die Tödliche Doris (The Deadly Doris) released their fourth album, which was titled, somewhat ironically, *Our Debut*. When the follow-up album, released in 1986, was called *Six*, this didn't make things any easier. In 1987, the band published a note that explained the 'missing' fifth album. *Our Debut* and *Six*, the note read, 'are constructed so that they correspond to one another in music, text and arrangement and comprise a unity if one plays them at the same time from the first piece on, on two record players with their respective A- or B-sides. The parallel pieces are the same length to the minute, from one track to the next, and offer a variety of textual, musical and semantic interactions. By playing both LPs together the invisible fifth LP, an immaterial LP emerges in the mind of the listener' (Tödliche Doris 2019). I have tried to achieve a similar effect with *Gilles Deleuze's Luminous Philosophy* and *Félix Guattari's Schizoanalytic Ecology*. Although each book can be read as an individual text, the two correspond to one another in such a way that when they are read together, an immaterial book emerges in the mind of the reader. Within the overall field of structural and thematic resonances between the two books, I will mark specific conceptual overlaps and cross-references by: square brackets, arrow, Guattari, page number. Where I discuss co-written texts, I will reference them as Deleuze and Guattari in *Gilles Deleuze's*

Luminous Philosophy and as Guattari and Deleuze in *Félix Guattari's Schizoanalytic Ecology*.

While Gary Genosko noted in 2002 that when Deleuze and Guattari is 'reversed as Guattari and Deleuze, it is a political reordering, an act of resistance, a dangerous heterodoxy' (42), in light of the growing interest in Guattari, especially after the ecological turn, this is, fortunately, no longer necessarily the case today. As Franco Berardi notes, 'there is a Deleuze without Guattari, and a Guattari without Deleuze, and then there is the rhizomatic machine put in motion by the encounter between the two' (2008: 43). If I reverse the conventional order of names in *Félix Guattari's Schizoanalytic Ecology*, therefore, I do so purely for reasons of symmetry.

Acknowledgements

It is impossible to note all of the influences that have shaped my image of Deleuzian philosophy. Much of what I say in this book has been said elsewhere, in more detail, and often better. There are so many excellent studies of specific aspects of Deleuze and of his encounters with other philosophers such as David Hume, Henri Bergson or Lucretius, that it is difficult for a more general study to be as meticulous and circumspect as these in-depth works. In other words, I consider the emergence of my text from within the overall field of Deleuze scholarship as a given. While writing, as happens so often, readings that converged with mine have tended to be both consoling and depressing, while diverging readings tended to be both scary and exhilarating. Which of these were more productive, and which to reference? Sometimes I found sentences in the work of other scholars that seemed to express perfectly what I needed a whole book to express. I can only hope that the resonant field I construct around them leads to a better understanding of these miraculous sentences. Sometimes I wished that I could write into the margins of other studies to add something about light or crystals that I thought might help to make that text clearer. I can only hope that in some situations, other scholars will find my text helpful in their reading of Deleuze.

There are at least three intersecting generations of Deleuze scholars. One cannot do Deleuze without encountering the groundwork: Ronald Bogue, Constantin Boundas, Tom Conley, Manuel DeLanda, Eugene Holland, Brian Massumi, Dorothea Olkowski, Paul Patton, John Protevi, Charles Stivale. Even where I have not referenced them directly, all of these have shaped my thought. I consider myself as a small part of the second generation: Rosi Braidotti, Ian Buchanan, Claire Colebrook, Paul Harris, Jay Lampert, David Rodowick. Cutting transversally across the generations, there is the group of philosophy-driven scholars, such as Keith Ansell-Pearson, Jeffrey Bell,

Levi Bryant, Miguel de Beistegui, Christian Kerslake, Daniel Smith, Alberto Toscano and James Williams.

The work of all of these scholars has influenced my text by way of what Arkady Plotnitsky calls modes of resonance or of interference. Although there are inevitably points of disagreement, in terms of shared interests, references and questions, their work provides the milieu from within which my text is constructed. If one takes seriously that concepts 'are forms of vibrations and are defined by resonances, through which they may amplify or temper each other' (Plotnitsky 2012: 20), every concept is, in the best of cases, charged by other concepts. In my case, these charges were sometimes an elaborate conceptualization, sometimes an insight, sometimes just a seemingly throw-away sentence or a reference to a specific passage in Deleuze. Had I engaged in detailed discussions with all such conceptual feedbacks, my text would have become even more ponderous than it already is. I have noted it, therefore, only where I think there is a productive link, mostly in reference to more recent work. This, however, does not imply that unmentioned feedbacks were in any way less important. Sometimes it was a remark that came just at the right time, or a passage that struck a chord: *kairos*. As scholarly work on Deleuze is immensely rich and diverse, there will always be both agreement and disagreement. What I mean by productive link is that, even where I am critical, I have tried to find a positive, good reason to engage with the work of other scholars. As Deleuze states in *Dialogues II*, 'objections have never contributed anything' (1).

While much of the following text was written with actual music playing in the background – Conor Oberst, The National, Mazzy Star, Sigur Ros – the communal work on Deleuze formed the conceptual music that played in the background while I wrote. In fact, the music did more than play in the background. Coming from within the computer, it seemed to literally pervade the text, as if the writing itself were musicalized. It felt similar with the conceptual music.

In the light of more recent philosophical trends, I should note that my text does not claim to prove that Deleuze's philosophy can explain the world and the ways in which it functions. More humbly, it aims to portray Deleuze's view of the world and to show that his philosophy forms a coherent figure of thought; that it is what Heinz von Foerster, who coined, in reference to the German mathematician David Hilbert, the term eigentheory, would perhaps have called an eigenphilosophy: a philosophy that in its own terms and in its inherent organization forms a coherent image (1993: 368–9). Even if Deleuze's concept of an anonymous life, for instance, might at first seem to run counter to common scientific differentiations between the animate and the inanimate, it is a concept that has a seminal position and function in the overall architecture of his philosophy. It is only after delineating this position and function that one can fruitfully address the question of the scientific viability of Deleuze's philosophy. For better or worse, my text will take the reader only to the beginning of such an investigation. Also, I should note that I take comfort, both conceptually and personally, in the conviction that my text is inevitably site- and time-specific. It has its own *chiaroscuro*, and its own diffracted consistency. It presents one image of Deleuzian philosophy that is actualized, for a moment, within a series of other images: *one click in a conceptual kaleidoscope*.

Apart from the ecology of scholarly influences that have shaped this text, there is an ecology of people who have helped it along and who are directly present in it in various ways. Marlene Mück and Jonas Neldner have helped formatting the text. Pauline Kosasih and Olga Tarapata worked tirelessly against my deplorable inability to provide exact references and complete bibliographical data. Sandra Danilovic and Wolfram Nitsch were kind enough to help with translations. Julius Greve and Jasmin Hermann read the text at various stages, providing feedback, and pointing out moments at which I lost the reader. The two anonymous readers provided extremely helpful input and ideas, while my copy editor Tim Clark was not only a joy to work with but also caught many potentially embarrassing mistakes. Finally, there were many discussions with my friend David DeSanctis, who gave me the space to explain, in the first place to him but ultimately to myself, what my project was all about, and who provided many invaluable insights, even though he might not have realized it at the time. He is the true Deleuzian. I am particularly grateful and happy that my brother Jürgen allowed me to use two of his paintings that, quite miraculously, worked perfectly as covers for the two books. As if he had known all along what I wanted to express. While I write about art, he is the true artist.

The publishing history of the two books started a long time ago in a far-away country. It was in a courtyard of Istanbul University that I first told Carol Macdonald, who has become a good friend between then and now, about the project. Her encouragement, advice and continuing support of the project, as well as her good spirit, have carried me through the writing of the text. Carol and the extended team at Edinburgh University Press, in particular James Dale, Naomi Farmer and Rebecca Mackenzie, have made the process of publishing it a truly joyful one. Joyful for me, I should add, if not for the three people who have in many ways suffered through the writing of the two books. My children Keyla and Dahlia have, too often, encountered a Dad who was lost in thought and sadly incommunicado. Sorry, kiddos! Then there is my wife, Nadine, who has not only provided countless ideas and inspirations for the project, but who has also, with infinite grace and patience, invited Deleuze to live with us in our home for far too long. If each of the books is dedicated to one of my kids, the whole project is dedicated to her. It is her presence that suffuses the project, as well as my life, like the warm rays of golden-hour sunlight.

*

Parts of this text have been published before, in different form or language. Parts of 'Philosophical Times and Spaces' were published in German as 'Unsichtbar werden: Die Mathematik des Verschwindens bei Gilles Deleuze' (2008), parts of 'Philosophy's Joy' were published as 'Crystal History: "You Pick Up the Pieces. You Connect the Dots"' (2012a). Parts of 'Luminous Philosophy' were published as 'Light, Camera, Action! The Luminous Worlds of Jacques Lacan and Gilles Deleuze' (2012b).

Abbreviations

Abbreviations used throughout the text correspond with the key below.

- AO: *Anti-Oedipus*
- B: *Bergsonism*
- C1: *Cinema 1: The Movement-Image*
- C2: *Cinema 2: The Time-Image*
- DI: *Desert Islands*
- DII: *Dialogues II*
- DR: *Difference and Repetition*
- EP: *Expressionism in Philosophy*
- ES: *Empiricism and Subjectivity*
- F: *Foucault*
- FB: *Francis Bacon: The Logic of Sensation*
- LB: *The Fold: Leibniz and the Baroque*
- LS: *The Logic of Sense*
- N: *Negotiations*
- PI: *Pure Immanence: Essays on a Life*
- PS: *Proust and Signs*
- S: *Spinoza: Practical Philosophy*
- TP: *A Thousand Plateaus*
- TRM: *Two Regimes of Madness*
- WP: *What is Philosophy?*

All translations from German sources are my own.

INTRODUCTION: LIGHTNING AND CRYSTALS

... a lightning storm was produced which will bear the name of Deleuze: new thought is possible; thought is again possible.
Michel Foucault, 'Theatrum Philosophicum' (908)

Difference is light, aerial and affirmative.
Gilles Deleuze, *Difference and Repetition* (54)

To believe, not in a different world, but in a link [*lien*] between man and the world, in love or life, to believe in this as in the impossible, the unthinkable, which none the less cannot but be thought.
Gilles Deleuze, *Cinema 2* (170)

WHEN I TALK about Gilles Deleuze's luminist philosophy, this luminism concerns two aspects of Deleuze's work. The first, conceptual aspect has to do with how Deleuze develops concepts from within registers of light, and with his use of both philosophical and scientific theories of light to position his philosophy within the overall philosophical field: *his philosophy's conceptual light*. The second aspect concerns the overall sentiment of Deleuzian philosophy. In this context, luminism stands for affirmation and for joy. For the warmth that, at all times and everywhere, suffuses Deleuze's thought. For a love of the world and of the living, and for a philosophy that aims, at all moments, to be adequate to the luminosity of that world: *his philosophy's affective light*. Although Deleuze's thought never shies away from coldness and cruelty, and although it knows pain, illness, suffering and death on a very intimate and personal level, it is never on the side of and it never celebrates negativity, or what Spinoza would consider to be bad encounters. It is a fundamentally positive thought. There is no dark romanticism in Deleuze's philosophy. No apocalypticism.

My intuition is that it is possible to develop a coherent image of Deleuze's philosophy from two of its conceptual leitmotifs: light and crystals. While each of these can function as an Ariadne's thread through Deleuze's work, if taken together, they can be more than that. As a figure of the complementarity of the plane of immanence and of the plane of consistency, which I will also call the plane of consistencies [→ **Guattari 11**], they can become a figure of not only that philosophy's conceptual architecture – its conceptual spine, that is – but also of its overall sentiment, mood or vibe; of the philosophical spirit I described above. Of its positivity and its affirmation of the world and of life. The notion of the complementarity of the plane of light and of the plane of crystals is one figure of this affirmation. As the complementarity of these two planes suffuses Deleuze's thought from its beginning to its very end, it allows us to draw a line of light through his work: a line of white light refracted by crystals.

After introducing the two motifs, I delineate Deleuze's theory of the crystal meeting of an actual with its virtual, as well as the crystallization of Deleuzian philosophy itself. Its dark precursors, perhaps. Having established the crystal spine of Deleuze's work, I trace his conceptualization of time and space, in particular his use of the topology of the real projective plane as the adequate space of thought from within which to conceptualize the formal difference between, but ontological identity of, the luminous plane of immanence and the plane of consistencies. In a final step, I draw on the complementarity of the photon to show that, for Deleuze, the most comprehensive plane of immanence is the photonic plane. Although the three steps concentrate on different aspects of their relation, the conceptual complementarity of light and of crystals forms the central problematic of my text.

Although the notion of light and luminosity is already present in 'Bergson's Conception of Difference' from 1956, and thus from the very beginning of Deleuze's thought, and although it remains an important motif, for instance in *Difference and Repetition*, it becomes especially intense in his work from the late 1970s onwards: *Les Cours de Gilles Deleuze: Spinoza* (1978), *Francis Bacon: The Logic of Sensation* (1981), *Cinema 1 & 2* (1983 and 1985), *Foucault* (1986) and *The Fold: Leibniz and the Baroque* (1988). While this luminism pervades my text at all times, it suffuses in particular its third part, in which I follow Deleuze's philosophical luminism into his work on painting and on the cinema. In the latter in particular, the crystal and the photonic series converge, not only in the sense that in the emulsion of celluloid film, light is caught by silver halide crystals.

Lightning

Difference and Repetition (1968), Desert Islands: and Other Texts 1953–1974 (2004), Gilles Deleuze from A to Z (1996, posthumous)

One image to which Deleuze returns repeatedly, from 'The Method of Dramatization', *Difference and Repetition*, *Cinema 1 & 2* and *What is Philosophy?* to the very last minutes of *Gilles Deleuze from A to Z* (*L'Abécédaire de Gilles Deleuze*), is that of a lightning bolt. While the Etruscans read ominous, divine messages into a flash of lightning, already Epicurus, as well as Lucretius in his epic poem *De Rerum Natura*, is critical of such religious divinations. To do science means: 'To investigate thorough the thunderbolt's nature . . . | Not to unroll the mystical verses of Tyre for nothing, | So to search out the sure prescription of god's hidden planning' (1973: 207). Lucretius sets the poetry of empiricism against fate. 'Fire's phenomenon must be grasped and the system celestial | Meteorology must be versified, lightning electric, | What end results they effect, from whatever cause they are carried' (199).

There is something in the air. You say this when you feel an electric charge in the atmosphere that affects your skin. Something makes the hairs on your arm stand up. Static. An initially diffuse electrical tension has built up. An electric potential. At a moment that is impossible to pin-point exactly, that electric charge has become perceptible. It has crossed the threshold from the unconscious to the conscious, which does not mean, of course, that it wasn't there before. Not only that: no atmospheric condition is ever without electric charge. There is no situation without a given electric intensity. Always already, everything is a complex interaction of electromagnetic fields, forces and intensities: barometric pressures, temperatures and humidities. Sometimes, however, through what a Freudian would call processes of condensation and displacement, the charged elements create a field with immense differences in intensity that somewhere and at some moment can no longer keep itself in balance. Its electrostatic dynamics reach a critical point of what might be called an electric potentiality or, less positively, an electric crisis. (On lightning and electricity, see also Barad 2015.)

Lightning is the figure of such an electric tension that has become unbearable within a specific meteorological situation and that discharges itself, as Lucretius would say, 'at an indeterminate place and an indeterminate moment' (1973: 53). This unpredictable, sudden and spectacular discharge, which can happen either within a cloud, between clouds or between clouds and the earth, resolves the tension between the differently charged electric fields. Within these dynamics, the specific branchings and spasms of the lightning bolt result from the electric fields through which the bolt finds the easiest way: the path of least resistance. In the case of a lightning bolt hitting the earth, the electric field builds up from the ground, which means that the bolt might be said to trace the path of least resistance quite literally in reverse.

To describe lightning as a part of and agent in highly unstable electric circumstances concerns first of all meteorology and physics, which measure and register electric fields down to the finest levels of technological perception. Today, it is a platitude to note that these registrations can never be infinitely precise, although the differences in intensity that make up the electric landscape are ultimately infinitely fine. In other words, they are continuous or analog. Every digital registration, therefore, is a reduction and a simplification that implies blackboxing. It reduces analog givens to digital data. It reduces the given to the given as given in order to make it scientifically manageable and mathematically countable. That both machinic and human perception are in themselves difference engines is something to which I will return.

The experience of being hit by lightning has been described as a discontinuity in the curve of life. As a differential. It is this affinity to questions of difference that makes lightning an interesting figure for a number of philosophies that not only have the notion of difference at their conceptual core, but that have also defined themselves as philosophies of difference. For good reason, Deleuze's philosophy has been included in this group. Keith Ansell-Pearson calls Deleuze a difference engineer; Deleuze himself has written *Difference and Repetition*. Still, I will argue that although difference is a crucial aspect of Deleuzian philosophy, it is not a philosophy of difference. What I will propose, instead, is that it is a philosophy of the complementarity of difference and indifference. As Niels Bohr noted on his coat of arms, contraries are complements, *'contraria sunt complementa'* (quoted in Capra 1982: 175).

In 'Difference in Itself', the first chapter of *Difference and Repetition* from 1968, Deleuze illustrates difference in itself by way of a sentence that has all the characteristics of a conceptual koan: 'Instead of something distinguished from something else, imagine something which distinguishes itself – and yet that from which it distinguishes itself does not distinguish itself from it' (28). The next sentence explains this logic by way of a lightning bolt that differentiates itself against the night sky, which does not, however, distinguish itself from the lightning bolt. 'Lightning, for example, distinguishes itself from the black sky but must also trail it behind, as though it were distinguishing itself from that which does not distinguish itself from it. It is as if the ground rose to the surface without ceasing to be ground ... Difference is this state in which determination takes the form of unilateral distinction' (28): *luminous philosophy*.

How can different energetic potentials and disparate electric elements within an energetic landscape be made to communicate? How do they become related differences, like the night sky and the lightning bolt? Deleuze calls the 'difference operator'

(DI: 97) that brings about this communication the 'dark precursor'. (The French original, *sombre precursor*, is also translated as obscure precursor). 'Thunderbolts explode between different intensities, but they are preceded by an invisible, imperceptible *dark precursor*, which determines their path in advance but in reverse, as though intagliated' (the word means, among other things, ornamented with a sunken or incised design, as opposed to a design in relief) (DR: 119). In 'The Method of Dramatization' Deleuze uses the same image. 'A lightning bolt flashes between different intensities, but it is preceded by an *obscure precursor*, invisible, imperceptible, which determines in advance the inverted path as in negative relief [intagliated], because this path is first the agent of communication between series of difference' (DI: 97). 'Intagliated', then, perhaps in the sense of invisible, indirect and dark, rather than in relief and clearly visible. Concave rather than convex. The French original's stress on invisibility is difficult to translate – '*en détermine à l'avance le chemin renversé, comme en creux*' (Deleuze 1968: 156), with *chemin renversé* as fractured path (an obscure, sunken road) and *en creux* as in the background (concave, discreet or imperceptibly) – 'It determines, imperceptibly and from the beginning, the obscure path', the fractured path taken by the lightning bolt.

The dark precursor is Deleuze's name for the invisible, subtle and unconscious tensions that precede the visible, less subtle and conscious phenomenon of the lightning bolt. It is the figure of the pre-individual dynamics out of which the individual lightning bolt emerges. It operates in what Deleuze calls the diverse, the field of great variety or multiplicity, as opposed to the field of the different. While the different, as related difference, belongs to the individual, the diverse, or difference in itself, belongs to nobody. It is anonymous. In Kantian terms, it belongs to the world as a thing-in-itself (*Ding an sich*) rather than as a thing-for-us. Leaving aside the question of whether the diverse might also be imagined as being 'in and for itself' (*an und für sich*), which will interest me in my conclusion, I will maintain for now that it belongs to, or quite literally is, *the world-in-itself*. To express this complicated state of affairs, Deleuze provides a second koan-like sentence, or perhaps zentence, which is a variation of the first: 'Difference is not diversity', he notes. 'Diversity is given, but difference is that by which the given is given, that by which the given is given as diverse' (DR: 222). Again: Deleuze's philosophy is not a philosophy of difference, but of the asymmetrical relation between difference and indifference or diversity.

The dark precursor operates infinitely fast, which means that it shows itself in perception only after the fact. It becomes visible only at the time of the phenomenon of lightning, although that phenomenon has started much earlier. As such, the dark precursor can only be deduced. It is, however, neither metaphor nor allegory. It is real and productive (see also, Lampert 2011: 66–9). In relation to the phenomenon of lightning, it is the name for the small, imperceptible degrees of tension from which the perceptible lightning develops, or from which it emerges. In other words, the dark precursor is the energetic, intensive unconscious of lightning. The sky is the unconscious of the lightning bolt, not its difference. That is what Deleuze notes in the above passage. Lightning is that which differs, but, at the same time, that from which it differs, the sky, does not differ from it.

One might transpose the description of lightning onto what one calls, in the field of mental phenomena, a flash of insight – a lightning bolt or a flashing light bulb as the image of a sudden inspiration or intuition [→ **Guattari 151**]. From a diffuse ecology of psychic fields, a mental milieu develops that is far-from-equilibrium. Suddenly, at an indeterminate place and moment, and 'in a period of time shorter than the shortest continuous period imaginable' (DII: 148), the psychic tensions discharge themselves into a bright idea. Albert Einstein stirs milk into his coffee cup. August Kékulé discovers the ring shape of the benzene molecule after day-dreaming the image of a snake seizing its own tail (*ouroboros*). The result of such processes is what one calls a sudden inspiration or intuition, which Deleuze calls, in 'Bergson's Conception of Difference', 'the joy [*jouissance*] of difference' (DI: 33).

In analogy to the development of a lightning bolt, one should imagine the sudden, unexpected intuition to be the result of smaller, infinitely networked and recursively stacked micro-thoughts, in the same way that every perception is the result of smaller, networked and recursively stacked micro-perceptions. As with real lightning, for every flash of insight there are fields of disparate micro-thoughts and imperceptible dark precursors. For Deleuze's philosophy, these pre-philosophical, pre-differentiated levels are of fundamental importance.

Although dark precursors bring disparate, not-yet-differentiated series into electric or intuitive communication, it is important that they are not synthetic. If they were, the ground of the world would not be a true multiplicity. In fact, Deleuze describes them as deterritorialized operators that create the potentiality for change. 'Once communication between heterogeneous series is established all sorts of consequences follow within the system. Something "passes" between the borders, events explode, phenomena flash, like thunder and lightning' (DR: 118). Yet, although there 'is no doubt that *there is* an identity belonging to the precursor, and a resemblance between the series which it causes to communicate' (119), this '"there is" . . . remains perfectly indeterminate' (119). Indifferent. In other words, in these dark dynamics there is neither a Hegelian sublation – in this context, Deleuze talks, in *Difference and Repetition*, of passive syntheses – nor predestination; neither teleology nor theology. Although 'the dark precursor is sufficient to enable communication between difference as such, and to make the different communicate with difference: the dark precursor is not a friend' (145). The heterogeneity and disparity that defines its beginning persists in the result of the process it brings about. Every harmony is a '*discordant harmony*' (146).

The American philosopher Charles Sanders Peirce deals with these problematics in his theory of abduction as the intuitive creation of a hypothesis. Peirce argues that the 'first premiss [sic] of all critical and controlled thinking' (1965d: 181) is what he calls the unconscious, intuitive perceptual judgement. A conscious abduction 'shades into perceptual judgement without any sharp line of demarcation between them' (181), so that the abduction is the making visible – the flash of insight – of the unconscious perceptual judgement. For Peirce, the beginning and the end of this process are not only connected, they are literally identical, or better: complementary. The perceptual judgement is the other side of the abduction and vice versa. Suddenly, again at an indeterminate place and moment and in a period of time shorter than the shortest period imaginable, from within a larger conceptual field, disparate elements orient themselves along a virtual axis of thought. As if the conceptual field was electromagnetically oriented, elements of thought gather along a mental vector, with intuition nothing but the name used to veil the existence of such unconscious perceptual and quasi-cognitive processes. The perceptual judgement brings about the seemingly intuitive flash of insight.

Man tends to guess right because the mind is immanent to nature and its operation. Drawing on a term he finds in Galileo, Peirce ascribes the natural sympathy or analogy between mind and nature to the *lumen naturale* (*il lume naturale*): 'If the universe conforms, with any approach to accuracy, to certain highly pervasive laws, and if man's mind has been developed under the influence of those laws, it is to be expected that he should have a natural light, or light of nature, or instinctive insight, or genius, tending to make him guess those laws aright, or nearly aright' (1965c: 604).

There are good reasons to criticize Peirce's tendency to idealize the natural light that makes clear and distinct abductions possible, and Deleuze criticizes Descartes for his conviction, in 'The Search for Truth by Means of the Natural Light', that such a natural, in Descartes' case religious, light exists. Against Descartes, according to whom the *lumen naturale* allows for clear and distinct perception, Deleuze, echoing his description of lightning, argues that Ideas 'are not illuminated by a natural light: rather, they shine like differential flashes which leap and metamorphose' (DR: 146). In fact, the philosophical question is inherently a question about light. 'The very conception of a natural light is inseparable from a certain value supposedly attached to the Idea – namely, "clarity and distinctness"; and from a certain supposed origin – namely, "innateness"', both of which are instruments of 'every orthodoxy, even when it is rational. Clarity and distinctness form the logic of recognition, just as innateness is the theology of common sense: both have already pushed the Idea over into representation' (146). Already here, Deleuze stakes a philosophical *chiaroscuro* against the postulate of the clarity of thought. 'The restitution of the Idea in the doctrine of the faculties requires the explosion of the clear and distinct, and the discovery of a

Dionysian value according to which the Idea is necessarily obscure in so far as it is distinct, all the more obscure the more it is distinct' (146). I will come back to the fact that if the light of philosophy is refracted and diffuse, the faculties should be as well. For now, let me stay with light. 'Underneath the large noisy events lie the small events of silence, just as underneath the natural light there are the little glimmers of the Idea . . . Problematic Ideas are not simple essences, but multiplicities or complexes of relations and corresponding singularities' (163). As Deleuze and Guattari note in *What is Philosophy?*, 'in the eighteenth century, what manifests the mutation of light from "natural light" to the "Enlightened" [*sic*!] is the substitution of *belief* for knowledge' (53). Philosophy, Deleuze implies, must find the adequate light in which to think. This light of thought should be refracted and diffuse. It should include darkness not as its negative other, but rather as its unconscious. It should not emanate from a divine source or figure, as in the radiant, golden aureole or nimbus that emanates from the body of a God, or the halo that radiates from the heads of Gods or saints. Although the sun has often taken the place of such a superior being, and although the notion of an aureole, as the inner disk of a corona, is also the name of a meteorological phenomenon that is caused by the diffraction of light, for Deleuze, light is neither a divine, religious light, nor the light of a philosophical principle such as reason. From Cicero, whose *naturae lumen* denotes the intrinsic seed of an a priori knowledge, to Thomas Aquinas, who considers the *lumen intellectus agentis* as an inborn, a priori principle of knowledge and intelligibility whose origin lies in God, the notion of a *lumen naturale* has denoted a transcendental light that allows for and guarantees intelligibility and the clarity of philosophy. In opposition, Deleuze's light is an immanent light; the given sunlight, but also moonlight or starlight. A light that suffuses reality, and that in its multiple diffractions, refractions and absorptions, scatters into all directions and creates, from within a given, pure multiplicity of light rays, the ordered multiplicities of illuminated objects. If there is a philosophical principle in Deleuze of which light is the figure, it is the principle of diversity and of difference: *light as the figure of multiplicity*.

At this point, however, Peirce's reliance on a *lumen naturale* should not distract from the parallelism of Deleuze's and Peirce's overall figure of thought. The perceptual judgement is faster than conscious deliberation, which merely tries to catch up with it after the fact. Like the dark precursor, the perceptual judgement is faster than both thought and philosophy. It operates on the pre-philosophical level of intensive differences and thus forms the unthinkable ground of perception that even the finest threads and filters of conscious thought cannot catch. Its intensity comes as a shock to thought and produces a philosophical vertigo, which 'reveal[s] to us that difference in itself that depth in itself or that intensity in itself at the original moment at which it is *neither qualified nor extended*' (DR: 237, emphasis added). This state of pure, intensive quantity makes up the vertigo of qualitative, differentiated thought, in and by which it is cancelled. 'Difference of intensity is cancelled or tends to be cancelled out in this system, but it creates this system by explicating itself' (228).

Let me pause to take a breath: Deleuze develops thought from within the unthought. Thought is not the difference of the unthought, it is its result. Its individuation. The unthought is not really unthought, in fact, in the same way in which the obscure is not really obscure. It is merely thought unconsciously, in the sense that the finer systems from which humans are assembled think and perceive in themselves. As Deleuze notes in *Cinema 1*, evoking an anonymous atomic perception, an atom 'perceives infinitely more than we do and, at the limit perceives the whole universe' (64). Similarly, in *The Fold* he stresses that 'if life implies a soul, it is because proteins already attest to an activity of perception, discrimination, and distinction' (92). The real lightning bolt is not an actual flash that stands in opposition to a flash of virtual thought. The chiasm that defines the logic of individuation is that every actual is always already virtual, and every virtual always already actual. Contemplations are operative in the actual, electric lightning bolt, in the same way that synaptic electricity is operative in virtual thought. Lightning is always already virtual, thought is always already electric: *flash philosophy*.

Deleuze stakes the level of an obscure unconscious out of which the conscious field emerges against the clarity of conscious thought. Despite his notion of the unconscious, nightly pit of the intelligence, Hegel sees the arbitrariness of the sign as heralding the absolute freedom of thought, while Deleuze sees it, in particular in *The Logic of Sense*, as a symptom of the closure of thought from the intensive world. Below the complexity of the discussion about difference and identity, Deleuze conceptualizes the complementarity of phenomenal world and noumenal thought. 'Difference is not phenomenon but the noumenon closest to the phenomenon' (DR: 222). Philosophy and art involve the purely quantitative phenomenon, because the phenomenal world is not their other; it is that out of which philosophy and art emerge in the first place. Their unconscious. If art and philosophy separate themselves from the world, they become irrelevant. Below difference, there is always complementarity: *the resonance between phenomenon and noumenon*.

The luminosity of the philosophy of lightning will suffuse Deleuze's theory and practice of philosophy, but also his practice of life. *Gilles Deleuze from A to Z*, the long interview with Claire Parnet, ends with a wonderful passage about 'Z as in Zigzag'. Deleuze connects the letter Z to the genesis of the world and to the emergence of thought from the unthought. Once again, Deleuze describes electric currents in relation to the phenomenon of lightning. How does a communication develop between different potentials within an energetic landscape? 'And once the journey of the dark precursor takes place, the potentials enter into a state of reaction, and between the two the visible event flashes, the bolt of lightning. So, there is the dark precursor and then a lightning bolt.' The relation between philosophy and world, Deleuze proposes, is similar to that of lightning and sky. Although philosophy distinguishes itself from the world, the world does not distinguish itself from philosophy. To be adequate both to itself and to the world, philosophy must trail the world behind: *the lightning of philosophy*.

Crystals: Actual X Virtual

Cinema 1 (1983), Cinema 2 (1985), 'The Actual and the Virtual' (1996, posthumous)

IN *CINEMA 2: The Time-Image* from 1985, Deleuze notes that 'life will no longer be made to appear before the categories of thought; thought will be thrown into the categories of life' (189). From within the Deleuzian terminology that forms the structural spine of my text this reversal concerns the relation between the virtual and the actual, the metaphysical and the physical. The immediate reference of Deleuze's statement is the demand of what he calls 'physical cinema' (204) to 'give me a body' (189). For that physical cinema, 'the categories of life are the attitudes of the body' (189), its affects, dispositions and postures in a larger ecology of the living. As such, the implications of its demand for a body go beyond the cinematic field. Ultimately, to throw thought into the categories of life is a 'formula of *philosophic* reversal' (189; emphasis added) that stakes physical philosophies against idealist philosophies that repress the body not only as a material matter-of-fact, but, more importantly, as a biophysical medium. (On the relation between materialisms and idealisms see Olkowski 1999: 103–4, 129.)

Idealisms tend to develop their conceptualizations from what Slavoj Žižek calls, taking up Hegel's concept of the 'immanence of the notion [*Immanenz des Begriffes*]' (1894: §451), the 'immanence of our thought' (2004: 53), while materialisms tend to share the belief that thought is a direct emanation of biophysical operations. Classic idealisms as well as more recent non-idealist idealisms have developed two ingenious figures of thought to negotiate the matter of the body. The first is inspired by Freud's topological figure of the unconscious as an inner exclusion (*inneres Ausland*), the second by the chronological figure of belatedness (*Nachträglichkeit*), which is captured by the expression 'always already'. The conceptual beauty of the image of an inner exclusion is that it relegates the material body to the space of the unspeakable; the conceptual beauty of a retrospective logic is that it considers the body as always already integrated into the fields of perception and cognition.

At moments when Deleuze becomes polemical, his polemics are often directed against the idealist tradition that disregards the ways in which our thought is attributed to life and vice versa. It is tempting, therefore, to read Deleuze as leaning towards the physical logic of corporeal production. Towards what Deleuze and Guattari call, in *Anti-Oedipus*, the factory as opposed to the theatre. Deleuze's physicalism, however, is not a simple materialism. Deleuze is equally critical of any materialist reduction of consciousness to a physics of thought and of its reliance on the hard sciences, in particular the neurosciences, to implement these physics. If there is a habit of thought in idealisms to repress the body, there is a complementary habit of thought in materialisms to repress the field of consciousness, which tends to evaporate within the logic of a pure physics. As Brian Massumi notes, materialisms set a 'natural a priori' against the 'cultural a priori' of idealisms (2002: 68). While idealisms celebrate the beauty and intricacy of thought, materialisms celebrate the beauty and intricacy of the body. Thoughts are complex firing patterns of neurons, images are complicated patterns of optical stimulation. There is no freedom of and in the mind because every thought is predetermined by physical operations. Ideas are purely electric, feelings merely chemical. For Deleuze, a shift from an idealist to a materialist logic is not an alternative to the idealist logic of an immanence of thought. If it were to promote the belief in a smooth, continuous progression from the physical to the metaphysical, considered for the moment as any realm that transcends the purely physical, Deleuzian philosophy would be nothing but a weak version of the philosophy of nature (*Naturphilosophie*).

One way for Deleuze to evade the impasses of the dualism of idealism and materialism is to conceptualize what I propose to call an intelligent materialism, in that such a materialism extends processes of perception, cognition and consciousness infinitely deep into the physical phylum. (Later, I will explain why the term infinitely, like the terms idealism and materialism, should be read within invisible quotation marks.) According to such an intelligent materialism, the world is pervaded, down to its infinitely small levels, by perceptual and cognitive machines, and thus by processes of discrimination and differentiation. As such a living, intelligent phylum forms the ungrounded conceptual ground of Deleuzian philosophy, Deleuze opposes any logic that takes matter to be an inherently lifeless material to be formed and animated by the virtuality of the spirit. There never was a time when matter was purely matter. The planes of life and of a philosophy that aims to be adequate to life have always been filled with machines that are simultaneously extensive and intensive or, in Deleuzian terms, simultaneously actual and virtual: *with crystals*.

This complementarity is why, a number of pages later in *Cinema 2*, Deleuze sets against the physicalist demand for the 'cinema of bodies' (198) an equally pressing demand – 'give me a brain [*cerveau*]' – that defines an 'intellectual cinema' as 'the other figure' (204) of mid-twentieth-century movie-making. It is never a question of choosing one position over the other, but of finding an adequate figure of thought to describe their complementarity. (Lynn Margulis notes that Descartes' fault was precisely 'splitting reality into human consciousness and an unfeeling, objective, "extensive" world that could be measured mathematically' (Margulis and Sagan 1995: 38, see also Ruyer 1952: 80).) Actual cinema and virtual cinema, actual philosophy and virtual philosophy: *transcendental empiricism*.

Deleuze's refusal to choose between the two sides implies that although he is deeply critical of the reduction of a logic of immanence to Žižek's immanence of our thought – both in the sense of the contention that immanence is purely of the mind, and in the sense that thought is in essence our thought – he never argues against the power and the importance of that field of thought, nor against the fact that the psychic reality of human beings is constructed within that field. What he is deeply critical of is the conceptual reduction of life, and of philosophy as a mode of conceptualizing life, to the operations of human thought and, more specifically, to the operations of the natural light of reason, as for instance in the philosophical and more generally cultural project of the Enlightenment. Invariably, Deleuze argues against the exclusion of a presumably obscure and dark physics from a clear and luminous metaphysics. Not in order to celebrate that darkness, however, but in order to show that this darkness is not at all dark. The paradox of Deleuze's luminism is: *the more light, the darker; infinite darkness equals infinite light.* The project of Deleuzian philosophy, one might say, is to complicate the common philosophical distribution of the registers of darkness and light.

At the same time, Deleuze invariably differentiates conceptually, or, as he will also call it, formally, between a physical and a metaphysical series that together make up the machinic plane of life, between the actual and the virtual. The question is what exactly is meant by together and by simultaneously. How exactly to think the alignment of the actual and the virtual? What does it mean when Deleuze notes, in *Difference and Repetition*, that 'every object is double without it being the case that the two halves resemble one another, one being a virtual image and the other an actual image. They are unequal odd halves' (209–10)?

I use the term crystal as one of my text's conceptual refrains because it is fundamental in Deleuze's conceptualization of the complementarity of the actual and the virtual. Deleuze takes the term from Gilbert Simondon, who uses it as a figure of the beginning of the individuation of living beings. Although it resonates in many ways with other Deleuzian terms, such as germinal life or larval subject, these latter highlight the chemo-biological aspects of individuation, while crystals and precursors highlight its more abstract aspects. The term is complicated, not least because its connotations are ambiguous. Sometimes, as when Deleuze refers to a crystal ball, or to the snow globe in Orson Welles's *Citizen Kane*, the crystal is a medium of either prescience or remembrance. (On the crystal of time, see Deleuze's lecture 'Image

Mouvement Image Temps' (1983b).) Deleuze also relates it to the precious, elusive ruby glass in Werner Herzog's film *Heart of Glass*. At other times, it is a jewel whose complex cut figures the fractures of the Kantian faculties that Deleuze stakes against the *lumen naturale*. In *A Thousand Plateaus*, Deleuze and Guattari talk of minorities as 'crystals of becoming whose value is to trigger uncontrollable movements and deterritorializations of the mean or majority' (106). For Alain Badiou, Deleuze himself 'appears as a fine point or a crystal that is at once translucent and timeless – just like the crystal ball of clairvoyants' (2000: 95).

At other times, the connotations of the crystal are more sinister. D. H. Lawrence maintains in 'Poetry of the Present' that 'there is no plasmic finality ... Life knows no finality, no finished crystallization' (1998: 76). This observation is mirrored in *A Thousand Plateaus*, where Deleuze and Guattari describe such a terminal crystallization in terms of the solidification of a 'representative' unconscious that has 'crystallized into codified complexes' (12). In the same book, however, they compare the function of the crystal in terms of interactions that living beings maintain with their sonorous and luminous environment to that of the crystal pick-up of a record-player, which 'acts upon that which surrounds it, sound or light, extracting from it various vibrations, or decompositions, projections, or transformations'. In these interactions, it 'has a *catalytic function*: not only to increase the speed of the exchanges and reactions in that which surrounds it, but also to assure indirect interactions between elements devoid of so-called natural affinity' (348, emphasis added; see also Ansell-Pearson 1999: 177).

Perhaps the most important structural characteristic of the crystal, however, is that crystallization denotes the process of 'taking on consistency' (TP: 433). This concerns both actual and virtual processes, as when a face 'crystallizes out of "different varieties of vague luminosity without form or dimension"' (168), or when Guattari talks about the 'crystallization of desire' (DI: 269). (On the crystal, Deleuze and Guattari also reference Olivier Messiaen and Paul Klee (TP: 551).) In *The Logic of Sense* from 1969, Deleuze talks of the processes of the individuation of singular events that are 'like crystals' in that 'they become and grow only out of the edges, or on the edge' (9). The last three examples, one might argue, already imply a first crystal series: *extraction, catalysis, consolidation*.

The references to consolidation and consistency evoke the image of a crystal as the figure of a specific aggregate state, or, in the case of the process of crystallization, as a figure of the shift from one aggregate state to another. From the amorphous to form; from anonymity to the individual. As in the case of a representational unconscious, however, there is always the danger of a 'too much' of crystallization. The crystal and processes of crystallization stand for the potentialities of individuation, but also for its dangers. (See also Jacques Lacan's reference to a 'crystalline style' in *Television* (1988: 45) as well its use in *Radiophonie*.)

A first link between the crystal and light is that the crystal is a medium of the refraction of light. It functions as a prism that turns white light into the spectrum of colours, like the liquid crystals of White Pond and Walden Pond in Henry David Thoreau's *Walden*, which are 'great crystals on the surface of the earth, Lakes of Light' (1906: 136). At the same time, Ralph Waldo Emerson describes the universe as 'a gigantic crystal, all whose atoms and laminae lie in uninterrupted order and with unbroken unity, but cold and still' (1850: 133). If the crystal is so ambiguous, why would Deleuze choose it as a figure of individuation?

The notions of the crystal and of crystallization are particularly prominent in *Cinema 2*, in which Deleuze develops the notion of the crystal-image, and in 'The Actual and the Virtual', a short text written shortly before his death and added in 1996 as a fifth chapter to the second edition of *Dialogues II*. In both texts, Deleuze relates the notion of the crystal and of crystallization directly to the relation between the actual and the virtual. Deleuze had envisioned 'The Actual and the Virtual' as the second chapter of a 'small book with very short chapters' (Dosse 2011: 455) to be entitled *Ensembles and Multiplicities*, of which 'Immanence: A Life' would have been the first chapter. It is a text that has all the hallmarks of a legacy. In crisp, telegrammatic sentences Deleuze draws up, from within the framework of individuation, a conceptual diagram of the twofold trajectory of the virtualization of the actual and of the actualization of the virtual. The text does not bother to develop its conceptual backgrounds or to argue its philosophical positions. At this stage of Deleuze's career, all of this has been done. In its almost staccato rhythm, the text is a fast-forward version of Deleuzism; a recapitulation that delineates in broad conceptual strokes the nucleus of Deleuzian philosophy. Perhaps, in that it describes its fundamental figure of thought, it might even be said to delineate its essence. (The term figure of thought should not be confused with Deleuze's term image of thought, which has mostly negative connotations, especially in opposition to 'a thought without image' (DR: 167). For diverging readings of the image of thought, see Beistegui 2004 and Bryant 2008.) To write about 'The Actual and the Virtual' is difficult, because every commentary runs the risk of violating its conceptual rigour and rhetorical austerity. Complicated arguments have given way to short statements that resonate conceptually with earlier texts. Written at the end of Deleuze's life, its simultaneously ascetic and bold style are the hallmarks of a late work. Much like 'Immanence: A Life', it is a complex conceptual echo chamber: *escrituras blancas*.

The manuscript of 'The Actual and the Virtual' is written in the same handwriting that, according to Badiou, Deleuze used in his correspondence: 'Long slanted, slashed letters that were trembling and determined at the same time' (2000: 4–5). The text begins with a refrain, a *nomos*, which Deleuze and Guattari describe in

A Thousand Plateaus as 'a prism, a crystal of space-time' (348). In the manuscript, this refrain, which aligns the three most fundamental elements of Deleuzian philosophy, is set off on the first, for the rest empty, page. Its melody forms both the conceptual kernel of the text that will follow, and of Deleuze's philosophy in general. Perhaps, it is this philosophy's most concise conceptual frame: 'philosophy is the theory of multiplicities, each of which is composed of a series of actual and virtual elements, there is no ...' (DII: 148). On the second page, the end of the sentence is repeated before it is completed: 'there is no ... purely actual object'. As Emerson noted, 'the soul is wholly embodied, and the body is wholly ensouled' (1950b: 218).

Setting out to be as comprehensive and abstract as possible, Deleuze talks, at the beginning of the text, of actuals and virtuals in the same way that he has talked, throughout his work, of multiplicities. They are not so much specified actuals and virtuals of something as they are actuals and virtuals *tout court*: material and immaterial elements. There is nothing else. The world's plane of consistency is made up of these pure actuals and pure virtuals: actual elements that show the characteristics of particles, and virtual elements that show the characteristics of waves, matter and memory, bodies and souls. Against the backdrop of this anonymous ground of the world, the text sets out to describe how this plane can be simultaneously both purely material and purely immaterial by tracing the process of the virtualization of actuals and the actualization of virtuals. While pure actuals and pure virtuals are the formally distinct elements that make up the plane, they are invariably collected into larger assemblages, each of which is, as Deleuze notes in 'On the Superiority of Anglo-American Literature', 'a multiplicity which is made up of many heterogeneous terms and which establishes liaisons, relations between them ... Thus, the assemblage's only unity is that of co-functioning: it is a symbiosis, a "sympathy". It is never filiations which are important, but alliances, alloys ... contagions, epidemics, the wind' (DII: 69). Such assemblages do not operate by way of natural affinities if these imply, like the *lumen naturale*, the idea of a natural or a metaphysical order, but according to the logic of elective, but also of forced affinities and resonances: Johann Wolfgang von Goethe's *Elective Affinities*, but also Witold Gombrowicz's infernalized version *Pornografia*. (On assemblages, see TRM: 179; on the replacement of the term 'desiring machines' by 'assemblages', see TRM: 177; on Gombrowicz and Deleuze, see my 'Fluchtlinien: Deleuze liest Gombrowicz' (2006).) If, as I noted, the conceptual challenge posed by Deleuze's philosophy is to think the mode of the alignment of the actual and the virtual series, then how to conceptualize living beings as assemblages of elements that are simultaneously purely material and purely immaterial? Is there a point where the two registers converge? Deleuze's philosophical rigour lies in refusing to accept such a point except at infinity. The crystal is the figure of this refusal of a convergence up to, but not at infinity, and thus of what I take to be the conceptual paradox that lies at the heart of Deleuzian philosophy.

In the text, the figure of the crystal defines the specific assemblages of in and of themselves unspecific, in Deleuzian terms, pure actuals and virtuals. 'This perpetual exchange between the virtual and the actual is what defines a crystal; and it is on the plane of immanence that crystals appear' (DII: 150). Parts of what Deleuze will later define as the luminous, informal plane of immanence, as the plane of pure light, are formed into crystals. At this moment, we are still far away from any human level. Crystallization should be imagined as happening between elementary particles in the sense that these denote, at specific scientific moments, the smallest elements possible; elements that are, ultimately, imperceptibly but not unthinkably small.

To define the very first moment of crystallization, Deleuze differentiates between three processes. Two of these describe movements that take place within already assembled crystals. Singularization describes the vector from actuals to virtuals and denotes the virtualization of actuals. Individuation tracks the opposite vector of the actualization of virtuals. As I will later argue, in relation to *Cinema 1* and *Cinema 2*, the first vector stresses the actual series in and of assembled crystals, while the second stresses their virtual series. Or: the first vector stresses processes of deterritorialization, the second those of territorialization. In the same way in which the actual never stops becoming virtual, 'the virtual never stops becoming actual' (DII: 150).

The third process, crystallization, concerns the first genesis of crystals *sui generis*. The creation of the field of potentiality that lies at the very beginning of individuation. It denotes the process of the very first conjunction of an infinitely small or faint actual, not just with any other infinitely faint virtual, but with its infinitely faint virtual. This moment I take to mark the beginning of Deleuzian philosophy. What specific, singular form does a field of moisture take on when the temperature drops below the freezing point? Crystallization is 'an individuation as process, the actual and its virtual: no longer an actualization but a crystallization' (150; see also C1: 81). The beginning of life is defined by such moments and processes of crystallization in which actuals are aligned with their virtuals and vice versa.

'The relationship between the actual and the virtual takes the form of a circuit, but it does so in two ways' (151), Deleuze notes. While all circuits run between actuals and virtuals, some run between a specific actual and other virtuals. 'Sometimes the actual refers to the virtuals as to other things in the vast circuits where the virtual is actualized' (151–2). In these cases, the relations between virtuals and actuals are those between different systems, as when a thought relates to a body in which it is not itself incarnated. In such cases, there is no crystallization. Sometimes, however, a particle-in-construction relates to a thought-in-construction in such a way that the thought is being incarnated in the body even while it virtualizes that body. In this case, 'the actual refers to the virtual as its own virtual, in the smallest circuits where the virtual crystallizes with the actual' (152). At such moments the two series converge towards or within one consistency to the point of becoming indiscernible.

Crystal convergences describe the genesis, but also the ongoing life, of living entities in that each lived moment is, quite literally, a new genesis. While one can conceptualize a superposition of the two series, in a formal sense, they must never, except at infinity, converge to a point of complete identification. Formally, the virtual never is the actual or vice versa. The two series converge only to the point of indiscernibility, never to the point of identity. There will always be infinitely small circuits between the two series, feedback loops by way of which they begin to assemble into crystal machines. The processes of crystallization, then, define processes of the genesis and the consistencing of living entities or, as Guattari calls them, consistencies [→ **Guattari 14**]. (On 'The Actual and the Virtual' see also Toscano 2006: 190–1; Olkowski 1999: 122.) Towards the end of his life Deleuze notes that he would be content to be remembered as a vitalist. This vitalism is already present in Deleuze's early work. As he notes in 'On Nietzsche and the Image of Thought' from 1968, 'we're looking for "vitality"' (DI: 142). Even earlier, in 'The Method of Dramatization' (1967), Deleuze writes that 'in systems of nature as well as artifice, we find intensive organizations, precursors, larval subjects, every sort of vitality, a vital character' (DI: 103). And, in *Nietzsche and Philosophy*, he notes that 'a thing, an animal or a god are no less capable of dramatisation than a man or his determinations. The method of dramatisation surpasses man on every side' (1983b: 79).

One might say, then, that Deleuze's philosophy rests on a sharp formal distinction between the categories of mind and the categories of matter – the virtual and the actual, the intensive and the extensive – and that it refuses to philosophically smooth out the differences between these series. As each series consists of a multiplicity of crystals, both are in themselves multiplicitous. As Deleuze and Guattari note in *What is Philosophy?*, 'it seems to us that the theory of multiplicities does not support the hypothesis of any multiplicity whatever . . . There must be at least two multiplicities, two types, from the outset. This is not because dualism is better than unity but because the multiplicity is precisely what happens between the two' (152). The complexity of Deleuze's philosophy lies in how it aligns the two series despite their formal distinction; in how it creates a space of thought within which they can be superposed onto each other without being conflated.

In *Cinema 2*, Deleuze evokes such an inherently chiastic conceptual space by treating the body in idealist registers and the mind in materialist registers. 'There is as much thought in the body', he notes, 'as there is shock and violence in the brain [*cerveau*]' (205). In other contexts, Deleuze calls this chiastic relation the 'reciprocal presupposition' (TP: 503; C2: 69) of two seemingly oppositional registers. On the one hand, 'the brain gives orders to the body which is just an outgrowth of it', on the other, 'the body also gives orders to the brain which is just a part of it' (C2: 205). Ultimately, the Deleuzian question recapitulates Spinoza's parallelism, of which more later. How to maintain a conceptual difference between the registers of mind and of matter even while maintaining that both series operate simultaneously, together and to an equal degree, not only within individual living beings, but within the world at large? If Deleuze is critical of both idealist repressions and materialist reductions, it is because both fail, although for exactly opposite reasons, to capture the specific form of inherent grace that belongs to both living movement and living thought. They are not adequate to conceptualize the way sentient matter expresses itself in both its material and mental aspects, and to the way it probes its way through the constantly changing set of circumstances that we call the world. If there is graceful movement in the body, there must be an equally graceful thought: *graceful philosophy*.

In his essay 'On the Marionette Theatre' Heinrich von Kleist defines grace as caught between the extremes of a pure materialism and a pure idealism. Between physics and metaphysics. In the text, the two positions are embodied by a puppet and a God respectively. As the narrator's acquaintance argues, in terms of grace, 'it would be almost impossible for a man to attain even an approximation of a mechanical being. In such a realm only a God could measure up to materiality, and this is the point where both ends of the circular world [*der ringförmigen Welt*] would join one another' (1972: 24, modified translation). The paradoxical meeting of the grace of God and that of a marionette. Humans, however, are neither puppets nor Gods, although, as both actual and virtual, they partake of both physics and metaphysics. Kleist negotiates these registers by way of unconscious and conscious movement, as the two series between which the game of grace plays itself out. In his fable about the inherent grace of the movements of the marionette, he describes the complicated relations between the puppeteer's consciousness, the puppet's body and the system of strings that quite literally mediate between them: consciousness, bodies, relations. (On Kleist's text, see DII: 125; TRM: 11–12.)

Humans lose their inherent grace when self-reflection intervenes in their unconscious, automatic corporeal movements. The narrator's acquaintance illustrates this loss of innocence by way of a young dancer's natural charm. He recounts that 'a short time before in Paris we had seen the statue of the youth pulling a splinter from his foot'. Later, after a swim, the young dancer was reminded of this statue when 'he placed his foot on the footstool to dry it and at the same glanced into a large mirror'. From 'that very moment on, an inexplicable change took place in this young man ... An invisible and inexplicable power like an iron net seemed to seize upon the spontaneity of his bearing, and after a year there was no trace of the charm that had so delighted those who knew him' (Kleist 1972: 25).

While materialisms and idealisms attempt to locate grace in the physical or the metaphysical extremes respectively, Kleist maintains that for humans, pure grace can only be regained at a conceptual point-at-infinity at which materialism and idealism become identical. In fact, Kleist might be said to evoke the one-sided topology of the real projective plane that will form Deleuze's plane of philosophy: 'We can see the degree to which contemplation becomes darker and weaker in the organic world, so that the grace that is there emerges all the more shining and triumphant. Just as the intersection of two lines from the same side of a point *after passing through the infinite* suddenly finds itself again on the other side – or as the image from a concave mirror, after having gone off into the infinite, suddenly appears before us again – so grace returns after knowledge has gone through the world of the infinite, in that it appears to best advantage in that human bodily structure that has no consciousness at all – or has infinite consciousness – that is, in the mechanical puppet, or in the God' (25, emphasis added). In the return of a grace that has gone through infinity, infinite unconsciousness equals infinite consciousness. Infinite actuality equals infinite virtuality. 'Therefore, I replied, somewhat distracted, we would have to eat again of the tree of knowledge to fall back into a state of innocence? Most certainly, he replied: That is the last chapter of the history of the world' (26, modified translation): *Kleist with Deleuze*.

While Kleist finds an ideal grace in the figure of a young male dancer, Deleuze finds moments of pure grace in the unreflected, light movements of children through their various milieus that he describes in 'What Children Say'. Girls especially embody a smooth, soft and elastic, dispersed elegance and plasticity. A dispersed essence, like the one Deleuze describes when he notes in *Proust and Signs* that 'there is, in the group of young girls, a mixture, a conglomeration of essences' (74). For Deleuze, both philosophy and art should not only celebrate but in fact embody the wild charm and grace of young girls, such as Pearl from Nathaniel Hawthorne's *The Scarlet Letter* or Priscilla from *The Blithedale Romance*. In the latter, Hawthorne's description of girls' light movements, which he opposes to the heavy clumsiness of boys, might in fact be read as an allegory of the relation between a minor and a royal philosophy. Priscilla is 'running and skipping, with spirits as light as the breeze of the May morning, but with limbs too little exercised to be quite responsive; she clapped her hands, too, with great exuberance of gesture, as is the custom of young girls when their electricity overcharges them' (1852: 72). As Hawthorne notes, 'girls are incomparably wilder and more effervescent than boys, more untamable and regardless of rule and limit, with an ever-shifting variety, breaking continually into new modes of fun, yet with a harmonious propriety through all. Their steps, their voices, appear free as the wind, but keep consonance with a strain of music inaudible to us. Young men and boys, on the other hand, play, according to recognized law, old, traditional games, permitting no caprioles of fancy, but with scope enough for the outbreak of savage instincts. For, young or old, in play or in earnest, man is prone to be a brute' (88). As Deleuze states in *Dialogues II*, 'charm is the source of life just as style is the source of writing . . . those who have no charm have no life, it is as though they are dead. But the charm is not the person' (5).

The probably most frivolously serious, and at first sight extremely unphilosophical Deleuzian provocation to philosophy is that it should install a becoming-girl in its conceptual heart because 'the girl is certainly not defined by virginity; she is defined by a relation of movement and rest, speed and slowness, by a combination of atoms, an emission of particles: haecceity. She never ceases to roam upon a body without organs. She is an abstract line, or a line of flight. Thus girls . . . produce *n* molecular sexes on the line of flight in relation to the dualism machines they cross right through . . . It is not the girl who becomes a woman; it is becoming-woman that produces the universal girl . . . Knowing how to age does not mean remaining young; it means extracting from one's age the particles, the speeds and slownesses, the flows that constitute the youth of *that* age' (TP: 266–7). (On haecceity and Duns Scotus, see Toscano 2006: 7; Ansell-Pearson 1999: 181; on haecceities as 'subjectless individuations', see TRM: 310, 351.)

At the centre of Deleuze's crystal alignment of the categories of thought and of life lies his belief that 'the identity of world and brain . . . does not form a whole, but rather a limit, a membrane which puts an outside and an inside in contact, makes them present to each other, confronts them or makes them clash' (C2: 206). In this paradoxical alignment, the body is 'no longer the obstacle that separates thought from itself, that which it has to overcome to reach thinking. It is on the contrary that which it plunges into or must plunge into, in order to reach the unthought, that is life. Not that the body thinks, but, obstinate and stubborn, it forces us to think, and forces us to think what is concealed from thought, life' (189). One might object that these are merely the playfields of philosophy and of aesthetics. Marx and Engels, however, proposed a similar reversal when they noted that 'life is not determined by consciousness, but consciousness by life. In the first method of approach the starting point is consciousness taken as the living individual; in the second method, which conforms to real life, it is the real living individuals themselves, and consciousness is considered solely as *their* consciousness' (1983: 15).

| THE BIRTH OF PHILOSOPHY

> ... to be present at the dawn of the world.
>
> Gilles Deleuze and Félix Guattari, *A Thousand Plateaus* (280)

> See now a star is born | Looks just like a blood orange | Don't it just make you want to cry?
>
> Conor Oberst, 'Ladder Song', *The People's Key*

> And that's how the world was born. There is always a dark precursor that no one sees and then the lightning bolt that illuminates, and there is the world. Or that's also what thought must be, that's what philosophy must be. That's the great Zed, but that's also the wisdom of Zen. The sage is the dark precursor, and then the blow of the stick comes, since the Zen master is always distributing blows. The blow of the stick is the lightning that makes things visible.
>
> Gilles Deleuze, *Gilles Deleuze from A to Z*

Becoming Crystal

'On Gilbert Simondon' (1966)

IT IS SYMPTOMATIC of Deleuze's twofold thought that some scholars read his work as a celebration of deterritorialization and schizophrenia, while others consider it a celebration of a vitalist monism that relies on the overall oneness of all things. In the light of my introduction, both of these readings miss the point. What makes Deleuze's work singular is precisely that it aligns these two extremes in such a way that at a philosophical point-at-infinity, schizophrenia and monism become identical. How to think the paradox of this conceptual simultaneity?

My initial proposition is that Deleuze defines the subject of philosophy as a living entity – an assemblage of crystals or desiring-machines as the 'molecular machines or micro-machines' that denote the 'non-organic system of the body' (DI: 219) – that negotiates its life-course within two complementary multiplicities. One physical, the other metaphysical; one actual, the other virtual. This twofold vectorization is why Deleuzian philosophy addresses to an equal degree both physical and metaphysical registers. In terms of physics, Deleuze develops a philosophical theory of the crystallization and individuation of molar material aggregates from within the extensive multiplicity of an anonymous, informal life that he conceptualizes variously as atomic (*The Fold: Leibniz and the Baroque, What is Philosophy?*), as molecular (*Anti-Oedipus, A Thousand Plateaus*) or as photonic (*Cinema 1 & 2*). In terms of metaphysics, Deleuze develops a complementary theory of the crystallization and individuation of molar immaterial aggregates from within the metaphysical, intensive multiplicity of a field of an anonymous, informal consciousness that is diffracted into the fields of sense (*The Logic of Sense*), sensation (*Francis Bacon: The Logic of Sensation, Proust and Signs*) and science (*Capitalism and Schizophrenia 1 & 2, What is Philosophy?*).

If one takes this twofold crystallization seriously, one is led to ask how exactly individual philosophies crystallize from within the fields of an actual and a virtual multiplicity. With Deleuze, this question is especially intriguing. As he himself never stopped pointing out, one of the most important inspirations for his philosophy was a text that itself proposes such a twofold assemblage theory: Gilbert Simondon's two-part study *L'individuation à la lumière des notions de forme et d'information* (*Individuation in the light of the notions of form and information*). Its first volume, published in 1964, concentrates on material, actual processes of individuation while its second volume, *L'individuation psychique et collective*, published in 1989, concentrates on virtual, immaterial processes. Despite the chronology, it is difficult to not feel this structure reverberate through Deleuze's equally complementary books *Cinema 1* and *Cinema 2*.

While Simondon's text forms part of what Simondon calls the adjacent milieu that provides the energy that allows the crystallization of Deleuze's philosophy, other milieus of crystallization precede this already academic moment. Earlier texts, but also Deleuze's youth, his visits to and encounters on the beach, school, the both meteorological and political atmosphere of France, his health, movies, courses taken at the university, discussions, books, a certain slant of light – the unregistered moments and processes that make up the uncharted plasma of Deleuzian philosophy, its pre- and non- or a-philosophical, unconscious hinterlands. (I will differentiate between the terms pre- and non- or a-philosophical in the same way that Deleuze differentiates, in *Francis Bacon: The Logic of Sensation*, between the pre-pictorial and the non- or a-pictorial.)

Two years after the publication of Simondon's book Deleuze writes an elaborate review that is in fact more of a homage: 'On Gilbert Simondon'. The text throws light on the debate about how much of Deleuzian thought is a translation of science into philosophy. In fact, Deleuze himself notes that Simondon's text 'demonstrates the extent to which a philosopher can both find his inspiration in contemporary science and at the same time connect with the major problems of classical philosophy – even as he transforms and renews those problems. The new concepts established by Simondon seem to me extremely important; their wealth and originality are striking, when they're not outright inspiring. What Simondon elaborates here is a whole ontology, according to which Being is never One. As pre-individual, being is more than one – metastable, superposed, simultaneous with itself. As individuated, it is still multiple, because it is "multiphased", "a phase of becoming that will lead to new processes"' (DI: 89). Simondon is seminal for Deleuze on at least two more counts. The first concerns conceptual couples such as actual and virtual as well as molecular and molar. The second concerns what Simondon's theory says, implicitly, about the crystallization of Deleuze's philosophy and its individuation as a composition of thought, or, in Deleuzian terms, as a philosophical plane of consistency. Simondon's scientific description of individuation as a crystallization is something Deleuze will draw on throughout his philosophy.

For Deleuze, to consider living beings as crystals might at first sight seem unusual, or even counter-intuitive in that unlike the terms germs and larvae, which evoke the field of the animate, one tends to think of crystals as inanimate. If that is so, then why choose crystals as figures of life? The reasons for Deleuze's seemingly surprising choice become clear in the light of Simondon's text. Simondon deals with the process of crystallization, which shares important characteristics with what science will later call emergent behaviour, as the first step in the genesis of form from chaos. As an 'elementary individuation' (2005: 91), crystallization concerns the formal discontinuity between 'crystalline and amorphous states' (73): between order and disorder; between form and chaos.

In terms of physics, the process of crystallization is defined by the development of a communal directionality among singular elements. Mathematically, this spatial and structural alignment, which, as I noted, Deleuze and Guattari define in *A Thousand Plateaus* as the process of 'taking on consistency' (433), can be described as the development, within an originary multiplicity, of specific eigenvectors that can be modelled in a vectorial phase-space. 'The crystalline state would be characterized by the existence of privileged directions in the crystallized substance . . . In opposition, the amorphous state, which includes the gaseous, the fluid or the solid amorphous (glassy) states, is characterized by the absence of privileged directions' (Simondon 2005: 73). Crystals are the effects of polarization, of the spatial orientation that defines, for instance, electromagnetic, gravitational or light waves. In terms of physics, crystals have, or at least can be given, specific eigenvalues. (I have dealt in detail with the terms eigenvector and eigenvalue in *Eigenvalue* (2018)). A crystal is not only the effect of polarization, however, it is also its cause. It is 'at the same time the effect and the cause of that polarization of matter without which it would not exist. Its structure is a given structure [*structure reçue*], because a germ has been necessary; *but the germ is not substantially different from the crystal*; it is included in the crystal, which has become a larger germ' (89, emphasis added). In other words, crystallization does not take place within a field of already formed matter. Rather, it is the very process of the organization of matter, and thus of the creation of form from chaos. 'Individuation as a process is not tied to the identity of a material, but to the modification of a state' (79).

As such, the process of becoming crystal denotes nothing less than the first moments of the creation of individual life from a life considered as anonymous, or, in mathematical terms, as uneigen. Singular voices emerge from the mad, anonymous clamour of being. In these voices, the sheer exuberance of that anonymous, chaotic life is bound and economized. Although there might be good reasons to read crystallization as a tragic process that subtracts from the pure energy of that anonymous life, Deleuze treats it, first of all, in terms of a philosophical proposition about the ultimate identity, at a conceptual point-at-infinity, of monism and multiplicity. A 'single and same voice for the whole thousand-voiced multiple, a single and same Ocean for all the drops, a single clamour of Being for all beings' (DR: 304). In a process that is comparable to the refraction of white light into the spectrum of colours, crystallization refracts monism into multiplicity. (See also Ruyer's use of William Stern's term *'unitas multiplex'* (1952: 15).) According to Simondon, crystallization happens only in 'metastable' (2005: 75) systems because only such systems provide a 'potential energy' (68) that forms a landscape of freely circulating energetic differences that is needed to fuel processes of crystallization: 'We call potential structural energies those that express the limits of the stability of a structural state, which form the real source of the formal conditions of the possible geneses' (77). In 'On Gilbert Simondon' Deleuze reads this state of energetic potentiality as a state of difference of and in intensity, which is a terminology that will find its way into his discussion of difference and diversity, or, in a different terminology, of quality and quantity, in *Difference and Repetition*. As he notes, 'a metastable system thus implies a fundamental *difference*, like a state of dissymmetry. It is nonetheless a system insofar as the difference therein is like *potential energy*, like a *difference of potential* distributed within certain limits. Simondon's conception, it seems to me, can in this respect be assimilated to a theory of intensive quanta, since each intensive quantum in itself is difference' (DI: 87).

As Simondon notes, in a terminology that aligns the biological and the abstract, all processes of individuation proceed from a 'crystal germ' (2005: 78). If the milieu that it still is allows it to draw enough potential energy from it, it chooses a possible mode of actualization from that milieu, which, in Deleuze's terminology is a virtual field of unlimited, infinite potentiality. 'The difference between the germ and the amorphous milieu that can be crystallized is not constituted by the absolute presence or absence of a structure, but by the state of actuality or virtuality of that structure' (Simondon 2005: 87). As Simondon notes, the relation does not arise between two terms that would already be individuals. As an aspect of the internal resonance of a system of individuation, it is part of the state of that system. The crystal is thus 'not just a result, but an *environment* of individuation' (DI: 86): *becoming before being*.

These genetic parameters concern both the moment at which a becoming crystal occurs, and the forms individual crystals take. Together with the germ, the amount of potential energy caught in the germ remains immanent to its energetic milieu. As a result of this continued involvement of an individual germ in the various stresses and constraints of its adjacent milieu, each crystal is singular. Each individuation depends on 'the compatibility of the crystalline systems of the germ and the substance that constitutes the milieu of that germ' (Simondon 2005: 87). Becoming crystal, therefore, relies on the two related dynamics of the capture and transformation of energy, and on the maintenance of a structural stability within the energetic, or intensive milieu. 'The stability of the individual is the stability of their association' (82).

Crystals, as 'intermediates between the amorphous and the purely crystalline states' (85), have three main characteristics: an 'active orientation', 'a true interiority' and an 'internal historicity' (86). To maintain that they have an active orientation is to say that they are, to some degree, self-organizing. To maintain that they have a true interiority implies that their formational and informational individuation concerns an internal architecture that defines the complex relations pertaining to its heterogeneous elements, as well as the relations between these elements and the crystal as a whole. 'The individuation exists on an intermediate level between the order of magnitude of the single elements and that of the molar ensemble of the complete system' (97). To maintain that they have an internal history implies that they have not only a spatial but also a chronological coherence and consistency. In other words, crystals have structural memories and biographies. (On Simondon and crystallization, see Beistegui 2004: 302–5; Bryant 2008: 217–19; on Simondon see Toscano 2006: 136–56; Massumi 2002; Ansell-Pearson 1999: 90–6.)

All of these characteristics, however, do not yet address the fact that we tend to think of crystals as inanimate. In the language of physics, this concerns Simondon's statement that 'the crystal milieu is a periodic milieu' (2005: 94). This strict periodicity links crystallization to the inorganic rather than the organic, and thus to physics rather than to biology. This incongruence does not escape Deleuze, who remarks specifically that in Simondon 'the differences between physical and vital individuation receive a profound exposition' (DI: 88). Deleuze addresses this directly in a passage of *The Logic of Sense* that provides a very concise summary of the most salient points of Simondon's theory of individuation: 'Everything happens at the surface in a crystal which develops only on the edges. Undoubtedly, an organism is not developed in the same manner' (103). Despite these differences between physical and biological crystallization, however, Deleuze maintains that '"larval" or "embryonic"' (DI: 94) subjects can be understood as the results of processes of crystallization.

Should this identification of the inanimate and the animate be read as a conceptual weakness in Deleuze, or is there a way to make sense of what I called his unusual choice? To answer this question, let me turn to *A Thousand Plateaus*, in which Deleuze and Guattari address that similarity as the one between physical and biological crystallization. In terms of physics, 'on a crystalline stratum, the amorphous milieu, or medium, is exterior to the seed before the crystal has formed; the crystal forms by interiorizing and incorporating masses of amorphous material. Conversely, the interiority of the seed of the crystal must move out to the system's exterior, where the amorphous medium can crystallize . . . To the point that the seed itself comes from the outside. In short, both exterior and interior are interior to the stratum. *The same applies to the organic stratum*: the materials furnished by the substrata are an exterior medium constituting the famous prebiotic soup, and catalysts play the role of seed in the formation of interior substantial elements or even compounds. These elements and compounds both appropriate materials and exteriorize themselves through replication, even in the conditions of the primordial soup itself. Once again, interior and exterior exchange places, and both are interior to the organic stratum. The limit between them is the membrane that regulates the exchanges and transformation in organization . . . and that defines all of the stratum's formal relations or traits' (49–50, emphasis added).

Apart from stressing once more that crystallization has to do with genesis, Deleuze and Guattari see the important similarity between physical and biological crystals in their membranic quality and in the projective topology, of which more later, that this quality introduces into the world. As membranes, 'they place internal and external spaces into contact without regard to distance. The internal and the external, depth and height, have biological significance only through this topological surface of contact. Thus, even biologically it is necessary to understand that "the deepest is the skin". The skin has at its disposal a vital and properly superficial potential energy. And just as events do not occupy the surface but rather frequent it, superficial energy is not localized at the surface but rather bound to its formation and reformation' (LS: 103–4). For Deleuze, as for Simondon, these similarities suffice to describe living beings as crystals. Today, some scientists indeed consider all biological membranes and cell membranes to be forms of liquid crystals.

German physicist Erwin Schrödinger addressed the problem of the inanimateness of crystals by proposing, in his 1943 essay 'What is Life?', that molecular assemblages are 'aperiodic crystals' (1967: 61), noting that 'the cases of a molecule, a solid, a crystal are not really different. In the light of present knowledge they are virtually the same' (58). Schrödinger therefore proposes to replace the common distinction between three states of matter by one basic distinction. Matter is either formless or formed. Either chaos, as in amorphous, or crystal. Either 'gas = liquid = amorphous' or 'molecule = solid = crystal' (59). In terms of these two series, molecules and crystals are quite literally identical. 'The atoms forming a molecule . . . are united by forces of exactly the same nature as the numerous atoms which build up a true solid, a crystal' (60). At the same time, inorganic and organic crystals follow different principles of assembly. While the growth of inorganic crystals into larger structures is periodic, which means that it proceeds by way of the simple repetition of a 'generative physical algorithm', organic crystals grow aperiodically. 'A small molecule might be called "the germ of a solid". Starting from such a small solid germ, there seem to be two different ways of building up larger and larger associations. One is the comparatively dull way of repeating the same structure in three directions again and again. That is the way followed in a growing crystal. Once the periodicity is established, there is no definite limit to the size of the aggregate' (60).

While periodic crystals concern non-organic assemblages, aperiodic crystals, which develop 'without the dull device of repetition' (60), concern organic assemblages, the 'more and more complicated organic molecule in which every atom, and every group of atoms, plays an individual role, not entirely equivalent to that of many others (as is the case in a periodic structure). We might quite properly call that an aperiodic crystal or solid and express our hypothesis by saying: We believe a gene – or perhaps the whole chromosome fibre – to be an aperiodic solid' (61).

In Deleuze's terms, one might say that while the growth of periodic crystals implies a process of pure repetition, that of aperiodic crystals implies processes of both difference and repetition. For Schrödinger, all singular lives are compounds of molecules that can be considered as organic crystals within which 'each atom and each group of atoms plays its specific role, which is not always equal to that played of many others' (110). Although Schrödinger considers some compounds to be more aperiodic than others, formally, genes, cats, plants and human beings are all aperiodic crystals. Despite shifts in science, Lynn Margulis subscribes to Schrödinger's notion of a crystal life. 'Life, Schrödinger held, is matter which, like a crystal – a strange, "aperiodic crystal" – repeats its structure as it grows' (Margulis and Sagan 1995: 12; see also Kauffman 2000: 5–8; for a critique of Schrödinger, see Ruyer 1952: 172).

There are aperiodic differences, then, in the periodic repetitions that make up the individuation of living beings. Deleuze and Guattari talk about a similar deregulation of the periodic order in *A Thousand Plateaus* when they state that an organism is *'more deterritorialized* than a crystal: only something deterritorialized is capable of reproducing itself' (59–60, emphasis added). In the light of aperiodic crystals, however, the shift from allo- to autopoietic behaviour should be measured in degrees of aperiodicity, not in terms of a difference in kind between periodicity and aperiodicity. In fact, as inherently aperiodic, living organisms might be defined as liquid- or as quasi-crystals, in which the molecules do not show the strict orientation that defines solid crystals, although they have a certain degree of positional orientation. This distinguishes them from liquids, which have no directional order at all, as well as from solids, which are strictly oriented. Translated into physical terms, the molecules in liquid crystals do not point in the same direction all of the time, although they show a tendency to point, over time, in one specific direction. They have developed a habit of pointing in a specific direction, one might say. The aggregate state of liquid crystals, therefore, is an inherently intermediate one between free, liquid movement and strict, crystalline stability. What are called quasi-crystals are defined by a similarly aperiodic state, although that state has less to do with orientation than with the fact that they are not defined by one lattice but by a multiplicity of lattices.

Deleuze uses the notion of the crystal to align physical and biological parameters. In terms of today's notion of aperiodic crystals, there are structural similarities between physics and biology that transcend the common differentiation between the dead and the living. In questioning that categorical differentiation, Deleuze's vitalism recasts that difference as that between periodicity and aperiodicity. In many ways, Deleuzian philosophy is a challenge to invent concepts for such new differentiations. What is important beyond the difference between physics and biology, however, is that crystals are singularities. In fact, Simondon's theory of crystallization might be said to address the creation of singularities understood as alignments of actuals with their virtuals, as Deleuze had described in 'The Actual and the Virtual'. 'Today' Deleuze notes, 'we are uncovering a world of pre-individual, impersonal singularities. They are not reducible to individuals or persons, nor to a sea without difference' (DI: 143): *singular diversity.*

As the series of actual and virtual are formally distinct, one should consider crystallization as two parallel processes, or rather as two aspects of the same process. Although it seems at first sight to contradict the idea of complementarity, Deleuze maintains that philosophy must maintain this differentiation at all costs. Similar to the way matter crystallizes itself into specific forms from within a field of vectorial and energetic potentiality, mind crystallizes itself into specific thoughts from within a field of vectorial and intensive potentiality. In analogy to material bodies, immaterial thoughts come into being by way of an orientation that creates a conceptual vector-space from an originary multiplicity. This is why for Deleuze, philosophy, as the art of thought, needs to open itself up to the non-philosophical: to link its concepts to pre- and non-philosophical plateaus and parameters. Only under this condition does it make sense to talk of crystals as 'seeds of thought' (WP: 69).

Out of Turbulence, Philosophy; or: In the Light of Lucretius

'Lucretius and the Simulacrum' (1961)

In 1961, three years before the publication of Simondon's first volume, Deleuze published the essay 'Lucretius and the Simulacrum', in which he reads Lucretius' epic poem *De Rerum Natura* as an early example of the philosophy of nature (*Naturphilosophie*); a conceptual field not yet so clearly differentiated into the scientific, the philosophical and the artistic as it tends to be today. Although written about in a different mode, and almost two millennia earlier, Lucretius' topic is the same as Simondon's: the emergence of an order of things from within a state of pure multiplicity.

Lucretius' story of the genesis of the world aligns two givens. The first is a rain of atoms or '*corpora*' (Nail 2018a: iv) that fall vertically through an inherently empty space. In Lucretius' conceptual diagram, this fall designates a timeless state before the birth of the world; timeless because without change. The second given is the infinitely small deviation of one single atom from the universal vertical vector: a contingent, symmetry-breaking swerve that Lucretius calls the *clinamen*. This minimal swerve triggers a cascade of atomic collisions that brings about an overall state of atomic disorder, or, more positively, of atomic multiplicity from within which all things – all crystals; that is – emerge. The moment of the *clinamen* is of fundamental importance for the genesis of the world, as well as, on a much smaller scale, for the genesis of Deleuzian philosophy. Already 'Lucretius and the Simulacrum' contains *in nuce* much of what will become Deleuzian philosophy.

It is symptomatic of the positivity, grace, beauty and the affirmative erotics of his philosophy that Lucretius chooses Venus Anadyomene, the goddess of beauty, love and creation, as his muse. Born from the foam of the sea, Venus is quite literally the figure of the crystallization of form from chaos; the figure of a liquid-crystal life. As such, she presides over nature as the most fundamental field of multiplicity out of which philosophy emerges. In Lucretius' philosophy, Deleuze finds a philosophy of immanence that provides both a conceptualization and a celebration of nature. It has nature as its both 'speculative and practical' (LS: 266) object. It is a 'hymn to Venus-Nature' (267).

If the best philosophy is the one that has the best concept of nature, the strength of Lucretius' philosophy lies in his conceptualization of nature as infinitely varied and everywhere alive and productive. For Lucretius, nature 'must be thought of as the principle of the *diverse* and its production' (266, emphasis added). As a 'heterogeneity of elements' (266) that form a sum of 'parts which cannot be totalized' (267), Lucretian nature forms an infinitely complex assemblage that surveys its own planes of consistency and composition from within those planes by way of swarms of partial observers. As it is based on a multiplicity of singularities – what Lucretius calls *corpora*, although Deleuze stresses that Lucretius considers these also 'to be "specific seeds" or sperms' (271), which adds them to the Deleuzian series of germs, larvae and crystals – that constantly enter into new constellations, nature 'does not assemble its own elements into a whole' (LS: 266). In *A Thousand Plateaus*, Deleuze and Guattari will express this fundamental diversity by way of the formula $n-1$, which describes the topology of the rhizome as constituting 'linear multiplicities with n dimensions having neither subject nor object, which can be laid out on a plane of consistency, and from which the One is always subtracted [$n-1$]' (21).

In Deleuze's rich and obscure reading of Lucretius, each of its sentences, many of which have a syntactic and conceptual rigour and a staccato rhythm that is similar to that of 'The Actual and the Virtual', expresses a disposition and an attitude that is indispensable for an understanding of Deleuzian philosophy. Like Lucretius' text, Deleuze's text is suffused with a deep love of the given world and of nature; a love of life and diversity that everywhere values the multiplicity and complexity of the concrete situation over the simplicity of the abstract ideal. In fact, as Deleuze argues in 'Plato and the Simulacrum' – the companion piece which precedes the text on Lucretius in the appendix of *The Logic of Sense*, although it was published five years later – ideals are invariably the source of sadness. It is against this ideal sadness that Deleuze stakes a voice that celebrates nature as the source of joy, multiplicity, positivity and creativity. In all of its aspects and through all the phases of his work, Deleuze's philosophical plane of consistency is based on this deep love and affirmation of multiplicity and of life.

In terms of this affirmation, Lucretius and Deleuze share the same muse: the figure of Venus, graceful and loving, but also infamously vengeful and dangerous. Thomas Nail takes up Lucretius', Deleuze's and Michel Serres' praise of Venus in *Lucretius I: An Ontology of Motion*, which provides a reading of Lucretius that is informed by quantum field physics and contemporary neo-materialisms. Nail acknowledges that 'Deleuze's suggestion for an immanent reinterpretation of atomism has had an incredible influence on all subsequent philosophical interpretations of Lucretius' (2018a: 9), and that 'the echoes of a return to Lucretius can be heard in the footnotes of "new materialist" philosophers' (10), all of whom 'emphasise the original Deleuzean imperative to reinterpret Lucretius according to the creative and immanent power of matter itself against the modern atomist interpretations of mechanistic particles and psychological freedom' (10). This said, however, Nail, like most of these new materialists, stakes his reading against Deleuze's 'explicitly idealist' (16) position, as 'when he says that "the atom is that which must be thought, and that which can only be thought . . . it is the object which is essentially addressed to thought"' (16).

'More than Deleuze, it is the historical intuitions of Michel Serres that have inspired the present work' (9), Nail explains, and indeed, Serres is perhaps more of a materialist than Deleuze, although both align particles and waves from within a logic of complementarity, rather than putting, as Nail does, all of their conceptual trust in the fluid [→ **Guattari 45–50**]. Their elective affinity suffuses Serres' reading of Lucretius in 'The Solid, The Fluid, Flames' from *Hermes V*, in which he stakes the 'paradoxical topology' (1994: 65) of the flame against a logic that stakes a physics of solid-state crystals against the fluid. In a passage that refers back to Robert Musil's novel *The Man Without Qualities*, Serres describes a car accident in a superposition of the terminologies of lightning, the *clinamen* and information theory. 'Something had gone out of line, a transversal movement. This is local chance. And very exactly the *clinamen*. And even more exactly a deviation from equilibrium. The declination, the lightning that strikes from the cloud, or the signal that rises clearly above the overall noise' (72). Although it is in the footsteps of Serres that Nail reads Lucretius' text as an example of a fluid dynamics *avant la lettre*, arguing as he is from within the logic of quantum physics, he notes that Serres' *The Birth of Physics* 'focuses primarily on the description of vortical and turbulent motion in the text' (2018a: 9).

In fact, when Nail refers to fluidity, he is less concerned with a specific aggregate state than he is with neo-materialist readings of quantum physics that propose an overall quantum-field and wave-function ontology. 'Quantum fields are in a state of superposition' (84), he notes. Nail's notion of the fluid does not concern a typology of aggregate states in which gases, and in extension aerosolic atomisms, of which more later, share some characteristics of fluids and vice versa. His proposition about fluidity is purely ontological. For Nail, when light floods a room, this flow is fluid only in the sense that it is defined as a superposition of eigenstates that is collapsed by its measurement: *ontology collapsed into epistemology*.

Similarly, a wave is fluid in the sense that it shows behaviour that is incompatible with that of a particle and its adherent philosophical pointillisms. Ultimately, it is the proposition of the ontological antecedence of continuous movement over discontinuous, discrete states – of folds over lattices – that drives Nail's, as well as many other neo-materialist, readings: *becoming before being*. 'Bergson', Nail writes, 'who published his first book as a close study of *De Rerum Natura*, similarly writes "it is movement which is anterior to immobility"' (92): *process materialism*. As Nail exclaims, 'beneath the paving stones of atoms, the sandy loam of flux!' (4). Deleuze, perhaps, would use a slightly different slogan: *within the paving stones, the beach!*

Unlike Nail, Deleuze considers becoming and being as two aspects of a complementary ontology in which the actual and the virtual are in a relation of reciprocal presupposition rather than of conceptual or chronological antecedence, whether that means materialism before idealism or vice versa. The logic of complementarity allows Deleuze to circumvent the mutual simplifications that tend to define debates between materialisms and idealisms, such as Nail's argument that idealisms are reactions to the atomist notion of discrete entities: 'If the world is nothing but things then it is sterile, dead, and we must affirm the idealist principle of creation or change *ex nihilo*' (74), adding in a footnote that 'this is precisely the ontology of becoming put forward by Whitehead and partially adopted by Deleuze' (82). (See, however, Ruyer: 'An atom is not a completely installed mechanism that functions. It is incessant activity; it forms itself without stopping' (1952: 157).)

Nail claims that 'in its broadest interpretation the rejection of *ex nihilo* creation is synonymous with the rejection of all metaphysics *tout court*. This includes the notions of eternal forms, immaterial forces, and even theories of space and time as ontologically fundamental. What all metaphysical theories share in common is the notion that some ahistorical substance, which is not matter in motion, is responsible for the ontological origins of material motion' (2018a: 75). In *Being and Motion*, Nail argues that Deleuze is guilty of metaphysics because he does not give priority to the ontological flux of matter. While 'becoming means continual flux, matter, and motion for Deleuze', it equally 'means difference, thought, and stasis' (2018b: 37). Like Whitehead, Deleuze 'always ends up reintroducing stasis or immobility into his definition of motion' (37). Furthermore, Deleuze conceptualizes the realm of thought as immaterial and the plane of immanence as a-historical. Let me disregard, for the moment, that Nail misunderstands Deleuze on all three counts. More productively: how near is Deleuze to Nail's notion, via Lucretius, of 'a creative material flow [*genitalia corpora*] (1.58) from which things come' (2018a: 75)?

In the chapter 'The Pleats of Matter' in *The Fold: Leibniz and the Baroque*, Deleuze argues, via Leibniz, that, although for entirely different reasons, 'the atomistic hypothesis of an absolute hardness and the Cartesian hypothesis of an absolute fluidity are joined all the more because they share the error that posits separable minima' (6). From Leibniz, Deleuze extracts a figure of thought that is adequate to an elemental complementarity of particles and waves, rather than a figure of thought that prefers either one or the other. Leibniz posits a 'flexible', 'elastic body' that 'has coherent parts that form a fold, such that they are not separated into parts of parts but are rather divided to infinity in smaller and smaller folds that always retain a certain cohesion. Thus a continuous labyrinth is not a line dissolving into independent points, as flowing sand might dissolve into grains, but resembles a sheet of paper divided into infinite folds' (6). As in Lucretius, the world consists of elemental folds: 'Folds of winds, of waters, of fire and earth, and subterranean folds of veins of ore in a mine' (6). Folds are everywhere. 'Water and its rivers, air and its clouds, earth and its caverns, and light and its fires are themselves infinite folds' (140). This is why 'the model for the sciences of matter is the "origami", as the Japanese philosopher might say, or the art of folding paper' (7): *philosophy in the folds*.

When Deleuze notes the 'morphogenetic movements' of matter, biological 'invagination' (6), a 'motivating force' that resides in matter, an 'affinity of matter for life and a 'spirit in matter' (7), these decidedly immanent forces share much more with the notion of 'a creative material flow' than with what Nail considers as metaphysical theories. 'Corporeal flows are in constant stochastic motion and are therefore morphogenetic, bending, swerving, twisting, and so on' (2018a: 127), Nail notes. Let me highlight, therefore, the affinities between Deleuze's luminous philosophy and Nail's process materialism rather than their differences.

The beginning of *De Rerum Natura*, in which Lucretius describes Venus as a loving and protective force that calms the elements, stresses Venus' genetic power: 'Gracious Venus, who makes teem the sea with vessels astride it, | Makes the earth lush with vital crops under sky signs rotating, | Since through you is conceived every creature by kind having life breath; | Risen in birth they contemplate the sun's luminescence. | Scurry the winds before you, the clouds skirt and scud at your coming; | Sweet and wondrous manifold earth with bouquets praising your buds | Calm and unruffled the sea for you ripples smilingly waving; | While skies above gleam tranquil for you in your spreading refulgence' (1973: 13). Under her influence, the sunlight becomes, as in a luminist painting, diffuse and peaceful: *diffuso lumine caelum*. Venus is not only the goddess who can calm the elements, however, she is herself elemental. In and through her, the atmosphere, the world and, with it, philosophy, become plays of darkness and light: *philosophical luminism*.

In *Hermes V*, Serres notes that, in philosophical terms, 'the difference between light and dark can only be defined in exceptional circumstances. Only when there is no atmosphere and there are no turbulent gases' (1994: 60). As no atmosphere is ever 'homogeneous and isotrophic', light is everywhere 'scattered' and light rays are 'constantly diffracted'. The result is 'a mixture of confusion and clarity'. The 'clear opposition between light and dark exists only in a philosophy of empty, which means geometrical space' (60). What we need, Serres implies, is a field philosophy, whether the field is that of elemental space, topological space or the space of quantum gravity. (On Lucretius and Bergson, see Serres 1994: 59.) Elemental space does not allow for clear distinctions. Venus is the figure of this atmospheric, elemental *chiaroscuro*. She is 'a triple lumina: visibility, vision, and view all at the same time. The froth of matter floats ashore, like Venus, on a bubble, but the materiality of air, water, and earth only comes to appearance with the addition of the *lumina solis* [light of the sun], or fire ... Air, water, earth, and fire thus form the elemental body of Venus' (Nail 2018a: 31). An encounter between Nail and Deleuze can take place less in the context of Nail's process materialism in which Nail repels Deleuze, somewhat in the way a magnet repels the like pole of another magnet, than in his unfolding of Lucretius' luminous philosophy, although Deleuze links material force also, and specifically so, to 'the propagation of light and the "expulsion into luminosity"' (LB: 7). In careful and detailed readings, Nail delineates Lucretius' luminous philosophy, in which Venus is the figure of an immanent, elemental light that is in turn the figure of the conceptual multiplicity that suffuses Lucretius' philosophy. As such, Lucretius comes to pre-capitulate Deleuze's critique, vis-à-vis Descartes and Peirce, of a clear and distinct *lumen naturale*. It is from within Lucretius' *lumen veneris*, that Deleuze argues against later idealist theories of the emanation of light. As Nail argues, '*De Rerum Natura* does not aim to reveal some metaphysical truth by the transcendent light of god or reason, or some other abstract Platonic principle like the "rays of the sun and the clear shafts of the day [*radii solis neque lucida tela diei*]"' (2018a: 167). In contrast, Lucretius' 'transcendental empiricism' (168) is 'an entirely immanent philosophy in and through the senses which will nonetheless allow us to understand the transcendental structure ... of the things of sensation' (167): *Deleuze in Lucretius*.

Like Deleuze's, Lucretius' light is made up of a multiplicity of diffractions and absorptions that are sustained by a constant solar emission. 'Light is what is emitted, reflected, and absorbed by matter, but is also itself material. The permeating flow of light is the invisible material condition for visibility which all of matter partakes in and responds to as it receives and reflects its flows. The light given by the sun is thus re-given again and again on Earth, circulated and re-circulated' (36). While the turbulences of this light can be more or less subdued, as Serres noted, there is never a state without turbulence. 'The dust motes that we can see with the eye are like the rerum [*sic!*] that are driven by the invisible corporeal flows of air that swirl turbulently' (186).

This multiplicity of light, its diversity and the singularity of its instantiation, allows one to conceptualize a luminous philosophy. (On light and the elements see also Deleuze's 'Michel Tournier and the World Without Others', in LS: 301–21.) As Nail notes, 'the photonoetics of Lucretius' transcendental materialism is neither the light of god nor the light of the mind, but the real immanent light of things themselves in relation' (2018a: 168). As with the *clinamen*, this multiplicitous, diffracted light comes into being when the white light emitted by the sun is diffracted at the moment that the obstacle of the material world is put in its way. In an eminently Lucretian image, Dante begins his *Divine Comedy* with the image of a ray of light that, after having crossed the endless and timeless cosmic void, hits the periphery of a world at the smallest of angles. At this moment of a *clinamen*, the white light refracts into the infinite spectrum of colours. Before that? 'Lucretius could not be more clear on this point: there was no moment when matter was just a laminar rain and then swerved' (77): *white light, laminar rain*.

Like the quantum field, light forms a medium within which observations and measurements take place. 'Lucretius was more right than he realised about this problem in fundamental physics. Light allows us to observe but does not allow us to observe our observation independent of the light used to observe' (249). Knowledge is invariably an entangled knowledge, Karen Barad would say. 'Lucretius presciently defines colour as the waveform of light. Colours, he says, cannot exist without light' (248). Using 'the recurring poetic image of the "shores of light" [*luminis oras*], Lucretius argues that 'corpora never emerge into the light. This is the case precisely because the corporeal flows are also flows of light itself. Light does not emerge into the light without something else illuminating this light. Just as light is the material condition of visibility which itself is not visible to the eye as a thing, so the corpora are the material conditions of sensation and are therefore nothing sensible' (248). They are too fast for sensation, Deleuze would note. They are the unconscious of sensation. (I take the sensible to denote the material side of the perceptual process.) 'Corpora are the luminous flows of motion that connect things together with each other and allow them to illuminate one another. Just as we can learn more about the structure of light by examining the things which light illuminates (mirrors, paintings, windows, etc.), so we can learn more about the corpora through the folds or things which they create for sensation' (167). We learn about the invisible, dark precursors of lightning by way of lightning, Deleuze would say.

Deleuze's philosophical question vis-à-vis Lucretius is very basic: Where will Lucretius' love of life, of light, and of the given, elemental multiplicity take thought and philosophy? Where did it take Lucretius? All Deleuzian philosophy does, one might say, is to set out to answer, with full philosophical rigour, this basic question. Although Deleuze is often considered to be ambiguous or even contradictory, there is nothing in his work – not one sentence, not one word – that will ever put into question the dispositions he finds in Lucretius. They will be refined, they will be tested against other planes of consistency such as those of psychoanalysis and of capitalism, they will be applied to the cinema, to painting and to music, they will be expressed in different terminologies, but Deleuze will never betray them. Even in the face of the most horrible wars, of illness, of pain and of death, Deleuze's philosophy never wavers. All horrors, many of which Deleuze knows all too intimately and talks about with great passion and compassion, are immanent to the positivity and luminosity of a more profound anonymous life. Invariably, Venus should win out over Mars. (For recent dark readings of Deleuze see Kaufman 2012; Culp 2016).

The text's most beautiful passages are those in which Deleuze describes, via Lucretius, nature as a field of infinite variety. 'In our world, natural diversity appears in three intertwined aspects: the diversity of species, the diversity of individuals which are members of the same species, and the diversity of the parts which together compose an individual. Specificity, individuality, and heterogeneity' (LS: 266). Everywhere, there is change and becoming. 'Nature is not attributive, but rather conjunctive: it expresses itself through "and", and not through "is". This *and* that – alterations and entwinings, resemblances and differences, attractions and distractions, nuance and abruptness' (267). Everything and everybody is part of this conjunctive tissue 'formed out of connections, densities, shocks, encounters, concurrences, and motions' (268).

The singularity of each element is the result of the infinite variety of the world. As in Simondon, the elements are immanent to the milieu, which must allow for the conjunction of elements and is always implicated in the process of compounding. Playing with the double meaning of elements, Deleuze notes that in Lucretius bodies are born into an ecology of 'complex settings, each one of which gathers a maximum number of elements of the same shape: earth, sea, air, ether, the *magna res* or great strata which constitute our world and are connected to one another through imperceptible transitions' (271–2). Both the body and its milieu are determined by the diversity of causal series. 'A body is born not only of determined elements, which are like the seeds producing it; it is born also into a determined setting, which is like a mother suited for its reproduction. The heterogeneity of the diverse forms a sort of *vitalism of seeds*, but the resemblance of the diverse forms a sort of pantheism of mothers' (272, emphasis added). While Venus is mother, however, she is also the lover of Mars.

All attempts to contain the multiplicity of nature by way of ideals such as 'Being, the One and the Whole' are sadly inadequate to Lucretius' productive nature, and thus 'theological forms of a false philosophy' (267). In 'Plato and the Simulacrum', Deleuze will differentiate between 'two formulas: "only that which resembles differs" and "only differences can resemble each other"' (LS: 261). The first formula is Platonic, the second, although Deleuze does not explicitly say so, is Lucretian. The first promotes a logic of resemblance and of icons, the second a logic of 'deep disparity' (261) and of simulacra. In *Difference and Repetition*, Deleuze will argue that in philosophy, icons are figures of identity whose function it is to cover up the true world of *simulacra*, 'all identities are only simulated, produced as an optical "effect" by the more profound game of *difference and repetition*' (xiv, emphasis added). This is why '"to reverse Platonism"' means to 'make the simulacra rise' (LS: 262). As Deleuze states, 'resemblance proceeds from the diverse as such and from its diversity' (271). (On simulacra and light, see also LS: 273.)

Why and how does Lucretius' *clinamen* allow philosophy 'to think the diverse as diverse' (266) and to think of nature as always already multiplicitous? The first characteristic of the *clinamen* is that it occurs in an indeterminate place and at an indeterminate moment, the second is that it takes place in 'a smaller time than the minimum of continuous, thinkable time' (276). The first characteristic denies the possibility of a transcendentally grounded teleology, instigating in its stead an inexplicable spark of electric life. This is why Deleuze calls the *clinamen* 'a kind of *conatus*' (269). Quite inexplicably and without apparent reason, the *clinamen* introduces movement and change into stasis: *white noise before pink noise*.

This chronology, however, is complicated because its second characteristic is that the time of the *clinamen* has always already passed, because it has happened too swiftly for thought. This is why the *clinamen* cannot be thought of as randomly disturbing an initially ordered state of affairs. Rather, it designates the instantaneous moment of the genesis of multiplicity and as such an originary state of multiplicity and complexity. It has 'always been present: it is not a secondary movement, which would come accidentally to modify a vertical fall. It has always been present . . . The clinamen is the original determination of the direction of the movement of the atom' (269): *pink noise before white noise*.

From this point of view, the state of thought is always already to be in the middle of constantly changing circumstances. It will remain in this middle because every change, or bifurcation, implies a new swerve. These continuous changes are, like the dark precursor, too fast for thought. (Deleuze and Guattari describe this state of being from the beginning in the middle as rhizomatic. If the *clinamen* is invariably too fast for human thought, perhaps the singular, pure virtuals, the pure actuals and the fragile crystals that were present at the moment of genesis were more adequate to its speed.)

What is one to make of the fact that Deleuze states that this multiplicity 'manifests neither contingency nor indetermination' (270)? That a multiplicity cannot be fully determined and still remain a multiplicity is evident. It is more counter-intuitive to state that multiplicity cannot be fully contingent. Isn't multiplicity a figure of chaos, and hasn't contingency become the modern password to enter a non-essentialist worldview? The reason for Deleuze's dismissal of both necessity and contingency is his contention that both terms are equally inadequate to nature. Already at the moment of its genesis, the world is a deterministic chaos, because the atomic multiplicity already and invariably contains small pockets of order. Faint, fragile crystals have always already developed at the edges of chaos. Ordered vortices have always already emerged in the chaotic, stochastic turbulence. Pockets of order have always already emerged in the sea of disorder. *Corpora* are always already *res*. Because Lucretius' multiplicity is invariably more ordered than the pure chaos of Greek philosophy and less ordered than the pure order of the rationalists and the priests, both chance and necessity are equally inadequate terms to capture the natural processes of life that take place within the world's multiplicity and complexity. It is not the difference between the extremes of the fluid and the solid, therefore, that counts. What counts is the middle. The logic of flames. The in-between states of liquid crystals and aerosols. As all change can be measured in terms of the relative or the complete change of states of matter, such as becoming-aerosol, becoming-fluid or becoming-solid, Deleuze notes in *Bergsonism* that it might be wrong to conceive of 'vital differences or variations' as 'purely accidental' (98).

In other words, the logic of the *clinamen* replaces the logic of the opposition of 'contingency and necessity' (LS: 270) with a logic of 'probability' (271) and indeterminacy that is more adequate to the natural processes that it addresses, given the 'irreducible plurality of causes or of causal series, and the impossibility of bringing causes together into a whole' (270). Deleuze deduces a second concept from the infinitely short moment of the genesis of multiplicity that will continue to suffuse his philosophy: As the figure of a fundamental and irreducible multiplicity, the inherently creative *clinamen* designates a fundamental positivity. Deleuze draws a distinction between affirmation and joy, however, that will be eminently important for his thought. 'The multiple as the multiple is the object of affirmation, just as the diverse as diverse is the object of joy' (279). The political and ethical notion of affirmation is set against the pure joy inherent in the *jouissance* of the birth of the world. In both registers, it is the *clinamen* that ensures the fullness of a multiplicity from which and within which crystals emerge. Affirmation, however, is neither celebration of nor affinity with something outside of the given. Rather, the act of affirmation implies being an integral part of that genesis; of being what Spinoza calls a mode. The germ of everything Deleuze will say about the positive givenness of multiplicity lies in this joy and affirmation of a crystal creation: *Venus, Lucretius, Simondon*.

Another term that will hold a special importance in Deleuze's philosophy is infinity. Deleuze argues that Lucretius' multiplicity is infinite. As for Simondon, for Lucretius every object is a compound of a finite number of elements that are selected from an infinite number of given elements. In fact, the processes of the creation and individuation of systems – their crystallization, that is – not only involve the reduction of an infinite set of elements to a finite set, but literally consist of that very reduction. 'What is not infinite', therefore, 'are the parts of the body and of the atoms, the sizes and shapes of the atom, and above all, every worldly or intra-worldly combination' (272).

While all crystals are finite as extensive and corporeal, their virtual combinations are infinite. 'What is truly infinite' is the number of elements from which crystals are created and the potential relations between them: 'the sum of atoms and the void, the number of atoms of the same shape and size, and the number of combinations or worlds which are similar to (or different from) ours' (272). In other words, what is infinite is the virtual potentiality of this world to change into another world. In being able to think these new worlds, finite crystals partake of the infinite potentiality of the world, or better of worlds, in general. As in 'Plato and the Simulacrum', Deleuze sets the infinite power of the false against the finite fact of the true [→ **Guattari 183**]. The inherently false time-image is set against the inherently true movement-image: *false fiction against true fact*.

A final detail Deleuze singles out for commentary is Lucretius' parallelism of thought and perception, which Lucretius sets up by way of a conceptual similarity between the *clinamen* and the *simulacrum*, which concerns Lucretius' idea that sight is based on ultra- or infra-thin surfaces that peel off from the object and travel to the observer's eye with a speed that is too fast for perception; a logic that evokes, for us, the persistence of vision that ensures the movement of filmic images. As both happen too fast for the respective faculty, the *clinamen* is the outside of thought in the same way that the *simulacrum* is the outside of perception. While the *clinamen* moves too fast for thought, *simulacra* move too fast for perception, which mistakes them for the qualities of the objects from which they emanate. They are perceived as images of these objects rather than as material assemblages that travel from the objects to the eye. In both registers, the apprehended world, as what Deleuze will later call the world as given as given, is false in relation to the forever too fast truth of the world as given. The truth as infinitely fast quantity: *false quality against true quantity*.

There are, then, two analogous modalities of the relation between the unthought and thought, and the imperceptible and the perceptible. Two modes of swiftness. '1) a time smaller than the minimum of thinkable time (an *incertum tempus* brought about by the *clinamen*); 2) a minimum of continuous thinkable time (the speed of the atom traveling in a single direction)' (275). In analogy, the speed of the *simulacrum* is too fast for the senses, while the speed of the image can be sensed: '3) a time smaller than the minimum of sensible time (*punctum temporis*, occupied by the *simulacrum*); and 4) a minimum of continuous sensible time (to which the *image* corresponds, which assures the perception of the object)' (275).

The relation between *simulacrum* and image, therefore, is analogous to that between atomic swerve and atomic movement. 'Simulacra are not perceived in themselves; what is perceived is their aggregate in a minimum of sensible time (image). The movement of the atom in a minimum of continuous thinkable time *bears witness* to the declination, which nevertheless occurs in a time smaller than the minimum. Similarly, the image *bears witness* to the succession and summation of simulacra, which occur in a time smaller than the minimum of continuous sensible time' (277, emphases added). Although it sounds like science-fiction, the impossible ideal of philosophy would be to accelerate thought and perception to infinitely fast and rarefied states, while its practice is to make them as fast and rarefied as possible to allow philosophy to bear witness to the infinite speed and diversity of the given world.

The ethics of Lucretius' naturalism, which aims to denounce false myths as the source of negativity and to affirm affirmation, is related to this speed. 'Naturalism makes of thought and sensibility an affirmation. It directs its attack against the prestige of the negative' (279). Where does this negative come from? Deleuze argues that by misreading the *clinamen* and the *simulacra*, myth installs negativity by setting up false infinities. 'In the same way that the clinamen leads thought to false conceptions of freedom, the simulacra lead the sensibility to a false impression of will and desire. In virtue of their speed, which causes them to be and to act below the sensible minimum, *simulacra produce the mirage of a false infinite in the images which they form*' (277, emphasis added). In this way, two illusions insert themselves into a swift philosophy. The illusion of infinite 'freedom' inserts itself into the hiatus between the speed of the swerve and of the atom; the illusion of 'an infinite capacity for pleasure and an infinite possibility for torment' (277) inserts itself into the hiatus between the simulacrum and the image. The myth of an eternal, infinite life after death defines worldly life as negative in the sense of not infinite. Similarly, the illusions of infinite pleasure and of infinite torment after life steal infinity from worldly life and define worldly pleasure within parameters of negativity: again, *not* infinite.

Against these bad, inadequate myths, which set up extra-worldly, transcendental infinities, naturalism sets the good, adequate infinities that operate within nature rather than outside of it. While bad infinity is always outside of nature, good infinity is immanent to nature. It is folded from the outside into the inside of nature. In terms of time, for instance, an adequate infinity has to do with 'the correct appreciation of times nested one within the other, and of the passages to the limit which they imply' (277–8). The ideal of an eternity out of this world, then, is replaced by the scale from Nietzsche's eternal present to the infinite speed of the movement of particles on the plane of nature. This speed of the world will become part of Deleuze's conceptualization of passive syntheses, of his conceptualization of becoming imperceptible and of becoming unconscious, as well as of that of a plane of immanence, on which movements are, ideally, infinitely fast. It will also set the parameters for the logic of sense, which differentiates categorically between the levels of material matters-of-fact and of immaterial events, and which regulates their logical distribution and attribution from within this distinction. Rather than construct infinities that lie outside of nature, philosophy should bear witness to the infinities inside of nature. In other words, an infinity that is external to this world has to be replaced by an infinity within this world.

In terms of that inherent infinity, the aim of naturalism is to set actual, finite sensation and virtual, infinite thought 'into correlation' (279). If 'the pure positivity of the finite is the object of the senses ... the positivity of the veritable infinite is the object of thought' (279). While the senses are actually finite, thought is virtually infinite. This is why Deleuze will write towards the end of his career in *What is Philosophy?* that philosophy is the only one of the three modes of thought that commences from infinite multiplicity and is able to retain the infinite in its practice. 'Philosophy wants to save the infinite by giving it consistency ... Science, on the other hand, relinquishes the infinite in order to gain reference ... Art wants to create the finite that restores the infinite' (197). I will take up the notion of infinity in my reading of Deleuze and Spinoza. At this point, let me just draw attention to the terms Deleuze uses to relate the perceived image of objects with the *simulacrum* as a material emission from these objects. From the side of the metaphysical event, it is a question of bearing witness; from the side of the physical *simulacrum*, it is a question of leading to and of producing. The beginning of a series: *production, incarnation, expression, witnessing*.

Although this terminology is a first step towards Deleuze's logic of sense, there is a point at which Deleuze can no longer develop this logic from within Lucretian registers, because Lucretius does not internally separate objects and events according to causes and effects, or according to terms and relations. Rather, Lucretius considers them as part of a general field of a causal multiplicity. 'The Epicureans ... affirm the independence of the *plurality* of the material causal series, in virtue of a *swerve* which affects each' (LS: 270). Lucretius cannot conceive, therefore, of the relation between events and matters-of-fact from a perspective that considers them as both complementary and formally distinct.

It is one of the more exasperating aspects of reading Deleuze that, at such moments, he tends to abandon one philosophical model to switch over to a model that is better suited to advance his thought. Precisely when he has brought Lucretius' model to its limit, Deleuze hints at a more radical philosophical model that will form the basis for the logic of sense. 'The Stoics affirm a difference of nature between corporeal causes and their incorporeal effects. As a result, effects refer to effects and form a *conjugation*, whereas causes refer to causes and form a *unity*' (270). The Stoics, rather than position causes and effects on the same plane and organize their relations chronologically from causes to effects, as well as, in analogy, from matters-of-fact to events, relegated each series to a separate plane or domain, setting up a 'new dualism of bodies or states of affairs and effects or incorporeal events [which] entails an upheaval in philosophy' (6). Between 'states of things and compounds, causes, souls and bodies, actions and passions, qualities and substances on the one hand, and, on the other, events or impassive, unqualifiable, incorporeal Effects, infinitives which result from these amalgams, which are attributed to these states of things, which are expressed in propositions ... The attribute is no longer a quality related to the subject by the indicative "is", it is any verb whatever in the infinitive which emerges from a state of things and skims over it' (DII: 63–4). As he will note in *Dialogues II*, 'the Stoics' strength lay in making a line of separation pass ... between physical depth and metaphysical surface. Between things and events' (63).

Even while Deleuze sees that the Lucretian logic has its limits, the moment and logic of the *clinamen* is a conceptual germ from which Deleuzian philosophy will unfold. In particular, what Deleuze distils from *De Rerum Natura* is the idea of 'naturalism as the philosophy of affirmation; pluralism linked with multiple affirmation; sensualism connected with the joy of the diverse, and the practical critique of all mystifications' (LS: 279). Although Deleuze will never call himself a naturalist – in fact, his switch to the Stoics can be read as an evasion from the trap of the philosophy of nature – he takes over from Lucretius' naturalism it's fundamental affirmation of the diverse. Virtually at the same time, he finds that affirmation in *Nietzsche and Philosophy* from 1962. Nowhere else in Deleuze's work is light so tightly related to the notions of lightness and delight, and, at the same time, to a negation that Deleuze again relates to the notion of a natural light. 'The person who does not act considers that he possesses a natural light over action, that he deserves to derive advantage or profit from it' (1983b: 74). As in Deleuze, in Nietzsche the forces of negation, heaviness and passivity are invariably in the service of affirmation, lightness and activity. 'The negative becomes the thunderbolt and lightning of a power of affirming' (175). As Deleuze quotes from Zarathustra's hymn to light in 'Before Sunrise', 'I ... am one who blesses and affirms if "only you are around me, you pure, luminous sky! You abyss of light!"' (177): *Nietzsche's immanent light; amor fati*. (On 'Before Sunrise' and Deleuze, see Stevenson 2009). The first part of *Difference and Repetition* will continue, on a much larger scale, both Deleuze's celebration of affirmation as well as the polemics against the logic of negation and negativity.

At the end of reading Lucretius, Deleuze has developed, from within purely philosophical registers, the notions of an originary multiplicity and of immanence. Although Lucretius' theory is first and foremost philosophical, it also had important political implications. Marx wrote his dissertation on the difference between the Democritean and the Epicurean philosophies of nature (*'Differenz der demokritischen und epikureischen Naturphilosophie'*). Berthold Brecht planned to set the Communist Manifesto into Lucretian hexameters, and planned, in direct analogy to Lucretius' *De Rerum Natura*, a didactic poem that would have been called *De Rerum Hominis*. There is a direct line, then, from Lucretius' philosophy of nature to political philosophy.

Multiplicities

Bergsonism (1966)

At this early point of his career, Deleuze has already worked on two theories of genesis: one scientific, the other philosophical. Simondon and Lucretius. *Bergsonism*, another early portrait, adds a third theory of genesis. Although Bergson is by default related to Deleuze's *Cinema 1* and *Cinema 2*, which develop from within Bergsonian parameters, *Bergsonism*, which was written the same year as 'On Gilbert Simondon', is Deleuze's first important encounter with Bergson. It looks back to Lucretius, forward to *Difference and Repetition* as well as to 'The Actual and the Virtual', and already contains the overall conceptual setup of the cinema books. 'There can only be a simultaneous genesis of matter and intelligence' (B: 88), Deleuze notes in *Bergsonism*, echoing both Simondon's and Lucretius' notion of the simultaneity of the emergence of the actual and the virtual from a pure multiplicity in a single, infinitesimally short instant of crystal individuation. Similarly, Bergson's 'critique of the negative and of negation' (18) as badly constructed philosophical problems echoes Lucretius. *Bergsonism* conceptualizes the birth of living beings from within the 'creation of differences' (98) and installs the planes of immanence and of consistency as the stage for the production of the new.

An extended meditation on the relation between the actual and the virtual, *Bergsonism* stresses that these two realms should be conceptualized as formally distinct. From the beginning, Bergson conceives of 'two types of multiplicity' (38). One of them 'is represented by space' and is 'a multiplicity of exteriority, of simultaneity, of juxtaposition, of order, of quantitative differentiation, of difference in degree; it is a numerical multiplicity, discontinuous and actual. The other type of multiplicity appears in pure duration: It is an internal multiplicity of succession, of fusion, of organization, of heterogeneity, of qualitative discrimination, or of difference in kind, it is a virtual and continuous multiplicity that cannot be reduced to numbers' (38, see also 80, 85). Already here, the conjunction of dualism and monism has to be thought of in relation to the fact that 'the Absolute is difference, but difference has two facets, differences in degree and differences in kind' (35). With this, Deleuze sets up a categorical difference between the actual and the virtual; a difference in kind between a difference in degree (which defines the quantitative state of actuality) and difference in kind (which defines the qualitative state of virtuality).

In Bergson, the actual is developed from and in relation to movement and space, and thus precisely to what will become the movement-image in *Cinema 1*, while the virtual is developed from and related to duration and memory, and thus precisely to what will become the time-image in *Cinema 2*. 'Duration is always the location and the environment of differences in kind; it is even their totality and multiplicity. There are no differences in kind except in duration – while space is nothing other than the location, the environment, the totality of differences in degree' (32). As with the time of Aion, Bergsonian duration is 'defined less by succession than by coexistence' (60). In duration, 'the "present" that endures divides at each "instant" into two directions, one oriented and dilated toward the past, the other contracted, contracting toward the future' (52). As I will argue later, in extensive, actual time, there is only the chronic succession of instants: *temporal stutter*.

Deleuze's insistence on the separation of the two series mirrors Bergson, whose critique of Einstein's theory of relativity lies in what he considers its 'combination of space and time into a badly analyzed composite' (86). In opposition, Bergson maintains that one must always proceed from 'two divergent and expanded directions which correspond to a true difference in kind between soul and body, spirit and matter' (30). As Deleuze notes in 'On the Movement-Image', 'there's a marriage in *Matter and Memory* of pure spiritualism and radical materialism' (N: 48). This relation between two separate entities is taken up in that between Bergson's perceptual sensory-motor arc and the cone of memory, which are the two conceptual references in *Cinema 1* and *Cinema 2* respectively. 'There must be a difference in kind between matter and memory, between pure perception and pure recollection, between the present and the past' (B: 55). As with the moment of the genesis of the world, the two series are formally distinct. Their distinction, in fact, happens at once: a term Deleuze often uses to express the simultaneity of the genesis of the virtual and of the actual. 'Representation in general is divided into two directions that differ in kind, into two pure presences . . . that of perception which puts us at once into matter and that of memory which puts us at once into the mind' (26). (On this relationship see also 'Bergson, 1859–1941', in DI.) In a passage of *Bergsonism* that will flow directly into the chapter 'Asymmetrical Synthesis of the Sensible' of *Difference and Repetition*, Deleuze states that Bergson's categorical distinction between the actual and the virtual is complicated because the pure virtual pertains only to the realm of the virtual in-and-of-itself. 'The obsession with the pure in Bergson goes back to this restoration of differences in kind' (B: 22), Deleuze notes. There is a difference between pure virtuality and actualized virtuality. As I noted in my introduction, Deleuze will state in 'Asymmetrical Synthesis of the Sensible' that 'diversity is given, but difference is that by which the given is given, that by which the given is given as diverse' (DR: 222): *same problem, different context*.

Bergson takes up this distinction in his definition of pure virtuality as a 'pure recollection' that has 'no psychological existence' (B: 55), that is, in other words, 'virtual, inactive, and unconscious' (55). Pure recollection takes on a psychological existence only when it is 'outside itself and for us' (93), which means for and in actualized, active and conscious entities that perceive and remember. In this incarnation, pure recollection becomes actualized recollection. As perception itself is extensive and actual, the virtual is literally extended. 'Duration, memory or spirit is difference in kind in itself and for itself; and space or matter is difference in degree outside itself and for us' (93). The actualization of recollection, therefore, implies a shift from 'ontological contraction' (65) to 'psychological contraction' (65); what Deleuze will call, later on, contemplation. In this way 'a psychological unconscious, distinct from the ontological unconscious, is defined ... The former represents the movement of recollection in the course of actualizing it' (71): *a life becomes concrete life.*

In psychological recollection, the virtual past is actualized according to a process that is comparable to the meeting of the sensible and the intelligible. Deleuze describes it as an aerosol. 'Little by little it comes into view *like a condensing cloud*; from the virtual state it passes into the actual' (56, emphasis added); the virtual in the process of being actualized: 'the subjective, or duration, is the virtual. To be more precise, it is the virtual insofar as it is actualized, in the course of being actualized' (42–3). In this process, the shift from quantity to quality is accumulative; by degree rather than in kind. 'What, in fact, is a sensation? It is the operation of contracting trillions of vibrations onto a receptive surface. Quality emerges from this, quality that is nothing other than contracted quantity. This is how the notion of contraction ... allows us to go beyond the duality of homogeneous quantity and heterogeneous quality, and to pass from one to the other in a continuous movement' (74). As Bergson notes, 'the primal function of perception is to grasp a series of elementary changes under the form of a quality or of a simple state, by a work of condensation' (1911: 301): *complementarity as continuity, continuity as complementarity.*

From the point of view of the subject, the difference between the actual and the virtual is defined as 'the difference in kind between the present and the past, between pure perception and pure memory' (B: 58); translated into cinematographic terms, as that between the sensory-motor arc of *Cinema 1* and the cone of memory of *Cinema 2*. 'There is always extensity in our duration and always duration of matter' (B: 87). In being actualized, a pure, virtual memory touches upon a pure, actual apparatus of perception and vice versa. In terms of the cinema, a time-image touches upon a movement-image and vice versa: *crystal-images.*

According to Bergson's ontology of the virtual, the world is an infinite reservoir of virtuality and recollection; a heterogeneous unity of an anonymous memory. 'The virtual as virtual has a reality; this reality, extended to the whole universe, consists in all the coexisting degrees of expansion ... and contraction. A gigantic memory, a universal cone in which everything coexists with itself, except for the differences of level' (100). One might see in this universal memory a first glimpse of the plane of consistencies as the actualized virtual. 'There is only a single time, a single duration, in which everything would participate, *including our consciousnesses, including living beings, including the whole material world*' (78, emphasis added). Toscano derives from this the 'sufficiency of the virtual' and the notion that 'the asymmetry of ontogenesis entails that its process is a unilateral one, entirely driven by the virtual as its creative pole' (2006: 175). Also, 'we could thus say, with Simondon, that time, rather than being the envelope of all possible individuations, is the "first of all transductivities", "it emerges from the preindividual like the other dimensions in accordance with which individuation is effectuated"' (Toscano 2006: 188; Deleuze refers to this in F: 97). This virtual reservoir 'form[s] the potential parts of a Whole that is itself virtual. They are the reality of the virtual ... When the virtuality is actualized ... it does so according to lines that are divergent, but each of which corresponds to a particular degree in the virtual totality. There is here no longer any coexisting whole; there are merely lines of actualization, some successive, others simultaneous, but each representing an actualization of the whole in one direction and not combining with other lines or other directions' (B: 100).

Deleuze's famous claim that the virtual is not the possible rests on this ontology of the virtual. 'From a certain point of view, ... the possible is the opposite of the real, it is opposed to the real; but, in quite a different opposition, the virtual is opposed to the actual ... The possible has no reality (although it may have an actuality); conversely, the virtual is not actual, but as such possesses a reality. Here again Proust's formula best defines the state of virtuality: "real without being actual, ideal without being abstract"' (96, see also DI: 101).

One way in which the virtual differs from the possible is that the real does not have a genetic relation to the possible because the latter is different from the real, while the virtual and the actual do have a genetic relation as they emerge together in a process of crystallization. One can of course reverse this argument. In that case 'the possible is that which is "realized"' (B: 96) in the sense that 'the real is supposed to be in the image of the possible that it realizes' (97). In this case, the possible denotes a fixed spectrum from which only one element is realized. According to this logic, 'everything is already completely given' (98). Finally, from the retrospective position of individual information, the possible is created from the real by way of abstraction; a process by which the possible becomes a 'sterile double' (98) of the real: it is simply that which is not; that which could have come about but did not.

In all cases, the process of the realization of the possible operates by limitation, as only one possible is realized from a finite number of possibles (the number of possibles can never be infinite as there are also impossibles) and by resemblance, as the real and the possible are similar because the real is 'simply a possible that has existence or reality added to' it (97). The virtual, in opposition, 'does not have to be realized, but rather actualized; and the rules of actualization are not those of resemblance and limitation, but those of difference or divergence and of creation' (97): *creative evolution; crystallization.*

Deleuze takes up the difference between the possible|real and the virtual|actual in *Difference and Repetition* in terms to its relations to difference [→ **Guattari 75**]. 'The virtual is not opposed to the real but to the actual. *The virtual is fully real in so far as it is virtual* . . . Indeed, the virtual must be defined as strictly a part of the real object – as though the object had one part of itself in the virtual into which it plunged as though into an objective dimension . . . The reality of the virtual consists of the differential elements and relations along with the singular points which correspond to them. The reality of the virtual is structure. We must avoid giving the elements and relations that form a structure an actuality which they do not have, and withdrawing from them a reality which they have' (DR: 208–9, see also 211–12).

The difference between the possible and the real on the one hand and the virtual and the actual on the other is analogous to the one that, according to what Deleuze calls Bergson's first thesis, pertains between cinema and life, which is that between a fixed reproduction and a true evolution. 'In order to be actualized, the virtual cannot proceed by elimination or limitation, but must create its own lines of actualization in positive acts. The reason for this is simple: While the real is in the image and likeness of the possible that it realizes, the actual . . . does not resemble the virtuality that it embodies' (B: 97). Again, there is a difference in kind between the two. 'It is difference that is primary in the process of actualization – the difference between the virtual from which we begin and the actuals at which we arrive . . . the characteristic of virtuality is to exist in such a way that it is actualized by being differentiated and is forced to differentiate itself, to create its own lines of differentiation in order to be actualized' (97): *the virtual ontology of pure vibration.*

2 PHILOSOPHY'S JOY

> The self does not undergo modifications, it is itself a modification.
> Gilles Deleuze, *Difference and Repetition* (78–9)

Consolidation

Empiricism and Subjectivity (1953)

IF IT SEEMS surprising that Deleuze would choose to work, at the beginning of his philosophical career, on the philosophy of nature, his earliest work had nevertheless already paved the way for this choice. Before 'Lucretius and the Simulacrum' Deleuze had published, apart from a number of book reviews, five articles that François Dosse would consider as part of Deleuze's 'portraits' of other philosophers (2011: 108). Three of them were on Henri Bergson ('Bergson, 1859–1941', 'Bergson's Conception of Difference' and 'Les études bergsonienne'), one on Nietzsche's differentiation of 'signification and force' ('Nietzsche sens et valeur'), and 'Du Christ à la bourgeoisie'. Deleuze's reading of Lucretius shows that although 'On Gilbert Simondon' is an important moment in the gradual crystallization of Deleuzian philosophy, Deleuze had already found a philosophy of multiplicity in the philosophy of nature, five years before he rediscovered it in modern science. Apart from the above articles, Deleuze had written, in 1953, *Empiricism and Subjectivity*, a short book on David Hume. In that book, before he was to deal with the infinitely short moment of the genesis of actual and virtual multiplicities from within both philosophical and scientific registers, he had conceptualized what processes take place within the planes of consistency and composition that develop within the plane of immanence. In this progression, Deleuze moves from the atomic to the molecular level.

One could easily extract from Lucretius' text a concept of the natural world as a complex system of habits and customs. In fact, in 'Lucretius and the Simulacrum', Deleuze maintained that 'nature is not opposed to custom, for there are natural customs' (LS: 278). Perhaps this comment might be read as an echo of *Empiricism and Subjectivity*, in which Deleuze had dealt with Hume's philosophy as one of habit and habit formation that attributes to each other a 'physicalism' (ES: 119) and a perceptualism. For Hume, according to Deleuze, material history must be humanized and 'be construed as a physics of humanity' (32), while at the same time, human psychology must be physicalized. 'Since the mind is itself a collection of atoms', Deleuze notes, 'a true psychology is neither immediately nor directly possible' (27).

The true beginning of the individuation of Deleuze's philosophy lies in *Empiricism and Subjectivity*. The genetic vector goes from Hume to Lucretius and on to Simondon, and thus runs counter to the chronology of my text. According to this vector, everything is already in place in 1953. Although Deleuze's philosophy is sometimes considered to emerge from, and in many ways to resonate with, the hard sciences, in particular those of self-organization and nonlinear dynamics, the genetic chronology implies that it does not need these theories for its alignment of physical and psychic registers; or, in terms that will become central for Deleuze in *Anti-Oedipus*, for the alignment of productive and theatrical processes. Even when referring to naturalism, Deleuze conceptualizes it from within strictly philosophical registers, which is also true for his theory of the mode in which 'the subject is constituted within the given' (ES: 104; see also Beistegui 2004: 222).

I have reversed the genetic vector of Deleuze's texts because *Empiricism and Subjectivity* deals with the time after the genesis of the world; with the modes of the consolidation and the dissolution of crystals within the plane of consistency. Hume provides philosophical terms for these processes and programmes, which he defines as habit formations and as the dissolution of habits. According to two terminologies that Deleuze will develop later on, they are processes of territorialization and of deterritorialization, or of striation and smoothing.

Although Deleuze scholars often consider territorializations to be implicitly negative and deterritorializations to be implicitly positive, this evaluation, like that of schizophrenia and monism, breaks down as soon as one considers the terms systemically, as one does, for instance, when one talks of an element's positive and negative electromagnetic charges; that is, as soon as one considers them as quantitative rather than as qualitative. Before any ethical or aesthetic value is ascribed to them, the dynamics of territorialization, deterritorialization and reterritorialization describe quite simply the machinic operations by which an anonymous molecular multiplicity constitutes, consolidates and molarizes itself into a temporally and locally stabilized system, as well as the machinic processes involved in its constant dissolution. As Michel Serres notes in *Genesis*, they describe the operations by which parts of a pure multiplicity organize themselves into ordered multiplicities. As Serres defines it, 'the cosmos is not a structure, it is a pure multiplicity of ordered multiplicities and pure multiplicities' (1995: 111).

In this context, the terms molecular and molar diffract once again into the fields of both physical and metaphysical agglomerations, starting from the meeting of the smallest actual elements with the faintest traces of a virtual life; from the thresholds between what we use to think of as the animate and the inanimate, although for Deleuze there is, philosophically speaking, no truly inanimate state, as everything that can be said to exist emerges from a plane of an anonymous, virtual life. As Bergson imagined this genesis in *Creative Evolution*, 'of phenomena in the simplest forms of life it is hard to say whether they are still physical and chemical or whether they are already vital' (1911: 99). At some point of organizational complexity, however, something develops that we would consider as individual life and death – the emergence of individual consistencies from anonymity and their return to it: *individual life, individual death*.

For an account of what kind of human subject can be constructed from within the conceptual givens of Deleuze's philosophy, such as multiplicity and crystallization, the most important given that Deleuze extracts from his reading of Hume is that any living system is nothing but 'a *habitus*, a habit, nothing but the habit in a field of immanence' (WP: 48). This idea will inform all of Deleuze's work, as when, in *Difference and Repetition*, he describes processes of systemic organization as those of 'contracting a habit' (74), or when he maintains that 'in essence, habit is contraction' (73). Both physically and metaphysically, habit formations consist of iterated processes that create minute systemic nuclei – atoms, germs, larvae, crystals – to which more and more elements attach themselves, as in the assemblage of complex molecules from single atoms. Each of these elements has its own habits that are brought into resonance within the overall, molar organization of the emergent entity. In the case of human beings, these habitual contractions include conceptual habits such as 'the habit of saying I' (DII: 48). Even consciousness and the notion of the self are nothing but habitual systems.

Deleuze takes from Hume the idea that such habitual contractions start long before the emergence of reason, which Hume considers to be just one habit among others. Accordingly, it is not reason that creates principles. Rather, the reason for reason is the principle of habit formation. As Deleuze notes, 'the principle is the habit of contracting habits . . . Habit is the root of reason, and indeed the principle from which reason stems as an effect' (ES: 66). Already at this point, one can sense a faint conceptual spine in Deleuze's philosophy. An emergent habit of thought. Hume's '*atomism*' (27) will lead Deleuze to Lucretius and Simondon, while his notion of habit formation will lead him to the pragmatisms of C. S. Peirce and William James. Famously, Peirce noted that even natural laws are nothing but habits. 'Habit is by no means exclusively a mental fact. Empirically, we find that some plants take habits. The stream of water that wears a bed for itself is forming a habit' (Peirce 1965a: 342; on Peirce and habit, see Toscano 2006: 109–35; on habit, see Massumi 2002). In a similar vein, as Deleuze notes, Bergson maintained that 'habits are not themselves natural, but what is natural is the habit to take up habits' (ES: 44). This habitual naturalism or natural habitualism is the basic figure of thought from which Deleuze will develop his notion of subjectivity. Unlike laws, habits account for both change and permanence, for difference and repetition. On the one hand, each entity is nothing but a bundle of habits; on the other, as Vladimir notes in Samuel Beckett's *Waiting for Godot*, 'habit is a great deadener' (1956: 91): *crystals grow according to specific habits, not laws*.

The challenge for Deleuze lies in developing, from within Hume, a philosophy that implements habit formation as the basic model of the genesis and of the persistence of both human and non-human entities. Crucially, Hume finds the origin of habit formation in nature. Habit is 'nothing but one of the principles of nature' and it derives 'all its force from that origin' (ES: 66). If one takes this logic seriously, it involves a reversal that is as surprising as it is paradoxical. In fact, Deleuze's programmatic reversal of the categories of life and the categories of thought that I mentioned in my introduction echoes Hume's notion that reason, as a function of an embodied mind, is not only deeply invested in nature, but is in actual fact a direct result of the natural operations of habit formation. 'The mind is not reason; reason is an affection of the mind. In this sense, reason will be called instinct ... habit, or nature' (30). There is logical reasoning, and there is a mind that is open to the given world and its habits, which Hume calls customs. 'All inferences from experience ... are effects of custom, not of reasoning' (32). According to this logic, reason is merely one habit among others, all of which are used by the entity to successfully navigate the world. It is a habit developed by an embodied mind. In other words, what we call reason is simply a specific habit that highly developed embodied minds have taken on in order to effectively negotiate their milieu with the aim of persisting as living systems: *Darwin before Plato*.

Much later and much more laconically, Deleuze recapitulates this logic when he notes in 'Immanence: A Life' that 'transcendence is always a product of immanence' (PI: 31). In Hume and in Deleuze, reason is both logically and genetically a product of habit formation. The statement that 'habit is the constitutive root of the subject' (92–3) needs to be understood in all of its radicalness. Hume's habitual world is defined by the fundamental paradox of a transcendental empiricism, a term Deleuze will use later on to describe his own philosophy (DR: 56; on the origin of the term in Schelling, see Kerslake 2009: 84). Once more, Deleuze finds the origin of this transcendental empiricism in the subject's constitution within the naturally given world; in its immanence: *Deleuzian ecology*.

Already at this point Deleuze notes something that will be crucial in his texts on Simondon and Lucretius: 'The given is no longer given to a subject; rather, the subject constitutes itself in the given' (ES: 87). Hume's natural given shows all of the characteristics of Simondon's milieu and Lucretius' multiplicity. On the one hand, it is 'easy going' and 'immediate' (101), on the other, it is inherently machinic because 'the state of nature is always already more than a simple state of nature' (39). Most importantly, it is everywhere filled with living beings that are 'the biological source of . . . spontaneity' (97) and that Deleuze will later on define as centres of indetermination (see Bergson 1911: 36).

The specific position of the subject within the given opens up the question of the relation between the parallel series of physical and metaphysical assemblage. The transcendental realm of reason and thought is immanent to human nature as the given. 'Nothing in the mind', Deleuze notes, 'transcends human nature, because it is human nature that, in its principles, transcends the mind' (ES: 24). According to this radical immanence, 'instead of referring nature to the mind, the mind *must* be referred to nature' (84). Thought emerges from habit or custom, and as such it remains the latter's attribute. Simultaneously, the transcendental realm is formally separated from that natural given. Deleuze will negotiate this incompatibility as that between virtual relations and actual terms, where 'the relation is *transcendence*' (100), while terms belong to the realm of empirical physics.

The relation of the subject to nature is thus both direct and immediate and, in another aspect, indirect and mediated. Deleuze notes that, for Hume, in a curiously Spinozan mode, 'nature and culture, drive and institution, are one to the extent that the one is satisfied by the other; but they are also two insofar as the latter is not explained by the former' (ES: 49). Nature and culture satisfy each other, Deleuze will say, in that they are attributed according to a logic of reciprocal presupposition. Neither Deleuze nor Hume, however, believe that culture can be explained by nature. In fact, 'Hume's originality . . . derives from the force with which he affirms: *relations are exterior to their terms*' (DI: 163). To rigorously and formally separate relations from their terms, like virtuals are formally separated from their actuals and vice versa, is crucial because it explains why human culture cannot be explained by nature. Rather, as I will argue later on, human culture is an expression of nature. Similarly, however, it explains why nature cannot be explained by culture. As the Stoics had argued, effects cannot be explained by causes. Similarly, events cannot be explained by matters-of-fact. The false cannot be explained by the true, the true cannot be explained by the false. Hume is very aware of this invariably twofold logic. Causes and effects are fundamentally distinct. 'Every effect is a distinct event from its cause' (Hume 2007: 21). At the same time, they need to be attributed, or, as Hume puts it, 'the cause must be *proportioned* to the effect' (2007: 99, emphasis added).

While causes are related to the realm of quantity and to terms, effects are related to the realm of quality and to relations. Formally, the quantitative and the qualitative series are fundamentally distinct. Although Deleuze would perhaps have some reservations, he would in general agree with Hume that, somewhat counter-intuitively, the ultimate aim of science is to arrive at mere quantities. 'The only objects of the abstract science or of demonstration are quantity and number, and ... all attempts to extend this more perfect species of knowledge beyond these bounds are mere sophistry and illusion' (Hume 2007: 119). The contention that terms and relations never bleed into one another attests to Hume's conceptual rigour and it forms the conceptual ground of his empiricism. 'We will call "nonempiricist" every theory according to which, *in one way or another*, relations are derived from the nature of things' (ES: 109), Deleuze notes. Deleuze's immanent luminism relies on this strict separation as well. As the nature of things is to be multiplicitous and luminous, a light emanating either from a non-natural source or from a harmonious nature is inadequate to nature's luminous wildness. Like Lucretius' and Simondon's, the inherently refracted logic of Hume's transcendental empiricism relies on the complementarity of given quantities of luminous intensity and their qualifications in the relational field of the given as given: *Hume's wild philosophy*.

In Hume's words, 'as all reasoning concerning matters of fact arises only from custom, and custom can only be the effect of repeated perceptions, the extending of custom and reasoning beyond the perceptions can never be the direct and natural effect of the constant repetition and connexion' (*Treatise*, quoted in ES: 78). A truly radical empiricism can only function when 'the agreement between principles and the given within which the principles constitute the subject is given up' (ES: 119): *the fracture of philosophy; philosophy of nature against itself*.

Both despite and because of the conceptual gap between the relations and terms, 'the entire sense of the principles of human nature is to transform the *multiplicities* of ideas which constitute the mind into a *system*' (80). Although the mind emerges from nature, the complicity between the psychic world and nature is defined by a radical break. 'The system is completed in the identity between system and world. But, as we have seen, the system is the product of the principles of nature, whereas the world (continuity and distinction) is an outright fiction of the imagination' (80). As Deleuze will throughout his work, Hume stakes the facticity of the true against the powers of the false: *actuality against virtuality*.

The reason for the radical disagreement between the factual and the fictional lies in Hume's perceptualism, which posits the radical informational and operational closure of any kind of perceptual apparatus. This is another position that Deleuze will retain throughout his work. As 'the mind, the collection of perceptions cannot call upon anything other than themselves' (89), Deleuze notes, 'never do we seize the object independently of the perception that we have of it' (78). In cybernetic terminology: all objects are radically constructed. 'Nothing can ever be present to the mind but an image or perception' and 'the senses are only the inlets, through which these images are conveyed, without being able to produce any immediate intercourse between the mind and the object' (Hume 2007: 111). In a similarly constructivist vein, 'all the sensible qualities of objects, such as hard, soft, hot, cold, white, black, &c. are merely secondary, and exist not in the objects themselves, but are perceptions of the mind, without any external archetype or model, which they represent. If this be allowed, with regard to secondary qualities, it must also follow, with regard to the supposed primary qualities of extension and solidity; nor can the latter be any more entitled to that denomination than the former. The idea of extension is entirely acquired from the senses of sight and feeling' (113). As Deleuze will stress in his reading of Lucretius, 'the smallest impression is *neither a mathematical nor a physical point*, but rather a sensible one' (ES: 91, emphasis added). All experience is inevitably not only mediated but in actual fact constructed by the senses. Symptomatically, for Hume, as for Lucretius, the most minimal layer of impressions consists of the 'impression of atoms or corpuscles' (90). Ideas, therefore, 'are not the representations of objects, but rather of impressions' that are 'innate' rather than 'representative' (88). In other words, both perception and cognition are radically impressionistic. 'The collection of perceptions, when organized and bound', becomes 'a system' (98) that is constructed within and by perceptual and cognitive machines.

Deleuze follows Hume's perceptualism, according to which perception is more lively than thought. 'The most lively thought is still inferior to the dullest sensation' (2007: 13), Hume maintains. While 'ideas, especially abstract ones, are naturally faint and obscure . . ., all impressions, that is, all sensations, either outward or inward, are strong *and vivid*' (15). For Deleuze, who sees both virtual thought and actual perception as multiplicities, thought and sensation stand in a relation of reciprocal presupposition. If sensation of the real world is lively, the imagination's strength lies in its being a free agent that can construct its own virtual worlds, as in the case of Deleuze's reading of Proust, with which I deal later. For Deleuze, it is not so much that ideas spring from internally constructed perceptions – *nihil est in intellectu quid non erat in sensu* – but that virtual ideas and actual sensations are related according to a logical and ultimately a topological vector rather than a chronological one.

Already at this point, Deleuze uses Hume's topology of thought to turn classical philosophy upside-down and inside-out. Even though reason is a closed system, every system of thought, whether of a philosophy or a novel, remains, as a natural habit, attributed and immanent to nature. The term Deleuze will use to model this topology is intensity, which I will use for the moment to denote the other side of impression. In this context, intensity is the term used to think impression from a position outside of the entity. While perceptions are assembled inside the perceptual apparatus, the outside consists of intensities that impress themselves onto the perceiving entity and thus function as the causes of perception. These intensities cannot be perceived and known as intensities. Like nodes and relations, the given, Deleuze will note in *Difference and Repetition*, can only be perceived in terms of the given as given. Intensity can only be given as perceived and as cognitively patterned. Or: intensity can only be given as given in the mode of extensity. (On Klossowski as one origin of Deleuze's use of intensity, see TRM: 179.) As all knowledge is relational and constructed within the actual system of perception, 'there is no intensive knowledge; all knowledge is extensive and *between parts*' (ES: 127, emphasis added). In other words, knowledge is invariably embodied and relational. The empiricist fault line, therefore, runs between 'matters of fact and relations between ideas' (127). In *The Logic of Sense* Deleuze will say that it runs between things and words, or between matters-of-fact and events. Already with Hume, however, the paradoxical relation between knowledge and the given is that they are both formally and experientially separated.

The knowledge produced within the perceiving entity is not only fictional rather than factual, it is also functional, and thus expressive, rather than representational. Already here, immanence. It is 'inside the given' that 'we establish relations and we form totalities. But *the latter* do not depend on the given, but rather on the principles we know; they are purely functional' (ES: 133). As all knowledge of and in the world is invariably mediated, the problematics shift from questions of the truth of facticity to questions of viability. Knowledge consists of sets of relations within the subject that function practically to negotiate the dynamic field of intensities as the milieu to which the entity is immanent. It is because of this inherent pragmatism that every system of thought, including philosophy, is immediately and inevitably practical. 'If the subject is constituted within the given, then, in fact, there is only a practical subject' (104). In *Foucault*, Deleuze will talk of a 'pragmatics of the multiple' (70).

The fictional world that is constructed in and projected by the subject, then, is radically separated from the world in which it is physically constituted and to which it remains immanent, including its apparatus of perception and projection. The faculty that literally turns the multiplicity of intensities into coherent, albeit fully fictional and thus false images is the spontaneous imagination, or, in Hume's terms, the faculty of the fancy, which 'finds itself at the foundation of the world, that is, of the world of culture and the world of *distinct and continuous existence*' (ES: 131, emphasis added). Evoking the difference between the virtual and the actual, Deleuze notes that animals, which are generally considered to lack the faculty of virtualization, are 'being held by the instinct to the actual' (60). The habit of the spontaneous imagination, then, is to turn intensive, quantitative impressions into corresponding extensive, qualitative images.

As the Humean subject is quite radically the direct result of habits, 'to speak of the subject ... is to speak of duration, custom, habit, and anticipation' (92). Hume differentiates, however, between habits and customs, which denote how nature and thought are structurally coupled by way of specific infrastructures. Hume uses the term pre-established harmony to denote these customary infrastructures. This term, however, should not immediately be read as metaphysical, because it designates, as it does in Peirce, a natural rather than a divine harmony. There is 'a kind of pre-established harmony between the course of nature and the succession of our ideas' (Hume 2007: 39) and 'custom is that principle, by which this correspondence has been effected; so necessary to the subsistence of our species, and the regulation of our conduct, in every circumstance and occurrence of human life' (40). Rather than to a divine agency, this pre-established harmony refers to an evolutionary given in that, without it, there would be no evolution. Evolution and pre-established harmony, in fact, are one and the same thing. Both are the result of the immanence of thought in nature.

As habits are not laws, and because they develop in reaction to and resonance with intensive shocks coming from an outside that follows an uncomputable, nonlinear dynamics, habits constantly change in order to adapt to these shocks. As Hume notes, 'the falling of a pebble may, for aught we know, extinguish the sun; or the wish of a man control the planets in their orbits. It is only experience, which teaches us the nature and bounds of cause and effect, and enables us to infer the existence of one object from that of another' (2007: 119–20). Both the habits that we are and the habits that we take on need to be adequate to such a constantly surprising, dangerously out-of-balance world. They need to be elastic enough to be kicked. As Deleuze and Guattari note in *What is Philosophy?*, 'habit is creative. The plant contemplates water, earth, nitrogen, carbon, chlorides, and sulphates, and it contracts them in order to acquire its own concept and fill itself with it (enjoyment?). The concept is a habit acquired by contemplating the elements from which we come ... We are all contemplations, and therefore habits. *I* is a habit. Wherever there are habits there are concepts, and habits are developed and given up on the plane of immanence of radical experience ... That is why English philosophy is a free and wild creation of concepts' (105).

At this point, one might describe a Deleuzian subject as an assemblage of both physical and metaphysical machines that unfold in time and in space by way of both physical and metaphysical routines; by habits that branch out into complex morphogenetic architectures even while the subject maintains an overall consistency, which means that it is held within a temporarily and spatially stable envelope. From such a perspective, both the human body and the human mind are literally nothing but the sum of their respective spatio-temporal developments. Each consists of a series of routines of folding and unfolding. At any point, however, this folding sequence can shift into different attractors when tiny variations and bifurcations cascade into larger, more massive changes: *philosophical catastrophism*.

The Jouissance of Thought

Difference and Repetition (1968)

Throughout the unfolding of Deleuze's philosophy, the theory of habit formation that he extracts from Hume in *Empiricism and Subjectivity* will remain one of the most consistent leitmotifs. Deleuze, however, does more than simply assume Hume's position. (See also Kerslake 2009: 102.) In *Difference and Repetition* from 1968, Hume's transcendental empiricism is integrated into a truly Deleuzian figure of thought. At this moment in time, one might say, Deleuzian thought takes on its own habit. While Deleuze's earlier texts tended to revolve around the given concepts of other philosophers, *Difference and Repetition* develops from these concepts and their immensely complicated philosophical and scientific histories an inherently Deleuzian figure of thought. This is why *Difference and Repetition* has become one of the central texts in Deleuze scholarship. Even while the given concepts retain their historical and philosophical resonances, they come alive within a field that is now singularly Deleuzian. In other words, around 1968, Deleuzian philosophy comes into its own.

In attempting to contour Deleuze's conceptual machine, my wager is that the figure of thought that I extract from *Difference and Repetition* is indeed Deleuzian. The only test of this is empirical. Once this figure is in place, texts by Deleuze that one has not yet read should no longer propose something that comes as a complete surprise, or that could not be conceptually integrated into his other texts. There should be no passages in his work that are not in line with this overall figure of thought. As with Žižek, who very often seems to be surprising until one realizes that his statements invariably derive from Lacan, who was one of the most rigorous thinkers imaginable. Heinz von Foerster (1993) relates this to the fact that every viable theory – what he calls an eigentheory – must show an internal conceptual coherence. Given that there is no external truth by which to judge a theory, it must be judged by the degree of that internal coherence, and, by extension, its adequation to the world. In the case of Deleuze, the overall figure of thought should be so comprehensive that it envelops all of Deleuze's work, even while it constantly develops variations, and even while its incarnations continuously change in a dynamic of difference and repetition: *eigenphilosophy*.

Although it takes up both Hume and Bergson, *Difference and Repetition* is the first work that is not portraiture. 'Memory is essentially *difference* and matter essentially *repetition*' (B: 93, emphasis added), Deleuze had written in *Bergsonism*, evoking once more the difference between aperiodic and periodic crystals. (Between 'Lucretius and the Simulacrum' and *Difference and Repetition*, Deleuze had published *Nietzsche and Philosophy* in 1962; *Kant's Critical Philosophy: The Doctrine of the Faculties* in 1963; *Proust and Signs* in 1964; *Nietzsche* in 1965 and *Bergsonism* in 1966). Inaugurating the mature phase of Deleuzian philosophy, *Difference and Repetition* is a wide-ranging text that tests Deleuze's philosophical dispositions against other conceptual fields such as psychoanalysis and political theory. From the many threads that make up its conceptual fabric, I will isolate those that define it as a meditation on unconscious habit formation, on the relation between the actual and the virtual, and on processes of individuation.

The image of lightning that I used to introduce Deleuze's luminous philosophy was taken from *Difference and Repetition*. Conceptualized from within luminous registers in which light and light rays are figures of a field of multiplicity of refractions and diffusion, the image is a figure of an elemental, ecological relationship between the world and its creatures: 'We are made of contracted water, earth, light and air' (DR: 73), Deleuze notes. *Difference and Repetition* takes up Lucretius' luminous nature, one might say, and develops from it a philosophy that is adequate to the life of crystals in a both disparate and differential world: *diffracted philosophy*.

In fact, one might draw a line of light from Lucretius' luminism to Deleuze's 1963 portrait *Kant's Critical Philosophy: The Doctrine of the Faculties*. If Lucretius' immanent light is invariably diffracted, some of that light shines onto what Deleuze calls the 'fundamental discord' (xii) of the Kantian faculties, whose 'unregulated exercise' (xi) Deleuze considered to be 'the great discovery of the *Critique of Judgement*, the final Kantian reversal' (xiii). This 'deeply romantic' (xi) notion of a diffraction of the faculties 'was to define future philosophy, just as for Rimbaud the disorder of all the senses was to define the poetry of the future. A new music as discord, and as a discordant accord' (xiii). Not only a new sound, but also, perhaps, the cinema.

Difference and Repetition, which is pervaded by the notion of diffraction, not only takes up the notion of a *'discordant harmony'* (on the fracture of the faculties, see also Kerslake 2009: 76–80; Bryant 2008: 104) – when Deleuze notes that 'Ideas, far from having as their milieu a good sense or a common sense, refer to a para-sense which determines only the communication between disjointed faculties', he links this obscure communication directly to matters of light: 'The restitution of the Idea in the doctrine of the faculties requires the explosion of the clear and distinct ... Distinction-obscurity becomes here the true tone of philosophy, the symphony of the discordant Idea' (DR: 146).

Once more, Deleuze's notion of a luminous Idea stakes diffraction, as a figure of multiplicity, against both an emanating, 'interior light' (95) and against what philosophy considered to be a natural light. Deleuze critiques this notion by way of taking the notion of natural light literally rather than metaphorically: *the light of immanence.* Ideas are, like crystals, immanent to their milieu, and related to each other by dark precursors considered, one might say, as a dark light. 'All Ideas coexist, but they do so at points, on the edges, and under *glimmerings which never have the uniformity of a natural light.* On each occasion, obscurities and zones of shadow correspond to their distinction' (186–7, emphasis added). These glimmerings form a leitmotif in Deleuze's description of 'the Idea in all its domains of multiplicity'. Ideas themselves are 'unequal glimmers' that 'have nothing in common with any natural light' (190). Often, Deleuze relates these glimmers directly to the diffraction of the Kantian faculties, as when he notes that Ideas are 'multiplicities with differential glimmers' that reach 'from one faculty to another, without ever having the homogeneity of that natural light which characterises common sense' (194).

In its ideational *chiaroscuro, Difference and Repetition* already prepares the way for Deleuze's luminous Leibniz in *The Fold*, as when he talks about 'a distinctness which can only be obscure, the more obscure the more it is distinct' (DR: 214). The Idea 'is *precisely real without being actual, differentiated without being differenciated, and complete without being entire.* Distinctness-obscurity is intoxication, the properly philosophical stupor or the Dionysian Idea. Leibniz very nearly encountered Dionysus at the sea shore or near the water mill. Perhaps Apollo, the clear-confused thinker, is needed in order to think the Ideas of Dionysus. However, the two never unite in order to reconstitute a natural light. Rather, they compose two languages which are encoded in the language of philosophy and directed at the divergent exercise of the faculties: the disparity of style' (214). Even where it does not explicitly work from within luminous registers, *Difference and Repetition* can be read as a sustained argument against the notion of a natural light in philosophy. It develops, one might say, a philosophy that glimmers; an unconscious, obscure philosophy that develops, from that obscurity, the notion of an immanent, diffracted philosophy: *philosophy's chiaroscuro.*

It is literally in this light that *Difference and Repetition* adds to Hume a stress on unconscious habits. Human subjects are not only a bundle of conscious habits, such as Kant's seven o'clock walk, but, more importantly, of habits that take place on molecular, unconscious levels that concern 'the primary habits that we are; the thousands of passive syntheses of which we are originally composed' (74). This sentence raises at least three questions that I will address in the following. First: 'what are primary habits?' Second: 'why are primary habits syntheses?' Third: 'why are these syntheses passive?'

What are primary habits? In terms of the physical genesis and individuation of living beings, primary habits concern biomaterial, molecular routines, such as the habit of atoms to aggregate into specific molecules that in turn have the habit of contracting into larger, more molar aggregates. In terms of the metaphysical genesis of living systems, primary habits concern sets of immaterial routines, such as the habits of what Deleuze calls molecular contemplations, which are virtual operations that allow immaterial molecular systems to bond into larger, molar sets of images and thoughts. In both registers, the movement goes from the molecular to the molar. Secondary habits, in opposition, concern conscious habits, or habits that have become once more unconscious after having been conscious. They form the set of a conscious being's macroscopic habits rather than the microscopic habits of that being's parts, although the overall being is ultimately nothing but the integrated and harmonized ensemble of all of these parts. The first differentiation, then, is between conscious and unconscious habits, although, as I will show later on, Deleuze's unconscious differs decisively from the Freudian and the Lacanian one.

Why are primary habits synthetic? Actual as well as virtual molecular habits are synthetic in that they bring heterogeneous elements into conjunction in order to form larger operative units by way of operations of actual contraction and virtual contemplation. These pre-individual, unconscious, inattentive and productive processes concern the mode in which an atomic or a molecular medium expresses itself by way of its self-formation and self-organization. Within a dispersed field, heterogeneous elements synthesize themselves into systems. Dark precursors synthesize electric fields and currents into a lightning bolt. Such consolidations, which constitute both our 'habit of living' (74) and 'the *living present*' (81, emphasis added), are extremely precarious, unconscious evolutionary processes in which 'random developmental noise or more violent environmental disturbances' can 'push equilibrium over into another path, resulting in a very different final product' (84): *evolutionary catastrophism*.

Primary habits, then, are the contractive and contemplative processes that bring about an emergent system that is at first nothing but a very fragile, precarious set of material and immaterial routines that, although they are conjoined by 'harmonic resonances' (26), are very susceptible to catastrophes. How is resonance related to the question of primary habits as synthetic? An entity, Deleuze argues, feedbacks with its milieu through sub-individual processes of physical, actual contraction as well through sub-individual processes of psychic, virtual contemplation. Both of these formally distinct processes synthesize heterogeneous elements into operative units by suspending the elements within larger resonant fields, and by holding them in these fields.

In both series, what happens within the field of resonance is a shift from quantity to quality. Somewhat counter-intuitively, this shift is from noumenon to phenomenon. The formal distinction of that difference, however, is empirically undone in the field. As Deleuze had noted in *Bergsonism*, quality emerges from quantity by way of accumulative processes of contraction. This makes of quality 'nothing other than contracted quantity'. Heinz von Foerster notes about this continuity of movement between quantity and quality, that 'the two areas, the qualitative and the quantitative perspectives, should be seen as complementary. One needs the other in order to form a "totality"' (2014: 14–15). A similar logic defines the field of contemplation. Like Peirce's 'inattentive habit[s]' (1965a: 328), abduction 'shades' into perceptual judgement. As Peirce notes, 'as soon as we find that a belief shows symptoms of being instinctive, although it may seem to be dubitable, we must suspect that experiment would show that it is not really so' (1965b: 208).

In a resonant field, an as yet 'passive self . . . *contemplates and contracts* the individuating factors' (DR: 276, emphasis added). Within these contemplations and contractions, the emergent self 'constitutes itself at the points of resonance of their series' (276). As Deleuze notes, 'the act of individuation consists . . . in integrating the elements of . . . disparateness into a state of coupling which ensures its internal resonance' (246). In these processes, contraction and contemplation work hand-in-hand. And even though one might think that virtual contemplation comes first – in *Difference and Repetition*, Deleuze stresses the vector 'from the virtual to its actualization' (251) – one should imagine the dynamics as happening within infinitely short circuits and feedback loops. Ultimately, it is '*simultaneously* through contraction that we are habits, but through contemplation that we contract' (74, emphasis added). Contemplation is the virtual side of contraction, contraction the actual side of contemplation. The virtual comes with its actual and vice versa.

Just how deeply Deleuze anchors processes of contraction and contemplation into the field of the living can be felt in such rhetorical questions as 'what organism is not made of elements and cases of repetition, of *contemplated and contracted water*, nitrogen, carbon, chlorides and sulphates, thereby intertwining all the habits of which it is composed?' (75, emphasis added). In light of the second of our three questions – why are the primary habits syntheses? – the passive processes of contraction and contemplation are synthetic in that they bring about resonant arrangements of heterogeneous elements and series. These syntheses, however, are not Hegelian, in that Deleuze's passive syntheses are resonant rather than conceptual or formal. As Deleuze and Guattari note in *What is Philosophy?*: 'the plant contemplates by contracting the elements from which it originates – light, carbon, and the salts – and it fills itself with colors and odors that in each case qualify its variety, its composition: it is sensation in itself. It is as if the flowers smell themselves by smelling what composes them, first attempts of vision or of sense of smell, before being perceived or even smelled by an agent with a nervous system and a brain . . . Not every organism has a brain, and not all life is organic, but everywhere there are forces that constitute microbrains, or an inorganic life of things' (212–13). These 'silent contemplations . . . *bear witness to a brain*' (213, emphasis added), however rudimentary that brain might be.

This logic of synthetic resonance leads to the third question, which is why are these syntheses passive? The passivity of primary syntheses has to do with the fact that they operate without being organized or monitored by a conscious agency operating on what Deleuze calls a plane of transcendence: $n+1$. They are unconscious, $n-1$ processes that take place without the active control or intervention of human consciousness. In fact, it is only in relation to consciousness that they are passive. Instead of calling them passive synthesis, Deleuze might also have called them unconscious, obscure syntheses. An organism, for instance, does not feel its organs except when they cease to function properly, in which case they become painfully conscious: *passivity as unconscious resonance*.

While all living beings are assembled from passive, resonant syntheses, humans have developed a level of active, or secondary syntheses that are related to 'the principle of representation' (DR: 81) and to conscious processes of apperception. As with the gradual emergence of reason from natural habits, however, active syntheses, which are seemingly more Hegelian, are in fact assembled from passive syntheses. This is why virtual processes of contemplation, perception and cognition need to be extended infinitely deeply into the sub-individual levels of the actual world: *intelligent materialism*.

One of Deleuze's most persistent philosophical interests is to conceptualize the slow, intricate assemblage of complex systems from within a plane of anonymous multiplicity. How does active, conscious thought emerge from passive, unconscious thought? How to chart the passage from pre- and non-philosophical to philosophical thought? However, if this vector deals with the movement from the imperceptible to the perceptible, Deleuze is equally interested in the vector that charts the decomposition of active syntheses into the passive syntheses from which they have emerged; that is, the vector that goes from the perceptible to the imperceptible. Is it possible to reach back from within the realm of active syntheses to that of passive syntheses? Given that passive syntheses are imperceptible and sub-individual, is it possible for the subject to reach back to them despite of or even through the operations of conscious memory and thought?

In temporal terms, the question is 'whether or not we can penetrate into [*pénetrer dans*] the passive synthesis of memory; whether we can in some sense live the being in itself of the past in the same way that we live the passive synthesis of habit' (84, my revised translation). If our conscious lives are based on the passive, unconscious syntheses of habit, how can we relate, from within our conscious lives, to the unconscious past in-itself? Is it possible to reach and recreate not only a consciously memorized past, but also an unconsciously memorized one?

'The passive synthesis of habit constituted time as the contraction of instants under the condition of the present, the active synthesis of memory constitutes it as the interlocking [*emboîtement*] of the presents themselves' (81, revised translation): *Chronos and Aion*.

The complexity of Deleuze's conceptualization of passive and active syntheses increases even more when one considers that every system is assembled from a multiplicity of smaller systems that are recursively folded into one another. As Deleuze notes in *Dialogues II*, 'we are deserts, but populated by tribes, flora and fauna' (11). Although Deleuze does not always explicitly address this recursivity, it underlies, passively one might say, his thought at all times. One of the more difficult aspects of reading Deleuze, in fact, is to distinguish moments when he writes from within the logic of passive assemblage from moments when he writes from within an already integrated perspective.

The logic of assemblage implies that one has to imagine levels of unconscious and conscious habits and memories for each plateau of the assemblage. I will deal in detail with this recursiveness at a later point. For now, let me just note that unconscious contractions and contemplations are related to passive syntheses of habit and involuntary memory, while conscious contractions and contemplations are related to active syntheses and to the registers of voluntary memory and thought.

Together, passive and active habit formations make up the operational ground of beings that should be thought of as radically processual. In fact, as recursive biophysical, computational and metaphysical routines, habit formations are not only indicators of living beings. More fundamentally, all living beings are quite literally the products of these operations. The conceptualization of living entities as complicated contractions of both physical and metaphysical habits turns habit formation into the philosophical version of what the hard sciences consider as self-organization. While this analogy turns physics into a branch of philosophy, it also turns philosophy into a branch of physics. As William James noted, 'the philosophy of habit is . . ., in the first instance, a chapter in physics rather than in physiology or psychology' (1984: 138).

Through habit formations, living beings separate themselves operationally and informationally from the infinitely complicated molecular multiplicity that makes up the world to which they are structurally coupled and energetically immanent. Through these processes they take on, for other perceptual systems, the character of objects or subjects with singular properties. In fact, from a systemic standpoint, objects are nothing but a being's experience of repeated perceptual routines; of irritations that impinge upon it in a regular, iterated fashion. Within these operational eigenspaces, living beings are habitual clusters that are contoured, for other living beings, against the background of an infinite multiplicity. They are the being's images of recurrent irritations within the allover dynamics of a general multiplicity. (In the following, I will sometimes use 'allover' instead of overall to evoke the abstract expressionist strategy of all-over painting.)

If active syntheses emerge from passive syntheses and from 'our thousands of component habits' (DR: 75), thought emerges from passive contemplations like bodies emerge from passive contractions, and both remain each other's attribute. Invariably, 'below the level of active syntheses, [there is] the domain of passive syntheses which constitutes us, the domain of modifications, tropisms and little peculiarities' (79). This also implies that 'beneath the general operation of laws, . . . there always remains the play of singularities' (25) and that 'the lived reality of a sub-representative domain' (69) lies beneath both physical and psychic reality. Beyond active syntheses 'we find not the impersonal but the individual and its factors, individuation and its fields, individuality and its pre-individual singularities' (258). In this context, Deleuze echoes Offray de la Mettrie's idea that 'a soul must be attributed to the heart, to the muscles, nerves and cells, but a contemplative soul whose entire function is to contract a habit' (74): *transcendental materialism*.

If the genesis of living entities is modelled as a process of gradual spatial contractions and contemplations, in terms of relations of power it is modelled as a gradual territorialization. Symptomatically, the terms habit and habitat have the same etymological origin in the Latin *habere*, to have or to possess. Within the *'undivided "terrain"'* (TP: 328, emphasis added) of the plane of immanence, which consists ideally of completely unrelated molecular elements – or, as Deleuze and Guattari call it, of 'destratified, deterritorialized matter' (407) 'laden with singularities' (369) – habits create coded milieus, 'a code' being defined, like a habit, 'by periodic repetition' (von Foerster 1993: 313). Coded milieus or territories emerge within an uncoded terrain at the moment that 'milieu components cease to be directional, becoming dimensional instead, when they cease to be functional to become *expressive*' (TP: 315, emphasis added). By way of this vital expressionism, living beings extract 'a *territory* from the milieu' (503). In temporal terms, the consolidation of a consistency – to use Guattari's term to designate a consolidated entity – involves a local slowing down of the ideally infinitely fast and chaotic movements of elements on the plane of immanence. Every solidification implies a spatial orientation but also a temporal deceleration. Beings, in fact, are nothing but decelerations, and stable structures merely dynamic sets that have been decelerated to what seems to be zero. In the words of Friedrich Cramer, 'every structure is a piece of decelerated time' (1998: 32) [→ **Guattari 143**].

The addition of unconscious habit formation to Hume's philosophy returns Deleuze to the process of crystallization as the moment of the conjoining of an actual and its virtual, which leads me to the second theme I want to follow in *Difference and Repetition*: The relation between the actual and the virtual, which Deleuze deals with in the immensely complex and dense fourth chapter of *Difference and*

Repetition – 'Asymmetrical Synthesis of the Sensible' – in reference to the relation between extensity and intensity (for the latter term's relation to Maimon, see Lord 2010: 134). One of the many challenges of the chapter is that Deleuze's argumentation oscillates between epistemological and ontological registers, between the fields of the sensible and of the intelligible on the one hand, and the field of the in and of itself on the other. This double perspective results in a complicated layering of terminological pairs around the virtual and the actual: diversity and difference, intension and extension, intensive energy and extensive energy, quantity and quality, as well as what Deleuze calls differen*t*iation and differen*c*iation. The perhaps most challenging aspect of reading the chapter is to carefully keep these registers apart without losing a sense of their overall identity or complementarity.

Difference and Repetition is an extended, sometimes polemical argument against what I have earlier called idealisms. Or, in more positive terms, it is an alternative to the inherent negativity of idealist philosophies. In *Difference and Repetition* Lucretius' nature is recast as the field of pure intensity. Both are fundamentally positive and 'make . . . difference an object of affirmation' (DR: 234). Once again, the philosophical challenge is how to relate two series – one virtual and intensive, the other actual and extensive – without formally conflating them. How to think their relation? Deleuze sets out to negotiate this problem in terms of incarnation. There is a given field of pure diversity. In Deleuze's reading of Lucretius and of Hume, this diversity had been the product of nature. Deleuze now takes up this givenness, but complicates the term by stating that living beings perceive this diversity as a play of differences. The minimal but decisive conceptual gap between diversity and difference is why, when Deleuze talks of his philosophy as a 'philosophy of difference' (245), this should be understood in the context of a relation between unperceived and perceived difference, between infinite and finite difference, or: between virtual and actual difference. Along these relations, what many scholars call Deleuze's philosophy of difference shades into a philosophy of complementarity. Ontologically, it is a philosophy of diversity; epistemologically, it is a philosophy of difference. In the complementarity of ontological and epistemological registers, it should be understood as a philosophy of the complementarity of difference and diversity.

Already before *Difference and Repetition*, Deleuzian philosophy had replaced the relation between subject and object with that between habitual system and intensity. In *Difference and Repetition*, the fault line between these two registers runs between processes of what Deleuze calls differen*t*iation and differen*c*iation. Together, as processes of 'differen*t/c*iation' (209), these two series define processes of individuation from within the plane of immanence as a field of pure diversity. The notion of individuation ties the chapter back to Simondon. It is after a summary of Simondon's theory of the crystallization of forms, in fact, that Deleuze concludes: 'we believe that individuation is essentially intensive, and that the pre-individual field is a virtual-ideal field ... Individuation is the act by which intensity determines differential relations to become actualized, along the lines of differenciation and within the qualities and extensities it creates' (246). A page later, Deleuze refers specifically to Simondon's notion of the crystal: 'Qualities and extensities, forms and matters, are not 'primary; they are imprisoned in individuals *as though in a crystal*. Moreover, the entire world may be read, as though in a crystal ball, in the moving depths of individuating differences or differences in intensity' (247, emphasis added). If Deleuze noted in 'The Actual and the Virtual' that crystallization is the process of a virtual finding its actual, he now defines that genesis in terms of incarnation. It 'takes place in time not between one actual term, however small, and another actual term, but between the virtual and its actualization – in other words, it goes from the structure to its incarnation' (183).

Deleuze opens the chapter with the programmatic distinction that I used in my introduction. 'Difference is not diversity', he notes. 'Diversity is given, but difference is that by which the given is given, that by which the given is given as diverse' (222). This statement again raises a number of questions, such as: Given to what or to whom? A first answer might be: given to perception or to thought. There are, however, a number of caveats. In a state of an eternally unchanging intensity, such as Lucretius' steady rain of atoms, the given intensity cannot be perceived. One reason for this might be seen to lie in the functioning of the apparatus of perception itself, which operates in and through differentiation. As Gregory Bateson notes in *Mind and Nature*, 'human sense organs can receive *only* news of difference, and the differences must be coded into events in *time* (i.e. into *changes*) in order to be perceptible. Ordinary static differences that remain constant for more than a few seconds become perceptible only by scanning' (1979: 70). Even more fundamentally, however, a state of laminar order is not only imperceptible, it is not even imperceptible. As an either fully ordered or fully disordered state, it cannot contain perceptual entities, and as such it lies before the very possibility of a perceptual negation of perception.

Even when diversity is changing and when there are perceptual entities, however, pure diversity is still imperceptible because it can only be perceived by way of digital increments that miss its ideally infinitely subtle, analog changes. Again, Bateson can help to understand this. 'What happens is that a static, unchanging state of affairs, existing, supposedly, in the outside universe quite regardless of whether we sense it or not, becomes the cause of an event, a step function, a sharp change' (96). And further, 'our sensory system ... can only operate with *events*, which we can call *changes*' (97). If perception is defined as the process of making distinctions, the given diversity – in which changes happen infinitely fast and in which infinitely fine differences move about in a 'mad ... instantaneous, nomadic distribution' (DR: 224) – is invariably perceived in and as a slowed-down and reduced field of finite differences. In analogy to Lucretius' atomic multiplicity, the diverse is the reservoir from within which all formations and phenomena, but also all informations and noumena, are assembled. It is, in other words, the plane of immanence.

Intensive diversity, as imperceptible and unmeasured, is given to perception as extensive difference. The field of diversity for itself, however, is also implicated in a differential logic because it is defined by continuous changes in intensity. This is why Deleuze differentiates between intensive, virtual difference and extensive, actual difference. The former, which is 'the condition or fact of being unequal' (222), refers to what Deleuze also calls disparity. As a 'difference of intensity', disparity is 'the sufficient reason of all phenomena' (222) and forms the ungrounded ground of perception: 'disparateness as it is determined and comprised in difference of intensity, in *intensity as difference*' (223, emphasis added). Diversity as change of intensity, or change of energy, follows an analog logic. Although Deleuze takes the definition of energy from the hard sciences, he stresses that 'energy or intensive difference is a transcendental principle, not a scientific concept' (241). Evoking the Greek concept of *energeia* and Simondon's notion of potential energy, Deleuze defines energy 'in terms of *the difference buried in . . . pure intensity*' (240).

As with intensive and extensive difference, Deleuze sets up an internal difference within the notion of energy. To denote how intensity in itself is given to itself as continuous change, Deleuze uses the term 'pure energy' (241), a concept that reverberates with two connotations of the term intensity that one should always be aware of when Deleuze uses it. In terms of physics, intensity is a measure of the energy flux, averaged over the period of the wave. It denotes a given physical force. At the same time, as intension or as the intensive, it denotes the state of immateriality as opposed to material extension or the extensive. The difference between pure energy as intensive energy and extensive energy as perceived energy is that the latter can be a 'uniform energy at rest' (240), whereas the most important property of the former is that it is always and everywhere changing. The field of pure energy is one of continuous, infinite variation and analog modulation: *folded and folding energy*.

The difference between intensive and extensive energy is that perceived energy is invariably extensive and actualized. As perceiving systems cannot register infinitely small changes, they perceive energy, if its fluctuations are too small to be picked up, as stable or at rest. How often, for instance, does it seem that the temperature around us is stable, although it is of course continually changing by imperceptible, ultimately infinitely small degrees and increments? It is in this context that Jacques Derrida quotes, in 'Différance' (1982: 17), from Deleuze's *Nietzsche and Philosophy*: '*Quantity itself is therefore inseparable from difference in quantity*. Difference in quantity is the essence of force and of the relation of force to force. To dream of two equal forces, even if they are said to be of opposite senses, is a coarse and approximate dream, a statistical dream in which the living is submerged but which chemistry dispels' (1983b: 43). We never perceive the changes in the actual, physical pressure that light exerts. It is as continuously changing energy that intensity is given to itself, while in terms of perception the notion of stable energy is invariably the result of a reduction, of the levelling of infinitely small differences of *intensity* into infinitesimally small *differences* of intensity: *folds of energy and energetic cuts.*

There are thus two series that define how the given is given, once to perception (extensive, actual difference and energy: processes of differenciation), and once to itself (intensive, virtual difference and pure energy: processes of differentiation). The reversal Deleuze proposes in this context is that because all beings are, *qua* beings, invariably in extension, difference of *intensity* is a transcendental concept, while *difference* of intensity is the mode of empirical experience. In other words, difference of *intensity* belongs to the register of quantity, while *difference* of intensity belongs to 'the quality which *belongs to* quantity' (232, emphasis added). 'Intensity is simultaneously the imperceptible and that which can only be sensed' (230). This paradox, which echoes Deleuze's statement from 'Lucretius and the Simulacrum' that 'the atom is that which must be thought, and that which can only be thought' (LS: 268), throws into clear relief the radical reversal implicit in Deleuze's transcendental empiricism. Intensity is 'a "something" which simultaneously cannot be sensed (from the point of view of the empirical exercise) and can only be sensed (from the point of view of the transcendent exercise)' (DR: 236). As Deleuze notes, 'how could it be sensed for itself, independently of the qualities which cover it and the extensity in which it is distributed? But how could it be other than "sensed", since it is what gives to be sensed, and defines the proper limits of sensibility?' (230).

As given, the intensive field cannot be sensed (it is purely intensive and quantitative). As given as given, everything that is sensed (as extensive, differential and qualitative) is of the intensive field. This implies that from the position of the given as given, the intensive field, as given, is a transcendental concept while, as given as given, it is an empirical concept. Its chiastic logic is that intensity cannot be sensed from the empirical position while, from the transcendental position, it is all that can be sensed. The empirical exercise 'can grasp intensity only in the order of quality and extensity ... Only transcendental enquiry can discover that intensity remains implicated in itself' (240). As such, *intensive* difference, or difference of *intensity* forms the imperceptible and unthinkable ground of experience that invariably exceeds even the finest filters of the senses. This intensity comes as what Deleuze calls a shock to thought. As if he were already writing on Hitchcock and affect for his cinema books, Deleuze uses the notion of vertigo to illustrate how 'difference in itself, that depth in itself or that intensity in itself as the original moment at which it is neither qualified nor extended' (237), is revealed as a limit of sensibility: *intensity* (of difference) as the vertigo of life, of sensation, of thought and of philosophy.

The relation between intensity and individuation is that in becoming-entity, living beings actualize local fields from the global ecology of pure intensity. In this crystal extraction, pure intensity (difference of and in *intensity*) is cancelled out and replaced by what might be called *difference* of and in extensity. 'Difference in the form of intensity remains implicated in itself, while it is cancelled by being explicated in extensity' (228). Deleuze congeals these separate series into the terminology of differen*t*iation and differen*c*iation. Differen*t*iation describes a vector towards the virtual and the intensive, whereas differen*c*iation goes towards the actual and the extensive. In 'Ideas and the Synthesis of Difference' Deleuze notes repeatedly that differenciation invariably involves actualization. There must be actual, extensive beings to differenciate. In analogy, differentiation implies a virtualization that involves a dissolution of actual beings into heterogeneous elements. Of particles into waves. The formula of a Deleuzian philosophy, therefore, is: intensity before extensity, virtuality before actuality, or: differen*t*/ciation rather than differen*c*/tiation. The idealist formula, in contrast, is, somewhat surprisingly, extensity before intensity, actuality before virtuality, or: differen*c*/tiation rather than differen*t*/ciation.

This formula brings me to my third topic, which concerns processes of individuation. As complicated, both extensive and intensive assemblages, living beings reduce the infinite set of pure intensity (the virtual field of differen*t*iation) to finite sets (the actualized fields of differen*c*iation), and the purely intensive diversity of the given (the intensive phenomenon as noumenon) to the given as given (the differential noumenon as phenomenon). From within perception, therefore, difference holds the position of what might be called a quasi-phenomenon. It is 'not phenomenon but the noumenon closest to the phenomenon' (222).

In this reduction, the senses function as filters whose specific perceptual frames and thresholds reduce the infinity of irritating intensities to finite sets of perceptions. Perceptual systems themselves, in fact, are singular sets of reductions, decelerations and filterings. When Deleuze notes that every 'perception is not the object *plus* something, but the object minus something' (B: 24–5), this points not only to a difference from Hume's positive perceptualism but also, despite Deleuze's own frequent disclaimers, to a number of ties between Deleuzian philosophy and phenomenology, although that phenomenology is never a 'phenomenology in the "vulgar" sense of the term' (F: 89). In fact, one might consider Deleuze's philosophy to be another paradox. It is a phenomenology minus intentionality, in which, although the senses allow for intensities to enter the system, it is more important that and how this actualization reduces the range of intensities from an infinite virtual field: *anonymous phenomenology*.

Again, one can discern here the conceptual spine that runs through Deleuze's work, the conceptual routine that allows one to talk of a singularly Deleuzian figure of thought. In fact, if one considers every perceptual and cognitive process as one of pattern production and pattern recognition, a pattern of Deleuzian thought begins to emerge: Hume, Lucretius, Simondon, *Difference and Repetition*. All of these develop, in a logic that recapitulates that of difference and repetition proposed in *Difference and Repetition*, philosophical theories of the incarnation of the virtual in the actual. Virtual diversity (the field of differen*t*iation) determines and guides processes of individuation by providing the always changing conditions of actualization (the field of differen*c*iation). The organism's systemic differen*c*iations (difference of and in extensity), are in response to, attributed to and witnesses of the differen*t*iations (difference of and in intensity) that govern the given as 'a problematic field which conditions a differenciation within the milieu in which it is incarnated' (DR: 207). Differenciation, therefore, 'expresses the actualization of [the] virtual and the constitution of solutions (by local integrations)' (209). (See also 'life is essentially determined in the act of avoiding obstacles, stating and solving a problem. The construction of the organism is both a stating of a problem and a solution' (B: 16)): *the obscure pilots the clear; the dark pilots the light.*

Both physical and psychic integrations – a term I will return to in relation to Deleuze's reading of Leibniz – are solutions to the problems of organisms living within a global ecology of intensity. 'For the nature of the virtual is such that, for it, to be actualized is to be differenciated. Each differenciation is a local integration or a local solution which then connects with others in the overall solution or the global integration' (DR: 211). Deleuze couples the fields of the biological and the perceptual through the notion of a specific organicity of perception. Biological organs, as solutions to what Deleuze also calls the overall intensive 'problematic' (203), determine specific modes of perception. 'An organism is nothing if not the solution to a problem, as are each of the differenciated organs, such as the eye, which solves a "light" problem' (211). As he had noted in *Bergsonism*, 'the construction of an eye, for example, is primarily the solution to a problem posed in terms of light' (103). These solutions differ in form. 'An animal forms an eye for itself by causing scattered and diffuse luminous excitations to be reproduced on a privileged surface of its body. The eye binds light, it is itself a bound light' (DR: 96). As Deleuze will note in *The Fold*, 'a prehension: an element is the given, the "datum" of another element that prehends it. Prehension is individual unity. Everything prehends its antecedents and its concomitants and, by degrees, prehends a world. The eye is a prehension of light' (88).

Throughout this argument, Deleuze insists once more on two things: 1. There is a formal difference between the series of virtual intensity and actual extensity: 'Extensity can emerge from the depths only if depth is definable independently of extensity' (DR: 230). 2. As in Simondon, differential processes of the emergence of living beings come before differencial processes: 'Individuation precedes differenciation in principle, ... every differenciation presupposes a prior intense field of individuation ... Individuation does not presuppose any differenciation, it gives rise to it' (247). Once more in terms of 'Immanence: A Life': *transcendence is always a product of immanence.*

As I have noted repeatedly, Deleuze's philosophical project is to develop figures of thought within which to think the coupling of these heterogeneous series, and the paradox of their simultaneous operation within living beings. In a direct reference to constructivism in *Difference and Repetition*, Deleuze once more asks a question he had posed in *Empiricism and Subjectivity*. '"How can a subject transcending the given be constituted in the given?" Undoubtedly, the subject itself is given. Undoubtedly, that which transcends the given is also given, in another way and in another sense. This subject who invents and believes is constituted inside the given in such a way that it makes the given itself a synthesis and a system ... Here, the critical requirement is that of a constructivist logic which finds its model in mathematics' (DR: 86). (See also 'philosophy is a constructivism' (WP: 35); Bell 2008: 15.)

Mathematics is central in the argument about constructivism. In *The Logic of Sense* Deleuze quotes Albert Lautman as saying that 'the field of vectors on one hand and the integral curves on the other are two essentially distinct mathematical realities' (345). Already in his essay on Simondon, Deleuze had noted that 'in the theory of differential equations ... the existence and the distribution of "singularities" are of another nature than the "individual" forms of the integral curves in their neighborhood' (DI: 87). The state of pre-individual being 'is difference, disparity, "disparation". And the finest pages in the book are those where Simondon shows how disparity, as in the first moment of being, a singular moment, is in fact presupposed by all other states, whether unification, integration, tension, opposition, resolution of oppositions, etc. ... Simondon holds that the idea of "disparation" is more profound than the idea of opposition, and the idea of potential energy more profound than the idea of a field of forces' (87).

In both mathematical and genetic terms, pure intensity translates into continuous quantity, whereas extensity translates into discrete quality. Deleuze makes use of the mathematical routine of the Dedekind cut (*Dedekind'scher Schnitt*) to illustrate how to solve the logical problem of turning an intensive continuum, in Dedekind's case the continuum of numbers, into an extensive continuum [→ **Guattari 171**]. Deleuze uses the procedure to explicate his differentiation between intensive, virtual and extensive, actual numbers. In mathematical terms, this difference again concerns pure intensity as continuous quantity on the one hand and pure extensity as discrete quality on the other. 'Every number is originally intensive and vectorial in so far as it implies a difference of *quantity* which cannot properly be cancelled' (DR: 232, emphasis added), Deleuze notes. The image of this state of numbers is the continuous line. The question is thus how to align intensive continuity (aionic duration; *durée*) with extensive discreteness (chronic instants; *temps*).

Dedekind's procedure consists of replacing the given, intensive continuity described by the line of numbers with an infinity of extensive cuts into that line. In this way, the given, continuous mathematical modulation is replaced by an infinity of extensive cuts by which the given continuity is given as mathematically given in the same way in which the given multiplicity of light is given as optically given as an infinity of different colours. Once the given, intensive continuity is translated into an infinity of particular cuts, it is 'extensive and scalar in so far as it cancels this difference on another plane that it creates and on which it is explicated' (232). (On Dedekind, Foucault and smooth space, see TRM: 398, in particular: 'it seems to me that both the distinction between irrational and rational cuts by Dedekind and the distinction between distances and sizes by Russell correspond to the difference between smooth and striated space in Boulez') Once again, the two series of intensive and extensive continuity, the given and the given as given, are complementary and related according to a logic of reciprocal presupposition rather than mutual exclusion. (I will deal with Leibniz's version of the fundamental analogy between mathematics and perception later.) Symptomatically, Deleuze returns to the notion of witnessing to describe the relation between intensity and extensity in terms of the relation between intensive and extensive numbers. 'The vectors or vectorial magnitudes which occur throughout extensity, but also the scalar magnitudes or particular cases of vector-potentials, are the eternal *witness to* the intensive origin' (DR: 231, emphasis added). Somewhat paradoxically: *the act of quantification consists of a qualification.*

To envision, by way of the concept of virtual numbers, a Lucretian, affirmative and virtual 'mathematics without negation' (234) – according to which 'perceived quality presupposes intensity, because it expresses only a resemblance to a 'band of isolatable intensities', within the limits of which a permanent object is constituted' (230) – is fully in line with Deleuze's intensive vitalism. At this point, Deleuze shifts to a systemic perspective, linking the conceptual problem of the relation between ontology and epistemology to chronological registers, in particular to a difference in temporal direction. In processes of individuation, intensity comes before extensity because 'extensity does not account for the individuations which occur within it' (229). As Deleuze had noted in 'The Actual and the Virtual', individuation concerns the actualization of virtuals. In terms of perception and cognition, intensity comes after extensity, as something that perception has always already qualified and differentiated. Processes of singularization reverse this vector in that they go from actuals to virtuals and denote the virtualization of actuals. As Deleuze notes, 'we know only forms of energy which are already localised and distributed in extensity, or extensities already qualified by forms of energy' (DR: 223). From the perspective of perception, therefore, 'we know intensity only as already developed within an extensity, and as covered over by qualities' (223). In this light, Bryant's criticism of Deleuze's 'tendency to treat the virtual as something other than the individual', and his argument that 'the individual precedes the virtual such that virtuality is always the virtuality of a substance' (2011: 30), considers only the epistemological side of 'formal, qualitative or semiological distinction' (DR: 35). This is why from Bryant's perspective 'Deleuze's monism must clearly be mistaken' (2011: 98). However, as I have shown in 'Out of Turbulence, Philosophy; or: In the Light of Lucretius', in terms of quantum physics, epistemology is defined as what one might call a collapsed ontology. This ontological side concerns an informal, quantitative or non-semiotic intensity: the indifferent and anonymous field of pure virtuals. Deleuze's polyphonous monism plays itself out within the complementarity of these two sides. He never chooses.

From the perspective of imperceptibility, a perceptual entity is immanent to pure intensity and emerges from it. From the perspective of the entity, that intensity is lost in its passage into perceptibility. To reach virtual intensity by way of dissolving into singularities would involve the virtualization of an actual system: *actual virtualization*. A virtual mode of reaching a virtual intensity would imply a dissolving of one's memory: Proust's literature as a literature for a dissolved self. The third, philosophical return to intensity would involve dissolving one's thought and concepts: Deleuze's philosophy as a philosophy for a dissolved self. The concept must be treated as a multiplicity; as an 'implicated order of constitutive differences' (229) considered as a fully virtual, luminous field: *the scattering of philosophy*.

In this dissolution into multiplicity, living beings become themselves expressive in their ideas and their conceptualizations. 'Intensity . . . *dramatises*. It is intensity which is immediately expressed in the basic spatio-temporal dynamisms and determines an "indistinct" differential relation in the Idea to incarnate itself in a distinct quality and a distinguished extensity' (245). As Deleuze notes, 'through dramatization, the Idea is incarnated or actualized, *it differentiates itself*. Nevertheless, the Idea in its proper content must already present characteristics that correspond with the two aspects of its differentiation. The Idea is in itself a system of *differential* relations and the result of a distribution of remarkable or singular points (ideal events). In other words, the Idea is fully differential in itself, before even *differentiating* itself in the actual' (DI: 94): *ontic disparity, differential ontology, differentiating epistemology*.

The space of virtual intensity is thus both pre- and non-mathematical and pre- and non-philosophical. Like the ideal realm of intensive numbers, it is an imperceptible and thus unconscious space of 'intensive quantity' (DR: 230). As a 'pure *spatium*'

(230), its 'intensive depths' (235) form a reservoir from which extensive, systemic space is actualized as the space of 'partial systems' (241); as what Deleuze calls 'spatio-temporal dynamism[s]' (214). Qualitative perception extensifies this intensive, topological spatium into measured, geometrical space, redefining it in two ways. First, it turns it inside out. 'Intensity is the uncancellable in difference of quantity, but this difference of quantity is cancelled by extension, extension being precisely the process by which the intensive difference is turned inside out and distributed in such a way as to be dispelled, compensated, equalized and suppressed in the extensity which it creates' (233). Second, it turns it upside down: 'Negation is the inverted image of difference ... the image of intensity seen from below ... *It is underneath quality and within extensity that Intensity appears upside down*' (235).

Perception constructs a false image of the intensive world, and thus a fundamentally false world. At this point, Deleuze's conceptual topology still differentiates between depth and surface. This will change in *The Logic of Sense*, which charts the shift from the one to the other. As Deleuze had noted apropos Simondon, the field of individuation 'is intensive, that is, it implies differences of intensity distributed at different depths. Though experience always shows us intensities already developed in extensions, already covered over by qualities, we must conceive, precisely as a condition of experience, of pure intensities enveloped in a depth, in an intensive *spatium* that preexists every quality and every extension. Depth is the power of pure unextended *spatium*; intensity is only the power of differentiation or the unequal in itself, and each intensity is already difference ... Such an intensive field constitutes an environment of individuation ... It is not enough to discover a difference of nature between individuation on the one hand, and specification or partition on the other. Because individuation is the prior condition under which specification, and partition or composition, function in a system. Individuation is intensive, and it is presupposed by all qualities and species, by all extensions and parts that happen to fill up or develop the system' (DI: 97). Deleuze's real question, then, is about the relation between the intensive and the extensive. Why is '*intensio* (intension) ... inseparable from an *extensio* (extension) which relates it to the *extensum* (extensity)' (DR: 223)? The answer is that difference of *intensity* and *difference* of intensity contract the fields of virtuality and actuality. As a process of crystallization, this contraction takes place in a time that is faster than the speed of thought and thus faster than both mathematics and philosophy. Deleuze's name for the agent that operates faster than thought and philosophy is, once more, the dark precursor. In fact, this is the sentence from which I took the term difference operator that I used in the context of the function of the dark precursor in the phenomenon of lightning to bring about a communication between differen*t*iations: 'Nevertheless, since intensity is difference, differences of intensity must enter into communication. Something like a "difference operator" is required, to relate difference to difference. This role is filled by what is called an *obscure precursor*' (DI: 97).

Simondon understands individuation as the process of the organization of matter and thus as the genesis of form from chaos. In order to auto-assemble themselves into individuals, heterogeneous elements need a far-from-equilibrium milieu, whose 'potential energy' (2005: 68) they can tap into to actualize themselves as an individual. As with lightning, the potential energies – what Deleuze would call the virtual energies – 'express the limits of stability' of a specific state and they are the 'real sources' of 'possible births' (77). The genesis of individual life, then, happens from within an energetic, luminous storm. As Simondon notes in 'The Genesis of the Individual', a relation does not develop between 'two terms that are already individuals [such as sky and lightning], rather, it is an aspect of the *internal resonance of a system of individuation*. It forms a part of a wider system' (1992: 306).

'It is nonetheless a system', Deleuze goes on to say, 'insofar as the difference therein is like *potential energy*, like a *difference of potential* distributed within certain limits. Simondon's conception, it seems to me, can in this respect be assimilated to a theory of intensive quanta, since each intensive quantum in itself is difference' (DI: 87). What you have to begin with is a given world of purely quantitative differences in themselves. Disparate levels of reality. A 'world packed with *impersonal individuations*, or even *pre-individual singularities*' ('On Nietzsche', DI: 137) that are 'not reducible to individuals or persons, nor to a sea without difference. These singularities are mobile, they break in, thieving and stealing away, alternating back and forth, like anarchy crowned, inhabiting a nomad space' (143).

In terms of the genesis of living beings, it is from this intensive *spatium* that individuation proceeds. 'The essential process of intensive quantities is individuation ... The act of individuation consists not in suppressing the problem, but in integrating the elements of the disparateness into a state of coupling which ensures its internal resonance ... Individuation is the act by which intensity determines differential relations to become actualized, along the lines of differenciation and within the qualities and extensities it creates ... Individuation precedes differenciation in principle ... every differenciation presupposes a prior intense field of individuation' (DR: 246). In evolutionary terms, the question concerns genetic couplings. Under what conditions do 'small, unconnected or free-floating differences become appreciable, connected and fixed differences' (248)? In other words, what is a specific entity's 'morphogenetic potential' (251)?

As it emerges from a purely intensive multiplicity, 'individuation is mobile, strangely supple, fortuitous and endowed with fringes and margins' (257). The ultimate reasons for this precariousness and fragility are the complicated topology and architecture of intensive differences within the field of diversity. 'The intensities which contribute to it communicate with each other, envelop other intensities and are in turn enveloped. The individual is far from indivisible, never ceasing to divide and change its nature' (257). From the position of the living entity, the pure multiplicity of intensities is modelled as the field of its dissolution. From the position of original nomadic distribution, however, it is a field of intensive play. 'We are made of all these depths and distances, of these intensive souls which develop and are re-enveloped. We call individuating factors the ensemble of these enveloping and enveloped intensities, of these individuating and individual differences which ceaselessly interpenetrate one another throughout the fields of individuation. Individuality is not a characteristic of the Self but, on the contrary, forms and sustains the system of the dissolved Self' (254). As the notions of I and self are themselves results of routines of individuation and habituation, Deleuze proposes another fundamental philosophical reversal. 'It is the I and the self which are the abstract universals' (258) proposed by an extensive philosophy. When they are proposed by an intensive philosophy, they are concrete universals, such as the light that suffuses the plane of consistency. As Deleuze states in *Difference and Repetition*, 'there is no abstract universal beyond the individual or beyond the particular and the general: it is singularity itself which is "pre-individual"' (176). This is why Ideas should also be 'concrete universals' (176).

In terms of intensity, the difference between more and less complicated living systems is that the latter are defined by a larger ratio of interiorization and a larger amount of passive and active syntheses. 'Complex systems increasingly tend to interiorize their constitutive differences: the centres of envelopment carry out this interiorization of the individuating factors' (256). Within the field of individuation of the living, the only operative level reserved for humans concerns the agency of the observer; the agency of transcendental apperception as opposed to the empirical apperception that defines all living beings. In these dynamics, 'language effectively represent[s] the manifestation of the noumenon, the appearance of expressive values ... the tendency towards the interiorization of difference' (261).

Although human language seems to be a system of active syntheses, it also emerges from passive syntheses. This is why Deleuze extends the notion of writing from the level of human language to include unconscious, biomaterial processes. Like all other philosophies of the immanence of life, Deleuze considers not only human cultures, but also non-human cultures such as bacterial or molecular cultures, as cognitive, and thus as semiotic aggregates [→ **Guattari 17**]. According to this extended notion of semiotics, human writing emerges from and is pervaded by an infinite number of intensive and productive writings. The inscriptions of these writings, however, never congeal into linguistic signs. In a world filled with 'signaletic material [*matière signalétique*]' (C2: 33), a semiotics of natural machines implies a fundamental critique of the idealist reliance on the conscious operations of a fully reasonable thought. As

Deleuze notes, another way to say that active syntheses emerge from passive syntheses is to say that artificial signs emerge from natural signs (DR: 77).

Difference and Repetition argues, then, that both individuation and philosophy start long before the consolidation of subjects and objects. Both emerge out of a pre-philosophical diversity made up of the fields of the innumerable machinic assemblages of communal, non-human ecologies and cultures. If classic philosophy turns this space upside-down and inside-out, Deleuze's reversals are reversals of these reversals that re-establish a topology that is more adequate to the true state of affairs. The question remains, however, as to how to operate as individuals within this diverse space and whether there is an adequate ethical position to take within its multiplicity. To answer these questions, Deleuze turns to Spinoza.

The Moment of Spinoza

Expressionism in Philosophy: Spinoza (1968), Spinoza: Practical Philosophy (1970)

Famously, Deleuze considered Baruch de Spinoza to be the philosopher who 'drew up and thought the "best" plane of immanence – that is, the purest, the one that does not hand itself over to the transcendent or restore any transcendent, the one that inspires the fewest illusions, bad feelings, and erroneous perceptions' (WP: 60). This makes Spinoza – who is a direct descendant of Lucretius and already present in 'Lucretius and the Simulacrum' as someone who argues, like Lucretius, against the 'avidity and anguish, covetousness and culpability' (LS: 271) of 'religious man' (271) – not only 'the prince' (WP: 48) but also, somewhat ironically, 'the Christ of philosophers' (60). Like Lucretius, Spinoza 'fulfilled philosophy because he satisfied its prephilosophical presuppositions' (48). As a figure of 'the vertigo of immanence' (48), he is of such importance to Deleuze that one might well consider Deleuze's *Expressionism in Philosophy: Spinoza* and *Spinoza: Practical Philosophy* as making up, together, the central conceptual panel of a triptych whose two side panels are *Difference and Repetition* and *The Logic of Sense* [→ **Guattari 8**]. Looking more closely at Deleuze's work on Spinoza will allow us to consider in more detail two terms that I have up until now used rather loosely, despite the fact that they play a crucial and well-defined role in Deleuze's philosophy: attribute and infinity. Also, Spinoza's parallelism of modes and the process of the individuation of these modes allows to revisit the alignment of the series of the actual and the virtual from yet another perspective.

Spinoza's philosophy is defined by the conceptual triad of attributes, essences and substances. The relation between these terms is that attributes are the 'qualit[ies]' (EP: 29) that express the essence of a substance. The most comprehensive substance, which Deleuze calls Spinoza's 'immanent God' (45), has an infinity of attributes of which humans know only two: virtual thought (*cogitatio*) and actual extension (*extensio*). (On attributes, see also S: 51–2.) The conceptually most important characteristic of attributes is that they are defined in two registers and aspects simultaneously. They are expressive of the essence of an allover substance, and they express themselves. According to this twofold vectorization, 'attributes are, indissolubly, expressive and univocal' (EP: 59). Spinoza calls the media, or carriers of attributes – the entities in which attributes embody or incarnate themselves – modes. Of these, humans also know only two: singular Ideas, which are modes of thought, and singular bodies, which are modes of Extension. While Ideas express the attribute of thought, bodies express the attribute of Extension. As Deleuze notes, 'the simplest bodies are the ultimate extensive modal division of Extension' (191). On this conceptual background, sentient beings are modal media whose bodies express the attribute of Extension and whose minds express the attribute of Thought or Intension; a claim to which I will return.

In his definition of the relation between these two attributes, Spinoza sets up a parallelism that Deleuze will continue to draw on throughout his philosophy. Although Spinoza maintains that there is an '*identity of order* or *correspondence*' (107) between 'modes of different attributes' (107) – which means for sentient beings: between minds and bodies – this correspondence is not causal in the sense that a body is the cause of a mind or a mind is the cause of a body. This idea, which echoes Hume's idea that the body cannot explain the mind and vice versa, is crucial for Deleuze. 'Spinoza never seems to have admitted the action of a real causality to account for the relation between modes of different attributes' (107).

Spinoza insists on a non-causal relation because it is adequate to model the complementarity of the series. 'One feels that soul and body have at once a sort of identity that removes the need for any real causality between them, and a heterogeneity, a heteronomy, that renders it impossible' (326). Already in his work on Lucretius, Deleuze had come to a similar conclusion. In fact, the logic of complementarity had brought him to switch from Lucretian to Stoic registers. In this aspect, both the Stoics' and Spinoza's planes of immanence are better than Lucretius' because they are more adequate to nature. One can begin to feel why Spinoza is so important to Deleuze. As Spinoza famously notes, '*the body cannot determine mind to think, nor can the mind determine the body to motion or rest, or to anything else (if there is anything else)*' (2002: 279). There is, perhaps, no better and more concise description of how Deleuze conceives of the relation between the virtual and the actual. Like Spinoza, Deleuze differentiates between the series of virtual intelligibility and actual sensibility. For Spinoza, perception, which has one side directed towards the mind and the other towards the body, is the threshold between these two realms. '*The human mind is capable of perceiving a great many things, and this capacity will vary in proportion to the variety of states which its body can assume*' (Spinoza 2002: 255). Although there is an ontological identity of mind and body, at the same time, Spinoza asserts 'the independence of the two series, the series of things and the series of ideas' (EP: 115, see also S: 87). This formal separation extends to infinity. 'Two attributes taken to infinity will still be formally distinct, while being ontologically identical' (EP: 64). While Spinoza's formal parallelism is geometric, the expressive vector is projective: *coincidentia oppositorum*.

Is one of the two series more important? No. If the parallel series of actual Extension and virtual Thought are at the same time 'autonomous and independent' (107) and identical, any logic that values one series over the other is inadequate to that logic. Accordingly, Spinoza 'refuses any analogy, any eminence, any kind of superiority of one series over another ... there is no more any superiority of soul over body, than of the attribute of Thought over that of Extension' (109). Taken to its conceptual limit, does this mean that the philosopher's body is as important as the philosopher's mind? Yes, if one considers that there is no disembodied philosophy (ontological unity), and No, if one considers the body of the philosopher to be the cause of his or her thoughts (formal distinction). The twist in Spinoza's logic is that the correspondence between the virtual and the actual series has to be thought of as between two different series rather than between two different things. There is an ontological unity of the series in relation to modes, because ideas are invariably embodied, while bodies are invariably sentient. 'No idea can exist unless the thing also exists' and 'there is no thing of which there is not an idea in the thinking thing' (EP: 116). Despite this ontological unity, however, the two series are neither identical nor causally related. Rather, they are defined by a unity of difference. Mind and body '*are one and the same thing*, conceived now under the attribute of Thought, now under the attribute of Extension' (Spinoza 2002: 280; emphasis added). Or, as Deleuze notes, 'actually there is only one term, Life, that encompasses thought, but conversely this term is encompassed only by thought' (S: 14).

'One of the most famous theoretical theses of Spinoza is known by the name of *parallelism*; it does not consist merely in denying any real causality between the mind and the body, it disallows any superiority of the one over the other. If Spinoza rejects any superiority of the mind over the body, this is not in order to establish a superiority of the body over the mind, which would be no more intelligible than the converse ... There is no primacy of one series over the other' (S: 18). This geometric diagram, to which I will return in terms of Deleuze's topology of the real projective plane, allows Spinoza not only to think the relation between the actual and the virtual as a truly reciprocal presupposition, but also to develop a parallelism of a virtual and an actual unconscious; of the unthought and the unperceived. 'The model of the body, according to Spinoza, does not imply any devaluation of thought in relation to extension, but, much more important, a devaluation of consciousness in relation to thought: a discovery of the unconscious, of an *unconscious of thought* just as profound as *the unknown of the body*' (18–19).

If the relation between the two series is not causal, then what is it? Before Spinoza, Deleuze had used the terms of witnessing, reciprocal presupposition or resonance to define this relation. Spinoza provides him with two new terms. The first, which Deleuze relates to the logic of 'resonance' (EP: 327), is *'noncausal correspondences'* (326). Stressing the difference between the merely representational and the truly expressive, Deleuze had noted in 'The Method of Dramatization' that 'the virtual and the actual correspond but do not resemble one another' (DI: 110). This difference is also crucial in Spinoza. The use of the word expressionism in *Expressionism in Philosophy: Spinoza* points to the importance, for Deleuze, of the difference between Spinoza's expressive philosophy and its aesthetics on the one hand (intensive philosophy), and representational philosophies and their aesthetics on the other (extensive philosophy). Spinoza's expressionism follows directly from his parallelism: It is its adequate figure of thought.

The second term Spinoza provides is adequation, which also has to do with expression. To work in unison, the two series must be adequate to each other. In fact, only truly adequate ideas are 'expressive' (EP: 133) while inadequate ideas are representational and 'inexpressive' (145). This differentiation resonates directly with Deleuze's differentiation between the logic of sense and the logic of representation. Inadequate ideas are *'representational and related to artificial signs'* (181). Unlike attributes, which are inherently expressive of a mode, inadequate ideas are merely propria. They are properties of something rather than attributes.

Propria foster a moral, 'extensive' teaching (56) that rests on fixed moral laws and as such is opposed to a truly ethical, 'intensive' teaching; a distinction that is the germ of Deleuze's legal philosophy and leads to a Deleuzian theory of education. Propria are related to images of thought – especially their relation to the *lumen naturale* – as 'dogmatic, orthodox or moral' (DR: 131), and to a closed-off thought that does not allow itself to be shocked from the outside by site- and case-specific encounters with a world that 'forces us to think' (139) and provides thought with its expressive power. In the field of art, the logic of propria translates into '*Estheticism*', which is 'that act by which an individual cuts him or herself off from the pre-individual reality from which he or she emerged' (DI: 89). In Deleuze's conceptual topology, *Francis Bacon: The Logic of Sensation* and *The Logic of Sense* are truly Spinozist, complementary books.

Spinoza's notion of infinity is directly related to this expressionism. God as the most comprehensive substance is defined by an absolute infinity (EP: 204) that, in relation to attributes, splits into two series. At this point, it is no longer surprising that these are a virtual, 'intensive infinity' (203) and an 'actual' (205), 'extensive infinity' (202). There is a conceptual resonance between these infinities and the conceptual pairs Deleuze had developed in *Difference and Repetition*, such as virtual energy and actual energy or differen*t*iation and differen*c*iation, 'an intensive quantity, which divides into intensive parts, or degrees, and an extensive quantity, which divides into extensive parts' (192). While intensive infinity is truly infinite, 'extensive infinity' (202) is merely 'indefinite' because its parts 'cannot be equated with any number, yet they can be conceived as greater or less' (192; see also 201–8). One can feel how much of Spinoza resonates with *Difference and Repetition*. Ontologically, '*intensive* infinity comes *before* extensive infinity' (202), in the same way that differen*t*iation comes before differen*c*iation and the virtual comes before the actual, while epistemologically, it is the other way around.

In terms of expressing the essence of a divine substance, attributes are the 'eternal and infinite [forms or] qualities' (191) of that substance. In terms of expressing themselves, however, they are related to modes in their state of actually existing as living, sentient beings. 'Leibniz by *monad*, no less than Spinoza by *mode*, understands nothing other than an individual as an expressive center' (327). A mode is an 'embodied individual' (257). Seen from the perspective of expressing a divine substance, the individuation of modes goes from an 'infinite quality' (119) to a '*corresponding* quantity, which divides into irreducible intrinsic or intensive parts' (199, emphasis added). In this aspect, modes are 'finite' and 'quantitative' (198). The virtual comes before the actual: *monism à la Spinoza*.

As living 'creatures' (199), however, in the aspect of expressing themselves rather than in the aspect of expressing an infinite, divine substance, individuation is a process of crystallization that operates without a transcendental agency. 'There is in Spinoza no metaphysics of essences, no dynamic of forces, no mechanism of phenomena. Everything in nature is "physical": a physics of intensive quantity corresponding to modal essences; a physics of extensive quantity, that is, a mechanism through which modes themselves come into existence; a physics of force, that is, a dynamism through which essence asserts itself in existence, espousing the variations of the power of action' (233). The actual comes before the virtual: *materialism à la Spinoza*.

In topological terms, the figure of a Necker cube might be taken as the conceptual figure of Spinoza's philosophy in that it contains two complementary but formally distinct realities. Depending on the point of view, expressive modes correspond either to the virtual qualities of a universal substance that actualizes itself in these modes, with their bodies being part of that substance, or they are singular actual quantities; bodies that develop their own qualities through processes of contraction that, as I mentioned earlier, are the source of qualities, with quality 'nothing other than contracted quantity': *divine thought against individual thought*. If there is a fundamental shift that Deleuze performs in relation to Spinoza, as well as, to a larger degree, in relation to Leibniz, it is from God to Nature. With Spinoza, this is easy: call Spinoza's universal substance an 'immanent God' (45) and define this God as an immanent Nature. With this move, the logic of expressionism becomes even more convoluted. Unity becomes multiplicity. Within a natural plane of immanence essence becomes singular essences: *the plane of immanence as the plane of consistency or consistencies*.

Although Spinoza does not develop this point explicitly, Deleuze argues that he might be understood as conceptualizing a 'singularity belonging to modal essences as such' (197). While the essence of a substance is expressed by its qualitative attributes, '*the essence of a mode is a pure physical reality*' (193). Modes, therefore, are naturally expressive – expressive of Nature, that is – rather than expressive of a supreme, unified substance. Their nature is to express Nature as a multiplicity. 'Expression in Nature is never a final symbolization, but always, and everywhere, a causal *explication*' (234). Against the 'qualitative identity of the absolute', modes set 'a quantitative distinction of being' (197): singularity. Spinoza segues into Simondon, differenciation segues into differentiation. 'Each finite being must be said to *express the absolute*, according to the intensive quantity that constitutes its essence ... Individuation is ... neither qualitative nor extrinsic, but quantitative and intrinsic, intensive' (197).

As in *Difference and Repetition*, Deleuze uses the term diversity to define the quantitative state of modal existence. 'There is a unity of the diverse in substance, and an actual diversity of the One in the attributes' (81, 104–5, 182). Caught between expressing the overall multiplicity of a substantial Nature, and expressing themselves as singular modal existences within a diversity of other modes, attributes have, once more, 'at once *identity of being* and *distinction of formality*. Ontologically one, formally diverse' (66, emphasis added).

Within Spinoza's plane of immanence, the universal substance is in no way prior to the modes, and as such it does not organize and survey individuation from a transcendental plateau ($n+1$). While Leibniz grounds the coherence of the world in a pre-established harmony, Spinoza's logic of attribution is based on a temporality and logic of immanence that is the direct and necessary result of the fact that, as with the Stoics, effects and causes make up the two parallel aspects of one and the same existing mode. Crystallization, as the process by which an actual relates to its virtual and vice versa, is an immanent process. 'A cause is immanent ... when its effect is "immanate" in the cause, rather than emanating from it. What defines an immanent cause is that its effect is in it – in it, of course, as in something else, but still being and remaining in it' (172, see also S: 54). This difference is analogous to that between theories of the emanation of light and an immanent light.

In 'Spinozistische Perspektiven: Die Ethik im Lichte der arguesianischen Geometrie betrachtet', Yvonne Toros (2009) relates Spinoza's inherently projective philosophy to Girard Desargues's development of projective geometry, and to an analogous theory of light. The former allows one to relate the formal logic of parallelism to the projective logic of expressionism. As Deleuze notes, 'it is because the body and the soul have no point in being inseparable, for they are not in the least really distinct . . . From this moment on any localization of the soul in an area of the body, no matter how tiny it may be, amounts rather to a projection from the top to the bottom, a projection of the soul focalizing on a "point" of the body, in conformity with Desargues's geometry, that develops from a Baroque perspective' (LB: 13). The latter sets up a luminism in which 'the finite modi of extension can . . . be understood as the result of a refraction of light, a modification of the white light (*lux*) that characterizes the eternal and infinite substance – a substance that is simultaneously *lux* and *lumen*' (189). In this context, the modi are 'the colors that result from the refraction of the white light in the prism that consists of stasis and movement' (189). Once more, this light is not a *lumen naturale*, but the light of an immanent Nature: *expressionist pantheism. Venus meets Spinoza; immanent versus emanating, expressive versus representational light.*

Expressionism, then, is the process of the actualization of an immanent logic. 'Immanence is revealed as expressive, and expression as immanent' (EP: 175). '*Natura naturans* (as substance and cause) and *Natura naturata* (as effect and mode) are interconnected through a mutual immanence' (S: 92). In this double movement, 'immanence is the very vertigo of philosophy' (EP: 180). In psychoanalytic registers, 'immanence is the unconscious itself, and the conquest of the unconscious' (S: 29). From the chapter 'What Can a Body Do?' onwards, Deleuze's text becomes a truly 'Lucretian' (EP: 270) celebration of an immanent ecology based on Spinoza's 'philosophy of pure affirmation' and joy: '*Non opposita sed diversa*' (60). A similarly Lucretian strain and rhythm runs through chapter six of *Spinoza: Practical Philosophy*, 'Spinoza and Us', in which Deleuze develops Spinoza's 'ethology' (S: 125) from within which it is no longer necessary to distinguish between God and Nature – '*Deus sive Natura*' (17) – nor to replace God by Nature. God is merely a name for the infinite substance that is expressed in and by an inherently heterogeneous Nature. 'A single substance with all its attributes really distinct' (EP: 61). God and Nature are no longer opposed, as God is no longer revealed in a transcendental light, but in 'the light of Nature' (59): *the luminosity of the world.*

Within his narrative of the individuation and existence of modes, Deleuze develops, with Spinoza, a theory of living beings as autopoietic. (For a critique of Maturana and Varela, see Toscano 2006; similarly, Ansell-Pearson 1999: 168–70, on the autopoiesis of concepts and philosophy, 202–3.) As Spinoza notes, 'the human mind does not perceive any external body as actually existing, except through the ideas of affections of its own body' (2002: 261). This is why the soul, as the 'idea of the body' (94), is mortal. 'The soul "endures" to the extent that it expresses the actual existence of a body that endures' (EP: 311).

A mode comes into existence 'when an infinity of extensive parts enter into a *given* relation: it continues to exist as long as this relation holds' (208). The given relation is 'a relation through which any of its parts belong to that particular modal essence' (208). Within its envelope of structural stability (209–11), the being's elements are defined according to a dynamic of 'movement and rest' (205) as well as 'speed and slowness' (208), which are terms Deleuze takes over from Spinoza. Its overall 'coherence' (S: 19) allows for a specific range of elasticity. Its structural spine, however, can also dissolve or break up. 'A given mode will continue to exist as long as the same relation *subsists* in the infinite whole of its parts' (EP: 208, emphasis added). At this point, subsistence takes the place of substance. As Deleuze notes, 'the existence of a particular thing is the thing itself, no longer as simply contained in its attribute, no longer as simply comprehended in God, but as having duration, as having a relation with a certain extrinsically distinct time and place' (213). As a subsisting '*res physica*' (303), each mode is invariably suspended in a specific, site- and time-specific ecology. As D. H. Lawrence, who will become important later on, notes, 'each continent has its own great spirit of place. Every people is polarized in some particular locality, which is home, the homeland. Different places on the face of the earth have different vital effluence, different vibration, different chemical exhalation, different polarity with different stars: call it what you like, but the spirit of place is a great reality' (1990: 5–6).

The question posed by living in a multiplicity and of expressing this multiplicity is 'how . . . to produce adequate ideas' (EP: 221), which means how to get from 'passive affection' (219) to 'active affection' (222). In this context, passive does not mean, as it did in terms of passive syntheses, unconscious or automatic. Rather, it is related to 'passion' (S: 27) as something that is being passively endured, as in the passion of Christ. 'Existence itself is still conceived as a kind of test. Not, it is true, a moral one, but a physical or chemical test, like that whereby workmen check the quality of some material, of a metal or a vase' (EP: 317, see also S: 41). The aim is to gain the most mental and physical 'power of action' (EP: 225, 226), of what today is called agency. This agency refers both to the body and to the mind. As Spinoza notes, 'our mind is in some instances active and in other instances passive. Insofar as it has adequate ideas, it is necessarily active; and insofar as it has inadequate ideas, it is necessarily passive' (2006: 279).

Spinoza calls the source of activity *conatus* or 'appetite' (S: 20), both of which designate the power of life operative within a mode. 'A *conatus* is indeed a mode's essence (or degree of power) *once the mode has begun to exist'* (EP: 230). As such, *conatus* denotes both 'desire' (231) and the will to cohere; 'our effort to persevere in existence, is always a quest for what is useful or good for us; it always involves some degree of our power of action, with which indeed it may be identified' (2006: 24). One can feel the positivity of Spinoza in the semantics of his definition of nature as the ensemble of the assembly and disassembly of living entities; a plane of composition in which, although they are conceptually complementary terms, dissolution is in the service of creation in the same way that pain is only the other side of joy, and individual death only the other side of genesis. 'Everything in Nature is just composition . . . Decomposition is only the other side of composition' (EP: 237). In fact, one of Spinoza's main lessons is proto-ecological. Individual modes are immanent to a nature that follows a 'common order' (245) rather than an individual one. Single individuals are of no concern to a nature in which everything is communal. Modes relate to each other through 'common notions' (275) that reach across their singularities in terms of biological co-adaptation and co-evolution. 'Spinoza's common notions are biological, rather than physical or mathematical, ideas. They really do play the part of Ideas in a philosophy of Nature from which all finality has been excluded' (278). These common notions should not be confused with common sense, with figures of thought, or with a *lumen naturale*; in short, with the abstract ideas developed from within an extensive philosophy. In fact, 'on all counts, abstract ideas are thoroughly inadequate' (277). 'Natural geometry' (S: 57), therefore, rather than mathematical geometry: 'geometric pantheism' (110). As '*general* rather than *abstract*' (EP: 278) ideas, common notions 'involve a certain generality without abstraction' (287, see also S: 114).

Nature is the plane of immanence and composition in which every living being exists according to its nature. Each one is in search of conjunctions with other beings, looking for relations and alliances that heighten its agency and happiness. As in Hume, reason is only an after-effect of the more fundamental 'effort to select and organize good encounters' (S: 55). Echoing *The Logic of Sense*, Deleuze notes that 'the body has a mechanism in reality, there is an automaton of thought in the order of ideality; but we learn that the corporeal mechanism and the spiritual automaton are most *expressive* when they find their "sense" and their "correspondence" in . . . necessary reason' (EP: 335). Once more, rationality is in the service of viability. As an existing mode, I look for those encounters with elements that are considered to '"agree with my nature", to be "good", that is, "useful", to me' (239). With each mode attempting to 'seek, soul and body, what is useful or good for them' (257), nature becomes an arena in which to find elective affinities.

Spinoza knows, however, that nature is never in balance and that there is a food chain. 'We will still be determined to destroy certain bodies, if only in order to subsist;

we cannot avoid all bad encounters, we cannot avoid death. But we can strive to unite with what agrees with our nature, to combine our relation with those that are compatible with it, to associate our acts and thoughts with the images of things that agree with us. From such an effort we have a right, by definition, to expect a maximum of joyful affections' (261). While Spinoza's philosophy is never utopian, it always aims to replace a morality of propria, which concerns only what is appropriate, with an ethics of adequation. 'The distinction between good things and bad provides the basis for a real ethical difference, which we must substitute for a false moral opposition' (254). From within such an ethics, an encounter that brings about 'the decomposition of a relation' (247) is bad. As in Lucretius, the moral dichotomy of good and evil is supplanted by the dichotomy of an ecological ethics of good and bad encounters (S: 23). In this shift, 'Spinozism is the becoming-child of the philosopher' (TP: 256): *ecological correlationism.*

Spinoza Now!

Capitalism and Schizophrenia 1 & 2 (1972, 1980)

One might consider the celebratory chapters on Spinoza to be the germ of *Anti-Oedipus* and *A Thousand Plateaus*, in which Deleuze and Guattari open philosophy up to the non- and even the pre-philosophical, to the unconscious realm from which philosophy emerges; the comprehensive field of anonymous thought – a general sentience – that puts philosophy in touch with all levels of contemporary life. The most adequate way to read the two books, in which philosophy is over long stretches implicit rather than explicit, is not as additions to Deleuzian philosophy, but as actualizations of the figure of philosophy that Deleuze had developed in *Difference and Repetition, Expressionism in Philosophy, Spinoza: Practical Philosophy* and *The Logic of Sense*. How can one propose an ethology of thought and remain within the traditionally and strictly bounded field of philosophy? In his work of the 1970s, Deleuze puts his philosophy to the test. Together with Guattari, he takes philosophy out of the philosophical laboratory and experiments with it in the extended field: *philosophy as an open system.*

Guattari is a crucial agent in the experiment of the opening-up of philosophy to other fields, but also of the diversification and opening-up of philosophical thought itself. Deleuze's philosophy is opened up, one might say, by Guattari's subversions of Lacanian psychoanalysis and its adherent politics. In their structural and stylistic stereophonics, the two books have the perhaps highest coefficient of conceptual deterritorialization. One cannot overestimate what it means for a philosopher such as Deleuze to write with somebody else, and thus to literally diversify his thought from without – to give up individual thought for a more general and more communal thought-machine and what Guattari would call a twofold assemblage of enunciation. With figures such as the rhizome, the books enact a true ecology of thought [→ **Guattari 5**].

The programme of this radical diversification rings through the famous polemic directed against closed systems that opens *A Thousand Plateaus*. 'The two of us wrote *Anti-Oedipus* together. Since each of us was several, there was already quite a crowd. Here we have made use of everything that came within range, what was closest as well as farthest away ... To reach, not the point where one no longer says I, but the point where it is no longer of any importance whether one says I ... We have been aided, inspired, multiplied' (3). (On their collaboration, see Guattari 2006; Dosse 2011.) A result of this both formal and conceptual openness has been that both *Anti-Oedipus* and *A Thousand Plateaus* have become important transdisciplinary pick-up machines. Political science, sociology, historical studies, literary studies, ethnography, psychoanalysis, film studies and the visual arts have found landing pads in the two books. Somewhat ironically, the only field that has not found a landing pad is philosophy, which has had its difficulties with how radically the two books open up the philosophical field to the allover milieu.

As the widening of the thematic range had a lot to do with the entry of Guattari into Deleuze's philosophical world, philosophy has tended to put the blame on Guattari. Even today there is a general agreement, or at least a lingering suspicion, both within Deleuze studies and beyond, that up to their later collaboration *What is Philosophy?*, Guattari's thought has been detrimental to Deleuzian philosophy. In *Organs without Bodies*, for instance, Slavoj Žižek attempts to save a true Deleuze from Guattari, although, in a second step, he then turns the true Deleuze into a closet Hegelian (see my 'Is it Possible not to Love Žižek?' (2005)). The claim is that with the entry of Guattari, the inherent complexity of Deleuzian philosophy is given up for a set of simple oppositions. What this claim misses, however, is that the complexity of Deleuze's system is also based on a system of simple oppositions, such as that of the virtual and the actual. It is not oppositionality that is simple. What is simple is to simply choose between the opposites rather than to consider them as complementary.

Guattari brings to Deleuze not only an opening up of frames of reference, but also a more polemical attitude and style. Against psychoanalysis and capitalism in *Anti-Oedipus*, against arborescent thought in general in *A Thousand Plateaus*. These polemics are owed to the fact that the two books are explicitly political, whereas the politics in Deleuze's singular works tend to be implicit. They are, however, the same politics. In fact, *Anti-Oedipus* reads as if one had picked Spinoza up from seventeenth-century Amsterdam and set him down in the Paris of the 1960s. As if Spinoza were the philosophical weapon of choice against the psychoanalytic, the capitalist and the cultural machines operative in the books' real time. As if Spinoza was the necessary tool to restore 'the syntheses of the unconscious to their immanent use' (AO: 112). As if, through Spinoza, one might counteract the colonization of 'the immanent unity of the earth' (146) by the combined forces of 'transcendent unity' (146) of the despot and later on of capital. (On the relation between Spinoza and *A Thousand Plateaus*, see Beistegui 2010: 105–17. Symptomatically, Hardt and Negri's *Multitude: War and Democracy in the Age of Empire* (2005) runs on Spinozist fuel.)

Spinoza's shadow falls onto *Anti-Oedipus* early on. 'The fundamental problem of political philosophy is still precisely the one that Spinoza saw so clearly ... "Why do men fight *for* their servitude as stubbornly as though it were their salvation?"' (AO: 29). There is no better way to describe the conceptual and political thrust of *Anti-Oedipus*. If one remembers that according to Deleuze Spinoza attempted to uncover an unconscious of rather than in thought, the immediate question in *Anti-Oedipus* is how such an unconscious would look. How does it compare and contrast to the Freudian and the Lacanian unconscious? Which of the two notions of the unconscious is wilder and more radical? Spinoza's unconscious – what can a body do? – is an unconscious of bodily affects and the ideas of these affects. It is productive, physical and expressive rather than representative. Much of *Anti-Oedipus* is about the ways in which this 'orphan unconscious' (82) that knows neither mother nor father can dismantle the both familiar and familial triangulations of desire performed by psychoanalysis. Throughout the book, the question is eminently Spinozian. How can one avoid 'the three errors concerning desire' (111); those of 'lack, law, and signifier' (111)? How can one change this negative, representational series into one of affirmation, composition and expression?

In *A Thousand Plateaus*, Spinoza is maybe even more present than in *Anti-Oedipus*. Symptomatically, the more or less precise middle of the book is made up of the two complementary chapters 'Memories of a Spinozist, I' and 'Memories of a Spinozist, II'. The general topic of the chapters is the body without organs as a plane of immanence. Already in *Anti-Oedipus*, Deleuze and Guattari had noted that 'the body without organs is the immanent substance, in the most Spinozist sense of the word; and the partial objects are like its ultimate attributes' (327). Their description of the body without organs as an egg recapitulates almost literally the description of Spinoza's plane of immanence in chapter six of *Spinoza: Practical Philosophy*, 'Spinoza and Us'. (On the egg, see also TRM: 21; Ansell-Pearson 1999: 8–9, 93–5.)

As it will become increasingly important in my text, some words about the plane of immanence: On one dense page of *A Thousand Plateaus*, Deleuze and Guattari define it as a plane that is made up of elements that 'no longer have either form or function' (253). They are 'abstract' (254), neutral and anonymous in the way pure events are, as I will argue later, neutral and anonymous. As such, the plane of immanence is fully virtual. At the same time, these elements are 'perfectly real' and, as elementary particles, indivisible. They are 'infinitely small, ultimate parts of an actual infinity' (254). Everything is composed of these elements, which enter into and leave compositions at an infinite speed. They are the smallest elements of nature understood as a 'multiplicity of perfectly individuated multiplicities' (254). This actual aspect of the plane of immanence is 'peopled by anonymous matter, by infinite bits of impalpable matter entering into various connections' (255). The plane of immanence forms the ungrounded ground of any 'plane of consistency' (255). It is the most general medium of material formation. When it is formed – and it is always formed – the plane of immanence is the plane of consistency. It is at this point that the world is split into the two aspects of the virtual as actualized and the actual as virtualized. Although the planes are formally distinct, they should, at the same time, be thought of as ontologically complementary. At infinity, the planes of immanence and of consistency are in actual fact the same plane. Perhaps this is why Deleuze would talk about nature as 'the plane of immanence *or* consistency, which is always variable and is constantly being altered, composed and recomposed, by individuals and collectivities' (S: 127–8, emphasis added). In a variation on Spinoza, in fact, the plane of immanence and the plane of consistency might be said to be one and the same thing, conceived first under the attribute of the virtual and intensity, secondly under the attribute of the actual and extension. In other words, ontological indifference, epistemological difference: *philosophical complementarity.*

Anti-Oedipus and *A Thousand Plateaus* do not develop a new figure of philosophy. Rather, they provide a number of new terminologies, such as the plane of immanence, the body without organs and the abstract machine [→ **Guattari 75**]. Using these terminologies as catalysts, they show how philosophy is actualized in specific milieus. They are variations on a theme. They chart experiments about how well the Spinozist figure of thought functions in the open range. How viable are its interventions in deeply inadequate political and cultural circumstances?: *practical philosophy.*

What the books dramatize is what happens to Deleuze's philosophy when it is suspended into the elements and circumstances of the concrete world. When Deleuze and Guattari take over the term plateau from Bateson, it is partly in this context. 'Gregory Bateson uses the term *plateau* for continuous regions of intensity ... A plateau is a piece of immanence' (TP: 158). *Anti-Oedipus* and *A Thousand Plateaus* are testing grounds for the adequacy of Deleuzian philosophy in the ecology of the contemporary world's planes of consistency and composition. They chart its agency and its alliances in its specific milieus. How could it not do this, when it advocates, at all points, such an immanence in the world? To say that this milieu is Paris before the backdrop of structuralism and poststructuralism would be true, but much too restricted. On less perceptible levels, the milieu also comprehends the myriad influences and meetings that have shaped Deleuze's life. Influences that go from the very personal to the academic. All of these levels create an infinitely complex field of resonance. Infinitely many chance encounters. The atmosphere in France; its meteorological and conceptual weather. The constantly changing light. Visits to the cinema. Becoming a father. Deleuze's philosophy emerges from his readings and from teaching courses in Vincennes, from minute decisions, from an overheard sentence, from cultural, biological and chemical influences. As everybody knows, this is how thought functions. As the mind is embodied, it is spread out within the milieu of the actualization of thought. Deleuze's thought emerges from the dynamics of the milieu to which his life is immanent. Ultimately, the pre-philosophical field encompasses the whole world as a field of intensities and resonances. It is the milieu out of which consistencies emerge as local expressions of that world.

In Deleuze's singular works, figures of thought are developed mainly from within philosophical milieus and registers. That it is not concerned explicitly with present philosophy and politics but rather with a virtual philosophy and politics as virtual figures of thought gives his singular work its air of timelessness. The feel of what Badiou calls 'philosophical eternity' (2000: 3). Maybe one might differentiate between Deleuze's works as a *scriptura contemplativa,* as opposed to the *scriptura activa* of some of his essays and interviews, but mainly, of his work with Guattari: *Anti-Oedipus, A Thousand Plateaus, Kafka* and *What is Philosophy?* In another sense, however, this distinction is much too general. Maybe it is simply a question of how else to write after having published *Spinoza: Practical Philosophy*?

In *Anti-Oedipus* and *A Thousand Plateaus,* the philosophical figure of thought is folded onto the milieu out of which it has emerged in an attempt to counter-actualize the operations of that milieu, to explicitly intervene, both formally and in terms of content, in this milieu in order to change it. Ultimately, to delineate a philosophy that is adequate to the world: *transcendental empiricism becomes political philosophy.*

One political intervention is Deleuze's essay 'Postscript on Control Societies' from 1990, which traces the shift in the logic of control from repressive structures to a field of open systems connected by the universal platform of a computerized reality that is pervaded by what Deleuze calls 'ultrarapid forms of apparently free-floating control [*les formes ultra-rapides de contrôle à l'air libre*]' (N: 178). In control societies, which have replaced the repressive societies described by Foucault and Althusser, the subject's desire for its own submission can no longer be understood from within a sadomasochist logic, which Deleuze had addressed in 'Coldness and Cruelty' from 1967, where coldness relates to masochism and cruelty to sadism. That essay is one of Deleuze's most sustained meditations on sexual complementarity, once as symmetrical and dialectical, once as a-symmetrical and paradoxical. It also marks the first moment of the institution of the difference between literary and singular syndromatology, as opposed to theoretical and abstract symptomatology: *literature against psychoanalysis*.

A control society seems to be everywhere equally liberal and to form a network that allows for free movements between a multiplicity of nodes. While disciplinary societies follow a logic of confinement, control societies seem to follow a logic of dispersion and of free movement. Heterogeneity seems to have won out over repression. 'Money, perhaps, best expresses the difference between the two kinds of society, since discipline was always related to molded currencies containing gold as a numerical standard, whereas control is based on floating exchange rates, modulations depending on a code setting sample percentages for various currencies' (N: 180). However, although money has lost its strict coupling to a natural standard of value, it remains, even under the new conditions of floating value, the measure of societal determinations. Every encounter is a capitalist encounter. The seemingly heterogeneous, dynamic network remains under the influence of a 'single modulation, a sort of universal transmutation' (179) [→ **Guattari 213**].

The French original gives universal transmutation as *déformateur universel*, which points more directly to the notion that the assumed freedom exists in a field or network that is everywhere defined by one stressor. As such, freedom is not at all free, because the network is not a true network, which would be based on a logic of free self-regulation under given, constantly changing circumstances. In even scarier terms, its freedoms work only from within a general capitalist logic. In its *faux* multiplicity, there can only be similarly *faux* lines of flight. Whether one calls this universal stressor Integrated World Capitalism, neo-liberalism or infinite economy, is sadly beside the point. Still, there is hope. Deleuze notes that 'one of the most important questions is whether trade unions still have any role' (N: 179). If this question seems to have been answered in 2019, Deleuze stresses that 'it's not a question of worrying or of hoping for the best, but of finding new weapons' (178). As Guattari notes in *Schizoanalytic Cartographies*, 'the future remains largely open' (2013: 15): *Spinoza 2.0*.

In this light, we would need, for 2020, a new, updated version of *Anti-Oedipus*, rewritten perhaps as a *Postscript on Control Sexualities*, which would critique the contemporary landscape of the modulations of sexuality from within the registers of its universal capitalist deformation. Similarly, we would need an updated version of *A Thousand Plateaus*, which would trace today's tilted rhizomatics of the capitalist implementation of flat hierarchies and their short-term, task-force dynamics; the co-option of strategies of ad-hoc organization and de-centralization by strategies of the implementation of continuous credit-card debt and continuous work-from-home precarity: *life in times of faux-fluid capital*.

The Event of Philosophy

The Logic of Sense (1969), What is Philosophy? (1991)

The perhaps most concise description of Deleuze's transcendental empiricism comes from Michel Foucault's *The Order of Things*. In the chapter 'The empirical and the transcendental', Foucault talks about 'a discourse whose tension *would keep separate the empirical and the transcendental, while being directed at both* . . . a discourse, in short, which in relation to the quasi-aesthetics and quasi-dialectics would play the role of an analytic . . . and perhaps enable them to articulate themselves in that third and intermediary term in which both the experience of the body and that of culture would be rooted' (1989: 320–1, emphasis added).

Like *Anti-Oedipus* and *Thousand Plateaus*, *The Logic of Sense* is structurally deterritorialized in that the text assembles a number of heterogeneous series rather than one coherent argument. Within this conceptual multiplicity, Deleuze provides a further variation on how to think the reciprocal attribution of the actual and the virtual. Matters-of-fact refer to the actual, events refer to the virtual. The original French term, *états de choses*, is translated into English variously as 'matters of fact' or as 'states-of-affairs'. I will follow Deleuze, who uses the English 'matters of fact' (LS: 7), but I will carry over the hyphenation of states-of-affairs. (On the relation of the term to Péguy, see Beistegui 2004: 225.)

The notion of the event is one of the most important, but also one of the most contested terms in Deleuze's oeuvre. Its position within the crystal logic that I have begun to develop in the preceding chapters is very precise. The relation between matters-of-fact and events has to do with the question of how to align language and the material world. Against the Saussurean linguistics that defined the theoretical field around Deleuze, the text develops a semiotics that is not based on the unstable attribution of signifiers and signifieds, but on the unstable attribution of the fields of the semiotic and the energetic. 'We should never oppose words to things that supposedly correspond to them' (TP: 67), Deleuze and Guattari note in reference to the logic of a classical semiotics. Instead, 'what should be opposed are distinct formalizations in a state of unstable equilibrium' (67). As Deleuze notes in 'Letter to Uno on Language', 'language has no self-sufficiency . . . signs are inseparable from . . . a non-linguistic element, which would be called "the state of things" or, better yet, "images"' (TRM: 201). Language is 'always a heterogeneous system, or, as physicists say, a system far from equilibrium' (202). Its polyvocality and anonymity are figured by the mode of 'free indirect discourse' (202, see also 367). In *The Logic of Sense*, this semiotics is set into place through the way sense will be defined against signification. This new semiotics allows for the adequate alignment of words – the realm of propositionality that is made up of 'denotation, manifestation and signification' (LS: 12) – and matters-of-fact, of immateriality and materiality, as well as of relations and terms. It allows us to make sense of the paradoxical statement that echoes both Lacan and the Stoics: the event '*subsists* in language, but . . . *happens* to things' (24, emphases added).

What are matters-of-fact, what are events, and how are the two related? In *What is Philosophy?*, Deleuze and Guattari differentiate between matters-of-fact, things and bodies. Matters-of-fact refer to a milieu of spatially and structurally oriented, but heterogeneous, unrelated elements. Things refer to these elements as 'variables that are functions *of each other*' (WP: 122, emphasis added), which means that things are heterogeneous elements that are functionally related and organized into sets. Bodies, finally, refer to fully individuated systems that result from 'a cascade of actualizations' (123). Bodies are crystals with 'internal milieus (endoreference)' that enter into 'probabilistic functions with external variables of the outside milieu (exoreference)' (123) [→ **Guattari 84**]. Within this progression, 'states of affairs are ordered mixtures, of very different types, which may even only concern trajectories . . . things are interactions, and bodies are communications' (123).

The contexts to which Deleuze and Guattari relate these three phases of individuation are instructive. Matters-of-fact 'refer to geometrical coordinates of *supposedly* closed systems, things refer to energetic coordinates of coupled systems, and bodies refer to the informational coordinates of separated, unconnected systems' (123, emphasis added). Matters-of-fact concern mixtures of heterogeneous, supposedly indivisible elements (supposedly closed systems), things concern resonant interactions of elements (structurally coupled systems), and bodies concern informational interactions (operationally closed systems): *geometry, formation, information*. In the case of bodies, the closure is no longer simply supposed. It now denotes a fully actualized operational and informational closure. In terms of Deleuze's transcendental empiricism, the geometric and the intensive define the abstract, transcendental side, while the informational defines the concrete, empirical side. If matters-of-fact refer to the reservoir of singular, oriented but not yet systematized actual elements, let me, already here, propose an analogous definition of events: events refer to the reservoir of singular, oriented but not yet systematized virtual elements.

The importance of the notion of the event in Deleuzian philosophy can be seen in this flash-forward to *What is Philosophy?* in which Deleuze and Guattari differentiate, famously, between three basic modes of thought: 'from sentences or their equivalent, philosophy extracts *concepts* (which must not be confused with general or abstract ideas), whereas science extracts *prospects* (propositions that must not be confused with judgements), and art extracts *percepts and affects* (which must not be confused with perceptions and feelings)' (24). Deleuze and Guattari note that art creates affective assemblages from pure affects, while philosophy invents concepts from pure events. Art creates surfaces of sensation, while philosophy creates surfaces of sense. In order to explain how these two surfaces can be brought into resonance, I will first deal with the differences between the three main practices of dealing with the infinite multiplicity of the world. What is philosophy? What is science? What is art?

Deleuze and Guattari maintain that philosophy, science and art differ mainly in their relation to infinity. 'By retaining the infinite, philosophy gives consistency to the virtual through concepts; by relinquishing the infinite, science gives reference to the virtual, which actualises it through functions. Philosophy proceeds with a plane of immanence or consistency; science with a plane of reference. In the case of science it is like a freeze-frame' (118). Although art operates by way of actual monuments, it is able to create 'a plane of composition that is able to restore the infinite' (203).

While philosophy and art retain the infinite, the relentless integrations of science reduce the infinite to the finite – the infinitesimal – in order to make its objects calculable and functional. In other words, there is no scientific unconscious. Or better: science represses its unconscious. In a nicely alliterative series, Deleuze and Guattari note that 'the philosopher brings back from chaos ... *variations* that are still infinite but that have become inseparable on the absolute surface', the scientist 'brings back from the chaos *variables* that have become independent by slowing down ... finite coordinates on a secant plane of reference', and the artist 'brings back from the chaos *varieties* that no longer constitute a reproduction of the sensory in the organ but set up a being of the sensory ... on an anorganic plane of composition that is able to restore the infinite' (202–3). Accordingly, the three modes of thought assemble different planes: 'plane of immanence of philosophy, plane of composition of art, plane of reference or coordination of science' (216). The three modes of thought are described further by way of another alliterative series: '*form* of concept, *force* of sensation, *function* of knowledge; concepts and conceptual personae, sensations and aesthetic figures, figures and partial observers' (216, emphasis added). In this conceptual triptych, philosophy stands out as the guardian and custodian of the purely virtual and of the infinite. It assembles its concepts from the pre-philosophical micro-concepts that populate the virtual plane of immanence. Philosophy, one might say, is the art of concepts and thus of the virtual.

The Event of Literature

Proust and Signs (1964)

In his early, 1964 study *Proust and Signs*, Deleuze had found the potential to construct purely virtual assemblages in the ability of literature to construct worlds of pure recollection, such as Proust's invention of the purely virtual world of

Combray, populated by purely virtual lives: *infinite, non-psychological memory*. By the time of *What is Philosophy?*, this has changed. Although art can still touch the infinite, the planes of art are planes of composition that relate to infinity only indirectly, because they take the detour through affects and percepts. They are not so much about the form of infinity as they are about its force; that is, not so much about virtual infinity as they are about actual infinity. Art can still touch the infinite, although only the actual infinite, because it creates works from out of the field of anonymous affects and percepts. As with affects and affectations, Deleuze differentiates between percepts and perceptions: 'Percepts are no longer perceptions; they are independent of a state of those who experience them. Affects are no longer feelings or affections; they go beyond the strength of those who undergo them. Sensations, percepts, and affects are *beings* whose validity lies in themselves and exceeds any lived. They could be said to exist in the absence of man because man, as he is caught in stone, on the canvas, or by words is himself a compound of percepts and affects. The work of art is a being of sensation and nothing else: it exists in itself' (WP: 164). In creating surfaces of sensation such as the page, the canvas, the stage or the screen, art is indebted to and frees the non-human affects of its material media. Sensation is 'the percept or affect of the material itself' (166). This is why affects can be 'metallic, crystalline, [or] stony' (167). It is only on a second level that these affects and percepts are related to the human spectrum of affections and perceptions.

That said, a return to Proust remains important, not only because it is from *Proust and Signs* that the term resonance will find its way into *Difference and Repetition*. (On resonance, see Olkowski 1999: 102.) While in his later work Deleuze will look for the truth of essences in philosophy, as the art of the invention of concepts, when he looks for it in literature in 1964, the similarity between philosophy and literature is that their measure is equally how adequate each is to life. How much it is in resonance with the world. As Deleuze maintains in *Dialogues II*, 'the only aim [*fin*] of writing is life, through the combinations which it draws' (6).

In *Proust and Signs*, Deleuze develops a resonant poetics in the context of how art, in particular literature, can express the truth of essence, which is something that at first sounds very unlike Deleuze [→ **Guattari 138–41**]. In fact, like many of Deleuze's arguments, this one is at first quite counter-intuitive. The search for the truth of essence becomes Deleuzian, however, under the premise that for Deleuze, essence is nothing but difference as such. (Later, I will differentiate between virtual differences that make up essences, and actual differences that make up substances. For the moment, however, it suffices to talk of difference as such.) The truth of this differential essence is not what one would generally call the truth, but the truth of the resonances between heterogeneous elements.

The resonance between life and literature lies in that both the literary machine and the machine of life produce fields of resonances and that they operate by the 'effects of resonance' (PS: 133) rather than those of 'simple vibration' (FB: 55). If living crystals are essentially bundles of heterogeneous elements in resonance, the power and beauty of art lies in the way it suspends a number of heterogeneous resonant assemblages into an allover resonant field, and in how it captures this field from a vantage point that is superior to that field only in that it is not empirically involved in it – it has no existential stake in it, that is – but is, at the same time, fully immanent to it. This twofold vantage point is that of the powers of the false when they create a fictional, subjunctive world. 'What is produced by the process of resonance, in the resonance machine, is the singular essence, the Viewpoint superior to the two moments which set up the resonance' (PS: 134).

It is once more counter-intuitive that Deleuze calls the register within which the assemblage of this resonant field can be conceptualized as 'style', because one would assume that a style expresses a specific subject or a specific literary genre. For Deleuze, however, style is the way in which a specific work captures 'a chaotic and multiple impersonal reality' (138) rather than an individualized one. Literature as a resonance machine creates a resonant field that consists of fictional characters, objects and landscapes. Against the Lacanian, psychoanalytic notion that style is the man himself, which Lacan picked up from Buffon, Deleuze stakes the idea that style consists of the capture of a particular resonant field. Style is the artistic machine of capture, one might say (see also TRM: 369). Each pebble, each flower, each animal and each human being has its own style, which consists of the interactions that define it within a resonant field, as well as the result of these interactions. Most forms of life express their style in their very living. As Deleuze notes in 'Bergson's Conception of Difference', 'animal behavior exhibits instinct as the dominant tendency, whereas in human behavior it is intelligence' (DI: 36). Only humans have developed levels such as philosophy, science and art to express their style, although the Deleuzian lesson is that this style should trail their style of life behind.

Especially in the case of Proust, literature is able to be more truthful to the essence of life – which means to difference as such – than actual life in that it creates a resonant field from within the fully virtual registers of memory and of the imagination: remembrance of things past. In the corked-up room in which Proust lives and writes, remembered and imagined life can emerge and unfold within a literary machine that is insulated from the actualities, the noises, the affects and the interferences of real, present and actual life: *Proust with Bergson*.

Memory and recollection are the media of the virtual as 'a pure recollection, and pure recollection is difference. Pure recollection is virtual because it would be absurd to look for a mark of the past in something actual and already actualized' (DI: 44).

(For the notion of recollection in Bergson see 'Bergson's Conception of Difference'.) Proust's remembered, recollected world of Combray is a purely virtual world, and it is only in such a fully virtual world that a lost time can be 'regained, by resonance' (PS: 142): *the world of and in literature*. In that recreation, however, it is not Proust who expresses himself. Rather, he allows the truth of a past to assemble itself in his writing; the truth being the resonances of the differences that make up the field. Only such an anonymous, resonant literature allows for the production of an immaterial, asubjective and singular field of recollected resonances; of a virtual past in which it is possible to fully 'affirm ... irreducible difference' (143). Through and in the medium of memory, Proust assembles a fully virtual life that shines forth without interference or contamination by the actual and the present. In terms of *Cinema 1* and *Cinema 2*, Proust creates pure time-words: *a field of pure events in resonance.*

As the media of philosophy, concepts are similarly nothing but clusters of philosophical events. 'Philosophical concepts have events for consistency whereas scientific functions have states of affairs or mixtures for reference: through concepts, philosophy continually extracts a consistent event from states of affairs ... whereas through functions, science continually actualizes the event in a state of affairs, thing, or body that can be referred to' (WP: 126). As Deleuze and Guattari note in *What is Philosophy?*, 'the concept is an incorporeal, even though it is incarnated or effectuated in bodies' (21). As always, Deleuze and Guattari stress the difference between the series. The concept is '*not mixed up* with the state of affairs in which it is effectuated' (21, emphasis added). In a passage that refers directly to *Difference and Repetition*, Deleuze notes that the concept 'does not have spatiotemporal coordinates, only intensive ordinates. It has no energy, only intensities, it is anenergetic (energy is not intensity, but rather the way in which the latter is deployed and nullified in an extensive state of affairs). The concept speaks the event, not the essence or the thing' (21). Concepts, as clusters of events, are fully virtual.

The Event of History

What is Philosophy? (1991)

How would the logic of the Deleuzian event be implicated in a Deleuzian notion of historiography? The perhaps most elegant definition of the Deleuzian event comes again from Foucault. In his 1970 lecture 'Discourse on Language', which is filled with echoes of *The Logic of Sense*, Foucault notes that 'an event is neither substance, nor accident, nor quality or process; events are not corporeal. And yet, an event is certainly not immaterial; it takes effect, becomes effect, always on the level of materiality.

Events have their place; they consist in relation to, coexistence with, dispersion of, the cross-checking accumulation and the selection of material elements; it occurs as an effect of, and in, material dispersion. Let us say that the philosophy of event [*sic*] should advance in the direction, at first sight paradoxical, of *an incorporeal materialism*' (1972: 231, emphasis added).

What is the function of events in that incorporeal materialism? One might see events as the smallest and most loosely coupled elements of conscious thought. Such a definition, however, would exclude unconscious events, which operate on levels that are quite literally unthinkable to humans. Even more, a seminal characteristic of Deleuzian events is that they are not immediately and necessarily tied to human thought. All levels of the infinite scale of life, from conscious to chemical plateaus and from the perceptible to the imperceptible, are pervaded by relations, observations, contemplations and thus eventualizations. In fact, quite apart from being elements of processes of conscious, cognitive integration, singular events are first of all elements of an unconscious, anonymous and pre-individual virtual multiplicity. They are the atoms of the virtual. The atoms of thought. (On the virtuality of the event see Ansell-Pearson 1999: 124–5, 132.) As such, Deleuze's events differ decisively from what Badiou calls events as specific, critical moments of bifurcation at which a system changes and thus develops a new landscape of constraints and potentialities. This fundamental structural difference makes it difficult to align their respective systems of thought. While Badiou considers events as exceptional moments, for Deleuze they are, as pure singularities, the smallest virtual elements that make up the fabric of sense. (On Badiou, see WP: 151–3; on events, Bell 2008: 74.)

Concerning the misunderstandings between Badiou and Deleuze, one should think, perhaps, of their 'nonrelationship' (Badiou 2000: 1) as the enactment of a lost tragi-comedy by Samuel Beckett. In confronting Deleuze's philosophy, Badiou proceeds like somebody who mistakes a bicycle for a wheelbarrow and then complains about how badly constructed that wheelbarrow is as a mode of transportation. Reading Badiou's account of their correspondence, one can literally feel Deleuze's incredulity, and his attempt to make the best of such a colossal misunderstanding; up to a point at which the encounter becomes simply too sad, and Deleuze feels that he has to stop responding. There might be some truth in Badiou's claim that Deleuze's thought is 'profoundly aristocratic' (12), but it is certainly not 'a philosophy of death' (13) and his 'conceptual productions' are only 'monotonous' (15) if one considers variations and modulations to be monotonous.

Maybe with enough conceptual Lacanian contortions, one might somehow translate Deleuze's formal distinction between formal distinction and ontological identity into a 'distinction of the formal and the real' (25) in which 'the One alone is real' (25), although I doubt that it can be done. In fact, although there might be some truth somewhere in Badiou's reading, one can feel that in actual fact, it is all utterly and sadly wrong. In a curious vertigo, one might argue, everything is so utterly wrong as to be almost completely true again. In this light, Badiou's statement that the 'power of the false' is what Deleuze considers as 'truth' (59) is doubly ironic. What to say about a sentence like 'whatever is spontaneous is inferior to thought, which only begins when it is constrained to become animated by the forces of the outside' (86)? Like all other claims, this one is so blatantly against the spirit of Deleuze that it only begins to make sense once it is completely inverted. But enough of this. (On Badiou's Deleuze, see Toscano 2000: 236, on Badiou and Deleuze, Kaufman).

When Deleuze notes that language is the only place in which events subsist, this centres on, but is not limited to, human language. As there are events on all levels of entitarian organization and disorganization, it includes the allover semiotic field, all levels of life that involve cognition in any way, shape or form. If you believe that life entails or even is sentience, events take place on all levels of life. It is out of an unconscious, anonymous multiplicity of events, in fact, that individual consciousness emerges as a specific mode of the virtual organization and arrangement of matter-of-factual, actual architectures. The only characteristic of singular events is that they have specific geometric coordinates. They have longitudes and latitudes within the allover virtual milieu. In regard to this milieu, however, they are neutral, in that they are not yet caught up in and organized by relational networks. At this point, they are what Deleuze calls pure events. Like dark precursors, pure events are not friends. The more such pure events become part of relational processes – of the individuation of singular events into a thought, for instance – the less neutral they become. To use a Deleuzian terminology, molar events are assemblages of pure, molecular events. 'The singularity belongs to another dimension than that of denotation, manifestation or signification. It is essentially pre-individual, non-personal, and a-conceptual. It is quite indifferent to the individual and the collective, the personal and the impersonal, the particular and the general – and to their oppositions. Singularity is *neutral . . . Peguy clearly saw that history and event were inseparable from those singular points*' (LS: 52–3, emphasis added).

These pure, neutral elements that are formed into more or less stabilized, informational assemblages, are the 'true transcendental events' (102–3). As 'impersonal and preindividuated nomadic singularities', pure events, like the diverse in *Difference and Repetition*, 'constitute the real transcendental field' (109). To define their neutrality, Deleuze in fact returns to the notion of nomadic distribution that he used in *Difference and Repetition* to designate diversity. 'What is neither individual nor personal are . . . emissions of singularities insofar as they occur on an unconscious surface and possess a mobile, immanent principle of auto-unification through a *nomadic distribution*, radically different from fixed and sedentary distributions as conditions of the synthesis of consciousness' (LS: 102). (On the relation of the event to Sartre, see WP: 47; Beistegui 2004: 243.)

Pure events form the surface of the multiplicity of an anonymous thought and an anonymous consciousness. When Deleuze notes that pure events as sense are 'impassive ... sterile' (LS: 20), 'indifferent to opposites' (35) and 'neutral' (19) in that they pertain to 'pre-individual, non-personal, and a-conceptual' levels of thought, this should be read in analogy to the notion of passive syntheses. Since pure events make up the non-essential essences of the virtual field – its differentiality, that is – 'to reverse Platonism is first and foremost to remove essences and to substitute events in their place, as jets of singularities' (53). While this claim might seem to be quite innocent, to consider events as the free elements of an anonymous consciousness pushes philosophical thought to its limit: *philosophy at the point-at-infinity*.

Events, then, are the most elementary virtual singularities out of which sense, meaning and narratives are assembled. Deleuze's logic of events, however, goes beyond this virtual assemblage theory. Events are not only the smallest atoms of virtual life and thought, they are, at the same time, attributed to actual, material, matter-of-factual life, and they express this life: *to each virtual, its actual*. In terms of *Difference and Repetition*, they are incarnated in bodies. Together, the two series form a surface on which the realms of thoughts and of bodies are reciprocally attributed: *incorporeal materialism*.

In *What is Philosophy?*, Deleuze and Guattari use Lewis Carroll's conceit of the smile of the Cheshire cat to illustrate the logic of this incorporeal materialism. A 'consistent event' is the 'smile without the cat, as it were' (126). In the same manner in which the de-materialized smile of the Cheshire cat is formally separated from the material cat even while it remains its attribute, in that it is the smile of the Cheshire cat, the immaterial, virtual event is formally separated from its material, actual matter-of-fact even while it remains its attribute. (In order to underline this chiasmic logic, I will sometimes refer to the level of materiality as the level of *matters-of-fact* and to the level of propositions and words as the level of matters-of-*fact*.) In the plotting of a complex topology of the material and the immaterial, the philosophical concept is on the side of the virtual. It 'is neither denotation of states of affairs nor signification of the lived; it is the event as pure sense' (WP: 144): *expressive philosophy*.

In Deleuze's theory of history, the complementarity between the series of events and of matters-of-fact can help explain why one should resist two complementary temptations. The first is to dissolve actual history in virtual historiography, the second to dissolve virtual historiography in actual history. In terms of *Difference and Repetition*, the first is an empirical exercise (history can only be thought), while the second is a transcendental one (history cannot be thought). If history and historiography should be kept as formally separate registers, how can historiography be made adequate to history? To address this question, one needs to go back to Deleuze's notion of two complementary multiplicities. The first is the material multiplicity as a given, extensive plane of anonymous, singular and heterogeneous matters-of-fact. It is defined solely by the movements of more or less loosely coupled material particles. On this plane, history is the history of pure changes in-and-of-themselves, changes in direction and speed, or, as Deleuze and Guattari also say, of 'latitudes and longitudes' (AO: 19). It is a level of what American historian Henry Adams called 'chance collisions of movements imperceptible to his senses, perhaps even imperceptible to his instruments, but perceptible to each other' (1961: 381–2). The habits of this particular, matter-of-fact history are those of corporeal affects, such as propulsion and propagation. Its time is that of material pulses of being that know neither future nor past. The time of the unrelated succession of pure presents-as-actions. A chronic history of pure causes. The term chronic history, however, is somewhat of an oxymoron. On the level of things and bodies, a chronic history is an actual history that operates on planes of material consistency that are defined by contractions, agglomerations, resonances and by infinitely subtle, continuous modulations of frequency. The plane of a chronic history is made up of pure, extensive matters-of-fact: *endo-consistent history*.

If the actual plane emerges out of matters-of-fact as the elements that populate a given actual field, the immaterial, virtual plane is related to pure events, as the material out of which narratives about actual things and bodies emerge. It is an intensive plane of anonymous, singular events, filled with more or less loosely connected relations and patterns. History, on this plane, consists of the temporal and spatial relations between the actual matters-of-fact and their agglomerations. Of the relations that are exterior to the actual, historical terms. The habits of this history of surfaces, which is set against the laws of actual depth, are the habits of relation, affects and contemplations. This plane of immaterial historiography is the plane of virtual history: *exo-consistent history*.

The question for the historian is how the actual and the virtual, which I will take to stand for the physical plane of history and the metaphysical plane of historiography respectively, can be made to resonate. (On the difference and relation between these two forms of history, see DeLanda 2002: 155; in more general terms, Lambert 2002.) According to the Deleuzian formula that 1. every virtual is at least minimally actualized, that 2. every actual is at least minimally virtualized, and that 3. both actual and virtual history emerge from the originary multiplicity of the twofold plane of immanence, how to bring about an adequation of actual history and virtual history? If there are material contractions on the one side and immaterial contemplations on the other, and if these two series are to be kept formally distinct, how to create a crystal history? In the following, I will argue that a Deleuzian historical studies needs to diffract the Kantian a priori of space, time and causality; to work from within an in itself multiplicitous space, a multiplicitous time, and a multiplicitous causality.

Deleuze and Guattari develop the notion of an in itself multiplicitous space in the chapter 'The Smooth and the Striated' of *A Thousand Plateaus*, in which they define space as a fractal, Riemannian manifold that is assembled from patches of local spaces that cannot be abstracted, which means that they cannot be separated from the elements of which they are composed. Space is an 'amorphous collection of juxtaposed pieces that can be joined together in an infinite number of ways' (TP: 476). Deleuze and Guattari note specifically that it was 'a decisive event when the mathematician Riemann uprooted the multiple from its predicate state and made it a noun, "multiplicity." It marked the end of dialectics and the beginning of a typology and topology of multiplicities' (482–3). In order to operate within such an inherently tattered space, historical studies need to become radically site-specific. They need to work from within a tangle of local spaces, which means from specific sets of local circumstances and milieus. From within what Serres calls a 'local topology [*topologie locale*]' (1994: 63). From this position, they need to provide 'a detailed analysis of the local multiplicities' (63). A similar multiplicity defines the a priori of time, which, Deleuze separates, formally, into the two temporal registers of the virtual, aionic time of the event and the actual, chronic time of matters-of-fact. In Deleuze, both time and space are fundamentally heterogeneous and specific.

If space and time are multiplicitous, it follows that the concept itself must also be 'a *multiplicity*, an absolute surface or volume, self-referents, made up of a certain number of inseparable intensive variations according to an order of neighborhood, and traversed by a point in a state of survey. The concept is the contour, the configuration, the constellation of an event to come' (WP: 32–3). In 'The Method of Dramatization', Deleuze answers a question about whether he is returning to Plato. 'If we think of the Plato from the later dialectic, where the Ideas are something like multiplicities that must be traversed by questions such as *how? how much? in which case?*, then yes, everything I've said has something Platonic about it. If you're thinking of the Plato who favors a simplicity of the essence or a ipseity of the Idea, then no' (DI: 116).

Because of these characteristics, the philosophical concept, and equally the historical concept, does 'not refer to the lived, by way of compensation, but consists, through its own creation, in setting up an event that surveys the whole of the lived no less than every state of affairs' (WP: 33–4). Ultimately, the brain itself 'is an absolutely consistent form that surveys *itself* independently of any supplementary dimension' (210) [→ **Guattari 180**]. In such a survey (*survol*), historical studies encounter complex living aggregates and their interactions in all of their unpredictability, and address the historical weather in all of its complexity; its climate, its geology, the currents and forces that traverse it. (On the notion of *survol*, see Ruyer 1952: 95–109.)

The multiplicitous character of time, of space and of the concept has a number of conceptual consequences. 1. Historical studies cannot create solid historical objects. 2. It cannot itself be treated as a solid object or a stable system. 3. Everything, especially the pre- and non- or a-historical, is part of history. This is why, 4. historical analyses must encompass the activities of non-human agents and levels. There is no singular point of view. No 'total observer' (WP: 129). Rather, as Deleuze and Guattari note in *What is Philosophy?* 'science brings to light *partial observers*' that 'swarm' (129) through conceptual space. These partial observers are '*sensibilia*' (131) whose role is '*to perceive* and *to experience*, although these perceptions and affections are not those of a man, in the currently adopted sense, but belong to the things studied' (131). The function of these partial observers, therefore, is not so much to integrate – 'partial observers belong to the neighborhood of the singularities of a curve, of a physical system, of a living organism' (130) – but to perceive on molecular levels that are part of the overall system. They are pick-up machines. 'Sources of molecular perception and affection' (130). Such partial observers operate on all levels of the living phylum. 'Wherever purely functional properties of recognition or selection appear, without direct action, there are observers' (130). In the extreme case, they are '*infinitely* subtle' (131, emphasis added). Even scientific functives have partial observers because '*ideal partial observers are the perceptions or sensory affections of functives themselves*' (131). As Deleuze and Guattari note, 'particle physics needs countless infinitely subtle observers' (131). Every one of these partial observers is a machine that transfers quantity into quality. 'The nonsubjective observer is precisely the sensory that qualifies . . . a scientifically determined state of affairs, thing, or body' (131). A minor history proceeds by way of such '*probe-heads* (tetes chercheuses, guidance devices)' (TP: 190); survey-machines that move not over but through the terrain, which means that the concepts created by a minor history develop from within the surveyed terrain: '*n*–1' immanence.

'The concept is in a state of *survey* [*survol*] in relation to its components, endlessly traversing them according to an order without distance' (WP: 20), Deleuze and Guattari note. On all levels of the living, the multiplicity of matter-of-factual, particular points that make up the terms of the rhizome of extensive history is translated, by a multiplicity of partial observers, into the eventual lines that make up the relations of the rhizome of virtual history. Surfaces of historiographic sense are extracted from the geological strata of material history by way of transforming recurrent material irritations or shocks into immaterial universes of meaning and signification. The tremors of an actual, true history need to be seismically registered by the apparatuses of the falsely virtual. In the same way that our measuring of actual history emerges from and is pervaded by an infinite number of minor actual histories, virtual history emerges from and is pervaded by an infinite number of minor virtual histories. If the series of actual history is transformed into the series of virtual history through processes of registration and integration, the historical irony is that the more a system integrates, the further it separates itself from the ungrounded ground of history. Deleuze conceptualizes this process as an increasing interiorization. The more levels of integration are in play, the more ponderous the system becomes. In Deleuzian terms: the aim of linking virtual history to actual history should not lie in reaching universal theories of history, but rather in reaching back, through the mass of historical integrations, to the a-historical becomings from which these integrations have emerged, and to create from them concepts that are concrete universals. Ultimately, these becomings form 'a congenial chaos, a creative disorder that is irreducible to any order whatsoever. It is this chaos of which Nietzsche spoke when he said it was not the contrary of the eternal return, but the eternal return in person. The great creations depart from this supra-historical stratum, this "untimely" chaos, at the extreme limit of what is livable' (DI: 126). (On *chaos as the virtual* see Plotnitsky 2010: 256.)

Informal Diagrams: 'The History before History'

Foucault (1986), Francis Bacon: The Logic of Sensation (1981)

How, for historical studies, to reach the anonymous, uncomputable and, as Nietzsche would say, forever shifting grounds of both actual history and virtual historiography? How to reach what Deleuze calls the complex informal diagram embodied by historical haecceities? According to Deleuze, the only way to do this is to become diagrammatic. To find ways to create, by way of counter-actualizing, what Deleuze calls a-historical, informal diagrams, which provide the asignifying ground from within which historical studies can develop historical Figures that trail that a-historical ground behind. (On the origin of the term diagram with Guattari, see TRM: 238; on the diagram TRM: 253; on Deleuze's and C. S. Peirce's diagrams, Vellodi 2014.)

Deleuze develops the notion of the informal diagram in *Foucault* as well as in *Francis Bacon: The Logic of Sensation*. In general, unlike formal diagrams, which retain only the abstract blueprint of a structure or a situation, informal diagrams retain the concrete complexity, as well as the time- and site-specificity, of a structure or a situation. They do not offer a view of the situation from above, that is, but from within. This is why, as Deleuze notes in *Foucault*, an informal diagram is, like the situation within which it operates, 'unstable, agitated and shuffled around' (F: 71). Furthermore, as part of the situation, it has effects in and on that situation. It is 'fluid, continually churning up matter and function... in a way likely to create change' (30). As a map of 'intensity' (36) and of 'the relations between forces' that are 'virtual, potential, unstable, vanishing and molecular' (37), it expresses a situation rather than representing it. In that expressive function, an informal diagram is inherently generative. As both heuristic device and generative force, the informal diagram is a 'non-unifying immanent cause' of 'concrete assemblages', with which it shares a logic of 'mutual presupposition' (32): In terms of history, the informal diagram is the asignifying ground of historiography: *the unconscious of historical studies*.

In its expressionist logic, an informal diagram turns the representational logic of a formal diagram upside-down and inside-out. It is not a structural blueprint as much as it is, in Deleuze's words, 'an atmospheric element, a "non-stratified substance"... The informal outside is a battle, a turbulent, stormy zone where particular points and the relations of forces between these points are tossed about. Strata merely collected and solidified the visual dust and the sonic echo of the battle raging above them... Each atmospheric state in this zone corresponds to a diagram of forces or particular features which are taken up by relations: a strategy... But it is the strategy's job to be fulfilled in the stratum, just as it is the diagram's job to become stratified. To be realized [better: actualized] in this way means becoming *both integrated and different*' (F: 121–2). An informal diagram is an actualized diagram of forces rather than of forms. It is in this light that it is informal.

In the chapter 'The Painting before Painting' from *Francis Bacon: The Logic of Sensation*, Deleuze calls Bacon's first, a-figurative brush- or hand-strokes across the canvas the informal diagram that provides the site- and time-specific ground out of which a concrete pictorial Figure might or might not arise. 'Bacon defines it in this way: make random marks (lines-traits); scrub, sweep, or wipe the canvas in order to clear out locales or zones (color-patches); throw the paint, from various angles and at various speeds' (FB: 99–100). As such, the diagram is 'the operative set of asignifying and nonrepresentative lines and zones, line-strokes and color-patches. And the operation of the diagram, its function, says Bacon, is to be "suggestive". Or, more rigorously, ... it is to introduce "possibilities of fact"' (101): *the dark precursor of painting*.

Although these marks and traits are 'irrational, involuntary, accidental, free, random' (100), they slow down the infinite speeds with which virtual elements traverse the plane of immanence. Perhaps the first stroke across the white canvas might be seen as a first *clinamen*. As an infinitesimally faint slowing down of the world's überfast virtual intensity, in which the deceleration would lie in the friction between pigment and canvas that allows for the first emergence of an actualized landscape of pigment. It might be seen as a first chromatic reduction of the non-colour whiteness of the canvas, as an actualization of the virtual chaos of light into colour: a slowing-down of the luminous chaos by actualizing it in a site- and time-specific chromatic milieu. The first, faint actualization and composition of the pictorial, pigmented world. Crucially, however, and in accordance with the notion that the plane of immanence is not converted into the plane of consistency but rather that it persists in it, part of the informal diagram does not stop not being actualized. As an excess virtuality or intensity, it remains outside of its own actualization and thus its own extensity. It is in this sense that the plane of immanence can be considered to be the most internal outside of the plane of consistency. This informal surplus ensures and literally contains the infinite potentiality of change and of becoming. It is why and how newness enters the world. An informal diagram attempts to capture purely virtual, intensive forces in surplus of being actualized, relationalized and formed into extensive matters-of-fact *by means of and from within the field of the actual*.

Bacon's brush- and hand-strokes, then, mark the passage from infinite speed to finite speed. 'The diagram is indeed a chaos, a catastrophe, but it is also a germ of order or rhythm. It is a violent chaos in relation to the figurative givens, but it is a germ of rhythm in relation to the new order of the painting' (102). Its function lies in this asignificant, purely pigmental composition. It consists of traits that do not follow a logic of sense. Rather, they are 'traits of sensation, but of confused sensations (the confused sensations, as Cezanne said, that we bring with us at birth). And above all, they are manual traits' (100), nonrepresentative, 'nonillustrative and nonnarrative' (65). Bacon's Figures might be said to be born from this asignifying, minimally sloweddown chaos. Already here, there are parallels to the overall theory of history: *painting the clinamen as the possibility of history*.

Bacon's informal diagram has to do with the birth of the pictorial world. Deleuze's notion of the informal diagram might be inspired by Peirce, but perhaps also by *art informel*, and certainly by Bacon himself, who speaks of his strategy in relation to a graph or a diagram. Crucially, the birth of painting does not lie in the probabilistic givens of the canvas, which 'express a prepictorial state of the painting' that 'will not be integrated into the act of painting' (95). Rather, it lies in the first moment of the manual, pictorial chance that is instantiated by Bacon's brush-strokes. Although these are asignifying, they are already pictorial. As Deleuze notes, 'the chance choice made at each move' is not pre-pictorial but rather 'nonpictorial or a-pictorial: it will become pictorial, it will be integrated into the act of painting, to the extent that it consists of manual marks that will reorient the visual whole, and will extract the improbable Figure from the set of figurative probabilities' (95).

If the a-pictorial is the site of the genesis of the pictorial Figure, might one consider the a-historical as the site of the genesis of history? The a-pictorial space from which the Figures emerge is not that of cultural clichés (*disegno*), but of 'a manual space, a space of active, manual strokes, which works through manual aggregates' (130). The wager is that a Figure emerges from this diagram that will trail this diagram, as the dark precursor of the Figure, behind. Like the dark precursor, 'this preparatory work is invisible and silent, yet extremely intense, and the act of painting itself appears as an afterward, an *après-coup* . . . in relation to this work' (99).

Crucially, the informal diagram is always in the service of the Figure or of the concept. At the same time, the concept is not adequate to the world without it, in that the concept must trail the informal diagram behind. This is why 'Bacon will never stop speaking of the absolute necessity of preventing the diagram from proliferating, the necessity of confining it to certain areas of the painting and certain moments of the act of painting' (109).

In more general, semiotic terms, signifying language must trail its asignifying, dark precursors behind. The digital code must trail the analog world behind. The digital and the analog denote, in fact, the registers of the informal and the formal diagram. '"Analogical language", it is said, belongs to the right hemisphere of the brain or, better, to the nervous system, whereas "digital language" belongs to the left hemisphere. Analogical language would be a language of relations, which consists of expressive movements, paralinguistic signs, breaths and screams, and so on. One can question whether or not this is a language properly speaking. But there is no doubt, for example, that Artaud's theater elevated scream-breaths to the state of language. More generally, painting elevates colors and lines to the state of language, and it is an analogical language. One might even wonder if painting has not always been the analogical language par excellence' (113).

It is in this context that Deleuze refers to Peirce's notion of the diagram: 'Peirce first defined icons by similitude, and symbols by a conventional rule. But he acknowledged that conventional symbols are composed of icons (by virtue of phenomena of isomorphism), and that pure icons range far beyond qualitative similitude, and consist of "diagrams." But it is still difficult to explain what an analogical diagram is, as opposed to a digital or symbolic code. Today we can relate it to the sonorous example of synthesizers. Analogical synthesizers are "modular": they establish an immediate connection between heterogeneous elements, they introduce a literally unlimited possibility of connection between these elements, on a field of presence or finite plane whose moments are all actual and sensible. Digital synthesizers, however, are "integral": their operation passes through a codification, through a homogenization and binarization of the data, which is produced on a separate plane, infinite in principle, and whose sound will only be produced as the result of a conversion-translation' (116). The diagram as an analogical language does not act as a code, but as a modulator; as the given ecology of pigment.

Painting can go into either one of these directions. 'What abstract painting elaborates is less a diagram than a symbolic *code*, on the basis of great formal oppositions.

It replaced the diagram with a code. This code is "digital"' (104). The other direction is instantiated by 'abstract expressionism or *art informel*', which 'offers an entirely different response, at the opposite extreme of abstraction. This time the abyss or chaos is deployed to the maximum. Somewhat like a map that is as large as the country, the diagram merges with the totality of the painting; the entire painting is diagrammatic' (104). In another way, 'perhaps *art informel* also borders on the impossible, for by extending the diagram to the entire painting, it takes the diagram for the analogical flux itself, rather than making the flux pass through the diagram. This time, it is as if the diagram were directed toward itself, rather than being used or treated. It no longer goes beyond itself in a code, but grounds itself in a scrambling' (117). Both of these extremes, however, are dead ends. 'The "middle" way, on the contrary, is one that makes use of the diagram in order to constitute an analogical language' (117). As such a paradoxical language without a code, the informal diagram is neither stasis nor flux, neither digital signal nor analog noise. It is the becoming flux of stasis, but this becoming flux is in the service of the Figure: *The Figure of painting. The Figure of history. The Figure of philosophy.*

In *Foucault*, Deleuze notes that the informal diagram is an 'abstract machine' (34). As such, Deleuze describes the informal diagram, quite beautifully, as a diagram 'that is almost blind and mute, even though it makes others see and speak' (34). This is also the operational receipt for philosophy, which must try to perceive the a-philosophical diagrams from which it emerges, in the same way that history must try to perceive as much of the a-historical 'diagram' (36) that is the source of history. It 'does not function to represent, even something real, but rather constructs a real ... Thus, when it constitutes points of creation or potentiality it does not stand outside history but is instead always "prior" to history' (TP: 142).

It is in this sense that Foucault's historical work is truly diagrammatic. One of Deleuze's most concise definitions of a diagram, in fact, comes from *Foucault*. It 'makes no distinction between content and expression' (34). It is 'highly unstable or fluid', 'it never functions in order to represent a persisting world but produces a new kind of reality ... It is neither the subject of history, nor does it survey history. It makes history by unmaking preceding realities and significations, constituting hundreds of points of emergence or creativity, unexpected conjunctions or improbable continuums. It doubles history with a sense of continual evolution' (35). Its 'realization is equally an integration, a collection of progressive integrations that are initially local and then become or tend to become global' (32).

There is a moment at which 'the informal diagram is swallowed up and becomes embodied ... in two different directions that are necessarily divergent and irreducible' (38). This is why Deleuze's theory of history argues against a global panorama that provides an overview of the multiplicity of local circumstances. When it claims to provide such an overview, science becomes royal science only. In analogy, historical studies become an exclusively royal history [→ **Guattari 30**]. According to Deleuze, all sciences should become diagrammatic 'in certain areas and certain moments' of doing science, although these diagrammatizations should always be in the service of, or suggestive of, specific Figurations. As Deleuze notes in *Dialogues II*, 'science is becoming increasingly event-centered . . . instead of structural. It follows lines and circuits, it takes leaps, rather than constructing axiomatics . . . Scientists are more and more concerned with singular events, of an incorporeal nature, which are effected in bodies, in states of bodies, in completely heterogeneous assemblages . . . science will be increasingly like grass' (67–8).

The third Kantian a priori that needs to be diversified in a Deleuzian historical studies is causality. One way of doing this is to introduce contingency into historiography. In fact, for Deleuze and Guattari 'there is no good reason but contingent reason; there is no universal history except of contingency' (AO: 93), and further, 'universal history is the history of contingencies, and not the history of necessity. Ruptures and limits, and not continuity' (140). History is 'not only retrospective, it is also contingent, singular, ironic and critical' (140). If Badiou saw only very specific events as critical, for Deleuze, every event, even a pure event, is critical because every single event changes the overall diagram. Whenever historians mark specific events as critical, this can always only be a pragmatic and never an ontological move.

A second mode of disrupting the logic of cause and effect is to set up a causal topology according to which, as with the Stoics, causes and effects do not follow each other chronologically. Rather, there is a material realm of deep causes (the plane of actual history) and an immaterial plane of surface effects on which imagined sets of relations function as 'quasi-causes' (LS: 86); the 'metaphysical surface' (125) of virtual history. The quasi-cause is an 'operator and it is defined not by its giving rise to multiplicities but by its capacity to affect them' (DeLanda 2002: 76). As Deleuze notes, it 'does not create, it "operates"' (LS: 147). The truly historical question, therefore, is about the attribution of quasi-causes to causes and vice versa. As the Stoics stress, although the two series are radically separate, 'everything happens at the boundary between things and propositions' (8): *between actual history and virtual historiography.*

Deleuze and Guattari transpose this topology to the verticality of the milieu; to its geography and to its circumstances. In Deleuze, these are the actual matters-of-fact that define extensive history and its vertical sedimentations, which have to be attributed to the horizontal durations of intensive history and vice versa: The circumstances 'wrest . . . history from the cult of necessity in order to stress the irreducibility of contingency. Contingency wrests historical contemplation from the cult of origins in order to affirm the power of a "milieu", of 'an ambiance, an ambient atmosphere' (WP: 96).

While virtual history is chronologically spanned out between past, present and future, actual history is geologically spanned out between strata. It forms 'haecceities' (TP: 507) that are defined by a superposition of 'imperceptible' (2) metamorphoses, which is why 'in becoming, there is no past nor future – not even present, there is no history' (29). If historical studies are 'to make perceptible the imperceptible forces that populate the world, affect us, and make us become' (WP: 182), they must find their place in the transversal space between, on the one side, an actual, vertical history, and, on the other, a virtual, horizontal history: *historical transversality*.

The perhaps most crucial element in maintaining that history emerges from an originary multiplicity concerns the fact that the historian him- or herself is immersed in the field and as such in a constant energetic exchange with the universe of forces. The historian is both observer and energetic assemblage. Every history is a history of the living. Given Deleuze's theory of history, the reason for doing history cannot be defined from within the usual historical parameters. Rather, it is to find the conditions under which something new is produced; to 'arrive at the unhistorical vapor that goes beyond actual factors to the advantage of a creation of something new' (WP: 140, see also C1: 7). The question how does newness enter the world? introduces a force into historical studies that has been called, in various places and times, *appetitus*, *conatus*, desire, *élan vital* or energy.

Historical change is the result of deviations from habits, of the difference buried in repetition, of the local negentropies that are operative within the allover entropy that defines The Nature of Things. As the unthought, unthinkable and imperceptible ground of virtual history, actual history provides the living stuff from which virtual history is constructed. Deleuze's project is precisely to align materialist and idealist aspects according to a transcendental empiricism; to reciprocally attribute the actual and the virtual machines; matters-of-fact and events: *crystal history*.

According to this crystal history, the difference is between two fields. On the one hand, a material, productive field (an informed physical medium, originary world or factory whose dynamics concern structural change) that is defined by: matters-of-fact, quantities, bodies, affects, causes|agents, being, the living|full present (chronos), continuity (fullness), analogicity, imperceptibility, intensity and forces. On the other hand, an immaterial, transcendental field (an informational psychic medium, derived milieu or theatre whose dynamics concern behavioural change) defined by: events|sense, qualities, mind, affections, effects|results, subsistence, the perceived present (aion), discontinuity (emptiness), digitality, perception, cognition and relations. Positioned in-between these realms are: crystals, quasi-causes, attributes, contractions, contemplations, signals, movements of singularization and subjectification.

The probably most intriguing space in this logical distribution is the in-between space of quasi-causes, which form another of Deleuze's conceptual hinges between the causal world of matters-of-fact and the effectual world of events. Recapitulating the operation of material causes on an immaterial level, quasi-causes denote the field of the immaterial causations between events. 'Immaterial sense is the result of corporeal things, of their mixtures, and of their actions and passions. But the result has a very different nature than the corporeal cause. It is for this reason that sense, as an effect, being always at the surface, refers to a quasi-cause which is itself incorporeal' (LS: 86).

How can a quasi-cause be both the effect of material causes and at the same time be itself fully immaterial? How can it be both quantity and quality? Max Ernst's and the surrealists' technique of *frottage* might help to visualize this paradox. Like Lucretius' *simulacrum*, a *frottage* – the rubbing off of the surface of physical objects onto a carrier medium such as a sheet of paper – captures the surface of a material object, which is, in turn, the superficial aspect of its deep organization. A *frottage*, therefore, is neither copy nor representation. It is the expression, by pigment, of the surface of the object on a plane or screen of registration, much like a photograph of the surface of an object is the optical *frottage* of that object. *Frottages* function somewhat like informal diagrams. They slow down the material plane of immanence into a plane of consistency and composition. Through the *frottage*, Ernst attributes his compositions to the level of matters-of-fact as their material cause. His paintings are actually constrained in that they pick up physical givens and develop images from within this given. John Cage does something similar when he attributes the placement of notes to minute irregularities on the paper as his recording medium. The only difference is that this paper is already a cultural product, whereas the *frottages* refer directly to the informal diagrams of the natural world.

Programmatically, the development of images from within the *frottage* happens on a radically different level, and according to a radically different logic from that which governs the rubbing off of the object. Through Salvador Dali's film *Impressions de la Haute Mongolie*, which is a cinematographic *frottage*, Leonardo's advice to young painters to find figures in the random irregularities of an uneven wall – in the same way that there is no general red, there are no even walls – has entered the surrealist world. The *frottage* and its subsequent virtualization and composition into Figures folds the level of physical formation and metaphysical information or Figuration onto one plane, marking the boundary between the realm of pure causes and events, as well as that between causes and quasi-causes: *the real projective plane.*

As with a *frottage*, which provides the surface aspect of a deep organization, the example Deleuze uses to illustrate the relation between physics and metaphysics concerns the dynamics that define the formation of a surface. His choice of a liquid as the example highlights that the logic of matter-of-facts and events extends far beyond conscious, human levels. The context is that these dynamics rely both on the laws that define the material givens of the liquid as a volume, and on a different set of laws that regulate its surface dynamics: 'The events of a liquid surface refer to the inter-molecular modifications on which they depend as their real cause, but also to the variations of surface tension on which they depend as their [ideational or "fictive"] quasi-cause' (LS: 94–5): *Deleuzian quasi-history*.

Again, the relation is between a material level of causation (inter-molecular modifications) and a level on which the surface itself forms, out of and in direct relation to these deep causes, its own surface causes (surface tension). Deleuze calls this 'an entire physics of surfaces as the effect of deep mixtures' (125). It is to this surface physics that the transcendental field (the 'metaphysical surface') corresponds. As a '*doubling up*' (125) of the deep physics, both the surface physics and the metaphysical surface retain a genetic relationship to the deep space of materiality. Perhaps one should imagine a Deleuzian historical studies as a series of historical *frottages*.

What is still missing at this point is a definition of matters-of-fact and events in relation to their different temporalities. In this context, it is a sign of Deleuze's conceptual rigour that he takes up the conceptual topology that negotiates the duality 'of causes and effects, of corporeal things and incorporeal events' (23) as the coupling of two mutually exclusive but reciprocally presupposing series in a temporality that consists of a coupling of two equally exclusive but reciprocally presupposing times. One of these times is material, the other immaterial; one of them is matter-of-factual, the other eventual. 'Whereas Chronos expressed the action of bodies and the creation of corporeal qualities, Aion is the locus of incorporeal events, and of attributes which are distinct from qualities. Whereas Chronos was inseparable from the bodies which filled it out entirely as causes and matter, Aion is populated by effects which haunt it without ever filling it up' (165).

3 PHILOSOPHICAL TIMES AND SPACES

> ... the present is an invisible electron.
> Annie Dillard, *Pilgrim at Tinker Creek* (79)

> All consciousness is a matter of thresholds.
> Gilles Deleuze, *The Fold* (88)

> The pure is the impure and the obscure is the clear. We live and think within the mix.
> Michel Serres, *Genesis* (132)

> horizontal weather
> Gilles Deleuze, *The Logic of Sense* (11)

Philosophical Times (Strobe and Clom)

Difference and Repetition (1968), The Logic of Sense (1969)

THERE ARE TWO theories of time in Deleuze, or three, if one counts the one that Deleuze develops in *Cinema 1* and *Cinema 2*. The most elaborate of these concerns the three syntheses of time in *Difference and Repetition*. First synthesis: the time of perception as the synthesis of 'the lived, or living, present' (DR: 70). Second synthesis: the time of memory as the synthesis of the present and the past. Third synthesis: the time of consciousness as the synthesis of the present, the past and the future. (On time, see also James Williams' indispensable *Gilles Deleuze's Philosophy of Time* (2011).) The first synthesis is a passive synthesis that defines and makes up the lived and living present. Its time, which 'contracts ... successive independent instants into one another' (70), lies outside of both memory and consciousness. Deleuze relates this time to the 'spontaneous imagination' (77) which contracts, in the same way in which the first synthesis contracts singular temporal points into clusters, heterogeneous instants into the temporal surface of the present. For all sentient beings, such an unconscious and habitual synthesis forms the general 'foundation of time' (79): *the time of being as continuous contraction.*

While the first synthesis concerns only the present, the second synthesis, which involves the notion of memory, concerns the present in its relation to a past. Deleuze splits this synthesis up into 'the passive synthesis of memory' (79), which operates from within the 'succession' (83) of the presents that is given to it by the temporal contraction of first synthesis, and the active synthesis of memory, which operates from within the contemplation of the 'coexistence' (83) of a present and a past. The passive synthesis of memory is nearer to a material, actual memory – it concerns involuntary memories and moments when one is suddenly overwhelmed by a feeling of being in a specific slice of the past, where this past is often a traumatic slice, but sometimes just a madeleine moment – while the active synthesis of memory is nearer to an immaterial, virtual memory; to the state that, by default, denotes that of remembrance, of the specific image triggered by the world of sensual perception involuntarily evoked in the madeleine moment.

The third synthesis of time is directed towards the future as the time of 'memory and understanding' (80). From within the Freudian terms that provide the backdrop to Deleuze's argument, the first synthesis concerns the Id, the second the Ego and the third the 'superego' (115). In Lacanian terms: the Real, the Imaginary and the Symbolic. Although Deleuze maps the three syntheses onto this Freudian triad, he might equally have mapped it onto Leibniz's differentiation of monads into naked monads as defined by perception and appetition (*conatus*), animal monads as defined by perception, appetition and memory, and human monads as defined by appetition, perception, memory and consciousness. (On the syntheses of time, see Bryant 2008; Olkowski 1999: 104–17, 179.)

If the three syntheses align three temporal modalities, the second theory of time, which Deleuze develops in *The Logic of Sense*, operates with only two temporal modalities, Aion and Chronos, which raises the question of how to turn three into two and vice versa. How to turn a temporal triptych into a temporal diptych? The solution is strictly mathematical and deceptively simple: 3 divided by 2 equals 1.5. In other words, the symmetry between the two theories lies in Deleuze's differentiation, within the field of the second synthesis of time, between a passive and an active mode of memory. A folding of the three syntheses of time along the difference between these two forms of memory yields an actual side that concerns the first synthesis plus half of the second synthesis, and a virtual side that concerns the second half of the second synthesis and the third synthesis. As Deleuze notes about the two forms of repetition in *Difference and Repetition*, 'one is bare, the other clothed; one is repetition of parts, the other of the whole; one involves succession, the other coexistence; one is actual, the other virtual; one is horizontal, the other vertical' (84): *crystal time*.

According to this twofold definition, the actual side of the three syntheses of time is analogous to chronic time, which belongs to the purely causal world of matters-of-fact. As Deleuze notes in *The Logic of Sense*, it is 'made up purely of passions, physical qualities, bodies, tensions and actions' (4), and it concerns 'the *living present*, [which] happens and *brings about* the event' (63, emphasis added). As he also notes, the 'only time of bodies and states of affairs ... is the present. For the living present is the temporal extension which accompanies the act' (4). In terms of light, it is a time that breaks up the glow of the light that suffuses a situation into the stutter of a chronic strobe. Deleuze sets up a direct complementarity between the temporal differentiation of Chronos and Aion and the spatial differentiation of causes and effects that he had developed in his reading of the Stoics. Against this background, one might imagine chronic time as a succession of purely causal, endo-consistent moments, each of which is closed onto itself. In the chronic world, 'a cosmic present embraces the entire universe; only bodies exist in space, and only the present exists in time. There are no causes and effects in bodies. Rather, all bodies are causes – causes in relation and to each other and for each other' (4). The chronic world is made up of a multiplicity of temporal pulses of different lengths and rhythms. In DeLanda's terms, it is made up of 'the objective time scale of oscillators' (2002: 89).

In this pulsating present, living entities are what Serres and Friedrich Cramer call bundles of time. As assemblages of heterogeneous machines with different temporal plateaus, intensities and rhythms, they are defined by a heterogeneity of temporal pulses. All of these, however, are entrained by the overall eigenpulse of the specific entity. In fact, each entity is itself the result of its entrainment, organization and regulation of a temporal heterology; of the integration of a multiplicity of chronic pulses into an overall operative pulse. DeLanda calls this 'the ability of nonlinear oscillators to synchronize or entrain one another's temporal behaviour' (2002: 92). Circadian clocks and lunatisms are examples of the literally cosmic character of these pulses, of their immanence to the allover plane of nature. 'When not in isolation, circadian clocks become entrained with the planet's own rotational period of twenty-four hours, a synchronizing capacity with obvious adaptive value since it allows a flexible coordination of internal rhythms and seasonally changing day lengths. Thanks to entrainment, biological oscillators can mesh, or form a heterogeneous assemblage, with the daily and seasonal rhythms of their external environment. Entrainment displays the typical characteristics of an intensive process, stimulus-independence and mechanism-independence' (93). By way of this entrainment, each living system territorializes and molarizes the chronic multiplicity. It subjects the multiplicity of pulses to a dominant pulse. Or, more correctly: each living entity is itself nothing but a territorialization of time. Even while they create, and are created by, an internal temporal resonance, however, living entities never stop being coupled to and in resonance with the more comprehensive temporal pulses that define their medium. (On a theory of a heterology of molecular pulses and 'non-pulsed time' in biology, see TRM: 17–18.) The two extremes that define the chronic world are, at one end of the spectrum, a series of infinitely short pulses of presents that follow each other in infinitely fast succession and that form an infinite density of singular pulses, and, at the other end, an infinitely long, cosmic pulse. A present that literally stretches out over eternity. The extremes are either being in the strobes or being in the strobe.

While all living entities are immanent to the totality of these chronic pulses in terms of their biomaterial energetics, they live within an immaterial, aionic time in terms of their memorial and cognitive operations. In terms of light, this immaterial time sets a diffuse aionic glow that suffuses a scene against the stuttering of the chronic strobe. Whereas chronic time, as the time of full, matter-of-fact presents without past or future, is the time of being – 'for to be present would mean to be and no longer to become' (LS: 164) – aionic time is 'the instant without thickness and *without extension*, which subdivides each present into past and future, rather than vast and thick presents which comprehend both future and past in relation to one another' (164, emphasis added). (To stress that it always relies on a duration, however minimal, between past and future, I will sometimes refer to aionic time as chronological time.)

As an empty, intensive, virtual duration that is open to both a past and to a future, chronological time is the time of becoming, and as such it is related to processes of deterritorialization and molecularization. As DeLanda notes, in reference to *The Logic of Sense*, 'a pure becoming involve[s] both directions at once, a melting-freezing event which never actually occurs, but is *always forthcoming and already past*' (2002: 107, see also LS: 80). In the context of the temporality of the Deleuzian event, chronic time brings about the event, while chronological time is the time of the event. It is the qualitative time that is a witness to the the quantities of chronic time.

In chronological time, the cyclical time of chronic pulses is unrolled into perceptual durations that are plotted on a straight line. 'Aion is the eternal truth of time: *pure empty form of time*, which has freed itself of its present corporeal content and has thereby unwound its own circle, stretching itself out in a straight line' (LS: 165). On this chronological line, time is 'subdivided ad infinitum into something that has just happened and something that is going to happen, always flying in both directions at once' (63). In his conceptualization of the infinite divisibility of chronological time, Deleuze draws once more on the mathematical conceit of the Dedekind cut, which, as I noted earlier, treats mathematical continuity as an infinite number of cuts into an unmeasured, ideally continuous line. On that line, an interval between past and future can become so minimally small that it is impossible to be thought. It cannot, however, at least not in the embodied world, become infinitely small. This echoes the time of the Stoics, about which Samuel Sambursky notes in *Physics of the Stoics* that 'we have thus to regard the stoic present as a shrinking duration of only indistinctly defined boundaries. The physical significance of such a duration is that it still represents an eventlike structure, it is an elementary event, and macroscopic time is composed of the succession of such events . . . There is no such thing [as the instantaneous present] to be found in nature. As an ultimate fact it is a nonentity. What is immediate for sense-awareness is a duration' (1959: 105).

The relation between chronic strobe and aionic glow, which brings Deleuze's thought once more to the threshold between an ideal, a mathematical, a physical and a perceptual notion of infinity, consists of an alignment of material pulses and immaterial intervals [|←|→|←|→|←|→|]. In this iambic or trochaic meter of time respectively, the chronic stress lies on the directed, irreversible pulses of full, material, lived presents [| | | | |], while chronological, unstressed time designates the multidirectional, reversible time of empty, immaterial, and neutral durations, which brings into operation the intervals between the full presents, and which opens up, between the chronic stresses, chronological becomings [←|→]; lines of flight between chronic pulses. The time travels within the fixed arrow of chronic time. Flashbacks and flashforwards. There are various modes of conceptualizing the alignment of circle and line, such as incarnation, interpenetration, mutual presupposition or superposition. In all of these cases, chronological time designates the empty, virtual time of becoming between full, actual pulses of being. In the topology Deleuze will overthrow, although he still uses it at this point, Aion, as a chronological surface, is built up from and spanned out over the depth of Chronos.

While Deleuze's philosophical differentiation between chronic and aionic time, as strobe and glow, pulse and duration, or point and line, is categorical and formal, it is complementary from an ontological point of view. As the temporal logic is scale-dependent within living entities, from a perceptual point of view each plateau has a threshold beyond which durational intervals are registered as momentous pulses, somewhat in the way a surface is registered, from a certain perceptual distance, as a mere point. In other words, there are perceptual thresholds where aionic durations are perceived as chronic moments. At such moments, they become literally unconscious in the sense of Deleuze's and Serres' notion of the unconscious. Conversely, momentous points can also, at specific thresholds, be perceived as durations, and thus become conscious. When one approaches a physical, as in non-mathematical, temporal pulse, one at some point perceives that it is in actual fact a temporal duration. To reduce the duration to a pulse would mean for the system a fall into the depths of chronic time. Such a fall would imply a becoming schizophrenic. A return to the non-subjective, deep and sterile body without organs; to 'the undifferentiated abyss of a groundlessness which only permits the pulsation of a monstrous body' (LS: 120). It would involve the collapse of the virtual surface. In order to perceive chronic presents, in fact, the perceptual apparatus would need to operate in chronic real-time, which would mean that it would have to literally cancel itself out in a movement analogous to that of becoming a pure, unformed medium.

Chronological time, therefore, can never become fully chronic. What it can do, however, is become finer, faster, more plastic and more anonymous. For this to happen, the perceptual apparatus needs to enter formerly imperceptible intervals of duration: *perception à la Dedekind*. The more levels of cognition intervene between the perceptual apparatus and the intensive medium, in fact, the more mediated and coarse perceptual time becomes. In a terminology that echoes Leibniz, the more integrated aionic time becomes, the more it becomes extensive and hermetic [→ **Guattari 171**]. One should note, however, that despite such temporal zooms, the formal difference between the two modes of time remains. The categorical difference is operative even on very microscopic levels, because each minimal, faint memory and each crystal act of cognition creates a virtual duration or temporal surface. The brain 'divides up excitation infinitely' (52) and 'in relation to the motor cells of the core it leaves us to choose between several possible reactions' (53).

To define a brain as an interval between stimulus and response seems at first sight to be extremely reductive. What this very abstract definition shows, however, is that elementary systems perceive faster and more than complicated ones, which is why atoms are best at perceiving small durations. They operate, one might say, fully within the level of tiny perceptions. Because all complicated, more ponderous systems are made up of atoms, however, they participate in the speed of atomic perception, although this concerns levels that are unconscious to the overall entity. From a perspective that looks at the brain as nothing but a machine for the deceleration and the mediation of perception, the sheer mass of cognition tends to make perception more and more ponderous. From a perspective that looks at the brain as a complex virtual machine, however, it also allows for virtual freedom and for complexity. Thought is staked against what we call instinctual response. In analogy to Peirce's idea that intuition is just a form of unconscious ratiocination, instinct is just another name for very short, seemingly instantaneous virtual operations. Humans are immanent to the whole spectrum of perception, from instant, accelerated responses to depressed decelerations such as Hamlet's; from an assemblage of molecular brains|minds to the unity of a molar brain|mind.

In this context, becoming imperceptible and becoming unconscious means to speed up perception into increasingly smaller slices of time, with an escape velocity that is ultimately faster than the speed of thought, and thus ultimately beyond the event horizon of classical philosophy. The end of this infinite acceleration marks also the end of individual perception. As smaller temporal intervals become increasingly imperceptible to entities with higher thresholds of perception, the perspective-point of an anonymous thought is a completely imperceptible, unreduced, anonymous thought|consciousness: *perception at the speed of light*.

Similar to the way that the surface of events forms a network of quasi-causes, the surface of chronological time might be said to form quasi-pulses. Chronic pulses and chronological durations – the real pulses of being and the quasi-pulses of becoming – might be said to be attributed according to a cinematographic logic; long stills and short motion. Deleuze calls the temporal modality that negotiates these dynamics the instant, 'the aleatory point, the nonsense of the surface and the quasi-cause' (LS: 166) which 'extracts singularities from the present' (166). Perceptual duration is constructed from these singularities that are extracted from the multiplicity of chronological instants in pre-individual, complex interaction. However, as the instant, qua quasi-cause, links the perceptual system and its chronic history in a reciprocal attribution, perceptual histories are not only constructed from aionic singularities, they are also extracted from and witnesses of the chronic, quantitative field.

As in the topology of the event, the paradoxical, complementary alignment of chronic and chronological time recapitulates the fact that in terms of energetics, living entities are immanent to the realm of deeply chronic pulses of successive presents that are analogous to material causes, while in terms of perception, they live and operate within an architecture of temporal surfaces that are made up of the immaterial spaces between these pulses and that are analogous to immaterial effects. There is thus a radical simultaneity of two temporal modalities. 'Time must be grasped twice, in two complementary though mutually exclusive fashions. First, it must be grasped entirely as the living present in bodies which act and are acted upon. Second, it must be grasped entirely as an entity infinitely divisible into past and future, and into the incorporeal effects which result from bodies, their actions and their passions' (5). For all living entities, 'there are two times, one of which is composed only of interlocking presents: the other is constantly decomposed into elongated pasts and futures. There are two times, one of which is always definite, active or passive; the other is eternally Infinitive and eternally neutral. *One is cyclical, measures the movements of bodies and depends on the matter which limits and fills it out; the other is a pure straight line at the surface, incorporeal, unlimited, an empty form of time, independent of all matter*' (62, emphasis added).

Once chronic and chronological time are defined as complementary, and once living beings are defined in temporal terms as particular modes of their alignment, the *chrono*logic of the event comes to recapitulate its *topo*logic: 'the always limited present, which measures the action of bodies as causes and the state of their mixtures in depth (Chronos); . . . the essentially unlimited past and future, which gather incorporeal events, at the surface, as effects (Aion)' (61). Deleuze specifically relates the two temporal modalities to the twofold vectorization of the event between matter-of-*fact* and *matter*-of-fact: 'The Aion is precisely the border of the two [tables|series], the straight line which separates them; but it is also the plain surface which connects them, an impenetrable window or glass . . . It makes one and the same event the expressed of propositions and the attribute of things' (64).

In a further parallel to the *topo*logic of the event, chronic pulses form the material ground of the assembly of the surface of chronological time according to aionizing programmes that are programmes of becoming interval. These allow for the construction of an architecture of chronological surfaces to emerge from the chronic depths of material pulses without ceasing to be their attribute, just like the eventual *topo*logic allows the immaterial event to emerge from the depths of material matters-of-fact. In fact, the chronological time of the event is a surface time assembled from chronic depths. 'We seek to determine an impersonal and pre-individual transcendental field, which does not resemble the corresponding empirical fields, and which nevertheless is not confused with an undifferentiated depth' (102). The paradox of the new topology is beautifully described in *Difference and Repetition*: 'It is as if the ground rose to the surface without ceasing to be ground' (28).

Within this overall topology, chronic time addresses the realm of physical, formational processes and movements, while chronological time addresses the level of informational, operational and relational procedures that integrate these processes into data and durations. Although it emerges from the realm of the chronic, every perceptual system invariably creates its own internal chronological dynamics and modes of formation. While the operational surface of chronological time is the plane of immaterial integrations, that of chronic time is the depths of material impulses and propagations. Once more, these two levels are radically separated. 'How could the sage be the quasi-cause of the incorporeal event, and thereby will its embodiment, if the event were not already in the process of being produced by and in the depth of corporeal causes . . . The quasi-cause does not create, it "operates", and wills only what comes to pass . . . Corporeal causes act and suffer through a cosmic mixture and a universal present which produces the incorporeal event. But the quasi-cause operates by doubling this physical causality – it embodies the event in the most limited possible present which is the most precise and the most instantaneous, the pure instant grasped at the point at which it divides itself into future and past [Aion], and no longer the present of the world which would gather into itself the past and the future [Chronos]' (LS: 147). As Deleuze notes, the 'present of the Aion representing the instant is not at all like the vast and deep present of Chronos: it is the present without thickness' (168). Surface time: *the fractal architecture of temporal planes.*

In 'The Actual and the Virtual', Deleuze relates actual Chronos and virtual Aion to the process of crystallization. In this context, the text resonates in particular with Deleuze's text on Lucretius and with *The Logic of Sense*. Taking up the definition of the chronic as a multiplicity of pulses, and of chronological time as linear time, Deleuze describes the chronic pulse as a resonant time without duration. The chronic pulse is an inherently timeless moment – it is smaller than the smallest period of continuous time – that replaces a chronological, linear direction with a chronic circle that is either expanded or contracted but that, at infinity, can be simultaneously infinitely short and infinitely long. 'The period of time which is smaller than the smallest period of continuous time imaginable in one direction is also the longest time imaginable in all directions' (DII: 151). During the process of crystallization, the two reciprocal forms of time become indiscernible. 'The two aspects of time, the actual image of the present which passes and the virtual image of the past which is preserved, are distinguishable during actualization although they have unassignable limits, but exchange during crystallization to the extent that they become indiscernible, each relating to the role of the other' (151). In terms of light and of the cinema, one might perhaps relate the stutter of Chronos to the cinematic apparatus, which is based on 24fps strobes, and the flow of Aion to the glow of the falsely durational cinematic image: *cinema as life.*

The fractal architecture of chronological time is that of counter-actualization. If the chronological event is actualized as an attribute of the chronic, then counter-actualization, as the operation by which entities actively produce material causes, is an actualization from within the chronological. To describe this process, Deleuze uses the image of the actor, which refers it back to the idea that 'it is intensity which *dramatises*' (DR: 245). In counter-actualizing, the actor 'actualizes the event, but in a way which is entirely different from the actualization of the event in the depth of things. Or rather, the actor redoubles this comic, or physical actualization, in his own way, which is singularly superficial' (LS: 150).

The challenge of counter-actualization lies in re-attributing the chronological event to its matter-of-factual chronics. When Deleuze notes in *Nietzsche and Philosophy* that 'to the famous positivity of the negative Nietzsche opposes his own discovery: the negativity of the positive' (1983b: 180), the first is dialectical and reactive, the second dramatizing and active: *Nietzsche against Hegel.* Philosophy is not affirmation of the real (primary affirmation: 'affirmation itself is being' (186)), but affirmation of the false. 'There is no truth of the world as it is thought, no reality of the sensible world, all is evaluation' (184). Qualification. To 'affirm is ... to create new values which are those of life, which make life light and active' (185).

The time of dramatization aligns aionic becoming and chronic being in the affirmation of their complementarity. 'Multiplicity, becoming and chance are the properly philosophical joy in which unity rejoices in itself and also in being and necessity' (190). Even more paradoxically, 'becoming is being, multiplicity is unity, chance is necessity. The affirmation of becoming is the affirmation of being etc.' (189). This, then, is the twofold time of philosophy: 'Being ought to belong to becoming, unity to multiplicity, necessity to chance, but only insofar as becoming, multiplicity and chance are reflected in the second affirmation which takes them as its object' (189). The 'moment of reflection where a second affirmation takes the first as its object' is when philosophy takes life as its object, when the false trails life behind. When Aion trails Chronos behind. 'In this game of becoming, the being of becoming also plays the game with itself; the aeon (time), says Heraclitus, is a child who plays' (24): *a philosophy of the false against false philosophies.*

Philosophical Spaces (The Real Projective Plane of Philosophy)

A Thousand Plateaus (1980), The Fold: Leibniz and the Baroque (1988),
The Logic of Sense (1969)

Let me switch from registers of time and history considered from within luminous registers as the times of strobe and glow, to those of space and architecture considered from within the luminous registers of light surface and dark depth. Again, similar to the way in which Deleuze considers chronic strobe and aionic glow as complementary, he breaks up the formal difference between light surface and dark depth by transposing the differentiation between surface and depth into an allover fractal space in which this differentiation defines every spatial plateau of that space equally, and as such sets up everywhere a relation of spatial complementarity.

In Deleuze's spatial fractalism, the opposition of light surface and dark depth is diffracted into the spectrum of a spatial *chiaroscuro*. In 'Lucretius and the Simulacrum', Deleuze talks about this new space in relation to 'a brilliant, though difficult, Epicurean theory' according to which 'bodies or atomic compounds never cease to emit particularly subtle, fluid, and tenuous elements' (LS: 273). These simulacra or, in Epicurean terminology idols (*eidola*), can either 'emanate from the depth of bodies or they detach themselves from the surface of a thing'. While 'sounds, smells, tastes and temperatures' are emitted from the depths, 'visual determinations, forms and colors refer to the simulacra of the surface' (273). Again, Deleuze stresses the complementarity of surface and depth, 'since each sense seems to combine information of the depth with information of the surface. Emissions arising from the depths pass through the surface, and the superficial envelopes, as they detach themselves from the object, are replaced by formerly concealed strata' (273–4). In the same way that light voices that operate on the surface of articulation rely on the dark realm of deep, sonorous noise, according to the theory of emanation, 'simulacra of the surface are able to provide colors and forms only if there is light, which is emitted from the depths' (274). The fractal complementarity of surface and depth can help understand why it is deceptive to talk of the famous flatness of Deleuze's ontology. The surfaces of thought and of life are not really flat, because they consist of an infinity of plateaus that lie in fractal dimensions between the three dimensions that are normally used to describe space: *fractal chiaroscuro*.

In the last chapter I argued that the architecture of the series of matters-of-fact and events is scaled, in that each event is a complex assemblage of pure, elementary events. Molar events are constructed from molecular events in the same way that molar bodies are constructed from pure, elementary particles. While the second, actual series goes from elementary particles to atoms, molecules and further to complex organisms, the first, virtual series goes from elementary thoughts to molecular thoughts and further to complex ideas. Both the virtual and the actual, therefore, should be understood as being scaled from the infinitely large to the infinitely small.

In 'Letter to a Harsh Critic', from 1973, Deleuze writes that 'one might ... note, looking at my fingertips, that I haven't got the normal protective whorls, so that touching anything, especially fabric, causes such irritation that I need long nails to protect them' (N: 5). The remark is Deleuze's subjunctive answer to a snide accusation that his exceptionally long fingernails give him the air of a diva. Immediately, however, Deleuze shifts from this physiological explanation to a philosophical one. 'Or one might say, and it's true, that I dream of being, not invisible, but imperceptible, and the closest I can get to the dream is having fingernails I can keep in my pocket' (N: 5). (See Dosse 2011 for the biographical background.)

The two answers are more than deeply self-ironic responses to a sadly unironic affront. In fact, the highly ambiguous notion of becoming imperceptible is of such importance to Deleuze that he includes it in his alternative set of cardinal virtues. If the Christian virtues are belief, love, and hope, Deleuze's 'three virtues' are 'imperceptibility, indiscernibility, and impersonality' (TP: 280). Each of these implies the dissolution of a system into its medium: 'the (anorganic) imperceptible, the (asignifying) indiscernible, and the (asubjective) impersonal' (279): Optically (as imperceptibility), categorically (as undifferentiability) and systemically (as impersonality), the idea is to ecologically blend into the world by way of a philosophical mimicry. A fish, for example, 'worlds with the lines of a rock, sand, and plants, becoming imperceptible' (280). In terms of birdsong, 'the imperceptible appears as such' (284) when the song separates itself from the bird and blends into the world's allover soundscape. 'No longer the songbird, but the sound molecule' (248). (On birdsong and Uexküll, see Ruyer 1952: 217.) In both examples, the vector of virtuosity goes from the molar to the molecular, and from the individual to the singular; 'from the howling of animals to the wailing of elements and particles' (TP: 249).

A first implication of the logic of scaling is that for sentient beings, phenomena that are imperceptible, undifferentiable or impersonal from one perceptual point of entry are perceptible, differentiable and personal from a more microscopic point of perceptual entry. This is why the formal distinction between the two registers blurs in the practice of life. Who would have thought that what looks like a mote of dust is in actual fact a human being? The most common way to make the imperceptible perceptible, therefore, is to enhance the given scales of the senses by way of technical machines of perception, such as microscopes or slow-motion cameras. The result would be similar, however, if one were to change one's own scale in a movement of downsizing, which is what happens in the science-fiction movie *The Incredible Shrinking Man* from 1957. The movie, which Deleuze comments on briefly, takes such a becoming imperceptible literally. Adapted by Jack Arnold from Richard Matheson's novel *The Shrinking Man*, the film is one of the earliest examples of a series of science-fiction movies interested in pre-nanoscale miniaturization, such as *The Phantastic Voyage* (1966), *The Incredible Shrinking Woman* (1981) and *Innerspace* (1987), in all of which people are artificially shrunk in order to perceive formerly imperceptible plateaus of life. In the beginning of *The Shrinking Man*, the process of shrinking is triggered by particles of a mysterious cloud that sublimate on the body of the protagonist, Scott Carey, during a boat ride. According to a favourite formula of 1950s science-fiction, Matheson's novel identifies the dust as insect spray 'hideously altered by radiation' (1969: 102).

Carey's process of becoming imperceptible can be read not only in subjective but also in cinematographic terms. In fact, the movie version recapitulates quite literally Bergson's and Deleuze's comparison of the time of becoming as the time of the interval between still film images. Becomings take place in the durations between singular, still instants. From this perspective, Carey's gradual process of vanishing resonates directly with Deleuze's discussion, in *The Logic of Sense*, of Lewis Carroll's *Alice in Wonderland*, which contains the perhaps most famous vanishing act in the history of literature. '"I wish you wouldn't keep appearing and vanishing so suddenly; you make one quite giddy!" the girl Alice tells a cat. "All right", said the Cat; and this time it vanished quite slowly, beginning with the end of the tail, and ending with the grin, which remained some time after the rest of it had gone' (93). The Cheshire cat's slow-motion vanishing act shows that every sudden change – now you see it, now you don't – is in actual fact a continuous process, which opens up the question of what happens in or during the interval. How does the passage from seeing to not-seeing function? What happens between t[ime]1 (now you see it) and t[ime]2 (now you don't)? In relation to the logic of cinematic perception, what lies in the interval (Δt) between two images on a strip of celluloid? In relation to Leibniz's integrational calculus, which I will deal with later, what lies in the infinitesimal interval between t1 and t2?

Mathematically, the question of what happens between the Δts evokes, once again, the procedure of the Dedekind cut, whose affinity to the process of vanishing lies in the fact that the interval between two digital measurements on a continuous line gets increasingly smaller the more numbers are added – in the ideal case, it gets infinitely small – but that it never, except at infinity, vanishes completely. Similarly, the temporal interval between t1 and t2 becomes increasingly smaller, but something never stops vanishing in-between any two cuts. Every vanishing happens in a spatial and temporal interval that converges towards zero, but that will never reach the point of convergence, except at the point-at-infinity. All it does is to forever become zero. As each vanishing remains processual, one can set up increasingly more powerful slow-motion devices to make the time of vanishing perceptible. Every point in time can always be slowed down into a duration. Except in a mathematical, abstract sense, there is no point in time.

Although one can think of a whole array of modes of vanishing, such as fading in terms of density, or structural disintegration, there are two default modes. The first concerns a change of position, the other a change of size. The visual strategy to address the first mode is to use a slow-motion device, for the second, to perform a zoom. Both strategies show that something vanishingly small is only vanishingly small on a particular level of perception, and thus from a specific perceptual distance. As I noted, both temporally and spatially, the moment of vanishing can always be stretched out. Every sudden disappearance is in actual fact a gradual fading or a becoming imperceptible. While the formal distinction between point in time and duration is strict, in practice, the perceptual problem is that specific technologies of perception are too coarse to register certain fadings.

If the process of vanishing lies invariably in the interval between the measuring points according to which specific levels and technologies of perception operate, what has vanished has only vanished in relation to the specific coarseness of the plateau of observation. The finer and faster the perceptual apparatus, the narrower the intervals. However, it is always possible to imagine even smaller intervals because, both mathematically and perceptually, each interval can be segmented into even smaller cuts. Read in psychological registers: for every perceptual level there is a lost, unconscious interval, such as the intervals on the celluloid that the human apparatus of visual perception cannot register because that apparatus is too slow: *persistence of vision*.

Becoming imperceptible, therefore, is ultimately about opening oneself up to as many fine, quasi-analog levels as possible. To become increasingly anonymous. A slower perception, in fact, would change the fluid movement of a film into a perceptual flicker, which means that the film would have to be speeded up in order to reconstitute the effect of continuous movement. In order to succeed in truly simulating movement, the film would indeed have to run at an infinitely fast speed. At the end of this perceptual series, then, lies an infinitely fine and infinitely fast, completely unconscious perception; a perception in real time: *perception at the speed of light and anonymous life*.

While the movement of becoming imperceptible stresses continuity and the analog, becoming perceptible stresses discontinuity and the discrete. (On the relation between digital and analog, see Massumi 2002: 133–43.) Symptomatically, Carey first perceives that he is shrinking during a completely automatic and unconscious routine. At some point, the imperceptible process of his gradual shrinking reaches a significant threshold of perception at which Carey registers it for the first time. While he dresses, he suddenly notices that his shirt has become too large. A series of unconscious and imperceptible differen*t*iations have become a conscious, perceptible differen*c*iation. A dark precursor has become perceptible after the fact. Such moments of discretion – as in: making something discrete – are inevitable. In fact, neither the book nor the movie can represent the continuity of becoming or of vanishing by way of an in itself gradual, analog movement. Both represent a continuous sliding as a stumbling or stuttering. They approach the continuity of vanishing through specific cinematographic and literary punctuations. Although both artistic regimes are about a process of continuous vanishing, they represent this vanishing by way of noteworthy moments.

While the becoming imperceptible in the movie is first of all about becoming invisible, it is also about becoming unconscious. In this context, Carey's initial panic about his shrinking might be read as an allegory of the panic of Lacanian psychoanalysis when it confronts the Deleuzian unconscious, which resides precisely in the 'microintervals' (TP: 281) between two points on a line, and thus participates in 'unconscious micropercepts' (213) and 'microperceptions' (283). If perception is always already discrete, then something that is unconscious can only be retrieved if perception reaches a level that is finer than the threshold of perception on which that specific unconscious lies. According to this recursive chain, one will never become fully unconscious. Deleuze's serialization of becomings-unconscious relies on this scaled logic. For now, let me just note that in the Deleuzian unconscious, psychoanalysis's categorical differentiation between the conscious and the unconscious is replaced by an infinitely recursive series of nested differentiations of conscious and unconscious levels; the schizoanalytic point being to make the thresholds of perception as fine as possible. Becomings happen always between discrete levels. This idea of the fractal and thus infinite series of becomings – which is too easily hijacked from the mathematical and philosophical into the merely metaphorical realm – is why becoming imperceptible is such a positive movement in Deleuze.

Deleuze and Guattari develop the concept of vanishing in the section 'Memories of a Molecule' in the chapter 'Becoming-Intense, Becoming-Animal, Becoming-Imperceptible' from *A Thousand Plateaus*, in which they describe 'becomings-elementary, -cellular, -molecular, and even becomings-imperceptible' (248) as the terminal points of processes of becoming. 'A fiber stretches from a human to an animal, from a human or an animal to molecules, from molecules to particles, and so on to the imperceptible' (249). The realm of the unconscious and the vanished, in which fixed points are dissolved into lines, and representations into productions, is defined by the ideal of the imperceptible.

In both the book and the movie version, the phases of Carey's becoming imperceptible are not only shown by critical moments that mark his material shrinking, but also by analogous moments that show a simultaneous cultural shrinking. Carey is gradually expelled from the social field, for instance through his change from loved and desired husband to emasculated toy-man, and further to a child. Although he can, for a short time, re-gain his lost masculinity on the level of smaller people, eventually, that threshold is crossed as well. Ironically, he becomes aware of this just when he has set himself up more or less comfortably on the new, smaller level of reality. Again, as with the moment of dressing, the film depicts a critical moment to show this shift. Sitting down next to his new love on a park bench, Carey realizes that, although he used to be larger than her, he is now smaller.

When Carey is the size of a child, he moves into a doll house that is set up fractally in the house he has lived in before, and thus within grown-up reality. If there are bodies in bodies, why not houses in houses? This relativity of scale is taken up by the fact that, in direct proportion to his becoming smaller, Carey's senses and perceptions become more and more molecular, which means that, from a more molar position, they become more acute. From within his new perceptual scale, he experiences grown-up perceptions at first comparatively, and later as oppressively large and molar. First, he begins to perceive things that his wife cannot perceive, then the sound of her movements and the noises in the house become gigantic and overwhelming. Quite literally, he sees (now you see it) what is unconscious for his wife (now you don't). 'He remembered how, toward the end of his stay in the house, he had been incapable of listening to music unless it was played so low that Lou couldn't even hear it. Otherwise the music was magnified into a clubbing noise at his ears, giving him a headache' (Matheson 1969: 104). The molar whisper is a molecular scream. The fact that spatial measures are similarly relative is shown in the way Carey carries the objective scale of measurement over into his new level of scale. As he notes, a piece of bread lying on a ledge is 'two hundred yards' (149) away.

At this point, the plot of the movie has already shifted from questions of human relationships to Carey's adventurous fights with animals; a series in which each fight marks a further moment of shrinking. The first enemy is a cat, the second a mouse, the third a spider. Through a series of further thresholds, the film tracks Carey's continuing descent into smaller scales of life. After it has gone beyond even the level of animals, Carey's vanishing proceeds towards the microscopic levels that are generally considered as inanimate. In the end, he enters the molecular and atomic levels. Before him lies the plane of immanence or, in the terminology of *A Thousand Plateaus*, the body without organs, as an impossible-to-reach limit. 'If the BwO is a limit, if one is forever attaining it, it is because behind each stratum, encased in it, there is always another stratum' (TP: 159).

The model of such a recursive universe is that of a fractal sponge whose structure is, like the Dedekind universe, defined by an infinite regress. As Deleuze notes in *Foucault*, 'if the world is infinitely cavernous, if worlds exist in the tiniest bodies, it is because everywhere there can be found "a spirit in matter"' (7). Even the atomic level, or that of elementary particles, therefore, are merely pragmatic limits. The particles on the plane of immanence are 'not atoms, in other words, finite elements still endowed with form' (TP: 254). Ultimately, the plane has 'nothing to do with a form or a figure'. It is a completely formless medium. Although the plot of the movie is relentlessly straight in that it follows Carey's gradual shrinking until the moment before he reaches Deleuze's actual infinity, the movie shows merely a number of significant thresholds within that process. The progression in the novel is more complicated. Descriptions of Carey's last six days are juxtaposed with inserted retrospective situations, which have as headings simple measurements in inches: 68, 49, 42, 35, 21, 18, 7. Mathematically, this series of subtractions of rational numbers will end with zero.

Before I get to the infinitely small, let me return to the different registers that are evoked by the movie. In relation to a subject, the unconscious consists of analog intensities and anonymous affects, of the imperceptible continua of intensities that lie between the discrete moments of the perceptible. In terms of both the body and the mind, the unconscious is related to unmeasurably fine shifts within molecular force-fields. Becoming-imperceptible implies not only becoming-unconscious, therefore, but also becoming-intensive. Not in the sense of becoming-excessive, however, but rather in the sense of becoming more and more unmeasurable, subliminal and anonymous. Becoming-intensive, one might say, implies becoming-medium. In becoming-unconscious, -imperceptible and -intensive, individual life dissolves into *a life*. 'The important thing is to understand life, each living individuality, not as form or a development of form but as a complex relation between differential velocities, between deceleration and acceleration of particles' (Deleuze 1992a: 626). Against the background of this dissolution, Carey becomes part of an overall intensive *haecceity*, of the itness of the world. From his descent into the molecular world onward, his shrinking can only be treated in the subjunctive, as if he had grown too small for both the camera and for the narrator to discern. All of the apparatuses of representation lose him because they are too coarse. Carey leaves the levels of the human and the animal in order to become part of a powerful non-organic life. At the end, he becomes part of the plane of immanence: invisible, undifferentiable and asubjective; an anonymous, vanished particle.

A difference between Deleuze's philosophy and the movie, however, is that in the movie Carey remains, even on the molecular and atomic levels, a coherent individual. In opposition, Deleuze considers the individual itself as a universe that is made up of an infinite number of recursive plateaus and that is immanent to the allover plane of nature. In fact, the individual is a plane of consistency within the plane of immanence. The closer one zooms into the plane of consistency, the more formerly unconscious levels become perceptible. At the end of the process, there are only crystals without qualities, purely quantitative elements.

In Deleuze, the perceptual paradox lies in that the more one sees, the less one is oneself. As Deleuze and Guattari state, quite programmatically, 'the imperceptible itself becomes necessarily perceived at the same time as perception becomes necessarily molecular' (TP: 282). For Deleuze, an atom perceives more than a human simply because it is faster and finer. 'The first material moment of subjectivity . . . is subtractive. It subtracts from the thing whatever does not interest it'. As I noted in the introduction, an atom, for instance, 'perceives infinitely more than we do and, at the limit perceives the whole universe' (C1: 64): *anonymous atomic perception*.

In her book *Pilgrim at Tinker Creek*, Annie Dillard describes the same idea from within the hard sciences: 'Donald E. Carr points out that the sense impressions of one-celled animals are not edited for the brain. "This is philosophically interesting in a rather mournful way, since it means that only the simplest animals perceive the universe as it is"' (1976: 19). From a Deleuzian perspective, one would have to imagine Carey, who does not stop vanishing, as dissolving into the infinitely fast and the infinitely small.

By the end, Carey has overcome his initial panic. He has separated himself from everything that had bound him to his former life, and he looks towards his infinite vanishing with high expectations. The novel's structure is organized around the switch from a finite logic of subtraction to an infinite and infinitesimal logic. Carey is no longer afraid of death because he realizes that he will never reach zero, because Nature does not know the concept of zero. It was only as long as he, and the novel with him, still believed in a finite, subtractive mathematics that he had reason to be afraid. 'In six days he would be gone' (Matheson 1969: 6), because, he had wondered, 'what reality could there be at zero inches?' (11). At the end of the novel he has realized that nature operates according to a recursive logic. According to its infinite, fractal mathematics, his becoming imperceptible is not 'a curse' but 'a thing of potential value' (143). 'How could he be less than nothing?' (188) Carey asks himself. 'To a man, zero inches mean nothing. Zero meant nothing. But to nature there was no zero . . . He would never disappear because there was no point of non-existence in the universe. There was food to be found, water, clothing, shelter. And, most important, life. Who knew? . . . Scott Carey ran into his new world, searching' (188).

'To become imperceptible oneself, to have dismantled love in order to become capable of loving' (TP: 197), Deleuze and Guattari note. And further, 'if becoming-woman is the first quantum, or molecular segment, with the becomings-animal that link up with it coming next, what are they all rushing toward? Without a doubt, toward becoming imperceptible. The imperceptible is the immanent end of becoming, its cosmic formula. Matheson's *Shrinking Man* passes through the kingdoms of nature, slips between molecules, to become an unfindable particle in infinite meditation on the infinite' (279). On this level, 'flows of intensity, their fluids, their fibers, their continuums and conjunctions of affects, the wind, fine segmentation, microperceptions, have replaced the world of the subject. Becomings, becomings-animal, becomings-molecular, have replaced history, individual or general' (162). The end of the novel shows Carey's becoming natural not in the sense of a return to a natural nature, but to Nature as a living, infinitely complex communal machine. Carey enters the world of elementary particles: *worlding with the universe.*

Unlike the novel, the movie refracts this descent into the infinitely microscopic into religious registers. Symptomatically, it is now God rather than Nature who does not know zero. In the movie, to shrink means literally to become nothing, although this implies existence in terms of a melting, of an existence without being there: 'I was continuing to shrink, to become . . . what? The infinitesimal? . . . So close – the infinitesimal and the infinite. But suddenly, I knew they were really the two ends of the same concept. The unbelievably small and the unbelievably vast eventually meet – like the closing of a gigantic circle . . . And in that moment, I knew the answer to the riddle of the infinite. I had thought in terms of man's own limited dimension. I had presumed upon nature. That existence begins and ends in man's conception, not nature's. And I felt my body dwindling, melting, *becoming nothing*. My fears melted away. And in their place came acceptance. All this vast majesty of creation, it had to mean something. And then I meant something, too. Yes, smaller than the smallest, I meant something, too. To God, there is no zero. [*shouts*] I still exist!'

If the motto for the novel was that Nature knows no zero, the movie can think Carey's infinite becoming imperceptible only in terms of a return to, or better a dissolve into, a divine being, although it does evoke the point-at-infinity where opposites become one. More than the movie, the novel shows that becoming imperceptible is a movement not away from but towards a perception that is increasingly finer, more acute and more anonymous. At the same time, it is a movement into the intensive spaces between even the smallest of perceptual discriminations; a movement that brings into play the infinity of intensive, unconscious levels that operate in-between the intelligible and the perceptible. One might be tempted to lay a voice-over of the novel's closing monologue over the cinematic ending.

For Deleuze, becoming-imperceptible implies becoming-intensive, becoming-unmeasurable and becoming-unconscious. Ultimately, the difference between the perceptible and the imperceptible is nothing but the difference between the conscious and the unconscious. Deleuze's critique is not directed at perception and its constructions, therefore, but at the fact that philosophy does not perceive enough; that it does not contain within its figures of thought the imperceptible, unconscious intensities and irritations that at every moment disturb the binary architectures constructed by the various technologies of perception. The main thrust of Deleuze's philosophy is towards the conceptualization of an infinitely recursive series of levels of the unconscious, each of which consists of unregistered virtual and actual machines. In this return to the non-philosophical, philosophy becomes a witness to the intensive forces that cannot be integrated into any form of cultural and cognitive calculus.

Judging from his fascination with Leuwenhoek's newly invented microscope, Leibniz would, in all probability, have loved *The Shrinking Man*; the novel for its mathematics, and the movie for its deflection into religion. In the context of Leibniz's belief that nature is defined by an infinitely recursive, fractal descent into more and more non-human levels, the story is, in fact, in many ways an allegory of Leibniz's philosophy. As Leibniz notes in the *Monadology*, 'every portion of matter may be conceived as like a garden full of plants and like a pond full of fishes. But every branch of every plant, each member of every animal, each drop of its liquid parts is also some such garden or pond' (1998: 256).

As such, it is not surprising that many of the concerns that lie at the centre of the previous section also define *The Fold: Leibniz and the Baroque*, which is another of Deleuze's portraits. The study provides an extremely complicated and highly condensed account of the encounter between Deleuze and Leibniz in the light of the philosophical, the scientific and the artistic Baroque. The concept that allows Deleuze to draw these seemingly heterogeneous cultural practices together into the Baroque is that of the fold, a figure of thought that informs, according to Deleuze, all three modes of Baroque thought – science, art and philosophy – to an equal degree, and thus allowed, during Leibniz's time, for resonances and encounters across their disciplinary boundaries. As Deleuze notes in the very first sentence, 'the Baroque refers not to an essence but rather to an operative function . . . It endlessly produces folds' (LB: 3). Deleuze reads Leibniz's work as one example of such a production. It emerges from the figure of the fold. Simultaneously, it is one of its most complex actualizations: *the becoming unconscious of philosophy.*

As in his other portraits, Deleuzian philosophy is present in *The Fold* implicitly rather than explicitly. It can be felt in the way Deleuze modulates Leibniz, in the things he finds remarkable in Leibniz's thought, in the way he stresses that thought, in the concepts he uses to structure the text – such as calling the first two chapters 'The Pleats of Matter' and 'The Folds in the Soul', which echoes once more the twofold structure of Simondon's individuation – and in the Leibnizian concepts he refers to most frequently. One of these is the notion of infinity and its conjunction with the infinitesimal and the imperceptible, which is seminal in the double definition of Leibniz's calculus as a simultaneously mathematical and perceptual routine. Mathematically, a function is continuous when it is defined by infinitely small increments, which accords to the logic of diversity, while a discontinuous function is defined by finitely small increments, which accords to the logic of difference. Infinitesimals, which are unmeasurably small although their size is larger than zero, are quasi-continuous. As both perception and cognition are difference engines, our concept of continuity, such as that of infinite diversity as continuous, is an ideal. As long as it is conceptualized as infinite rather than as infinitesimal, however, diversity can be conceptualized as either fluid or as an aerosol made up of an infinity of particles, because from within a logic of complementarity these are, at a point-at-infinity, identical: *infinity as the unconscious of the infinitesimal.* Much of Leibniz's genius, in fact, lies in the way he conceives of the calculus as a both mathematical routine and as a 'psychic automatism' (89); in his refraction of mathematics into aesthetics as the science of perception, and vice versa. Three questions that Deleuze raises in *The Fold* are especially important for me. In what way does perception operate like the mathematical calculus? What is the relation between obscure and clear perceptions? What is the relation between the sensible and the intelligible? A fourth question, which creates a conceptual bridge to the next chapter, 'Luminous Philosophy', has to do with the luminous nature of monads. Can monads be conceptualized as photons?

In what way does perception operate like the mathematical calculus? First, similar to the way the calculus cuts a continuous curve into infinitesimally small mathematical segments, perception cuts a continuous world up into infinitesimally small increments of perceptual differences. In terms of *Difference and Repetition,* for Leibniz, perception might be said to cut into the plane of consistency by way of processes of clear differenciations that have emerged from the overall chromatic spectrum of obscure differentiations. The apparatus of visual perception, for instance, differentiates within the continuous changes across the chromatic scale of colour, from the optical spectrum, that is, by way of clear perceptual increments: *infinitesimal optical intervals:* Δos.

In a second step, the imagination sums up the infinitesimal differences into an integrated plane, into individual colours and their respective shades. In Lucretian terminology, it turns material simulacra into immaterial images. Something similar occurs within the chromatic scale or spectrum of sound, where the apparatus of perception first isolates, by way of differentiation, individual frequencies, which it then integrates into specific notes or words. If one considers the imagination as the immaterial side of the perceptual operation, it smooths out an agitated photonic or auditive multiplicity into less perturbed, imagined optical or auditive surfaces. The analogy between mathematics and perception, then, lies in the fact that both cut up quantitative continua into digital segments. In a second step, these discriminated segments are summed up, or, in Leibniz's doubly connoted term, are integrated, into qualities. These calculations are recursive in that the integrations can be more or less coarse, which leads directly to the second question. What is the relation between obscure and clear perceptions? According to Leibniz, the perceptual apparatus extracts clear perceptions from obscure perceptions by way of increasingly coarse integrations. The perceptual vector goes from 'molecular perceptions to molar perceptions' (100). In order to produce clear perceptions, it is necessary to first descend into the realm of obscure perceptions, which is why 'differential calculus is the psychic mechanism of perception, the automatism that at once and inseparably plunges into obscurity and determines clarity: a selection of minute, obscure perceptions and a perception that moves into clarity' (102).

When Leibniz's distinction between clear and obscure perceptions is conceptualized in analogy to the relation between active and passive syntheses, as well as in analogy to the relation between differenciation and differentiation, clear perceptions are conscious perceptions that emerge from unconscious, obscure perceptions in the same way that active syntheses emerge from passive syntheses, and differenciations emerge from differentiations. Deleuze had commented on this analogy in *Difference and Repetition* in the context of intensity or difference in itself. Within the field of pure intensity, 'all the intensities are implicated in one another, each in turn enveloped and enveloping, such that each continues to express ... the variable ensemble of differential relations' (DR: 252). In the shift from intensity as given to itself to intensity as given to something or somebody, this twofold definition is itself differentiated. As enveloping, 'each intensity *clearly* expresses only certain relations or certain degrees of variation' (252). In other words, the price perception pays for clarity is reduction. In terms of colour, for instance, the price paid for the distinction between red and orange is the loss of a more comprehensive, intensive chromatics. 'Orange is just a collage, the spatial gluing together of a yellow and a red multiplicity which are not separated and cut off from one another. A spatial chiasm of light' (Serres 1994: 57). As the perceiving entity remains immanent to the overall field of intensity, however, 'in its role as *enveloped*, it still expresses all relations and all degrees, but *confusedly*' (DR: 252).

While Leibniz is interested mainly in the production of clear perceptions from obscure ones, Deleuze is interested in the double vector of the emergence of clarity from obscurity (in Deleuzian terms: the vector from molecular to molar perceptions), even while clarity remains implicated in obscurity (in Deleuzian terms: the immanence of the molar in the molecular). In fact, Deleuze sets up a *coincidentia oppositorum* in which light is darkness, and darkness is light. Already in *Difference and Repetition*, Deleuze had stressed Leibniz's thought in this way. Quite infamously, Deleuze describes this strategy as 'taking a philosopher from behind' and of making him say things he did not mean. 'No one has ever been better able to immerse thought in the element of difference and provide it with a differential unconscious, surround it with little glimmerings and singularities, all in order to save and reconstitute the homogeneity of a natural light à la Descartes' (213), Deleuze had noted about Leibniz in *Difference and Repetition*. It is a familiar gesture. A precursor has done everything that should have brought him to realize what only the new philosopher can bring to light from within a stressed reading of the work of the precursor. This logic ties in with Deleuze's less notorious remark that 'my ideal, when I write about an author, would be to write nothing that could cause him sadness, or if he is dead, that might make him weep in his grave' (DII: 119).

For Deleuze it is not enough simply to note Leibniz's belief in the homogeneity of a *lumen naturale* which allows one to see clearly and distinctly. Rather, his reading of Leibniz conceptually stresses Leibniz's belief to the point that 'a clear idea is in itself confused; it is confused *in so far as it is clear*' (DR: 213). Such a twofold logic plays directly into the logic of conscious and unconscious perceptions. Clarity is itself obscure because it emerges from elements that are distinct rather than differentiated (a conceptual pair that takes up the difference between the diverse and the different) and thus obscure. This makes for the perceptual *chiaroscuro*. 'The little perceptions are themselves distinct and obscure (not clear): distinct because they are not yet "distinguished", not yet differenciated. These singularities then condense to determine a threshold of consciousness in relation to our bodies, a threshold of differenciation on the basis of which the little perceptions are actualized, but actualized in an apperception which in turn is only clear and confused; clear because it is distinguished or differenciated, and confused because it is clear' (213). Paradoxically, 'the clear is confused by itself, in so far as it is clear' (254): *the chiaroscuro of immanence*.

In *The Fold*, Deleuze deals in detail with this paradox in the chapter 'Perception in the Folds', which argues that the microperceptions that form the medium of a perceptual, continuous unconscious form 'an infinity of tiny folds . . . endlessly furling and unfurling in every direction, so that the monad's spontaneity resembles that of agitated sleepers who twist and turn on their mattresses' (LB: 98). Clear perceptions create digital data from this reservoir of tiny perceptions according to a logic of what is '*ordinary*' (100) and 'what is *notable* or *remarkable*' (100). The chosen, relevant elements are no longer simple differences, but 'differences that make a difference' (Bateson 1979: 99). In other words, they are qualitative rather than quantitative. The process of perception is not merely one of simple differentiation, but of distinguishing and then summing up the distinctions into clear macroperceptions by way of repeated processes of perceptual integration. 'Inconspicuous perceptions constitute the obscure dust of the world, the dark depths every monad contains. There are differential relations among these presently infinitely small ones that are *drawn into* clarity . . . *Differential relations always select minute perceptions that play a role in each case*, and bring to light or clarify the conscious perception that comes forth' (LB: 102).

Deleuze relates these obscure perceptions once more to dark precursors, to the subtle, imperceptible dynamics that produce and lead both conscious actions and conscious thought. 'There exist minute perceptions that are not integrated into present perception, but also minute perceptions that are not integrated into the preceding one and that nourish the one that comes along' (99). The microperceptions that produce and pilot conscious perception and thought are the obscure precursors of digital, individual perceptions. These 'minute, obscure, confused perceptions that make up our macroperceptions, our conscious, clear and distinct apperceptions' (99) are 'little folds that unravel in every direction, folds in folds, over folds, following folds' (98). Deleuze's main point is that without these dark, folded precursors, 'a conscious perception would never happen' (99).

As I noted in reference to Lucretius, these folds are both continuous and discontinuous. Although there is a formal distinction between continuous folds and discontinuous particles, that distinction should be replaced by a figure of thought that posits a reciprocal presupposition of these two states: their conceptual complementarity. (For recent readings that, against mainstream Deleuze scholarship, stress the discontinuous in Deleuze, see Arjen Kleinherenbrink (2019), who considers Deleuze's 'machine ontology' (292) of 'individual and irreducible entities, and of discontinuity between such entities' (x), to be a forerunner of contemporary object-oriented ontologies; Nail (2018a, 2018b), and Kaufman (2012).) When one zooms into it, a fold, or surface, disintegrates into a tight net of tiny particles and relations. When one zooms out of such a network, it turns into a surface. Space, this zooming implies, is not either one- or two-dimensional, but fractal. Only such a fractal space, of which more later, allows one to conceptualize states of relative coherence and continuity. As Deleuze notes, the coherent, continuous folds are made up of 'an infinite sum of minute perceptions that *destabilize the preceding macroperceptions while preparing the following one*' (99, emphasis added): *fold into aerosol, aerosol into fold*.

Leibniz is aware of these subtle cohesions, and of the inadequacy of the formal distinction. How could he not be, when the calculus posits the adequation of the integrated sum and the original curve? 'The division of the continuous must not be taken as of sand dividing into grains, but as that of a sheet of paper or of a tunic in folds, in such a way that an infinite number of folds can be produced, some smaller than others, but without the body ever dissolving into points or minima' (Leibniz, quoted in LB: 6). When I noted Deleuze's critique that 'the atomistic hypothesis of an absolute hardness and the Cartesian hypothesis of an absolute fluidity are joined all the more because they share the error that posits separable minima' in reference to Nail's reading of Lucretius, that sentence is followed, in *The Fold*, by Deleuze's reference to Leibniz's concept that 'a flexible or *an elastic body still has cohering parts that form a fold*, such that they are not separated into parts of parts but are rather divided into infinity in smaller and smaller folds that always retain *a certain cohesion*. Thus a continuous labyrinth is not a line dissolving into independent points, as flowing sand might dissolve into grains, but resembles a sheet of paper divided into infinite folds or separated into bending movements, each one determined by the consistent or conspiring surroundings' (6, emphases added). As Peirce notes, 'breaking grains of sand more and more will only make the sand more broken. It will not weld the grains into unbroken continuity' (quoted in Toscano 2006: 130). When, somewhat paradoxically, cohering parts form folds, the world is neither fully continuous nor fully discontinuous: *elastic philosophy*.

That said, the aim of Leibniz's perceptual calculus is to produce clear perceptions. From subtle perceptions, 'increasingly numerous differential relations of a deepening order are determining a zone of clear expression' (LB: 105). This process, however, is problematic because the integrated zone is 'both more extensive and increasingly hermetic' (105) compared to the field of obscure perceptions. As more extensive, it is also more actual. Clear perceptions are particular and individual, while microperceptions are virtual and communal. Clear perceptions are more hermetic because the architecture of integrations is created within the system, which means that clear perceptions are bound by internal relations. In the same way that chemical elements that are bound in or captured by larger assemblages have less freedom of movement because they have less valence, clear perceptions are not as open to outside shocks as obscure perceptions, which are more fragile and elastic. Once I have decided that a specific colour is red, I will no longer perceive small differences in colour within the differentiated and integrated field. As Deleuze notes in *Difference and Repetition*, 'an Idea or multiplicity such as that of colour is constituted by the virtual coexistence of relations between ... differential elements of a particular order. These relations are actualized in qualitatively distinct colours, while their distinctive points are incarnated in distinct extensities which correspond to these qualities' (245). (On the difference between intensive and extensive colour see also Kerslake 2009: 232–3): *philosophy's loss of grace.*

According to the Baroque figure of thought, Leibniz considers the medium of perception to be a both philosophically and visually undulating landscape of tiny folds from which integrated perceptions emerge. The spatial image of the relation between obscure perceptions and clear perceptions is that of a double folding. A space made up of microperceptual folds is part of a larger fold between the levels of obscure perceptions and of clear perceptions. The large fold is the one between passive and active syntheses or, from within another frame, between the unconscious and the conscious.

The passage from obscure to clear perception splits the world into two causalities: ontological and epistemological, or, as Deleuze calls it in *The Fold*, metaphysical and psychological. 'The theory of minute perceptions is based thus on two causes: a metaphysical cause, according to which every perceptive monad conveys an infinite world that it contains; a psychological cause, according to which every conscious perception implies this infinity of minute perceptions that prepare, compose, or follow it' (LB: 99). By way of perception, the monad breaks the continuous world up into minimal differences. In terms of aggregate state, perception turns folds into the aerosol of integration. As Deleuze notes, 'the task of perception entails pulverizing the world, but also one of spiritualising its dust' (99): *the concrete virtual.*

It is only the second fold between obscure and clear perceptions that introduces the notion of coarseness or of molarity. The image of increasingly coarse processes of integration leads directly to one of the most fundamental concepts in Deleuzian philosophy: an unconscious that is 1. material and machinic, and 2. infinitely recursive. *The Incredible Shrinking Unconscious*, one might say. In 'The Origin of Language: Biology, Information Theory, & Thermodynamics', Serres describes such an unconscious as an assemblage of an infinite number of nested levels that denote the machinic levels below the integrations of the respective perceptual and cognitive apparatuses. In this image, the unconscious is the field of imperceptible and, from the position of the dominant monad, unintegrated machines. In Serres as in Deleuze, the lowest level of that unconscious is made up of exchanges of pure energy or intensity, of waves or folds of energy, that are made conscious by way of their their integration into systems of digital data and information [→ **Guattari 177**]. This unconscious 'gives way from below [recedes into the depths]; there are as many unconsciousnesses in the system as there are integration levels. It is merely a question, in general, of that for which we initially possess no information ... Each level of information functions as an unconscious for the global level bordering it ... What remains unknown and unconscious is, at the chain's furthermost limit, the din of energy transformations: this must be so, for the din is by definition stripped of all meaning, like a set of pure signals or aleatory movements. These packages of chance are filtered, level after level, by the subtle transformer constituted by the organism ... In this sense the traditional view of the unconscious would seem to be the final black box, the clearest box for us since it has its own language in the full sense' (Serres 1982: 80).

This conceptualization of the perceptual system as an integration machine defines the Deleuzian unconscious as well. As Deleuze and Guattari note in *A Thousand Plateaus*, 'there is always a perception finer than yours, a perception of your imperceptible, of what is in your box' (287). They elaborate on this in *What is Philosophy?* when they note, after having quoted Serres on Leibniz, that 'one could conceive of a series of coordinates or phase spaces as a succession of filters, the earlier of which would be in each case a relatively chaotic state, and the later a chaoid state, so that we would cross chaotic thresholds rather than go from the elementary to the composite' (206).

The Deleuzian unconscious is thus quite literally made up of what is imperceptible to the specific platform of perception under consideration. To retrieve something unconscious does not mean, therefore, to re-activate something formerly repressed, but rather to zoom into the infinity of unperceived plateaus, somewhat in the way Carey did in *The Incredible Shrinking Man*. In the infinite regress of a recursive unconscious, each lower level forms the obscure medium of the level of clear, digital perception above it and from which the unconscious level is experienced as analog or folded. Similarly, each level of clear and light perception forms, although it is a digital plane, an obscure and dark, seemingly analog level for the even grainier levels of perception above it: *the unconscious as a black box*.

Quite paradoxically, therefore, to make the unconscious conscious implies discriminating on finer perceptual scales, decomposing or decontracting molar into molecular perceptions. This is why the microscope is for the Deleuzian unconscious what the couch is for the Freudian. As I argued, such a refined perception goes hand in hand with the monad's increased anonymization. The further the monad zooms into the fields of formerly obscure perceptions, the more its coherence dissolves. From the perspective of the monad, the pure clamour and light of being is an obscure field that it has differentiated and summed up into clear, integrated sounds and images. These clear images, however, are obscure in their very clarity. From the other perspective, in fact, which goes from these clearly obscure perceptions to the formerly obscure perceptions, the clear perceptions and images are decomposed into forces, communal operations and communal affects: individuation versus singularization. Paradoxically, in the vector from clear to obscure perception, the formerly obscure field becomes, as the individual dissolves, increasingly clear and luminous: *the total obscurity of white light.*

In Deleuze, this communal, quantitative field is the truly transcendental one. The monad emerges from the textured surface of a both infinitely obscure and infinitely luminous backdrop. From the white light of the world. As the plane of consistency is infinitely folded, it contains, at the level of infinite imperceptibility, the conceptual point-at-infinity of perception. Pervaded by tiny living and perceiving entities and their perceptions, it is, somewhat like the towel in Witold Gombrowicz's novel *The Possessed*, always minimally vibrating and trembling. The plane of immanence lies at the point-of-infinity of this vibrating plane. As Deleuze notes, 'from a psychic point of view, chaos would be a universal giddiness, the sum of all possible perceptions being infinitesimal or infinitely minute; but the screen would extract differentials that could be integrated in ordered perceptions' (LB: 87). The plane of immanence is the oscillating, unconscious trembling Deleuze referred to when he talked of 'agitated sleepers who twist and turn on their mattresses', while the screen is the apparatus of perception: *the perceptual chora.*

Although Leibniz's calculus includes, both mathematically and perceptually, the infinitely and the imperceptibly small, Deleuze constantly stresses Leibniz's thought in order to stop it from going in one direction only; to retrieve from it moments where it evokes an unconscious, ungrounded ground. 'Leibniz: the image of murmuring, or the ocean, or a water mill, or vanishing, or even drunkenness: they all bespeak a Dionysian depth rumbling beneath this apparently Apollonian philosophy' (DI: 101). Unstressed, Leibniz might be said to make *The Incredible Shrinking Man* run backwards: *The Incredible Expanding Man*. This one-way vectorization also reverberates through Deleuze's question about the conceptual reach of the calculus. 'Is differential calculus adequate for infinitesimal things [*l'infiniment petit*]?'; to which 'the answer is negative' (LB: 110). As Deleuze notes, this time from an unstressed position, 'differential relations intervene only in order to extract a clear perception from minute, obscure perceptions' (110). And as Serres notes, Leibniz 'lumps everything into the differential. And under the numberless thickness of successive orders of integration. The mechanism is admirable. No one ever went so far in rational mastery, down into the innermost little recesses of the smallest departments. The straight line of reason that must turn its back on this chaos is the ascent into those scalar orders' (1995: 20–1).

This brings me to my third question, which is about the relation between the sensible and the intelligible. Between perception and thought. According to the

Deleuzian logic, the most important thing about this relation is that one needs to formally separate the psychic mechanism of the calculus from physical mechanisms. Precisely this is what Leibniz does. 'There can be no question of assuming it [the calculus] in what perception resembles, that is, by turning it into a physical mechanism, except through convention and by increasing the fiction' (LB: 110). This restriction of the calculus to the psychic realm is why it is, in Spinozan terms, so difficult to know what a body can do. Against this background, Deleuze's supplementation of Leibniz's infinitesimals with Newton's notion of fluxions, which echo Lucretius' turbulence, might be read as an attempt to detect a physical automatism that is analogous to the psychic automatism of Leibniz's calculus. As Deleuze notes, 'Leibniz's calculus is adequate to psychic mechanics where Newton's is operative for physical mechanics' (112). Within a physical assemblage theory, a fluxion denotes the infinitely small change that 'causes parts endlessly to leave their specified aggregate in order to enter into entirely different aggregates that are differently specified' (132).

In his distinction between the psychic and the physical, Leibniz formally separates, like Deleuze, the actual and the virtual series. 'Thus there exists a great difference between an always extrinsic physical causality . . . and an always intrinsic psychic causality' (111), Deleuze notes. And further, 'to these two causalities correspond two calculations – or two aspects of the calculus that, even if they are inseparable, must be distinguished'. The spatial figure of their relation is that 'these are like two halves of each other', while the conceptual one is that of resemblance. 'A quality perceived by consciousness resembles the vibrations contracted through the organism. Differential mechanisms on the inside of the monad resemble mechanisms of communication and propagation of extrinsic movement, although they are not the same and must not be confused' (111). Formally confused, that is. As Leibniz notes, they do not mix and they are each ruled by their own laws.

What fascinates Deleuze is that Leibniz, like Spinoza, sees an absolute heterogeneity between the worlds of thought and action, as there is no way to explain how the body could cause something to happen in the soul, and vice versa. In both Spinoza and Leibniz, there is a formal split between 'the psycho-metaphysical mechanism of perception, and the . . . physico-organic mechanism of excitation or impulsion' (111). Leibniz's differentiation between psychic mechanisms of cognition on the one hand, and physical mechanisms of propagation and propulsion on the other, is analogous to Deleuze and Guattari's distinctions between the theatre and the factory, as well as between quality and quantity. 'Physical mechanisms are infinitely tiny fluvia that form displacements, crisscrossings, and accumulations of waves, or "conspiracies" of molecular movements' (110), Deleuze notes. They 'do not work by differentials, which are always differentials of consciousness, but by communication and propagation of movement' (111).

In terms of ontology, these two formally distinct dynamics run through the human being simultaneously and to a similar degree. While the body belongs to the soul through processes of projection and contemplation, the soul belongs to the body through processes of entrainment and contraction. Structurally speaking, individual monads are agents of surveillance and integration as 'distributive units that follow a relation of part and whole', while bodies are 'collectives – flocks or aggregates – that follow a relation of the-ones-to-the-other' (114). A dominant monad is 'present to its body . . . *by projection*' (135). It contains and envelopes the actual multitude by contemplating the monadic collective into an overall survey. Perceptually, souled monads contract and integrate an intensive multiplicity into an imaginary surface, similar to the way the photonic multiplicity is contracted into an image or into a series of moving images. In cinematographic terms, the body is present to the soul through projection, which means that the perceived body is an imaged, or better, a cinematic body. It is a perceptual film in the physical sense of a thin surface: *a quasi-body*.

Deleuze stresses that for Leibniz, the 'organic body is precisely that which possesses the dominant, *a* body that here finds the determination of its specific unity' (128). All material aggregates require monads as operative units of integration. 'Every body is inseparable from the souls that belong to it, and that are present to it by requisition' (134). In other words, an organism is a multiplicity entrained by a dominant unit of integration. Margulis calls this 'the specialization of massive numbers of cells into integrated individuals' (Margulis and Sagan 1995: 127). This individual, however, remains part of a more general community. 'The belonging makes us enter into a strangely intermediary, or rather, original, zone, in which every body acquires individuality of a possessive insofar as it belongs to a private soul, and souls accede to a public status; that is, they are taken in a crowd or in a heap, inasmuch as they belong to a collective body' (LB: 136–7). Deleuze describes the double relation between a sensible body that can be affected and an intelligent soul that provides the ideas of the affections as a folding of two series onto each other. 'Is it not in this zone, in this depth or the material fabric between the two levels, that the upper is folded over the lower, such that we can no longer tell where one ends and the other begins, or where the sensible ends and the intelligible begins?' (137).

In *Dialogues II*, Deleuze describes an analogous reciprocal presupposition in relation to a recursive stacking of molecular individuals within a molar individual. 'Each individual, body and soul, possesses an infinity of parts which belong to him in a more or less complex relationship. Each individual is also himself composed of individuals of a lower order and enters into the composition of individuals of a higher order' (59). In *The Fold* Deleuze deals with this twofold, both actual and virtual, assemblage in terms of being a body and of having a body.

If one aligns Leibniz's recursive logic with the separation of the series of the actual and the virtual, the implication is that even within this infinite recursion of individuals, bodies and souls remain both present and separated. Neither of them goes away to leave the other as an uncontaminated origin. Neither materialism nor idealism. At the same time, they never become identical. Rather, on increasingly smaller levels of bodies, there are increasingly smaller souls. As Deleuze notes, a body 'is probably made of infinities of present material parts, in conformity with infinite division, in conformity with the nature of masses or collections. But these infinities in turn would not comprise organs if they were not inseparable from crowds of little monads, monads of heart, liver, knee, of eyes, hands' (LB: 123). Down to its most microscopic levels, nature is animated and thus monadic. 'If life implies a soul, it is because proteins already attest to an activity of perception, discrimination, and distinction – in short, a "primary force"' (129): *material intelligence*.

The biomaterial requisition of free-floating elements entrains an actual multiplicity of matters-of-fact on the one hand and a virtual multiplicity of events on the other into a complicated aggregate through processes of material contraction and immaterial contemplation: *crystallization*. As Toscano notes, 'it is in this passage between the realm of preindividual free matter [materia soluta] and that of bounded individuals or physical bodies [materia ligata] that the question of organized beings must be relocated' (2006: 55). For a specific amount of time, which we call their specific life span, individual monads entrain both material and immaterial media. At the point we call individual death, they once more dissolve into the anonymous medium. In less existential terms, when the molecular individuals escape the entrainment by the dominant monad, they stop being part of the 'texturology' (LB: 131) of a specific individual and begin to scatter. The organic elements become inorganic, in the same way that, vice versa, they become organic at the point of their crystal conception. 'No longer are they fabrics, but a felt that is obtained by simple pressing. Surely these inorganic, disorganized aggregates of felt continue to have organisms in their subaggregates. Every body has organisms in its folds; organisms are everywhere' (132). According to the logic of immanence, therefore, the true distinction is not between life and death. Rather, it is between an individual and an anonymous life. While the former opens up a logic of loss, such as the loss of self, the latter is seen from the perspective of anonymity, opening up a logic of plenitude and affirmation.

'How can a portrait be made of Leibniz's person without marking the extreme tension of an open façade and a hermetic inner volume, each being independent of the other and both regulated by a strange preestablished connection? It is an almost schizophrenic tension' (LB: 36–7). It is also, one might add, a spatial tension between surface and depth and a tension between light and darkness; a tension between two kinds of luminosity that lie at the centre of *The Fold*. As I noted above, in *Difference and Repetition* Deleuze stated that while Leibniz created a differential unconscious and surrounded it 'with little glimmerings and singularities' he did so, ultimately, 'in order to save and reconstitute the homogeneity of a natural light à la Descartes': *Leibniz's double bind.*

Deleuze does not mention the term *lumen naturale* in *The Fold*. Nevertheless, Leibniz's double bind plays itself out between two theories of light: *double light*. The first is the natural light Deleuze evokes when he notes that monads have a luminous soul. 'Since monads have no openings, a light that has been "sealed" is lit in each one when it is raised to the level of reason' (36). A second, more complicated theory of light, however, which Deleuze sets against the first one, allows us to read *The Fold* as a study about a new philosophical distribution of light and of darkness. Leibniz's philosophical schizophrenia, in fact, is inherently both spatial and luminous. In the section 'Baroque light' Deleuze relates that distribution, as he does in the example of lightning, to the relation of the conscious and the unconscious. As with lightning, in Leibniz darkness is the unconscious of light, not its opposite. From this follows a daunting reversal: vis-à-vis Leibniz, Deleuze develops a philosophy of light in which light is obscure, and the obscure is light.

There are two spaces: 'The continuous labyrinth in matter and its parts', and 'the labyrinth of freedom in the soul and its predicates' (3). The first is actual, the second virtual. Pleats and Folds. Body and Soul. In the Baroque house considered as a figure of both philosophy and of Leibniz himself, the ground floor, which is that of the senses, has windows that let in the light, while the soul lives in the upper floor, which is without doors or windows. 'To begin, we can consider light and shadows as 1 and 0, as the two levels of the world separated by a thin line of waters' (35), Deleuze notes, evoking once more the moment of genesis. In a stunning reversal of the common concept of the soul, the upper floor is 'very dark, in fact almost decorated in black, "fuscum subnigrum"' (35). In the history of painting, this darkening of the soul is the 'Baroque contribution: in place of the white chalk or plaster that primes the canvas, Tintoretto and Caravaggio use a dark, red-brown background on which they place the thickest shadows, and paint directly by shading toward the shadows. The painting is transformed. Things jump out of the background, colors spring from the common base that attests to their obscure nature, figures are defined by their covering more than their contour. Yet this is not in opposition to light; to the contrary, it is by virtue of the new regime of light' (35).

The monadic soul, however, does not live in complete darkness. Into a space ideally made of 'black marble', light enters 'through orifices so well bent that nothing on the outside can be seen through them, yet they illuminate or color the decor of a pure inside' (31). This architectural monadology is analogous to Baroque architecture, which 'erects chapels and rooms where a crushing light comes from openings invisible to their very inhabitants' (31). This light, which is neither the *lumen naturale* of God or reason, nor the immanent, refracted light that suffuses reality, is, quite literally, the light of and according to, a technical apparatus; that of the camera obscura, which refracts light by way of mirrors in order to project images of the outside onto the internal surfaces of the darkly marbled room: *Vermeer*.

This is why the monad is 'a cell. It resembles a sacristy more than an atom: a room with neither doors nor windows, where all activity takes place on the inside' (31). Monadic souls do not live in the light, because they 'have no windows, by which anything could come in or go out', nor do they have 'openings nor doorways' (30). At the same time, they do not live in darkness. The optical device of the camera obscura is the figure of how images of this outside are brought to the soul in its dark room. 'The camera obscura has only one small aperture high up through which light passes, then through the relay of two mirrors it projects on a sheet the objects to be drawn that cannot be seen' (31). It takes white light and refracts it. This is why the second floor is illuminated by 'all kinds of trompe l'oeil that adorn the walls: the monad has furniture and objects only in trompe l'oeil' (31). This is the figure of thought as the power of the false; of thought as an 'as if': *the world as photograph or cinema*.

Somewhat as the images of the outside pass through the mirrors of the camera obscura, the monad's images of the outside are caught by a multiplicity of tiny mirrors that function as resonating and reflecting surfaces. Everything would be easy if the light that shines into the first floor were to also illuminate the second floor. But it doesn't. Leibniz's philosophy is based on the strict separation of the two levels. The logic of the relation between the levels is not one of suffusion, but of resonance. 'There are souls down below, sensitive, animal; and there even exists a lower level in the souls', Deleuze writes. These differences in degree allow the relation between the 'the pleats of matter and the folds in the soul' (4) to be one of resonance: *fractal souls*. (When Deleuze notes that 'the upper floor, blind and closed', turns images into sounds, 'resonating as if it were a musical salon translating the visible movements below into sounds up above' (4), this is written from within the difference between the lighted first floor and the dark second floor. This distinction is no longer categorical when the darkness of the second floor is that of the camera obscura.)

Each actual perception 'evokes a vibration gathered by a receptive organ' (109). Each of the tiny actual vibrations is projected into the soul, whose white light 'does "not resemble a convex spherical mirror", but rather an infinity of "little convex mirrors such as there are seen in foam when we look at it closely"' (109). Each of these tiny convex mirrors, one might say, captures, by way of integration, a small surface of the overall vibration. In such a way, the overall vibration of the actual perception is transmuted, by way of resonance, into the virtual 'as if' of the soul, which sums the microperceptions up, by way of integration, and transmutes them into a clear and conscious image, somewhat like actual, chronic strobes are transmuted into an aionic glow. The actual depths are transmuted into virtual surfaces. The soul's white light, however, is always infinitely refracted and fractal. Its 'whiteness is produced through all the tiny inner mirrors' (36), Deleuze notes. 'This progressivity of light that grows and ebbs, and that is transmitted by degrees' stands in 'opposition to Descartes, who remained a man of the Renaissance, from the double point of view of a physics of light and a logic of the idea' (36). Light surface and obscure depths are transmuted into the fractal space of a philosophical *chiaroscuro*.

Deleuze describes this new space in one of the most painterly and poetic moments of *The Fold*: 'A dust of colored perceptions falls on a black backdrop; yet, if we look closely, these are not atoms, but minuscule folds that are endlessly unfurling and bending on the edges of juxtaposed areas, like a mist or fog that makes their surface sparkle, at speeds that no one of our thresholds of consciousness could sustain in a normal state. But when our clear perceptions are reformed, they draw yet another fold that now separates the conscious from the unconscious, that joins the tiny edges of surface to a great area, that moderates the different speeds, and rejects all kinds of minute perceptions in order to make from all the others the solid fabric of apperception: dust falls, and I see the great fold of figures just as the background is unfurling its tiny folds' (106). Leibniz's schizophrenia lies in the fact that this second fold destroys his new luminous regime, by suspending it in the extremes of a light emanating from God on the one hand and dark matter on the other. 'Clarity endlessly plunges into obscurity. Chiaroscuro fills the monad following a series that can move in either of two directions: at one end is a dark background and at the other is light, sealed; when it is lit, the monad produces white light in an area set aside, but the white is progressively shaded, giving way to obscurity, to a thicker and thicker shadow, as it spreads toward the dark background in the whole monad. Outside of the series we have God on one side, who said let there be light, and with it the white-mirror, but on the other side the shadows or absolute blackness, made up of an infinity of holes that can no longer reflect the received rays. An infinitely spongy and cavernous matter ultimately contains all of these holes' (36).

Leibniz's vector from darkness to a light that is still confused is usually read in the light of his tendency to not stop integrating; a process that would lead, at infinity, to a completely clear, as in fully conscious, light: *The Enlightenment*. Already in *Difference and Repetition*, Deleuze had proposed that there is 'another more radical interpretation, according to which there would be a difference between the clear and the distinct, not just of degree but in kind, such that the clear would be in itself confused and the distinct in itself obscure' (213). If clear and distinct, as in differentiated, perceptions are in themselves obscure, a philosophy of difference or integration, in which clarity and obscurity are treated as differences such as light and dark, needs to be supplemented by a theory of the complementarity of the distinct and the obscure; a theory in which clarity is obscure, because it is created from obscure, indistinct, as in indifferent, elements; a process that results in a perceptual *chiaroscuro*.

In *Difference and Repetition*, Deleuze had commented on Leibniz's notion that 'a clear idea is in itself confused; it is confused *in so far as it is clear*' (213). On two immensely dense and intensely beautiful pages, Deleuze illustrates this by way of Leibniz's famous image of the indistinct sound of the sea: 'Either we say that the apperception [the conscious perception] of the whole noise is clear but confused (not distinct) because the component little perceptions are themselves not clear but obscure; or we say that the little perceptions are themselves distinct and obscure (not clear): distinct because they grasp differential relations and singularities; obscure because they are not yet distinguished, not yet differentiated. These singularities then condense to determine a threshold of consciousness in relation to our bodies, a threshold of differenciation on the basis of which the little perceptions are actualized, but actualized in an apperception which in turn is only clear and confused; clear because it is distinguished or differenciated, and confused because it is clear' (213, my square brackets). As clear and obscure are not distinct, they need to be treated from under the conceptual shadow of a logic of complementarity: the clarity of obscurity and the obscurity of clarity. From which follows that one can never, except at infinity, return to the purity of opposites as identical: *contraria sunt complementa*. In being clear, difference is by necessity obscure. Or, put even stronger: in being difference, difference is by necessity false: *Hume*.

It is not the task of philosophy, however, to set a given truth against the false, which is only false as opposed to the undifferentiated. Already, in his essay 'On Truth and Lies in a Nonmoral Sense', Nietzsche had shown the strength of the lie, which Deleuze conceptualizes as the power of the false. To be truly powerful, however, the false must be in resonance with the intensive world. This implies that thought must reach back to the realm of unthinkable, non-philosophical dark precursors operating in the world. Ultimately, thought must, depending on its vector, become once more, or emerge from, the anonymous multiplicity that is the world.

To be adequate to that task, the monad needs to be equally extensive particle and intensive wave [→ **Guattari 131**]. Which leads to the question of whether, if its essence is luminous, the monad can be thought of as a photon, and as such as in itself complementary. In his essay 'Monade und Licht', Hubertus Busche excavates a luminous logic from Leibniz's work that rests on the both material and conceptual medium of the luminiferous æther – the element without characteristics that

Aristotle had postulated as the fifth element in addition to those of earth, sky, fire and water. Although the existence of a physical æther was later disproved, it remained a powerful figure of thought; so much so that even Hermann von Helmholtz would still refer to it when he noted that 'light only becomes light when it hits a seeing eye, without that it is only æthereal vibration' (1896: 98).

When Leibniz writes that monads have a 'luminous "nature"' (Busche 2009: 126), he refers to this complex conceptual context. In fact, Leibniz himself considered monads as souls of light. Although they are without extension, they have an inclination (*conatus*) to become extensive. As 'points of light' (125), monads move within an æther that is itself moving vortically. This vortex, which is reminiscent of Lucretius and Serres, is the result of the interplay between a *conatus rectus* and a *conatus circularis*. Within this luminous, vortical medium, monads are 'ensouled centers of æthereal spheres' (142), that consist of an 'indefinitely small interior of a fluidum of light ... in which an ensouled center is incarnated' (162). Through their spontaneous activity, monads bring the æther into 'vibrations' (160).

For Leibniz, the æther is a 'substantia spiritualis' (Busche 2009: 149). As 'the materiality in which light is propagated', it is 'the medium of the activity or movement of light' (145). In this context, Leibniz makes a crucial distinction. As what he calls the *prima materia* – 'the dynamic, first receptacle, the first substrate' (133) – the æther is the soul's 'medium of incarnation' (139), while the body as the medium in which the soul is incorporated is the *secunda materia*. While the second matter defines the 'organic machine [*machina organica*]' (160), the first matter is 'that which is found in the body when one disregards all principles of unity' (138). Leibniz's 'body without organs'. The idea of a *prima materia* allows Leibniz to state that a monad is material without being corporeal. 'The monad has a *materiality* but no *body*' (161). The first matter, in other words, is inorganic, while the second is organic. While the first is aerosolic, the second has a 'cohesion' (138) in the sense that the parts of a body cohere. Leibniz models the relation between the two forms of materiality in terms of space as a 'dynamic *interpenetration* of the second matter by the ætherial first matter' (149). The spiritual plane animates the physical plane so completely, and the physical plane incorporates the spiritual plane so completely, that 'both immensely *different series* relate to each other in the same bodily substance and are in full agreement [*vollkommen übereinstimmen*], even [*ebenso*] *as if* the one would be ruled by the influence of the other' (151, emphasis added). The first matter acts like an insubstantial ghost within the bodies of the second matter. It is the animated ghost in the corporeal machine.

The Deleuzian question is whether this relation can be conceptualized other than as a mutual interpenetration, in which the luminiferous æther forms the substantial link (*vinculum substantiale*) between body and soul. It is here that it might help to think of monads as photons, which are quite literally both particles and waves of light: *quanta*. If monads are photonic, the topology of the relation between the two planes of matter might be conceptualized from within the complementarity of the photon as both particle (*secunda materia*) and wave (*prima materia*). While the formal separation between the two would still be into two different planes or series, the ontological one would define them as one plane that is itself defined by a logic based on the complementary of the two formally distinct series. If this logic is plotted onto the projective, folded plane of immanence, its one side concerns actual particles, while its other side concerns virtual waves and vibrations. In this way, the complementarity of particle and wave would be another step towards the conceptualization of a photonic, and thus projective, plane of immanence, whose topology I will describe in more detail later on.

Deleuze projects such a fold between the world and the soul into the architectural conceit of the Baroque house that I dealt with earlier in terms of light. The two floors of this house denote the levels of body and soul respectively, and thus those of actual matters-of-fact and virtual events. The pleats of matter denote the second matter, while the folds of the soul denote the first. As Deleuze notes, 'a real distinction holds between souls and matter and between the body and the soul. One never acts upon the other, but each operates according to its own laws, one by inner spontaneity and action, the other by outer spontaneity or action' (LB: 135–6). The two floors are simultaneously distinct and inseparable because they are folded over or projected onto each other. 'For Leibniz, the two floors are and will remain inseparable; they are really distinct and yet inseparable by dint of a presence of the upper in the lower. The upper floor is folded over the lower floor. One is not acting upon the other, but one belongs to the other, in a sense of a double belonging' (136). Of course, Leibniz did not know about the complementarity of the photon, nor did he know about the fact that atoms can be split. By conceptualizing monads as points of light, however, he might be said to already point towards the modern notion of complementarity, which, had he known it, would certainly have found its way into his conceptualization of spatial interpenetration. His notion of a first and a second matter, in fact, goes a long way in that direction.

Deleuze's folded topology allows us to think the fundamental paradox to which I promised to return. On the one hand, monads are points without material extension, which means that they are, from a Deleuzian point of view, fully virtual. In the *Monadology*, Leibniz states that 'now where there are no parts, there can be neither extension nor form [*figure*] nor divisibility. These Monads are the real atoms of nature and, in a word, the elements of things' (1998: 218). On the other hand, and at the same time, monads have the faculty of perception and appetition. Although they are a-corporeal, they seem to literally hunger for perception. As Schneider notes, monads are defined as the 'the totality of their continually . . . evolving appetitions, which are the respective transitions between consecutive perceptions' (2001: 64). Symptomatically, Busche relates this appetite directly to the monads' luminous essence. As he quotes Leibniz, this luminous first matter 'does not consist of an extension, but in the desire for extension' because 'the nature of light is to desire to expand [*luminis natura se diffundere nititur*]' (2009: 130).

While one might argue that Leibniz's idea of an a-corporeal monad that has an appetition for extension implies that he considers the matter in which monads are inevitably embodied as dead and inert, Deleuze argues that the notion of a first and a second matter that completely interpenetrate each other allows Leibniz to sidestep this distinction. Leibniz addresses the question of a living, intelligent matter by way of displacing it into the question of whether matter can be ontologically separated from monads rather than in terms of epistemology, and thus formally. 'There is no cause to ask if matter thinks or perceives, but only whether it is separable from these little souls capable of perception' (LB: 123). Leibniz and Deleuze are in agreement about the formal distinction of the two series. Their difference lies in the figure of their ontological identity, for which Leibniz does not develop an adequate logic.

For Leibniz, although the soul and matter follow radically different laws, a universal harmony guarantees the alignment the two series. 'Souls act according to the laws of final causes, through appetition, ends, and means. Bodies act according to the laws of efficient causes or motions. And these two realms, that of efficient causes and that of final causes, are in harmony with each other' (Leibniz 1998: 263). (See also Ruyer, who notes that God is 'within the variety of dissonant agreements (*chords*), as much as in the perfect agreement (*chord*)' (1952: 267).) Leibniz imagines a God who can compute infinitely fast – the ideal is that of a computation in real time – and who has a complete overview of the world ($n+1$). As Rutherford quotes Leibniz, 'between the appearances of bodies given to us and the appearances given to God there is as much of a difference as between a perspectival projection [*scenographia*] and a ground plan [*ichnographia*]. For perspective projections differ according to the position [*situs*] of the viewer, [while] a ground plan or geometrical representation is unique' (1995: 235). From this transcendental position, God can overcome the limited perspectives of monads, who are inevitably in a position of an $n-1$ survol.

The belief in such a divine overview is why Leibniz fails to develop a logic of immanence. Unlike Spinoza, he does not identify God with an infinitely intricate and autopoietic Nature, which is the identification that makes Spinoza's plane of immanence more adequate. In order to develop a similar logic for Leibniz, one would need one more folding, beyond those of folding obscure perceptions onto clear perceptions and folding matter onto soul: a folding of transcendence onto immanence. God would have to be folded onto the innermost recesses of nature and the result of that folding would have to be called immanence. The infinite speed of God's computations would need to be folded onto the infinite speed of a living matter that makes up the plane of immanence, while the notion of divine harmony would need to be folded onto the habitual logic and spontaneity of self-organization. After such a topological operation, Leibniz's universe of monads could be integrated into that of modern physics. As Michel Serres notes in his book on Leibniz, 'coherent and diverse, a new approach to the notion of harmony' (2003: 385).

Deleuze advocates precisely such a topological torsion in relation to the topology of the monad. As with a crystal, the inside and the outside of the monad are aligned in a topology in which the outside is part of the inside. In fact, in this new topology, which I will argue is the topology of Deleuze's plane of immanence in general, the terms are aligned in such a way that they can be identical and different at the same time: 'Leibniz discovers that the monad as absolute interiority, as an inner surface with only one side, nonetheless has another side, or a minimum of outside, a strictly complementary form of outside. Can topology resolve the apparent contradiction? The latter effectively disappears if we recall that the "unilaterality" of the monad implies as its condition of closure *a torsion of the world, an infinite fold*, that can be unwrapped in conformity with the condition only by uncovering the other side, not as exterior to the monad, but as the exterior or outside *of* its own interiority' (LB: 127, emphasis added): *real projective philosophy*.

In his 1988 description of monads Deleuze operates explicitly from within the topology of the real projective plane. The first installation of that topology into Deleuze's thought, however, happens in *The Logic of Sense*, a book that charts, both conceptually and structurally, Deleuze's shift from Cartesian to projective space. In fact, this shift is arguably the most fundamentally new element *The Logic of Sense* brings to Deleuzian philosophy. While Deleuze's earlier texts had addressed the logical alignment of the virtual and the actual by way of figures of thought such as reciprocal presupposition, transcendental empiricism, witnessing, resonance or adequation, *The Logic of Sense* conceptualizes a completely new space of thought from within which to think the alignment of the two series. For the first time, Deleuze develops a conceptual topology that is fully adequate to his philosophy. A space of thought that functions as the analytic of the relation between the virtual and the actual.

The Logic of Sense not only traces the shift towards this new topology, it is itself an embodiment of it in that its beginning still argues from within the parameters of classical space. Events differ from matters-of-fact as surfaces differ from depth. Already early on, however, Deleuze confronts the reader with a topological image. 'Comparing the event to a mist rising over the prairie', he writes, 'we could say that this mist rises precisely at the frontier, at the juncture of things and propositions' (LS: 24). The mist of events rises from the surface on which material prairie meets immaterial air; where material causes meet immaterial quasi-causes. (On the vapor of events, see also WP: 127, 159.)

Although this image still relies on a topology that differentiates between depth and surface, such as material world and immaterial air or '"deep" bodies and ... "lofty" Ideas' (132), it already marks the beginning of a topological routine that will lead, as *The Logic of Sense* progresses, to the conceptualization of a one-sided plane of both thought and life. Early on, one of Deleuze's paradoxical conceits announces the result of this process: 'what is most deep is the skin' (10).

What exactly is a real projective plane, and how does it enter Deleuzian philosophy? The basic characteristic of the real projective plane is, first of all, that it is a plane. Projective geometry is not so much about depths and volumes as it is about surfaces and folds, which resonates well with Deleuze's interest in the superficial and in the construction of surfaces from a given *spatium*, from a deep volume of space. The notion of the real projective plane originates in painting as a conceptual space between mathematics and art that aligns projective geometry and the theory of perspective. As Ian Stewart notes, 'the geometry of perspective was published by ... Alberti in 1436, in his book *Della pittura*. It's called *projective geometry*, and it describes the way in which the eye sees the world. The basic surface is known as the *projective plane*' (1989: 441). Unlike classical geometry, which is objective and abstract, projective geometry describes the way a human subject perceives the world that follows the laws of classical geometry, and as such it is abstract and objective as well as subjective and concrete. As a geometrical model of how visual perception and the imagination project a world, it recapitulates the habits of the eye and of the mind. Its logic is that of embodied, topological space and of the central perspective rather than of the purely abstract, Euclidean logic of Cartesian space. It concerns the topology of a space that always has its own optical weather.

The fundamental difference between classical and projective geometry concerns the difference between plotting and seeing. In projective geometry, two parallel lines that are projected into the distance converge at a point-of-perspective considered as a point-at-infinity that designates, in terms of perception, the infinitely far away horizon. Anyone who has stood on train-tracks or has looked at paintings by Salvador Dali or Giorgio de Chirico knows this. In geometrical terms, the fifth axiom of Euclidean geometry, which states that parallel lines never meet, is put out of operation. In projective geometry, 'any two lines meet at a single point' (Stewart 1989: 158). In other words, projective geometry is an example of a non-Euclidean geometry having no parallel lines. In his poem 'The Definition of Love', Andrew Marvell used the fifth Euclidean axiom in a conceit about the impossibility of a perfect love. The starting point of his geometrization of love is the image of two lovers situated at opposite poles and thus at the opposite ends of the *axis amoris*. 'And therefore her [fate's] decrees of steel | Us as the distant poles have placed, | (Though Love's whole world on us doth wheel), | Not by themselves to be embraced.' As long as the three-dimensional world is not flattened into a two-dimensional surface, the lovers will never be able to meet: 'Unless the giddy heaven fall, | And earth some new convulsion tear. | And, us to join, the world should all | Be cramp'd into a planisphere.' The tragedy is that although an oblique love will always meet, a perfectly parallel love will never, like mathematical parallels, bring the two lovers together: 'As lines, so love's oblique, may well | Themselves in every angle greet: | But ours, so truly parallel, | Though infinite, can never meet' (109–11). In projective space, this would be different, and the lovers would actually be able to meet, at least after 1874, because before then, the projective plane accorded to our intuitive experience of space in that it was defined, like any other plane, as having two sides. In 1874, however, German mathematician Felix Klein proposed that 'the projective plane has only one side' (Stewart 1989: 158). An important result of this highly counter-intuitive definition is that the concepts of inside and outside are, as with Deleuze's monads, fundamentally undecided. The new plane, which came to be known as the real projective plane, models a space in which the differentiation between inside and outside holds only on a local level. In mathematical terms: the projective plane is 'locally like a sphere, but has a different global topology' (Weeks 1985: 61). It is locally two-sided, but globally one-sided. If one conceptualizes this plane as a logical plane, opposites are chiastically crossed on a global scale, while locally, a two-sided logic remains in operation.

To experience some of the beauty of the mathematical conceptualization of the real projective plane, one has to consider the boldness of Klein's conceit. If an unbounded plane is normally visualized as extending, at all points, to infinity, an infinitely extended real projective plane is, at all infinitely far away points, folded back onto itself. It is this folding that causes it to have only one side. In his book *Vorlesungen über Nicht-Euklidische Geometrie*, Klein describes it as a hemisphere with a line-at-infinity added to its periphery. 'We should attempt to imagine the projective situation long enough for it to be no longer too difficult to, for instance, pull some figure through the infinitely far away' (1928: 17). On this plane, opposite points are identified. 'To every infinitely far away point of the plane correspond . . . two points at the rim of the half-sphere; therefore, we have to regard . . . two of such diametrically opposed points as identical' (14).

To arrive at such a concept, one must entertain, simultaneously, two paradoxes. The first concerns the notion of infinity, a notion that, as I noted, also lies at the heart of Deleuzian philosophy. Although the real projective plane extends to infinity, it is imaged as a finite planisphere. For all intents and purposes, however, that planisphere is treated as infinite. To mark this paradoxically finite infinity, points on its periphery are defined as points-at-infinity. It is at these points that space is folded back upon itself. If this is already quite bold, the next conceptual step, which concerns this folding, is even bolder. On the real projective plane, two diametrically opposed points are no longer defined as infinitely far away from each other and thus as both spatial and logical opposites. Rather, and quite paradoxically, they are conceptualized as being identical. At the paradoxically finitely infinite periphery, space is folded back upon itself at points-at-infinity. On the real projective plane, two diametrically opposed points are no longer defined as infinitely far away from each other and thus as both spatial and logical opposites. Rather, they are conceptualized as being identical. Because of the plane's curvature, opposites meet at infinity. Once more, *contraria sunt complementa*. The challenge posed by the real projective plane is thus to imagine points-at-infinity at which, as Marcel Duchamp has called it, 'opposites are reconciled': Deleuze's *'torsion of the world, an infinite fold'.*

One of the difficulties inherent in the notion of the real projective plane concerns its visualization, because in our perceptually given three-dimensional space it cannot be rendered without moments of self-intersection, which is, geometrically speaking, cheating. To construct a real projective plane without self-intersection, one would need to imagine a four-dimensional space. This is why the Möbius strip – a two-dimensional figure that can be rendered in three-dimensional space and that shares most topological characteristics of the projective plane – is often used to visualize its main properties. As Klein notes, the Möbius strip is 'the simplest plane ... that shows the same behaviour as the projective plane' (15). Both, for instance, are not volumes. The only topological difference between the Möbius strip and the projective plane is that, unlike the real projective plane, the Möbius strip has a border, or edge. Historically, the Möbius strip was the first model of one-sided or unilateral space. The primal scene of its conceptualization comes from the *Collected Works* of German mathematician August Ferdinand Möbius. Klein, who was the editor of Möbius' works, dates this discovery to 'the last quarter of the year 1858' (Möbius 1886: 519). Geometrically, the creation of a Möbius strip can be defined, quite elegantly, as the 180° rotation of a line-segment over the radius of a circle.

The surface of the Möbius strip, which should be thought of as two-dimensional and thus as ideally depthless, can be visualized by considering it as a membrane. (For an account of this difficulty see Abbott 2013.) Hilbert and Cohn-Vassen define the unilaterality of a surface according to whether 'there is a way on the surface (which is considered as a membrane) that leads from the one side of the surface to the other without having to cross the edge and without having to pierce the membrane at the point that it is moving over. If there is such a way, the surface is called one-sided, otherwise, two-sided' (1996: 27).

It is easy to get lost in the topological intricacies of the various unilateral surfaces invented by mathematicians in the wake of the möbial moment. In order not to lose one's bearings, one should keep in mind that all of them share a number of fundamental characteristics. In fact, most of them are homeomorphic, which means that they can be transformed into one another by way of continuous, invertible mappings. To create a projective plane from a Möbius strip, for instance, one simply has to pull out the opposite edges and connect them. The Boy-surface, which was conceptualized by Werner Boy in 1901 while he was working for David Hilbert, is an immersion of the real projective plane in three-dimensional space. It is continuous, has threefold symmetry and is self-intersecting at a triple point. The cross-cap is a three-dimensional representation of a two-dimensional projective plane and as such also the result of a topological routine to which the projective plane is submitted. If the former relies on the abstract identification of opposite points – concerning the projective plane, 'we should think of a disc, whose opposite boundary points are identified mentally, rather than by actually bending the disc around to bring them together' (Stewart 1989: 162) – the latter is the result of their direct spatial identification. Another way to obtain a cross-cap is by gluing the edge of a Möbius strip to the edge of a disk. Two more surfaces that can be obtained in this way are the Boy-surface and the Roman surface. In fact, this direct identification shows that the projective plane cannot be realized in three-dimensional space without self-intersection. Another unilateral surface is the Klein bottle, which is, mathematically, the three-dimensional representation of a projective plane and as such also defined by a self-intersection.

All unilateral spaces fundamentally undecide the notions of inside and outside as well as the topological distribution of extremes, which are all laid out on the same plane and folded onto each other at infinity. Thought from within a unilateral topology of thought, opposites, such as the actual and the virtual, remain operative locally, but are identified at infinity. As Deleuze notes in *Difference and Repetition*, 'the extreme can be defined by the infinite, in the small or in the large. The infinite, in this sense, even signifies the identity of the small and the large, the identity of extremes' (42). Again: *real projective philosophy*.

It is quite safe to assume that Deleuze learned about the concept of the real projective plane by way of Jacques Lacan's elaborate filtering of psychoanalysis through topology [→ **Guattari 180**]. Lacan, whose work became increasingly suffused with topology, from the figure of the Borromean knot to his growing interest in and finally obsession with knot theory, used the topology of the projective plane to model psychic reality by way of a projective alignment of the signifier and the signified. The space of psychic reality, which is made up of the Imaginary and the Symbolic, is the unilateral space of the 'projective plan [sic]' (Lacan 2004: 223). As Lacan notes about his Schema R, '(the cut "ei", "MI"), are sufficient indication that this cut isolates a Moebius-strip in the field' (223). The context is the chiastic suture of the imaginary ideal-ego

(i) with the symbolic ego-ideal (I) and the ego (e) with the signifier (M). Schema L had already pointed towards this topology, although at that time the topology was not yet fully in place. As Lacan notes in a footnote added in 1966, 'this is why we have, in the meantime, introduced an adequate topology' (55).

Although Maurice Merleau-Ponty and Raymond Ruyer were also interested in projective topologies (Merleau-Ponty 1968; Ruyer 1952: 98–9, noted in Massumi 2002: 188), the Lacanian topology was the perhaps most generally visible reference, with Guattari serving as a mediator. The space Deleuze envisions for the 'phantasm' (LS: 31), for instance, is clearly developed from within a Lacanian topology. 'The phantasm covers the distance between psychic systems with ease, going from consciousness to the unconscious and vice versa ... from the inner to the outer and conversely, as if it itself belonged to a surface dominating and articulating both the unconscious and the conscious, or to a line connecting and arranging the inner and the outer over two sides' (217). At this point, Deleuze is not so much interested in the specific content of a phantasm, as he is in determining the kind of topology according to which the phantasm should be thought. 'The phantasm has the property of bringing in contact with each other the inner and the outer and uniting them on a single side' (220), he notes. In other words, the phantasm is stretched out over the surface of a real projective plane.

Although it is indebted to Lacan, *The Logic of Sense* not only charts Deleuze's own transition from classical to topological space, it also charts his reorganization of the Lacanian topology. As such, Deleuze's topology is both an acknowledgement of Lacan, as well as a critical response to his use of the real projective plane in psychoanalysis. The notion of a unilateral topology of thought had run through Deleuze's work in parallel with the gradual implementation of its conceptual spine. Already early on, it is implicit in the way Deleuze looks for a topology in which to think the alignment of the virtual and the actual, and in his interest in different spatial alignments of conceptual terms such as the Stoic relation between causes and effects. From *Difference and Repetition* onward, however, topology becomes an explicit reference. In *The Logic of Sense* Deleuze notes about the unilateral topology of the relation between events and matters-of-fact that 'the doubling up does not at all signify an evanescent and disembodied resemblance, an image without flesh ... it is rather defined by the production of surfaces, their multiplication and consolidation. This doubling up is the continuity of reverse and right sides, the art of establishing this continuity in a way which permits sense, at the surface, to be distributed to both sides at once, as the expressed which subsists in propositions and as the event which occurs in states of bodies. When this production collapses ... bodies fall back again into their depths; everything falls back again into the anonymous pulsation wherein words are no longer anything but affectations of the body – everything falls back into the primary order which grumbles beneath the secondary organization of sense' (125).

In terms of individuation, the aim is to shift from the difference between surface and depth to the concept of a unilateral surface in that the individuation of living beings literally consists of drawing the fields of physics and metaphysics onto the same projective surface of sense on which the actual and the virtual are aligned. This is why, when one of the series fails, the overall topology collapses. When the metaphysical side collapses, one falls back into the depths of actual schizophrenia, as in Deleuze and Guattari's description of the schizo stroll in *A Thousand Plateaus*; into the space called, philosophically, materialism. When, in analogy, the physical side collapses, one falls into the heights of a virtual phantasm; into the space called, philosophically, idealism. When Deleuze talks about 'the continuity of reverse and right sides, the art of establishing this continuity in a way which permits sense, at the surface, to be distributed to both sides at once', he stretches the spatial boundary between the two series out over the entire conceptual space of philosophy. This is a crucial move, because on a real projective plane there is no longer a fundamental threshold between two fields such as deep causes and superficial effects. Rather, the plane itself aligns them in its paradoxical topology. (Later, I will show how, by way of its fractality, a notion of quasi-depth is reconstituted within the plane.) Sense can span the whole spectrum from *matters*-of-fact to matters-of-*fact* because it is distributed on a projective surface. What was inherently paradoxical in classical space is no longer paradoxical in the inherently paradoxical topology of thought in real projective philosophy.

What, in this conceptualization, is the difference between Deleuze and Lacan? This question can be answered without having to delve too deeply into the topological Baroque of the late Lacan, as his thought relies, throughout his work, on the same fundamental projective operation of folding. In fact, this is a double folding. One concerns Lacan's folding of linguistics onto psychoanalysis, the other concerns the folding of the signifier onto the signified. This folding originates in Ferdinand de Saussure's visualization of the plane of the sign – which aligns the signifier and the signified and thus the materiality of language and the ideality of meaning – as the two sides of a sheet of paper; a plane that accords to the classical definition of a bilateral plane.

Lacan's fundamental conceptual move is to take this plane of the sign and to twist it into a unilateral, real projective plane. In this topological move, the Symbolic (the realm of the signifier) is situated on the one side of the plane while the Imaginary (the realm of the signified) is positioned on its other side, although what I just called the two sides are in actual fact only one, because it is possible to reach the other side without crossing a spatial threshold. The Real (the realm of the referent) is excluded from the projective plane in a similar way that the referent is excluded from language. It is crucial in the functioning of the plane, however, in that it stands for the 180° twist that brings about the unilateral topology in the first place. As such, it insists in the plane as both its origin and as its fundamentally excluded term. It is, quite literally, its constitutive lack.

Although Deleuze takes over the topology of the real projective plane, he uses it to align different terms. (On the chiasm in Irigaray and Merleau-Ponty, see Olkowski 1999: 86; on Deleuze's reference to the 'figure 8' in DR: 100 see Olkowski 1999: 155, 171.) Rather than positioning the signifier on one side of the projective plane and the signified on the other, he positions events on the one side, and matters-of-fact on the other. More generally, he positions the intensive virtual on the one side and the extensive actual on the other. In this alignment, the twist is provided by the logic of the reciprocal presupposition of the two series according to the logic of Deleuze's transcendental empiricism or incorporeal materialism.

This shift is the topic of a discussion during which Serge Leclaire, against the background of Lacanian psychoanalysis, questions Deleuze about his notion of what Lacan calls the Real, which Leclaire finds 'somewhat . . . totalitarian: no signifier, no flaw, no fissure, no castration. In the end, one wonders what makes the "true difference" . . . According to you, it must be situated . . . let's see, not between . . .' (DI: 223), at which point Deleuze interrupts Leclaire, coaxingly, '. . . the imaginary and the symbolic . . ', 'but', as Leclaire realizes, 'between the real on the one hand, which you present as the ground, the underlying element, and on the other hand, something like superstructures such as the imaginary and the symbolic' (223): *touché*.

As part of the Real, on Lacan's real projective plane materiality is an excluded field, while Deleuzian philosophy cannot be thought without the full implication of the actual machinics of physical reality in the virtuality of thought and vice versa. In fact, in *What is Philosophy?* Deleuze and Guattari note that the brain itself is a projective plane in that it 'has only a single side' (210). It is on this topological background that one can understand the full implications of Deleuze and Guattari's literally monstrous statement that 'the brain is the *mind* itself' (211). Deleuze's philosophical plane aligns the two sides of matter and mind – in Freudian terms, the id and the complex of the subject and the ego, while Lacan's psychoanalytic plane aligns symbolic logic and imaginary phantasm. In Freudian terms, it aligns the ego and the subject, with the id as the twist or fold. Ultimately, the topological difference between Lacan and Deleuze is that between an unconscious structured like a language and an unconscious structured like a crystal machine that aligns the actual and the virtual within a logic of complementarity.

While Lacan's real projective surface is that of the surface of the sign, Deleuze's surface is the surface of sense. This explains a curious sliding, in *The Logic of Sense*, from the logic of the event to the logic of sense. In fact, the Deleuzian plane of sense is related to the plane of events in that both the Deleuzian event and Deleuzian sense occur in the realm of *matters*-of-fact but *subsist* in matters-of-*fact*. Sense, therefore, cannot be thought without the event and vice versa. In fact, Deleuze folds the two onto each other in unilateral sentences such as 'the event has a different nature than the actions and passions of the body. But it *results* from them, since sense is the effect of corporeal causes and their mixtures' (LS: 94). In this folding, the event becomes the sense|event while sense becomes the event|sense: *the surface of sense as the surface of events and vice versa.*

The Logic of Sense provides a detailed account of the gradual establishment of the projective surface of the sense|event. The milieu of individuation is in itself creative. Deleuze notes that the deep world of pure *matters*-of-fact contains virtual superficializing programmes that, as in Simondon, run according to self-organizing processes inherent in the originary world's genetic setup. Like the narrative of *The Logic of Sense* itself, the transformation goes 'from depths to the production of surfaces' (186). As Deleuze notes, 'the depth acts in an original way, *by means of its power to organize surfaces and to envelop itself within surfaces*' (124). The individuation of topology, the topology of individuation: *crystal topology*. According to these processes, an individuated metaphysics might be said to percolate up from the material, physical depth. It can only do so, however, because this depth, down to its infinitely small elements, is pervaded, ontologically, by its own anonymous metaphysics. 'Things and propositions are less in a situation of radical duality', therefore, 'and more on the two sides of a frontier represented by sense' (24).

What does it mean, topologically, to align *matters*-of-fact and matters-of-*fact*, or things and propositions, on the real projective plane of sense? What kind of frontier does sense form? First of all, the surface of sense is no longer simply the surface of meaning, which means that it can no longer be encompassed by a Saussurean or a Lacanian logic, both of which remain squarely within the field of linguistics and of representation. Rather, Deleuzian sense designates a membrane on which, as Hilbert and Cohn-Vassen (1996) had noted, immaterial thought and material forces meet; on which words meet things and vice versa. This alignment allows for a new relation of the world of language and the world of matters-of-fact.

To illustrate the gradual implementation of the new topology, Deleuze uses what he identifies as an internal shift in the work of Lewis Carroll. (On surfaces and topology in LS see also TRM: 63–6.) This shift goes, like Deleuze's own shift in *The Logic of Sense*, from a vertical topology that differentiates fundamentally between the depth of things and the surface of propositions to a fractal topology: from *continuous spatium* to *discontinuous planes*. While 'the entire first half of *Alice* still seeks the secret of events ... in the depths of the earth' (LS: 9), which means that it recapitulates classical geometry's distinction between surface and depth, in its second half, the topology turns into that of a projective plane. 'The old depth no longer exists at all, having been reduced to the opposite side of the surface. By sliding, one passes to the other side, since the other side is nothing but the opposite direction . . . It suffices to follow it far enough, precisely enough, and superficially enough, in order to reverse sides and to make the right side become the left or vice versa' (9).

Deleuze argues that in Carroll's *Through the Looking-Glass* the concept of superficial sense|events is even more prominent. At this moment, the topology of the surface of sense is homeomorphic to that of the surface of sensation, on which affects are distributed. In 'Lucretius and the Simulacrum' Deleuze had noted that simulacra, 'insofar as they affect the *animus* and the *anima* . . . account for sensible qualities' (273). In fact, living systems are situated within the real projective planes of sense and of sensation. Like Ideas, 'simulacra are everywhere. We do not cease to be immersed in them, and to be battered by them as if by waves' (275).

In the construction of the new topology, Deleuze is very clear about three things. Formally, events remain radically different from material things in that they are immaterial and relational. Events and things are related by a logic of reciprocal presupposition. Events are superficial in the sense that the surface of the projective plane is inherently superficial. 'Events, differing radically from things, are no longer sought in the depths, but at the surface, in the faint incorporeal mist which escapes from bodies, a film without volume which envelops them, a mirror which reflects them, a chessboard on which they are organized according to plan [*échiquier qui les planifie*]' (9–10). In his book *Sylvie and Bruno Concluded*, Carroll, who was himself immensely interested in the relation between logic and topology, refers directly to projective topology in the conceit of what he calls Fortunato's purse, whose construction goes like this. '"You shall first", said Mein Herr, possessing himself of two . . . handkerchiefs, spreading one upon the other, and holding them up by two corners, "you shall first join together these upper corners, the right to the right, the left to the left; and the opening between them shall be the *mouth* of the purse . . . Turn one of them [the lower edges] over, and join the *right* lower corner of the one to the *left* lower corner of the other, and sew the lower edges together in what you would call *the wrong way*"' (1939: 521). According to this manual, 'whatever is *inside* that purse, is *outside* it; and whatever is *outside* it, is *inside* it' (523), so that, as Mein Herr stresses, 'you have all the wealth of the world in that leetle Purse' (523), which is why the purse is called *Fortunato's* purse. Carroll underscores the topological similarities between the purse, which is, topologically, a Klein bottle, and the Möbius strip when he has Mein Herr relate the purse directly to the '*puzzle* of the Paper Ring . . . Where you take a slip of paper, and join its ends together, first twisting one, so as to join the *upper* corner of *one* end to the *lower* corner of the *other*' (522).

Deleuze uses Carroll's topological conceit to mark the meeting of materiality and immateriality on the operating table of the surfaces of sense and of sensation. 'In *Sylvie and Bruno*, the technique of passing from reality to dream, and from bodies to the incorporeal, is multiplied, completely renewed, and carried out to perfection. It is, however, still by skirting the surface, or the border, that one passes to the other side, by virtue of the strip. The continuity between reverse and right side replaces all levels of depths; and the surface effects in one and the same Event, which would hold for all events, brings to language becoming and its paradoxes' (LS: 11). This paradoxical meeting of materiality and immateriality opens up the theatre of representation to material production and vice versa. In this twist, representation and production turn into elements of an overall expressionism. The unilateral, membranic surface of sense positions the field of events and the field of matters-of-fact on one plane on which sense, which subsists in language, functions as a hinge between '*the expressed of the proposition*' and 'states of affairs' (22). As the surface on which they meet, sense aligns words and bodies|things without being reduced to either. In *Francis Bacon: The Logic of Sensation*, Deleuze assembles, from a different perspective, an analogous surface of sensation. According to its unilateral topology, events and effects lie on the immaterial side of the surface of sense, while matters-of-fact and causes lie on its material side. Another term, whose conceptual importance for Deleuze I noted earlier, functions as a similar threshold. The quasi-cause lies on the immaterial side of the surface of sense, while the cause lies on its material side.

Much of Deleuze's topological conceptualization is already part of the complex Stoic topology that defines things as radically dynamic and as part of a genetic and dynamic view of the world (see Sambursky 1959). Had the Stoics known about the projective plane, chances are they would have used its topology because it allows one to resolve these topological complexities in an extremely elegant manner. Causes and effects are distributed on a projective plane. The topology of the projective plane, on which events are formally but not ontologically separated from matters-of-fact, replaces a topology of surface and depth. As Deleuze notes, 'it is rather the coexistence of two sides without thickness, such that we pass from one to the other by following their length. *Sense is both the expressible of the expressed of the proposition, and an attribute of the state of affairs*' (22). This quote brings me to the core of my argument. How can the plane of immanence be folded onto the projective plane, and why should it be?

As many scholars have noted, the plane of immanence is one of the most difficult but also one of the most central concepts in Deleuzian philosophy. It is described most clearly, as well as, perhaps, most poetically, in the chapter 'Spinoza and Us' from *Spinoza: Practical Philosophy*, where it designates a machinic 'plane of Nature' that 'does not make any distinction at all between things that might be called natural and things that might be called artificial. Artifice is fully part of Nature' (124). The plane of Nature is the largest individuated multiplicity. 'One Nature for all bodies, one Nature for all individuals, a Nature that is itself an individual varying in an infinite number of ways. What is involved is no longer the affirmation of a single substance, but rather the laying out of a *common plane of immanence* on which all bodies, all minds, and all individuals are situated. This plane of immanence or consistency is a plan, but not in the sense of a mental design, a project, a program; it is a plan in the geometric sense: a section, and intersection, a diagram' (122). 'This plane of immanence or consistency'. Again, one can understand this 'or' only on the condition that Deleuze considers the two planes as one, unilateral plane: *unilateral philosophy*.

Although the passages about the plane of immanence in Deleuze's work are quite heterogeneous, it has three intimately related characteristics. As Deleuze and Guattari note in *What is Philosophy?*, it has a 'variable curvature', it is 'fractal' (39), and movements on it happen at an 'infinite speed' (42). All three characteristics are implicit in Deleuze's description of the plane of Nature. Its variable curvature defines the plane as spatially irregular and thus as always and everywhere singular and site-specific. A sphere, for instance, which has a nonvariable curvature, is always and everywhere regular. (In this context, Deleuze makes use of Bernard Cache's notion of the projectile in *Earth Moves: The Furnishing of Territories*.) The variable curvature is owed to the fact that the plane is embodied and dynamic rather than ideally static. Topological rather than Cartesian. As Deleuze notes, it is 'always variable and is constantly being altered, composed and recomposed, by individuals and collectives' (S: 128).

The fact that it is fractal can explain how everything can happen within the plane. While a plane of transcendence 'always implies a dimension supplementary to the dimensions of the given' (128), $n+1$, the number of conceptual dimensions of the plane is always $n-1$, which means that the dimensions are always smaller than the dimension of the overall plane. Although it is defined as a two-dimensional membrane, the plane of immanence contains infinitely many plateaus that are situated on fractal dimensions within the plane rather than on higher or lower dimensions. It is defined as having a quasi-depth. Even while it is two-dimensional, it contains fractal plateaus; depths within a surface. In fact, the plane of immanence is the model of 'an infinitely cavernous or porous world ... Mandelbrot's fractal dimension as a fractional or irrational number, a nondimension, an interdimension' (LB: 17). In *What is Philosophy?* Deleuze and Guattari state that the plane is 'neither surface nor volume but always fractal' (36).

Another image of this both virtual and actual plane is the rhizome as an image of an infinite multiplicity of nodes and relations. As a horizontal plane that is still somewhat vertical it is a good, if not geometrically completely precise, image of this fractality. Similarly, the difference between smooth and striated space that Deleuze and Guattari set up in *A Thousand Plateaus* is defined in relation to such a fractality, which also links the real projective plane to the philosophical concept of infinity, because 'it is this fractal nature that makes the planomenon an infinite that is always different from any surface or volume determinable as a concept. Every movement passes through the whole of the plane by immediately turning back on and folding itself and also folding other movements or allowing itself to be folded by them, giving rise to retroactions, connections, and proliferations in the fractalization of this infinitely folded up infinity' (WP: 38–9). It is in order to think the transfers and shifts between these fractal plateaus that Deleuze and Guattari employ the notion of infinite scales and scalings: *fractal philosophy*.

The third aspect of the plane of immanence is that it is not only spatially, but also temporally infinite. Ideally, particles move over or, better, within it at an infinite velocity. This characteristic not only defines it as ontologically kinetic, it also implies that movement on some of its levels happens too fast to be thought. Deleuze and Guattari develop their notion of infinite speed from the fact that the movements on the plane follow the dynamics of a Lucretian chaos that 'is characterized less by the absence of determinations than by the infinite speed with which they take shape and vanish' (42); a chaos defined 'not so much by its disorder as by the infinite speed with which every form taking shape in it vanishes ... chaos is an infinite speed of birth and disappearance' (118). It is a chaos in which specific states are, paradoxically, actualized with infinite speed or at the speed of chaos: *a chaos that is faster than the speed of light*.

In terms of perception, finitely small, unconscious perceptions as well as conscious perceptions move over the plane as the plane of consistency at finite speed. As Guattari states, the 'plane of machinic interfaces' (1995: 58) is defined by 'a deterministic chaos animated by infinite velocities. It is out of this chaos that complex compositions, which are capable of being slowed down in energetico-spatio-temporal coordinates or category systems, constitute themselves' (59). It is always within this fundamentally multiplicitous plane that human movement – both physical and psychic – takes place. Subtractive and decelerating machines cut into the plane and assemble specific metaphysical and physical arrangements (see also Massumi 2002: 31) [→ **Guattari 62**]. Its infinite speed refers to the fact that on the plane of immanence 'there is no longer a form, but only relations of velocity between infinitesimal particles of an unformed material. There is no longer a subject, but only individuating affective states of an anonymous force' (S: 128). Deleuze adds another topological characteristic to the plane that defines it as a projective plane. On the plane, 'the interior is only a selected exterior, and the exterior, a projected interior' (125). In *The Fold*, Deleuze had evoked a similar space when he noted that 'the world must be placed in the subject in order that the subject can be for the world. This is *the torsion that constitutes the fold of the world and of the soul*' (26, emphasis added).

If it sometimes seems that Deleuze's conceptualization of the plane of immanence is inconsistent, because he sometimes stresses its actuality and at other times its virtuality, this is because of the conceptual contraction of its formally separated sides. When Deleuze and Guattari describe it as a field 'peopled by anonymous matter, by infinite bits of impalpable matter entering into varying connections' (TP: 255), the plane of immanence seems to be predominantly material and actual. It is the true 'body without organs' (154), a space of 'positive absolute deterritorialization' (134) and of 'uninterrupted continuum' (154). At other moments, Deleuze and Guattari describe it as a fully immaterial field of virtuality, as when they note that it is pervaded by '*haecceities*, events, incorporeal transformations that are apprehended in themselves; *nomadic essences*, vague yet riotous; *continuums of intensities* or continuous variations ... *becomings*, which have neither culmination nor subject, but draw one another into zones of undecidability; *smooth spaces*; composed from within striated space' (TP: 507; see also DII: 92). The two aspects of the plane – once as an anonymous, fully material, terminological plane, and once as an anonymous, fully immaterial, relational plane – however, denote its formal distinction into an actual and a virtual aspect. At the same time, they are the two complementary aspects of its overall projective topology. Stated more provocatively, at infinity the plane is both fully actual and fully virtual because at infinity, its two aspects are identical.

If that is so, why does Deleuze make the distinctions in the first place? This question can also be answered from within the overall topology. The formal distinction is related to the fact that the projective plane is locally bilateral, which means that one can, locally, maintain that it has two sides. At the same time, its ontological identity refers to its global unilaterality (see also Beistegui 2010: 49). The alignment of the topology of the projective plane of immanence and the topology of living beings within this plane can be performed along this differentiation. By slowing down the infinite speed of the elements that pass through the plane, all living beings create quasi-bilateral systems: crystals. Topologically, this corresponds to the fact that, on a local level, the projective space is bilateral. Idealisms take this quasi-bilaterality for granted. At the same time, however, living beings remain part of the plane of immanence and thus they partake, on a global level, of its aspect of unilaterality.

In other words, every living being forms planes of 'consistency' (TP: 255) and composition within the plane of immanence, which are the plane of immanence considered from the aspect of the crystallizations that take place within it. In the same way that 'the concept as such can be concept of the affect, just as the affect can be affect of the concept', the 'plane of composition of art and the plane of immanence of philosophy can slip into each other to the degree that parts of one may be occupied by entities of the other' (WP: 66). All three of these planes are inherently dynamic spaces through which fluxes, forces and intensities, 'continuums of intensity, blocs of becoming, emissions of particles, combinations of fluxes' (DII: 105), travel at various speeds and in various alignments. This is what distinguishes them from yet another plane; the 'plane of organization and development' (TP: 507).

Every living being is a cluster made up of a heterogeneity of actual and virtual series that cut through all of the fractal dimensions of the plane as long as they remain attributed to each other, which means as long as they operate as a coherent or consistent entity. The entity falls apart when the two series lose their specific reciprocal supposition; that is, when the projective plane breaks up. As the plane is made up of infinitely many living beings, no living being can be separated from the countless processes of production – both productions of productions and productions of representations – that pass through the plane on all levels and at all times. As the various movements taking place on, or better in, the plane are sensitive to initial conditions and, at each moment, open to unexpected changes and catastrophes, the plane forms an infinite, fractal space of potentiality and multiplicity.

Living beings navigate their life-course through the fractal plateaus of the plane of immanence. 'It is only in appearance that a plane of this kind "reduces" the number of dimensions; for it gathers in all the dimensions to the extent that *flat multiplicities* – which nonetheless have *an increasing or decreasing number of dimensions* – are inscribed upon it . . . Far from reducing the multiplicities' number of dimensions to two, the *plane of consistency* cuts across them all, intersects them in order to bring into coexistence any number of multiplicities, with any number of dimensions. The plane of consistency is the intersection of all concrete forms . . . The only question is: Does a given becoming reach that point?' (TP: 251). Whether a becoming develops a plane of consistency, or, in other words, a plane of individuation, 'has nothing to do with a ground buried deep within things, nor with an end or a project in the mind of God' (254). Rather, it has to do with the both material and immaterial plane of immanence within which it assembles itself: with the immanent, one-sided and fractal 'plane of life' (254): *fractal luminosity*.

In 'The Actual and the Virtual', Deleuze had addressed the twofold aspect of the plane of immanence as both actual and virtual, noting that the virtual continuity of the plane of immanence is literally cut up by actualizations. 'The virtual is never independent of the *singularities* which cut it up and divide it out on the plane of immanence' (DII: 149, emphasis added). It 'includes both the virtual and its actualization simultaneously, without there being any assignable limit between the two' (149). At this late point, Deleuze defines the plane of immanence by the true complementarity of the actual and the virtual.

The dimensionalities of the entities that emerge within the plane of immanence invariably remain within its fractal envelope. Because of this immanence, the plane is, somewhat like Freud's interior foreign country, 'that which must be thought and that which cannot be thought. It is the nonthought within thought. It is the base of all planes, immanent to every thinkable plane that does not succeed in thinking it. It is the most intimate within thought and yet the absolute outside. An outside more distant than any external world: it is immanence' (WP: 59). Like the atom in 'Lucretius and the Simulacrum' it 'is that which must be thought, and that which can only be thought' (LS: 268).

This topology, which Lacan calls *extimité*, lies at the heart of *Foucault*, which points to Martin Heidegger, but even more to the chiastic logic in Merleau-Ponty's *The Visible and the Invisible*, as an important moment for Deleuze's conceptualization of a projective logic. In Foucault, 'an Outside, more distant than any exterior, is "twisted", "folded" and "doubled" by an Inside that is deeper than any interior, and alone creates the possibility of the derived relation between the interior and the exterior' (91). 'Individual points' are integrated into curves: '*a statement is the curve joining individual points*' (66). The elective affinity Deleuze finds between his own thought and Foucault's lies in the fact that Foucault continually confronts thought with its interior outside. 'The outside is not a fixed limit but a moving matter animated by peristaltic movements, folds and foldings that together make up an inside: they are not something other than the outside, but precisely the inside *of* the outside' (80). In fact, 'to think is to fold, to double the outside with a coextensive inside. The general topology of thought . . . ends up in the folding of the outside into the inside' (97): *projective thought*. (On the term topology of thought, see Ansell-Pearson 1999: 79.)

The three final pages of *Foucault* are a rhapsody of Deleuze's conceptual topology of '*life within the folds*' (101). Although the topic is Foucault's diagram, what Deleuze describes is, in actual fact, his own projective plane of life. The stratified archives that we are, the turbulent diagrams within us that form the outside of our thought: the unformed, 'informal outside' (99); 'a life that is the power of the outside' (79). In this light, 'in philosophy, it is a question of an impossible thought, making thinkable through a very complex material of thought forces that are unthinkable' (TRM: 160). In fact, the 'supreme act of philosophy' (WP: 60) is 'to show' that this plane of immanence 'is there, unthought in every plane, and to think it in this way as the outside and inside of thought' (60–1). This philosophical project can only be thought from within a projective plane; 'the not-external outside and the not-internal inside – that which cannot be thought and yet must be thought, which was thought once, as Christ was incarnated once, in order to show, that one time, the possibility of the impossible' (61): *real projective Spinoza, the Christ of philosophers*.

4   LUMINOUS PHILOSOPHY

Most persons do not see the sun. At least they have a very superficial seeing. The sun illuminates only the eye of the man, but shines into the eye and the heart of a child.

Ralph Waldo Emerson, 'Nature' (6)

I cannot cause light; the most I can do is put myself in the path of its beam. It is possible, in deep space, to sail on solar wind.

Annie Dillard, *Pilgrim at Tinker Creek* (33)

sunflakes falling in the sea | Beyond the outer shore

Harry Crosby, 'Néant', in *Chariot of the Sun*

in luce ambulemus

The First Epistle of St John the Apostle

We are fluid, luminous beings made of fibres.

Carlos Castaneda, quoted in *A Thousand Plateaus* (249)

That light travels over the ground, that it pools – that there is a pool of luminescence which is very ephemeral, and which takes a relaxing of Western muscles in the eyes in order to be aware of. That light-streaks come down previous to rain – splitting the air – light-like phosphorescent streaks of . . . something! That I call light!

Stan Brakhage on *The Text of Light* (quoted in Wees 1992: 101)

In the light of light is the *virtù* | 'sunt lumina' said Erigena Scotus |. . .| all things that are are light.

Ezra Pound, *The Cantos* (429)

Years ago you said. Fundamentally, I am a matter of Light.
    Giorgos Seferis, 'On a Ray of Winter Light (quoted on Cy Twombly's *Gaeta*)'

> Our sun radiates heat and light beyond the farthest planet. And, on the other hand, it moves in a certain fixed direction, drawing with it the planets and their satellites. The thread attaching it to the rest of the universe is doubtless very tenuous. Nevertheless it is along this thread that is transmitted down to the smallest particle of the world in which we live the duration immanent to the whole of the universe.
>
> Henri Bergson, *Creative Evolution* (10–11)

As I noted in my introduction, the line of light that can be drawn through Deleuze's work from his early readings of Lucretius, Nietzsche and Bergson, becomes more and more distinct from the end of the 1970s onwards. Although differently so, the 'Lectures on Spinoza' between 1978 and 1981, *Francis Bacon: The Logic of Sensation* from 1981, *Cinema 1 & 2* from 1983 and 1985 respectively, *Foucault* from 1986 and *The Fold: Leibniz and the Baroque* 1988 are all eminently luminous.

In *Cinema 1: The Movement-Image* Deleuze notes that 'the plane of immanence is entirely made up of Light' (60). If the plane of immanence, as the projective plane of life and thought, is quite literally photonic, and as such luminous, Deleuzian philosophy is a luminous philosophy. While Deleuze tends, in other contexts, to consider the plane of immanence as atomic or molecular, the conceptually most adequate, as well as the most comprehensive plane of immanence, is that luminous, photonic plane.

How does that photonic plane differ from the other planes of immanence, and why is the photon an adequate notion to define the plane of immanence? A first difference between the three planes concerns the fact that the photon is an even smaller element than the atom and the molecule. The photonic medium contains the atomic medium, which in turn contains the molecular medium. Photons, as elementary particles that make up the sub-atomic building-blocks of the world's electromagnetic field, are the most minute elements of the world's luminous reality, which makes the photonic medium the most comprehensive of all Deleuzian media.

A second difference concerns the conceptual contexts of the three planes. For the atomic plane of immanence, these tend to centre on physics and, filtered through atomist philosophies, on questions of ontology. For the molecular plane, they tend to centre on modes of assemblage and disassemblage, such as the bureaucracies of consolidation and the possibilities of dispersion that Deleuze treats either from within the terminology of the molar and the molecular, or from within that of territorialization, deterritorialization and reterritorialization. While the conceptual context of the photonic plane centres around questions of visibility, it also embodies, more importantly, the topology of thought that is conceptually most adequate to Deleuze's inherently projective and luminous philosophy. If Bergson's notion of universal vibration seems to favour a collapse into the virtual, while atomism seems to favour a collapse into the actual, the photonic, which shows properties of both discrete particles and of communal waves, allows one to think the complementarity of the two series. Werner Heisenberg's statement that 'the quantum-theoretical dualism of waves and particles makes the same entity appear both as matter and as force' (140) translates quite seamlessly into the Deleuzian terminology of the actual and the virtual. (On 'an ontology of vibration' see Kerslake 2009: 236; see also Ruyer on the notion that 'the life-force is not of another nature than the physical force . . . The macroscopic force, for example the attraction of the sun or that of a large magnet, [is] the sum of an enormous quantity of molecular actions' (1952: 218–19).)

The second question about why the photon is an adequate notion to define the plane of immanence concerns the complementarity of those two states, which was already implicit in the scientific controversy about whether light is corpuscular, a belief held by, amongst others, Isaac Newton, Pierre Gassendi and Albert Einstein, or whether it was wave-like, as was thought by, amongst others, Robert Hooke, Christiaan Huygens and René Descartes. In the twentieth century, these opposites were reconciled in the paradoxical concept of complementarity, according to which the photon, a term coined in 1926 by Gilbert N. Lewis, has at the same time the properties of waves and of particles. Photons, which Einstein called light quanta, are discrete quantities of electromagnetic energy that have no measurable mass because they are never at rest, have no electric charge and have an indefinitely long life span. The de Broglie hypothesis extends the logic of complementarity to all of matter. With experimental proof of the existence of atomic waves that undergo diffraction, interference and that allow for quantum reflection, the logic of quantum mechanics has percolated onto a macroscopic scale of molecules and macro-molecules. Although this percolation implies that complementarity is no longer restricted to the photonic level, the photon is still the default figure of complementarity, in the same way that the atom, despite the fact that it consists of smaller elements, is still the default figure of assemblage theories.

Deleuze's photonic logic addresses three levels. The overall plane of immanence is that of electromagnetic radiation. Already in 1966, Deleuze had related this plane to Henri Bergson's description of the universe as consisting only of 'modifications, disturbances, changes of tension and of energy and nothing else' (B: 76). (See also 'a cosmology where everything is changes in tension, changes in energy, and nothing else' (DI: 71); what Kerslake calls Bergson's 'transcendental energetics' (2009: 236).) The luminous plane of immanence as the plane of given light is that part of the spectrum of electromagnetic radiation that affects living entities that have developed the optical machines we call eyes as light, which makes light one of the aspects of electromagnetic radiation. It can also be registered as warmth, however, or as a magnetic current.

The most immediate source of electromagnetic radiation is the sun, as the generator of light and warmth, and thus of the photonic plane of immanence as the plane of Nature. As Werner Heisenberg describes the origin of 'cosmic radiation' in *Physics and Philosophy*, 'the electromagnetic fields on the surface of stars extending over huge spaces are under certain circumstances able to accelerate charged atomic particles, electrons and nuclei' (1959: 138). When they reach the earth, they 'have already travelled through potentials of several thousand million volts' and 'in rare cases a million times this amount' (138). The result of this is 'the complete mutability of matter' (139): at sufficiently high levels of energy, all elementary particles can be transmuted into each other. There is a deep Spinozism in Heisenberg's idea that 'all the elementary particles are made of the same substance, which we may call energy or universal matter' and that they are just 'different forms in which matter can appear' (139). As Heisenberg notes further about the virtuality of energy, 'if we compare this situation with the Aristotelian concepts of matter and form, we can say that the matter of Aristotle, which is mere 'potentia', should be compared to our concept of energy, which gets into 'actuality' by means of the form, when the elementary particle is created' (139). Heisenberg's reference to Aristotle is particularly intriguing because Aristotle added the luminiferous æther to the elements, as the fifth element that brings the other elements to life and that is, at the same time, the medium in which all of them are immersed. Something like the aerosol of immanence, electromagnetic radiation is the most abstract natural habitat, in the sense that every landscape is suffused with an æthereal energy or light. A few pages later, in describing the realities of elementary particles, Heisenberg evokes something very like Deleuze's notion of the plane of immanence as a plane of pure potentiality. 'In the experiments about atomic events we have to do with things and facts, with phenomena that are just as real as any phenomena in daily life. But the atoms or the elementary particles themselves are not as real; they form a world of potentialities or possibilities rather than one of things or facts' (160). A line of light might thus be drawn through the history of science and through the history of philosophy.

Light also provides a link between philosophy and media studies, most strikingly, perhaps, in Fritz Heider's textually overlapping essays 'Ding und Medium' from 1923 and 'Thing and Medium' from 1959, in which he conceptualizes a luminous multiplicity as a luminous body without organs. Heider's initial point is that 'we do not perceive light waves as things that touch our eyes and refer to something else. We seem to see the mediated object directly' (1959: 2). In delineating the logic of optical perception, Heider differentiates between on the one hand the solid and semi-solid objects in our perceptual surrounding, and on the other 'the air-filled space through which we see and hear' (6). As in Lucretius, diffuse light is a photonic multiplicity or, in Heider's words, 'a manifold of light rays' (7; 2008: 323). It is 'a multitude of rays of different directions' (1959: 16) whose formation by objects is what makes these objects visible. Taking light as a medium of perception, Heider's basic idea is that 'the special state of the medium is *to a high degree* irrelevant for the form of the process in it' (4, emphasis added). As a loosely coupled set of elements – 'wave frequencies and other determinations are coupled only to a small degree, if at all' (16) – it invariably takes on the specific form (*'Eigenform',* 2008: 323) of the substrate in which it actualizes itself. Unlike the objects within it, the medium does not have its own 'free vibration' (1959: 4; *'Eigenschwingung',* 2008: 324) and as such it does not in itself form a coherent unity. Its only quality, one might say, is to be a substrate without qualities. As a pure multiplicity made up of parts that are 'independent of each other' (1959: 7), light rays form an 'atomistic manifold' (19). Only objects are unities with eigenforms and eigenfrequencies. As light is itself without form, is can easily be formed by the outside, such as the surfaces of the world of objects. As Heider notes, 'free vibration occurs in things, forced vibration in media' (15). Although 'a forced vibration has the same geometrical characteristics as a free vibration' and '*appears* to be unitary' (6, emphasis added), forced vibrations are 'composite events' (5), or, as Heider calls them, 'spurious units' (7). Only 'free vibration is a unitary event' (5). Thus, the structural difference between objects and light is that between eigenhood (*Eigentlichkeit*) and un-eigenhood (*Uneigentlichkeit*). Like Ulrich in Robert Musil's novel *The Man without Qualities*, light is, as an inherently formless carrier of optical forms, a medium without qualities.

Although Deleuze shares with Heider the idea of a given multiplicity of light, there are two crucial differences between them. For Heider, light operates best, both in terms of perception and of information, when it is completely under erasure. Secondly, although 'in the medium we find wave events and also movements of the small units' (13), these events are 'irrelevant for the things of our order of magnitude' (13). As Heider notes, 'neither molecular events nor wave events have coordinated effects within the thing order' (14).

Luminous Concepts

'Bergson's Conception of Difference' (1956)

Although Deleuze's luminism increased after the late 1970s, already at the very beginning of his career he had defined his philosophy, in 'Bergson's Conception of Difference', as one that not only talks about light, but that is itself inherently luminous; as a philosophy in which the luminous world can express itself not only in writing, in pigment, in marble or, as in the cinema, literally in light, but also in inherently luminous concepts. Deleuze defines luminous concepts in terms of the difference between two philosophical conceptualizations of colour and light. One philosophy, which operates in analogy to the logic of subtractive light, creates general concepts that, in a philosophical analogy to Heider's media studies, absorb or subsume the singular in the same way that the general concept of colour subsumes specific colours or, on a lower level of generalization, in the same way that the general concept of redness subsumes or absorbs the complex events of light from which the notion of redness emerges as their generalization. We talk of a red bag, for instance, rather than about a multiplicity of singular rays of light that are reflected and partly absorbed by and on the infinitely irregular surface of that bag.

In truth, however, the infinite and inherent irregularity of that surface implies that each of its points onto which a ray of light falls, or which it intercepts – each event of reflection and absorption, that is – is utterly singular. In pictorial terms, this singularity is especially striking with pastel drawings, or any painting in which pigment is applied in a pasty manner. While under certain conditions the surface of the red bag is optically smoothed out by the specific medium within which the light is dissolved, such as smooth leather or cloth, the surface of pastel drawings is made up of a multiplicity of singular grains of pigment, each of which refracts and absorbs rays of light differently. That effect of optical singularization becomes even more visible when several layers of pigment are superimposed, because in that case, different areas shade each other off, which results in an even more irregular landscape of light. When Heider notes that the 'microhappenings of the molecules' (2008: 329) are 'not important for what happens on our scale' (329), he follows the logic of what might be called a media studies of subsumption and absorption. Integrating the singular rays of light on an irregular surface into a general red implies considering the minimal differences between the singular events of light as irrelevant. In terms of Leibniz, it means that the multiplicity of light waves is integrated to such a degree that it becomes a clear and present red, which is a concept by which small, obscure perceptions are cancelled out.

In this light, a philosophy that relies on general notions is a philosophy of subsumption and absorption in that it subsumes particular ordered multiplicities of light into general notions, such as redness. '*Either* we extract the abstract and general idea of color, and we do so by "effacing from red what makes it red, from blue what makes it blue, and from green what makes it green": then we are left with a concept which is a genre, and many objects for one concept. The concept and the object are two things, and the relation of the object to the concept is one of subsumption' (DI: 43). Against such a philosophy, Deleuze sets a philosophy that creates, somewhat paradoxically, concepts that are singularizing rather than generalizing. In delineating a diffractive rather than a subsumptive mode of philosophy, he uses an optical phenomenon as a philosophical and conceptual allegory. If, according to the logic of additive light, all colours taken together make up a white luminosity, that luminosity can be considered as a white concept that, when it is diffracted into the spectrum of colours, expresses and incarnates itself in each singular colour. In Spinozist terms, the singular colours function as the modes that express the more comprehensive substance of that whiteness. 'Or we send the colors through a convergent lens that concentrates them on the same point: what we have then is "pure white light," the very light that "makes the differences come out between the shades." So, the different colors are no longer objects *under* a concept, but nuances or degrees of the concept itself. Degrees of difference itself, and not differences of degree. The relation is no longer one of subsumption, but one of participation. White light is still a universal, but a *concrete universal*, which gives us an understanding of the particular because it is the far end of the particular' (43, emphasis added). Such a luminous concept, rather than subsuming or absorbing singular colours, comes to function as their universal substance. Insofar as the single modes of colour express both themselves and that universal substance, such a concept is simultaneously both concrete and universal, as well as infinitely differentiable: *a luminous philosophy of concrete universals*.

When, in 'The Brain is the Screen', Deleuze provides a classification of light in the cinema, this is, in light of the above, at first sight surprising. Deleuze's classification, however, is true to the logic of luminous concepts, because this classification is itself infinitely differentiable. There is a light 'whose composition gives you white light, a Newtonian light that can be found in American cinema, and perhaps in Antonioni's films'. There is also 'a Goethe-light, an indestructible force that slams into shadows and picks things out'. Another light is 'defined by its contrast not with shadow, but with shades of white, opacity being a total white out'. Furthermore, you have 'a kind of light no longer defined either by composition or by contrast, but by alternation and the production of lunar figures'. Deleuze explicitly stresses that '*the list could go on forever, because new lighting events can always be created*' (TRM: 286; emphasis added).

Such an infinitely differentiable classification is also both universal and concrete. 'Because things have become nuances or degrees of the concept, the concept itself has become a thing. It is a universal thing, if you like, since the objects look like so many degrees, but a concrete thing, not a genus or a generality. Properly speaking, there is no longer many objects for one concept; the concept is identical to the thing itself. But it is not the resemblance of objects; the concept is the difference between them, to which they are related. This is internal difference: the concept which has become a concept of difference' (DI: 43). The content and form of such a luminous, white concept is difference itself. If light is a medium without qualities that does not show itself as itself – except as the sheer luminosity of disparate rays of light – but rather itself in the form of the objects from which it is reflected and by which parts of it are absorbed, the Deleuzian concept is that of a pure, universal difference without qualities that embodies itself in the singular differences that pertain between the totality of singular objects. In this way, Deleuze develops the concept of the concept in terms of light as a plane of given optical disparity, that is given as given, however, in the mode of the visibility of illuminated objects and their infinite differences and differentiability. While the first concerns again a luminous ontology, the second concerns a luminous epistemology.

To define Deleuze's philosophy as luminous brings into play the art-historical term Luminism, which was coined by John I. H. Baur in the 1950s apropos of American landscape painting of the nineteenth century. (When referring to the art movement, Luminism is capitalised.) Although it might easily be extended to photography and film, the term is closely linked to a genre of painting that is, both in terms of poetics and of *sujet*, in many aspects the analog to what is called, in terms of literature, local colour writing. Concerning its inherent poetics, Luminism marks one specific moment at which light is treated as the true medium of painting. Luminism will shade into Impressionism, which, although it differs formally from local colour luminism, is similarly concerned with objects given immediately in and by light. In terms of a painterly luminosity, in fact, one might construct a 'line of light' (LB: 32) from Lucretius' diffuse light to the baroque *chiaroscuro*, to Luminism, whether in America or in J. M. W. Turner's light-drenched, post-Tambora England, and further to Impressionism.

In its depiction of tranquil landscapes, calm, reflective water and soft, hazy skies, much of Luminist painting highlights the natural elements. These elements, however, are all seen and depicted under the given of light, which provides the movement with its name and which functions as the medium that encompasses all of the others. Invariably, the four elements are bathed in light as the fifth element. If Luminism can be understood as local colour painting, local colour writing can be understood as inherently Luminist. Not local colour writing, but local light writing. In fact, it might make sense to talk of a local light movement instead of a local colour movement. After such a conceptual upgrade, the cliché of the colourful characters in local colour stories is changed into something both more fundamental and local; into literally luminous characters.

If Luminism is based on a complex play between colour and light, one of its main painterly challenges is how to evoke the pure, immaterial luminosity of light by way of material, inherently coloured and therefore darkened pigment? How to create the illusion of immaterial light by way of material pigment? In terms of colour theory, the distinction between material colour and immaterial luminosity, and thus the distinction between local colour and local light, plays itself out between the two logics of additive and subtractive light. While additive light is defined by mixing light of two or more different colours and is measured in terms of the addition of differently coloured luminosities that together form white light, subtractive light is defined by subtracting parts of the spectrum of light that is virtually present in white light by means of coloured pigments and is measured in terms of rates of colour and the absorption of light. All pigments or filters together add up to black. The overall difference, then, is between virtual luminosity and actual pigment; between light and colour, which is a difference that has been read in analogy to the fields of the body and the mind respectively. Light is incarnated in a colour like thought is incarnated in a body. In the more focused context of painting, the distinction has to do with the pigmented bodies of the canvas and the resulting colours on the one hand, and the virtual luminosity of the scene that is depicted on the other. On this background, luminism might be defined as the strategy of using the subtractive logic of coloured pigment to simulate the additive logic of projected light.

The creation of the illusion of luminosity by way of coloured pigment is an inherently painterly challenge. The local light phenomenon is precisely the opposite of what is called local colour in terms of the visual theory of colour. In that theory, local colour denotes the specific colour of a specific object as unmodified by ambient light and luminosity. It denotes the pigmented colour of an object without the interference of its position within an overall optical milieu. In the local light phenomenon, in contrast, ambience and ambient light are the media that suffuse both the action and the objects that are being described. The ambient light suffuses the specific scene and, in extension, the whole world. Even more, it is the medium within which the action, the objects, the situation and the world emerge. In Luminist painting, every local colour is suffused by a specific ambient light, as in the proto-Luminist paintings of Nicolas Poussin or Claude Lorrain. Maybe one can sense the local colour through the ambient light as given as given, but to posit a pure local colour for the objects in Luminist paintings is, ultimately, an idealization. In fact, it is difficult to conceive, categorically, of the pure local colour of an object, because that would imply the erasure of ambient light. Ambient light, however, will, even in museums that try to limit its effects by white walls and neutral lighting, invariably interact with the specific local colour of objects. As with the inhabitants of a specific milieu, local colour and ambient light form complex optical mixtures: *in luce ambulemus*.

Spinoza on the Beach

Les Cours de Gilles Deleuze: Spinoza (1978, 1981), Foucault (1986)

There is electromagnetic radiation, then there is the aspect of radiation that is given as light, and then there is that given light as given, and as given as given. Erwin Schrödinger argues in his essay 'Mind and Matter' from 1944, there is an incommensurable gap between given light and light as given as given. Between, as Schrödinger calls it, the fact of being 'hit by and receiv[ing] light quanta' (1967: 123) and the experience of, say, the luminous beauty of a golden hour on an island beach. While the first concerns the experience of being corporeally affected by light, which is a level that Deleuze relates to affection, the second concerns the experience of having an image in light, which Deleuze relates to affect. Symptomatically, in relation to the gap between matter and mind, Schrödinger quotes Spinoza's statement that *'the body cannot determine mind to think, nor can the mind determine the body to motion or rest, or to anything else (if there is anything else)'* (2002: 279). In Schrödinger's version: 'Neither can the body determine the mind to think, nor the mind determine the body to motion or rest' (1967: 122).

To account for this gap, Schrödinger splits light up into two separate but parallel aspects: objective 'rays of light' and subjective 'rays of vision' (123). Being hit by light waves, and seeing specific colours. As Schrödinger notes, 'the sensation of color cannot be accounted for by the physicist's objective picture of light-waves' (154) and, in reverse, 'color in itself tells you nothing about the wave-length' (160). There is no objective correlation between objective and subjective measurement. 'The quality of the color sensation gives no direct clue whatsoever to infer the physical property, the wave-length' (160). In other words, 'the direct sensual perception of the phenomenon tells us nothing as to its objective physical nature' (162). As Francisco Varela will note much later in *The Embodied Mind*, 'if we actually measure the light reflected from the world around us, we will discover that there simply is no one-to-one relationship between light flux at various wavelengths and the colors we perceive areas to have' (Varela, Rosch and Thompson 1991: 160). Invariably, there is an irritating gap between locally reflected light and perceived colour [→ **Guattari 100**].

While Schrödinger considers this deeply Spinozist parallelism to be a 'horrible antinomy' (1967: 122), Deleuze comments on it in more favourable terms. 'One of the most famous theoretical theses of Spinoza is known by the name of *parallelism*; it does not consist merely in denying any real causality between the mind and the body, it disallows any superiority of the one over the other. If Spinoza rejects any superiority of the mind over the body, this is not in order to establish a superiority of the body over the mind, which would be no more intelligible than the converse ... There is no primacy of one series over the other' (S: 18). To conceptualize the relation between the parallel series is both a mathematical and a philosophical question. Deleuze, following Spinoza, resolves it by considering that relation as a 'reciprocal presupposition' (TP: 66, 503; C2: 69). As I noted before, the series are 'formally distinct, while being ontologically identical' (EP: 64).

Deleuze's philosophical luminism suffuses *Les Cours de Gilles Deleuze: Spinoza*, in particular his lectures on Spinoza and D. H. Lawrence, in which he literally folds the logic of light onto Spinoza's logic of affects. Like many of Deleuze's own philosophical concepts, Spinoza's concept of affect is seemingly paradoxical. As he notes, 'by emotion [*affectus*] I understand the affections of the body, by which the body's power of activity is increased or diminished . . . together with the ideas of these affections' (2002: 278).

Deleuze takes up Spinoza's terminology, affection (*affectio*) and affect (*affectus*), to differentiate between the two series, both of which differ, for Deleuze, from emotion or feeling (*sentiment*). 'Thus when I use the word "affect" it refers to Spinoza's *affectus*, and when I say the word "affection", it refers to *affectio*' (Lecture, 24.01.78). At other times, however, Deleuze uses the term affect quite loosely, as when he notes that 'every mode of thought insofar as it is non-representational will be termed affect' (24.01.78). (On affections and affects, see also S: 48–51.)

The term affection is taken up by Schrödinger's rays of light and Deleuze's notion of the actual, while the term affect denotes Schrödinger's rays of vision and Deleuze's notion of the virtual. (*Actual*: attribute1 extension; affection [*affectio*]: movement-image, body|particle, being|still, instants|chronos, corporeal images, terms, spatial extension. *Virtual*: attribute2 thought; affect [*affectus*]: time-image, mind|wave, becoming|flow, durations|aion, ideas, continuous variations, relations, temporal intensity.) As with the complementarity of the photon as both particle and wave, in order to express the logic of being formally distinct but ontologically identical Deleuze conceptualizes the two physical and psychic series as complementary rather than exclusive. In Deleuzian terms, although the series are formally distinct, what counts is the inherent complementarity of actual affection (what a body can do) and of virtual affect (what a mind can do). Because of this complementarity, both a call to a return to pure affections (materialism, empiricism) and a call to a return to pure affects (idealism, transcendentalism) are equally one-sided: 'transcendental empiricism' (PI: 25).

My argument about Deleuze's luminous affectology relies on his theories of space and time. While the space of affect – if that term includes, for the moment, both *affectio* and *affectus* – is that of the real projective plane, the time of affect is that of the complementarity of Chronos and Aion. In temporal terms, therefore, I am not so much concerned with the argument as to whether affect is faster than cognition or, as Hume would say, more lively, but rather with Deleuze's reading of affection and affect as analogous to actual being and virtual becoming. (On the speed of affect, see Massumi 2002.) The limit of both the temporal and the spatial logic lies at infinity, where the opposites in kind of inside and outside as well as *durée* and *temps* are reconciled in a philosophical koan.

There is an assemblage theory at the back of Deleuze's take-over of Spinoza's differentiation between virtual affect and actual affection. While in general, affect denotes the simultaneity of body and mind, in this context, the theory of affects (*affectus*) and affections (*affectio*) recapitulates the logic of the given and of the given as given; of pure diversity and of diversity as given in difference. Affect denotes the given, while affection denotes the given as given. Obscure affect, light affection. Analog, unconscious affect, digital, conscious affection: *intensive affect, extensive affection*.

As Deleuze notes, 'the affect is impersonal and is distinct from every individual state of things: it is none the less *singular*, and can enter into singular combinations or conjunctions with other affects' (C1: 98). Taken from within an affective multiplicity, singular virtual affects are entrained into the conscious affects of individual organisms; or, as Deleuze describes it, pure affects are enveloped by organisms. Each time, an aionic becoming is enveloped by two moments of chronic being. They become one only at the crystal point-at-infinity. 'What is it, the affect? Spinoza tells us that it is something that the affection envelops . . . For example perceptions are affections . . . There is a difference in nature between the affect and the affection. The affect is not something dependent on the affection, it is enveloped by the affection . . . What does my affection, that is the image of the thing and the effect of this image on me, what does it envelop? . . . *Every instantaneous affection envelops . . . a lived passage, a lived transition, which obviously doesn't mean conscious* . . . There is a specificity of the transition, and it is precisely this that we call duration . . . What is duration? Never anything but the passage from one thing to another, it suffices to add, insofar as it is lived' (Lecture, 20.01.81).

In this temporality, which is a modulation of aionic and chronic registers, Deleuze refers back to Bergson's use of Dedekind, as well as, in the background, his own discussion of virtual and actual numbers. 'When Bergson tries to make us understand what he calls duration, he says: you can consider psychic states as close together as you want in time, you can consider the state A and the state A', as separated by a minute, but just as well by a second, by a thousandth of a second, that is you can make more and more cuts, increasingly tight, increasingly close to one another. You may well go to the infinite, says Bergson, in your decomposition of time, by establishing cuts with increasing rapidity, but you will only ever reach states. And he adds that the states are always of space. The cuts are always spatial. And you will have brought your cuts together very well, you will let something necessarily escape, it is the passage from one cut to another, however small it may be. Now, what does he call duration, at its simplest? It is the passage from one cut to another, it is the passage from one state to another' (Lecture, 20.01.81).

These dynamics evoke both the notion of perception as a machine that cuts into reality, the difference between affects as given and affects as given as given, as well as the theory of luminosity, which differentiates between a digital light that oscillates between actual light and darkness as in between 1 and 0, and an analog light of a virtual *chiaroscuro*. In *Francis Bacon: The Logic of Sensation*, Deleuze notes that 'color itself is capable of two very different kinds of relation: *relations of value*, based on the contrast of black and white, in which a tone is defined as either dark or light, saturated or rarefied; and *relations of tonality*, based on the spectrum, on the opposition of yellow and blue, or green and red, in which this or that pure tone is defined as warm or cool. It is obvious that these two scales of color continually mix with one another, and that their combinations constitute powerful acts of painting' (132). It is as if Deleuze was talking about affect in terms of black and white affection and luminous affect. 'The passage from one state to another is not a state . . . but it is a really profound statute of living. For how can we speak of the passage, the passage from one state to another, without making it a state? . . . You have . . . two states which could be very close together in time . . . They are very close together. I am saying: there is a passage from one to the other, so fast that it may even be unconscious . . . The affect is what? It is the passage. *The affection is the dark state and the lighted state. Two successive affections, in cuts. The passage is the lived transition from one to the other*. Notice that in this case here there is no physical transition, there is a biological transition, it is your body which makes the transition' (Lecture, 20.01.81, emphasis added).

The aionic, durational affect is 'the lived passage from the preceding state to the current state, or of the current state to the following state' (Lecture, 20.01.81). In terms of both size and speed, this procedure goes towards infinity. 'However quickly I pass from one state to another, the passage is irreducible to the two states. It is this that every affection envelops. I would say: every affection envelops the passage by which we arrive at it. Or equally well: every affection envelops the passage by which we arrive at it, and by which we leave it, towards another affection, however close the two affections considered are' (Lecture, 20.01.81). At this point, Deleuze stresses the differences in kind between the two series rather than their convergence at infinity. One must remember, however, Spinoza's description of their formal complementarity as a temporal simultaneity. Affect concerns 'the modifications of the body, whereby the active power of the said body is increased or diminished, aided or constrained, and also [at the same time] the ideas of such modifications' (2006: 122). The temporal limit, which is at infinite speed, resolves the formal logic into Spinoza's paradoxical parallelism. Although they are different in nature, then – in optical terms the affection of light follows the line of rays of light, while the affect of light follows the line of rays of vision – affection and affect are complementary. In this complementarity, they form the *chiaroscuro* of life. Together, they darken the plane of pure, virtually white light. The radiant luminosity of the photonic plane of immanence.

This brings me to my third, central point about Deleuze's luminous affectology. The deeply Spinozist ground of Deleuze's philosophy is that darkness is not light's other, but rather its attribute. Everything changes, Deleuze notes, when you think 'light in terms of white light instead of shadow. From this perspective, you have a whole other world; shadow is only one result. There is no less harshness or even cruelty in this solution, but now everything is light. However, there are two kinds of light: the light of the sun, and the light of the moon' (TRM: 218). Without the play of actual affection and virtual affect, there is no individual life and consciousness, both of which are subtractions from the white light of immanence, and modes of its expression. Without that play, there are no planes of consistency and no planes of composition. No philosophy. In a deeply Spinozist and Bergsonian logic, dark consistencies, as surfaces of reflection and absorption, allow light to show itself as diffracted into colours, and thus they express it in its optical embodiment. In cosmic terms, the sun is the origin of the 'luminous plane of immanence' (C1: 68) in that it provides light and warmth. When Lynn Margulis talks about the beginnings of life, she notes, in reference to Vladimir Vernadsky's notion that life is 'a global phenomenon that transforms solar energy' (Margulis and Sagan 1995: 45), that 'living matter can ascend over common matter only by constant sun-bathing' (41). Not only are bacteria already 'light-sensitive' (136), even more, 'light sensitivity, in the rudimentary sense, even antedates life itself: colored compounds react in highly specific ways to visible solar radiation' (136). As Olkowski notes, 'the warm sun opens the senses like flowers . . . This desire *comes from the world*' (1999: 120). When I maintain that the pre-philosophical, life-affirming light and warmth that is given by the sun suffuses Deleuzian philosophy at all moments, this is not to say that Deleuze knows nothing of moments of seemingly utter darkness. The important thing is that darkness, coldness and even cruelty are invariably attributes or aspects of white light and warmth.

It is entirely fitting that the original title of Deleuze's article 'Zones of Immanence' is 'Les Plages d'Immanence'. During the Second World War, the young Deleuze had been sent to Deauville where, on the beach, he encountered a young teacher named Pierre Halwachs. In *Gilles Deleuze from A to Z*, Deleuze recounts their walks along the beach together. Halwachs would read. He was a good reader, Deleuze remembers, whose heroes were Anatole France, Charles Baudelaire and André Gide. Deleuze had found a master. He was Halwachs' disciple. Before that encounter, he was a mediocre student with no interest in anything at all. This encounter caused a total awakening. 'It was there that I ceased being an idiot.' Such concrete, particular encounters pose shocks to thought, and they have existential repercussions. For Deleuze, such encounters spark 'the creation of new concepts, the experience of unfamiliar affects, or the production of different practices of living' (Johnson 2017: 257).

Deleuze's discussions of Spinoza's theory of affects in 1978 and 1981 are pervaded by his luminist ontology and epistemology. The reference to light comes from D. H.

Lawrence's text '"Chaos in Poetry" Introduction to Harry Crosby's "Chariot of the Sun"', which Deleuze and Guattari describe in *What is Philosophy?* as 'violently poetic' (203). The text is an introduction to a collection of poems by American poet Harry Crosby, whose oeuvre is in its entirety an ode to the sun and to the 'shores of light'. Even in his celebration of light, however, Deleuze is aware of darkness. 'The two points common to Lawrence and Spinoza', he remarks, are 'light and tuberculosis' (Lecture, 24.03.81). Also, he knows that the sun is a *pharmakon* rather than a friend. A full, unfiltered immersion in the luminous intensity of the photonic plane of immanence would hurt the human. As he notes in 'Michel Tournier and the World Without Others' (LS: 301–21), there can always be too much light. Don't look directly into the sun, we tell our kids, or you'll go blind. As Deleuze notes in his first lecture on Spinoza, 'Lawrence said a directly Spinozist thing: an intensity which exceeds your power of being affected is bad . . . It's inevitable: a blue that is too intense for my eyes will not make me say it's beautiful, it will perhaps be beautiful for someone else' (Lecture, 24.01.78). Despite this caveat, however, Crosby's luminous poems, Lawrence's luminous poetics and Deleuze's luminous philosophy find their origin in the violent, cosmic energy of the sun as the provider of a radiant energy. All three emerge from solar storms. From storms of light.

The concrete image from which Lawrence develops his luminous poetics is that of people at a beach who have set up umbrellas to hide from the intensity of that wild, chaotic, luminous multiplicity. 'In his terror of chaos, he [man] begins by putting up an umbrella between himself and the everlasting chaos. Then he paints the underside of his umbrella like a firmament. Then he parades around, lives, and dies under his umbrella. Bequeathed to his descendants, the umbrella becomes a dome, a vault, and men at last begin to feel that something is wrong' (Lawrence 2005: 109). Both Crosby and Lawrence, however, are 'glad to get out of that church, and into the natural chaos' (110). Poets such as Crosby tear the fabric of the umbrella, and with it, the false firmament, in order to let the sun shine once more directly onto the pale and sickly humans. In *What is Philosophy?* Deleuze and Guattari compare this gesture to Luigi Fontana's slashing of the canvas in his series of paintings called *Attese*.

The parasol is first a sun-screen that simulates the sky, like the ceilings of some movie-theatres from the 1940s and '50s. 'Man fixes some wonderful erection of his own between himself and the wild chaos, and gradually goes bleached and stifled under his parasol. Then comes a poet, enemy of convention, and makes a slit in the umbrella; and lo! the glimpse of chaos is a vision, a window to the sun' (Lawrence 2005: 109). Whenever the power of such a poetry, or such a philosophy, for that matter, is destroyed by too much habit and explication, its luminous power is lost. An originally luminous art becomes pale and unhealthy. A poetics of representation wins out over a poetics of expression. 'But after a while, getting used to the vision, and not liking the genuine draught from chaos, commonplace man daubs a simulacrum of the window that opens onto chaos, and patches the umbrella with the painted patch of the simulacrum ... Homer and Keats, annotated and with glossary' (110). As long as this twofold movement goes on, a civilization 'will continue more or less happily, completing its own painted prison. It is called completing the consciousness' (110). The parasol turns first into a dome and then into a vault. More and more, it shuts out the light. If the sun can still shine through the fabric of an umbrella, no light can penetrate into the vault of a fully civilized, conscious poetry.

Lawrence sees the possibility for grace in immersing oneself in the chaos of the sun. Poets, in touching the vital, unconscious force of the living chaos, provide images of such a lost grace. 'A glimpse of the living, untamed chaos. For the grand chaos is all alive. And everlasting. From it we draw our breath of life. If we shut ourselves off from it, we stifle. The animals live with it, so they live in grace. But when man became conscious, and aware of himself, his own littleness and puniness in the whirl of the vast chaos of God, he took fright, and began inventing God in his own image' (112). In Lawrence's terms, a Deleuzian aesthetics relies on the ability to be receptive and adequate to the luminous chaos of life. 'Sun breathes its way into words, and the words become poetry, by *suffusion*. On the part of the poet it is an act of faith, pure attention and purified receptiveness' (114, emphasis added). The idea is to become a medium by which the 'nonorganic life of things' (WP: 180) can express itself. Of course, Lawrence does not propose to get out from under the umbrella completely and for good. As he notes, 'they are a necessity of our consciousness' (2005: 112). The danger, which is the danger of idealism, is to vault life by turning the umbrella into an ideal. As Lawrence also notes, 'never again shall we be able to put up the Absolute Umbrella, either religious or moral or rational or scientific or practical' (113): *Lawrence with Kleist.*

For Lawrence, the poet must be receptive to the chaos of life and to life's most gossamer threads. The idea of Cosby's poetry, as it is of Deleuze's philosophy, is to bring us back to our senses, and then beyond that, to the realm of pure affects and concepts. To express the 'powerful nonorganic life' (WP: 182) that creates us and that we create and counter-actualize. In celebrating 'the chaotic splendour of suns' (Lawrence 2005: 113), both Crosby's poetry and Lawrence's introduction follow a poetics that asks for an immanence in a living chaos. In his lectures on Spinoza, Deleuze links Lawrence directly to a philosophy of immanence. 'There are many Englishmen who are pantheists. I'm thinking of Lawrence. He had a cult of the sun' (Lecture, 24.03.81).

Deleuze's Spinozist reading of Lawrence traces Spinoza's theory of the three kinds of knowledge, which Deleuze relates to three modes in which humans relate to the sun: actual, virtual and immanent. The first mode, which is corporeal and actual, relates to Spinoza's notion of inadequate perception. 'There are people on the beach, but they don't understand, they don't know what the sun is, they live badly. If they were to understand something of the sun, after all, they would come out of it more intelligent and better. But as soon as they put their clothes back on, they are as scabby [*teigneux*] as before' (Lecture, 24.03.81). A purely actual, affective (*affection*) relation to the sun, which relates to Spinoza's first knowledge, concerns only the realm of extension. In relation to the complementarity of the photon as both particle and wave, it concerns only its character as a particle. This is why Deleuze talks explicitly of 'the corpuscules of sun, the corpuscules of heat act on my skin' and produce a 'mixture of bodies' (Lecture, 24.03.81). 'The "I" in "I like the heat" is an I that expresses relations of extensive parts of the vasoconstrictive and vasodilative type, that expresses itself directly in an external determinism putting the extensive parts in play. In that sense these are *particles* that act on my particles and the effect of one on the other is a pleasure or a joy. That's the sun of the first kind of knowledge, which I translate under the naïve formula "oh the sun, I love that." In fact, these are extrinsic mechanisms of my body that play, and the relations between parts, parts of the sun and parts of my body' (Lecture, 24.03.81, emphasis added). The actual level also refers to the body as that upon which outside forces impinge. 'An affection is what? In a first determination, an affection is the following: it's a state of a body insofar as it is subject to the action of another body. What does this mean? "I feel the sun on me", or else "A ray of sunlight falls upon you"; it's an affection of your body. What is an affection of your body? Not the sun, but the action of the sun or the effect of the sun on you' (Lecture, 24.01.78). An actual relation to the sun alone is inadequate to an understanding of the functioning of the world. 'One could say that affection-ideas are representations of effects without their causes, and it's precisely these that Spinoza calls inadequate ideas' (Lecture, 24.01.78). It concerns a passive life; a life of passions. 'I would say that the perception that I have of heat is a confused [inadequate] perception, and from it come affects which are themselves passions: "I'm hot!" At the level of the proposition "I'm hot!", if I try to distribute the Spinozist categories, I would say: an external body acts on mine. It's the sun. That is to say that the parts of the sun act on the parts of my body. All of that is pure external determinism, it's like the shocks of particles' (Lecture, 24.03.81).

In the next step, which corresponds to Spinoza's second knowledge, Deleuze shifts to virtual registers, and thus from the actions of many external particles to the virtual relations between these particles. In Humean terms, this shift marks the passage from terms to relations, in photonic terms, that from particles to waves. The mode of life is 'no longer essence insofar as it actually possesses an infinity of extensive parts, it's essence insofar as it expresses itself in a relation' (Lecture, 24.03.81). In this state, the sun is virtual and active. 'I am no longer in the effect of particles of sun on my body, I am in another domain, in compositions of relation. And at this very moment . . . I am not far from being able to say, "the sun, I am something of it." I have a relation of affinity with the sun. This is the second kind of knowledge' (Lecture, 24.03.81). Even a virtual relation to the sun, however, is not enough. The actual (particles: what a body can do) and the virtual (waves: what a mind can do) need to be aligned according to the logic of complementary and thus to be comprehended by the world. Only Spinoza's third knowledge of the sun concerns the sun of immanence: *Spinoza on the beach*.

'What would the third kind be? Here Lawrence abounds. In abstract terms it would be a mystical union. It's that at the level of the third kind one arrives at this mode of intrinsic distinction. It's here that there is something irreducibly mystical in Spinoza's third kind of knowledge . . . the rays by which the sun affects me are the rays by which I affect myself, and the rays by which I affect myself are the rays of the sun that affect me. It's solar auto-affection' (Lecture, 24.03.81). As Deleuze remarks, 'in words this has a grotesque air, but understand that at the level of modes of life it's quite different. Lawrence develops these texts on this kind of identity that maintains the internal distinction between his own singular essence, the singular essence of the sun, and the essence of the world' (Lecture, 24.03.81). At this point, the sun, which has taken the place of Spinoza's God, affects and expresses itself through its attributes and modes.

In *Expressionism in Philosophy*, Deleuze relates this third knowledge, which has to do with 'pure intensities', to what Spinoza calls 'beatitude' (310). As he notes in the lectures, 'if you arrive at a world of pure intensities, all these are supposed to agree with one another. At that moment, the love of yourself and at the same time, as Spinoza says, the love of things other than you, and at the same time the love of God, and the love God bears for Himself, etc. . . . What interests me in this mystical point is this world of intensities. There, you are in possession, not merely formally but in an accomplished way. It's no longer even joy, Spinoza finds the mystical word beatitude or active affect, that is to say the auto-affect. But this remains quite concrete. The third kind is a world of pure intensities' (Lecture, 24.01.78). It is here, in this accomplished rather than formal state, that Deleuze's philosophy becomes literally radiant: *beatitude on the beach*.

In *Nietzsche and Philosophy*, Deleuze had drawn a line of affirmation that goes from 'Lucretius' and 'Spinoza' (1983b: 190) to Nietzsche's notion of 'a thought that would affirm life instead of a knowledge that is opposed to life. Life would be the active force of thought, but thought would be the affirmative power of life. Both would go in the same direction. . . . Thinking would then mean discovering, inventing, new possibilities of life' (101): *luminous and light affirmation*.

Deleuze develops this line further in *Foucault*, which is another book pervaded by a conceptual luminism, Deleuze is fascinated by two of Foucault's conceptual gestures. The first is the topological problematization of the notions of inside and outside. He is even more fascinated by the second gesture, which concerns the way Foucault considers sound and light as the two media to which language and images are immanent. In loving detail, Deleuze traces how in Foucault's thought statements and visibilities emerge from these two media, which in turn emerge from the plane of immanence considered as a 'field of vectors' (F: 7). Over long stretches, Deleuze's text is literally suffused with sound and light. 'Just as statements are curves before they are phrases and propositions, so scenes are lines of light before they become contours and colors' (67), he notes. 'The statement-curve integrates into language the intensity of the affects ... But visibilities must then also integrate these in a completely different way, into light' (66). The two media each form a 'diagram of forces' that is 'realized' in 'description-scenes and statement-curves' (67). Before individual knowledge and before an individual gaze, 'there is' light, and 'there is' language. There is 'a "there is" of light, a being of light or a light-being' (58). Everything that exists emerges from a luminous and sonorous multiplicity. 'Visibilities are not forms of objects, nor even forms that would show up under light, but rather forms of luminosity which are created by the light itself and allow a thing or object to exist only as a flash, sparkle or shimmer' (45). Already in 'Michel Foucault's Main Concepts', which is the conceptual blueprint for *Foucault*, Deleuze had claimed that Foucault 'paints the most beautiful paintings of light in philosophy and traces unprecedented curves of utterances' (TRM: 260). This, in fact, is the difference between representational and, in Spinozist terms, conventional and expressive signs. While the former have cut the genetic cord between themselves and the given planes of luminosity and sound, the latter trail the luminous and sonorous planes of immanence behind.

In an extended passage on William Faulkner as 'literature's greatest "luminist"' (F: 68), Deleuze relates light to literature. As Faulkner explains about the origin of his title *Light in August*, 'because in my country in August there's a – a – a peculiar quality to light, and that's what that title means' (1957: n.p.). In painting, Foucault's philosophical luminism has a correlative in the luminism of Delaunay, about whose work Deleuze notes in *Gilles Deleuze from A to Z* under the letter 'N for Neurology' that in it 'light itself forms figures, there are figures of light'. Delaunay paints figures that are 'formed by light, light figures. He paints light figures, and not – which is quite different – aspects that light takes on when it meets an object'. This is how Delaunay 'detaches himself from all objects, with the result of no longer creating paintings with any objects at all ... So, regarding the elimination of objects, Delaunay substitutes figures of pure light for rigid and geometric figures.'

Actual Colour: Pigment

Francis Bacon: The Logic of Sensation (1981)

Apart from his cinema books, *Francis Bacon: The Logic of Sensation*, which is the companion piece to *The Logic of Sense*, is Deleuze's most elaborate treatment of visuality. It is also the text in which Deleuze traces Bacon's strategy of erasing cultural clichés and putting informal diagrams in their place that I described in 'The History before History'. *The Logic of Sensation* is a book about colour and light. About colour and light rather than light and colour, because in classical figurative painting, the illusion of virtual light is created by means of actual colour. Neglecting for a moment that paintings themselves are only visible in light, the adequate painterly medium is colour, as in pigment. Its ontology: *first painting*.

As he does in *Cinema 1* and *Cinema 2*, in *The Logic of Sensation* Deleuze narrates the history of a medium along a specific conceptual problematic. This problematic is complementary to that of *The Logic of Sense* in that both books set an aesthetics of expression against one of representation. In *The Logic of Sense*, this representative aesthetics concerns the realm of 'denotation, manifestation and signification' (LS: 12). Although they concern different contexts, in both books Deleuze sets a poetics of asignification, sensation and intensity against a poetics of narrative and symbolic figuration. In *The Logic of Sensation* Deleuze stresses that 'painting has neither a model to represent nor a story to narrate' (2). In pictorial terms, the hand is set against the eye, and an optical haptics against a strictly optical optics. If the medium of painting cancels itself out as a medium when it becomes fully representative and figurative, a sensational painting highlights its medium. In terms of sensation, for instance, painterly violence is not 'the bogus violence of the represented or the signified' but rather 'the violence of sensation – in other words, of the act of painting' (xiv). As Deleuze and Guattari note in *What is Philosophy?*, 'the smile on the canvas is made solely with colors, lines, shadow, and light. If resemblance haunts the work of art, it is because sensation refers only to its material: it is the percept or affect of the material itself, the smile of oil, the gesture of fired clay, the thrust of metal' (166). In the luminism of figurative painting, which creates a world that seems to be made up entirely of light, we forget the painterly medium and its sensational registers; we forget pigment, that is, to concentrate, instead, on pictorial exegesis and hermeneutics; on the scene and the story it tells: *iconography and iconology*.

In opposition to a logic of representation and of sense, 'sensation is not qualitative and qualified, but has only an intensive reality, which no longer determines with itself representative elements, but allotropic variations. Sensation is vibration' (FB: 45). In other words, in an expressive poetics, affects are carried by the medium, while emotions are carried by the message. As 'the color system itself is a system of direct action on the nervous system' (52), it creates what Deleuze calls the '"pathic" (nonrepresentative) moment of the sensation' (12). The history of painting goes back and forth between two opposite vectors. '*Either toward the exposition of a purely optical space*, which is freed from its references to even a subordinate tactility ... or, *on the contrary, toward the imposition of a violent manual space*, which rebels against and suppresses the subordination, as in automatic writing' (127). These extremes, which also create new possibilities in that 'one could say that the optical space has itself liberated new tactile values (and also the reverse)' (131), apply similarly to figurative and non-figurative art. In the latter, they apply to the optics of abstract painting as set against the haptics of abstract expressionism, although the two extremes again allow for in-between states. Bacon's aesthetics of abstract figuration, which denotes a strategy of figuration minus its adherent logic of representation, complicates the registers that define the difference between the former's optical abstraction and the latter's allover haptics. Bacon's art is set in a doubly in-between state. Between figuration and abstraction, as well as between optical and haptic space.

'It is in the triptychs that colors become light, and that light divides itself into colors' (xiv), Deleuze notes in his introduction, stressing that in the triptychs what he calls Bacon's Figures are positioned within a diagrammatic rather than a representative space; in a 'milieu [that] is no longer anything but light and color' (84). If in figurative and representational portraits the figures tend to be surround by attributes and representational space – even if that space is to a large degree diagrammed, as in Rembrandt or baroquely dark Spanish portraits of the seventeenth century – Bacon's Figures are surrounded by a fully diagrammed space that consists solely of coloured pigment. Across the spatial divide provided by its format, which sets both the Figures and the background apart from each other, the triptychs are allovered by the 'luminous or colored vivacity' (84) of the continuous informal diagram that forms their background. 'This then is the principle of the triptychs: the maximum unity of light and color for the maximum division of Figures' (84).

In his descriptions of these Figures and their pigmental milieu Deleuze is at his most poetic. In the triptychs, 'it is the separation of bodies in universal light and universal color that becomes the common fact of the Figures, their rhythmic being, the second "matter of fact" or the union that separates. A joining-together separates the Figures and separates the colors – such is light. The Figure-beings separate while falling into the black light. The color-fields separate while falling into the white light. Everything becomes aerial in these triptychs of light; the separation itself is in the air. Time is no longer in the chromatism of bodies; it has become a monochromatic eternity' (84–5; see also 'dark light' in TP: 228).

In this interplay, *The Logic of Sensation* is a book about 'white light' and 'black light' and about the play of light and darkness. This is why Deleuze would probably have liked the work of Pierre Soulages, in which light is derived from the blackest of reflective surfaces. In *Black: The Brilliance of a Non-Color*, Badiou uses Soulages' notion of beyond black (*Outrenoir*) to develop a dark ontology and a specific form of Badioublack that is less ultrablack or beyond black as it is a Realblack. Like the Lacanian Real, Badioublack 'consolidates one of its great affirmative functions: marking the location of what exists only by lacking' (2017: 73). It is the colour of satanic negation, Badiou notes. 'The pure soul clad in white says: *Vade retro, Satanas!* Which is proof of the primacy of black Satan, whom purity, clothed in white as battle armor, struggles to fight' (47). In luminous terms, it is what zero is to mathematics: the zero of colour. 'Black is the absence of light and therefore the absence of any wavelength in the analysis of what black negates' (42). In terms of psychoanalysis, it evokes the dark continent and the navel of the dream. Ultimately, 'dark' designates 'what is lacking in perception so that nothing should be lacking in thought' (85). Badioublack is the ontological *oscuro* to Deleuze's ontological *chiaroscuro*. As the 'noncolor of painting', Badioublack 'is not the opposite of light but the basis for a light other than light' (50). It colours the Enlightenment in an ontological darkness, unleashing an 'infinite luminosity, the new luminosity, latent in black' (51). Against the ontological dark, the phantasm of light; against death, the phantasm of life, 'some childish idolizing of Mother Nature, of the goddess Gaia, leads you straight to "the shadowy underside of the creation," to the blackness of which nature's greenery is both the product and the mask' (90). As in the correspondence between Deleuze and Badiou, there is no common ground. Badiou's black ontology is nothing like Deleuze's luminous ontology. Badiou's black light is the opposite of Deleuze's black light or Nietzsche's abyss of light.

While the play of light and darkness is Deleuze's shorthand for the milieu and for haptic space, the contour is Deleuze's shorthand for figuration and optical space. In short, while in classical figurative art the contour is in the service of representation and thus narrative, in Bacon 'the contour is in the service of vibration' (73) and thus of affect. 'It is as if the duality of the tactile and the optical were surpassed visually in this haptic function born of the diagram' (161), Deleuze notes. The viewer's affect and sensation are actualized in the haptic, close-vision aspect of the surface of the pigment. While the logic of representation plays itself out in the *chiaroscuro* of 'the "free" or disembodied play of light and color' (35), according to the formula of signification and narration, the logic of expressionism plays itself out, according to the formula of sensation, in the field of colour. 'Color is in the body, sensation is in the body, and not in the air. Sensation is what is painted' (35). This *chiaroscuro* is different from the *chiaroscuro* of philosophy in that painting puts it into the service of a regime of representation. As asignifying, corporeal sensation is quantitative rather than qualitative, which sets the actual, affective chromatism of colour against the *chiaroscuro* of a representative scene that erases chromatic affect. 'If it is true that relations of value, modeling in chiaroscuro, or the modulation of light appeal to a purely optical function of distant vision, the modulation of color, on the contrary, recreates a properly haptic function, in which the juxtaposition of pure tones arranged gradually on the flat surface forms a progression and a regression that culminates in a close vision' (132–3): *haptic philosophy.*

Painterly luminism, one might say, operates as if it were cinema. It submerges figures and stories in a narrative, luminous space made up entirely of the play of darkness and light. In stressing the relations of value between colours – rather than their tonality that I mentioned in talking about black and white affection and luminous affect – it creates a false, virtual light. 'It is through the oppositions of warm and cool tones that the colors used by the painter – without any absolute luminous quality in themselves – come to represent light and shadow' (133). In opposition, 'the painting of light or value ... conserves a menacing relation with a possible narration (we represent what we think we can touch, but we narrate what we see, what seems to be happening in the light or what we presume is happening in the shadows) in which narratives are enveloped' (134).

How, then, can painting evade narration and representation? For one, it can hollow luminism out from within. 'Luminism escapes from [the] danger of storytelling ... by taking refuge in a pure code of black and white, which raises inner space to an abstraction' (134). The other mode of escaping narration, which is by way of the asignifying, actual haptics of a chromatism of colour, is the more immediately painterly, and thus the more adequate mode. According to the analogical logic of painting, as opposed to the digital, coded language of literature, painting is continuous, as in undifferentiated: *pictorial chromatism.* It makes use of 'the analogical language of painting: if there is still molding by color, it is no longer even an interior mold, but a temporal, variable, and continuous mold, to which alone the name of modulation belongs, strictly speaking. There is neither an inside nor an outside, but only a continuous creation of space, the spatializing energy of color. By avoiding abstraction, colorism avoids both figuration and narration, and moves infinitely closer to the pure state of a pictorial "fact" which has nothing left to narrate. This fact is the constitution or reconstitution of a haptic function of sight' (134).

While optical space is the space of digital coding, in its chromatism haptic space is that of continuous sensation. It is only from within that chromatism that sensation can be painted. 'Light is time, but space is color. Painters we call "colorists" are those who tend to substitute relations of tonality for relations of value, and who "render" not only the form, but also shadow and light, and time, through these pure relations of color' (139). In painting, 'analogy finds its highest law in the treatment of colors. This treatment is opposed to relations of value, of light and shadow, of chiaroscuro. One consequence of this is that even black and white are liberated, they are turned into colors, so that black shadows acquire a real presence and white light acquires an intense clarity, which is diffused throughout all the ranges of color. But "colorism" is not opposed to relief, nor even to a drawn contour' (120): *Bacon*.

Colour, then, is the medium of painterly asignification, while colour used in the creation of the illusion of light is the medium of painterly signification. Crucially, this will be different in the cinema, in which light is the medium of asignification, while technicolour, or colour in general, might be said to be the medium of cinematic signification. This reversal shows that Deleuze is right in noting that 'it is through very different means that color is conquered in light, or that light attains color' (133).

In his comments on complementary colours, Deleuze flashes forward to the cinema books. Colour and space are to *Cinema 1* as light and time are to *Cinema 2*. Painting, as the more spatial rather than temporal narrative medium, stresses the actuality of pigment. 'Clarity no longer resides in the tangible form or the optical light, but in the incomparable flash produced by complementary colors. Colorism claims to bring out a peculiar kind of sense from sight: a haptic sight of color-space, as opposed to the optical sight of light-time' (139). A cinematic affect theory has developed from this differentiation, which finds a take-over of haptic colourism in a cinema that stresses close-ups and surfaces, as well as any other means by which it negates its representational register: *close-up, superficial optics*.

The footnote Deleuze inserts into the passage about the tonal values of complementary colours is important. It is taken from a letter by Vincent van Gogh to his brother. 'When the complementary colours are produced in equal strength, that is to say in the same degree of vividness and brightness, their juxtaposition will intensify them each to such a violent intensity that the human eye can hardly bear the sight of it.' As Deleuze comments, 'one of the principal interests of Van Gogh's correspondence is that Van Gogh turned color into a kind of initiatory experience, after a long trek through chiaroscuro, and black and white' (193). According to the painterly diagrammaticism of *The Logic of Sensation*, an aesthetics that is adequate to Deleuzian philosophy tends to centre on works of art that emerge from the field of non-human, non-artistic, anonymous affects and sensations. Everything perceives. 'Even when they are nonliving, or rather inorganic, things have a lived experience because they are perceptions and affections' (WP: 154). What is truly unformed lies at the imperceptible and unthinkable, pre-philosophical moment just before the informal diagram, which acts as its infinitesimally slowed-down witness. The diagram captures purely quantitative forces with only a minimum of qualification. As such, the gestures that create Bacon's diagrams are actualizations of the purely intensive movements of the plane of immanence, whose potentiality allows living beings to emerge: *abstract colourism*. This is how Bacon's painting is related to an anonymous life that is expressed by its Figures. All art that works from within informal diagrams is expressive rather than representative. Similarly, all signs that work from within diagrams are expressive rather than representative: *contour in the service of colourism*.

Bacon, one might say, is the Faulkner of painting, or: Faulkner is the Bacon of literature. In *Foucault*, Deleuze calls Faulkner one of literature's greatest luminists. Not a colourist. As Faulkner's medium is language, his writing emerges from the sonorous field, from the sound of language from which the literary image arises. That sound functions as a diagrammatic rendering of the milieu. In Faulkner, nothing is signifying symbol or allegory. The milieu is never black and white in terms of cultural signification. It is directly corporeal: *the colour of skin rendered as a literary sensation*.

Virtual Light: Celluloid

Cinema 1 (1983), Cinema 2 (1985)

If *The Logic of Sensation* approaches light and luminosity by way of colour, in the cinema books, it is the other way around. If painting deals in actual pigment, the cinema 'captures relations of light' (FB: 115). It approaches actual colour by way of virtual light and luminosity. As a medium, while painting is inherently colourist, the cinema is inherently luminist. In terms of the theory of colour and light, the painterly logic is subtractive and actual, although it can, from within the logic of actual pigment, create incredible effects of additive, virtual light, while the cinematic logic is additive and virtual. At the same time, the cinema also has an actual medium. While the actual medium of painting is pigment, the actual medium of the cinema was, until some decades ago, celluloid. While pigment embodies colour directly, celluloid film captures light. Today, when celluloid has been replaced by digital modes of capture, this at first sight puts the cinema, somewhat ironically, on the side of what Deleuze called, in *The Logic of Sensation*, digital coding rather than analog modulation. As that digital coding does not code a series of abstract elements, however, but rather luminous modulations, its digitality might be said to be in the service of an analog aesthetics.

In Deleuze's view, the cinema tends to follow, perhaps even more adequately so than painting, a narrative and representational logic. As with painting, however, there are ways to evade this logic. One of the ways to make cinematic images expressive has to do with the manipulation, or administration, of light; with the mode in which light is captured by celluloid. Obviously, there is no light in the celluloid in the sense that a film reel would glow in the dark. The film stock merely stores the chemical traces of the photons that hit the light-sensitive emulsion that is coated on the celluloid. This emulsion, which consists of insoluble, light-sensitive silver halide crystals that are dispersed in gelatin, functions as a medial substrate within the celluloid. The gelatin coating allows the subsequent chemical processing agents such as developer, fixer and toners, to enter the colloid without dislodging the crystals. The light that hits the emulsion is absorbed by and stored in chemical patterns that copy the initial pattern of the play of given light to which the silver halide crystals in the gelatin were exposed, and thus it creates, by way of the reversal of the latent images into the original images during the process of development, an analogous, chemical copy of the original economy and ecology of darkness and light. The emulsion transforms a natural, optical *chiaroscuro* into a chemical *chiaroscuro*. When the reel of celluloid is run through the movie projector, which replaces the luminosity provided by the sun with a technical source of light, the chemical circumstances are resurrected as once-again luminous circumstances: *chemical cinema.*

Both chemically and physically, with the passing of time, the medium that had more or less cancelled itself out in the original film becomes increasingly visible in that it deteriorates. As the ratio of that deterioration is fully contingent in relation to the narrative and the luminous patterns that are stored in the celluloided images, it functions as an increasingly dense layer of optical noise. The loss of meaning and signification caused by that chemical noise, however, is set off by a gain in the registers of both artwork-centred aesthetics and of *aisthesis*, defined by Alexander Gottlieb Baumgarten as the field of sensuous, affective judgements of taste [→ **Guattari 88**]. This gain in expressionism is inherent in what might be called the slow and persistent patination of light; a patination that is, as the material marker of its historicity, the inevitable effect of any object's presence in the material world. Dust settles on a canvas, lacquer loses its shine and transparency, chips of pigment flake off a painted surface, surfaces become brittle through the chemicals that make up acid rain. Colours fade. Cells deteriorate. Skin, like celluloid, becomes brittle. Although patination begins immediately after an object is introduced into and becomes part of the material world, it becomes visible only after a longer period of time, which is why it can be read as a marker of increased affect, but also, simultaneously, of aging and decay. Once it is exposed to the environment, chemical processes make it age. In fact, like a living body, the specific modes of deterioration of the celluloidal body are heavily dependent on the milieu in which it lives and with which it interacts.

From within this logic, how can the cinema escape the logic of representation? Bill Morrison's film *Light is Calling* (2004) consists of the cinematic administration of an old, deteriorated movie-reel that shows a scene from the 1926 movie *The Bells*. Morrison's poetics develop from the logic of celluloidal deterioration. Although one might initially think that his work consists simply of the given, found footage, for

Morrison, that found footage is a medium in the same way that found letters are the medium for the writer, found pigment for the painter, or found landscape for the land-artist. First, each frame is optically printed four times and stretch-printed at half exposure. This creates the movie's slow-motion effect. Then, a similarly stretched print is optically layered over the first, again at half exposure, so that each condensed frame is again as light as the original frame. This second layer is displaced by three frames, so that each frame 'would appear as the composite of two frames, either double exposed with an identical frame, or with an adjacent frame'. This makes for 'the film's unique pulsing blend' (personal email 02.06.15). After these optical alterations, the filmed figures seem to exist and act within or even behind the luminous layers of the deteriorated celluloid: *expressive light*.

The meeting of philosophy and the cinema takes place within a double contingency, as there is no information that travels between the two practices. While the practice of philosophy consists of the invention of virtual concepts, the practice of cinema consists of the creation of affective planes of luminous composition. If philosophy deals with the logic of embodied virtual sense, cinema deals with the logic of the virtualization of actual sensation. If philosophy thinks in concepts, the cinema 'thinks through affects and percepts' (WP: 66). Even while he aims to conceptually superpose philosophy and cinema, Deleuze is careful to always note the distinctions between the two fields. Cinema does cinema, philosophy does philosophy. At the same time, Deleuze and Guattari stress the complex set of resonances between the two practices. Within philosophy, concepts 'freely enter into relationships of nondiscursive resonance' (23). As they note, concepts are 'centers of vibrations ... This is why they all resonate rather than cohere or correspond with each other' (30). Such 'coadaptations' (82) also take place between the modes of thought of philosophy, art and science. Philosophy resonates with the cinema, just as the cinema resonates with philosophy. Although forms of thought never become identical, such resonances or also irritations are important because only the totality of resonating practices makes up the plane of the production of the new. 'It is at the level of the interference of many practices that things happen, beings, images, concepts, all the kinds of events' (C2: 280).

Before questions of individual style, before all differentiations into epochs and artistic media and before all schools of art, Deleuze favours art that is open to the plane of pure, singular affects, and that expresses, in human form, its immanence to this non-human, affective multiplicity: *luminist expressionism*. Painting emerges within the medium of pigment. In Foucault and Faulkner, writing emerges within the media of sound and vision. It is in the cinema, however, that the world can express itself in light, as the medium that is most adequate to it: *light is calling*.

Painting can evoke the white light of the plane of immanence only negatively or by contrast, as the absence of colour, or by way of the pigment called ultra white. In opposition, the cinema operates directly by and in light and as such, it participates directly in the optical plane of immanence, whose ultra white light it diffracts into a cinematic *chiaroscuro*. Symptomatically, it is in *Cinema 1* that Deleuze proposes that 'the plane of immanence is entirely made up of Light'. The protagonist of Jim Jarmusch's movie *The Limits of Control* (2009) flies Air Lumière, not only because the inventors of the cinema are called Lumière but also because light is the ultimate medium of the cinema. Derek Jarman's movie *Blue* (1993), which consists of one static shot of 'International Klein Blue', carries this inherent luminism to its limit. Without light, there is no cinema. It is for the same reason that a film-production company in Thomas Pynchon's novel *Vineland* is called 'Lux Unlimited' (1990: 370), and that in his novel *Against the Day* one of the characters moves to Hollywood because, as he notes, 'I want to know light ... I want to reach inside light and find its heart, touch its soul, take some of it in my hands whatever it turns out to be' (2006: 456). David Lynch is similarly enthralled by the luminous quality of Hollywood light when he notes 'I love Los Angeles ... The golden age of cinema is still alive there, in the smell of jasmine at night and the beautiful weather. And the light is inspiring and energizing ... It was the light that brought everybody to L.A. to make films in the early days' (2000: 31–2).

Whether in Hollywood or elsewhere, the ambient light that the cinema takes, administers and often intensifies by means of additional lighting, functions as a medium that is not only luminous but also voluminous. Douglas Sirk's melodramas, for instance, are literally soaked in a technicoloured and cinemascoped light. If one sometimes notes that people move as if they were under water, from Sirk's movies to Todd Haynes people often move as if they were under light: *in luce ambulant*.

Film studies usually reduce the question of light to questions of cinematic lighting and of characterization. By default, they tend to treat light as a technological or aesthetic element of the production of movies, similar to the way they tend to treat its characters as elements within a psychoanalytic field. What is less noted in film studies is that, beyond its symbolic and technological aspects, light is the ontological and epistemological medium of the cinema in the sense that it is the milieu within which the cinema quite literally embodies itself. The photonic plane is the optical plane of immanence and of composition of every filmic situation. If film studies lack both a photonic ontology and epistemology, Deleuze's cinema books provide precisely these two things.

Programmatically, *Cinema 1: The Movement-Image* and *Cinema 2: The Time-Image* describe movies as singular events or plays of light. In German, movies used to be called plays of light (*Lichtspiele*) and movie theatres houses of plays of light (*Lichtspielhäuser*); terms that stress that each movie emerges from within a photonic multiplicity and is, both during its production as well as in its later life, immanent to a constantly changing ambient light. This is why, especially when they are filmed on location, and despite the use of technical intermediaries such as additional lighting or coloured lenses, there are inherently Dutch or Italian movies. But then the differentiation into an inherently Dutch or Italian light is much too coarse. Every cinematic narrative is quite literally immanent to a very specific light, such as golden hour in Los Angeles on a specific summer day in 1978, or the cold, harsh light of a rainy New York morning on a specific day in 1984. In fact, each microsecond and each microsurface has its own light. In terms of Deleuze's reading of Bergson, the concept of white light was diffracted into an infinity of luminous nuances, which makes light the concrete universal of the cinema. In the same way that there are ultimately infinitely fine geographical differences in terms of ambient light, there are also infinitely fine temporal differences, such as the specific modulations of light at dusk and at dawn; light's incremental becoming darker or becoming lighter: *the twilight of the cinema*.

As assemblages of singular luminous events – perhaps each shot might be taken as an event of light, although each shot can again be broken down, *ad infinitum*, into ever smaller events of light – all movies form luminous planes of composition. In fact, movie-making might be described as taking light, understood as a luminous multiplicity of rays, and making it form itself by putting objects and people in its way. For the cinema, the given photonic multiplicity functions as its groundless ground; itself formless, it needs the 'proper form' (*Eigenform*) (Heider 2008: 323) of the objects it shines on to actualize itself. As I noted, one might say that the white, luminous multiplicity of light incarnates itself in objects in the same way that thought incarnates itself in a body. There is, then, a given luminosity with a continually modulated intensity, and there is that luminosity as incarnated in the surfaces of objects and people. In Deleuzian terms, there is a virtual light, and there is an actual light in which the virtual light embodies itself.

For artistic practices, the notion of a material medium has important ramifications. In fact, if one were to ask a sculptor about the essence of one of his or her figures, that essence would in the first place not be strength, beauty or pain, but rather marble, clay or wood. Because the strength would be a marbled strength, the beauty a clayed beauty and the pain a wooden pain. As Deleuze noted in *The Logic of Sensation*, a painted smile is made of oil. A smile drawn in crayon is made of coloured wax, charcoal or chalk. Similarly, in the cinema, the essence of a movie is not the narrative it tells, but the light in and by which that narrative is given. In every movie, every story emerges from, is told and falls back into shades of darkness and light. Light, then, is much more than a medium of representation. It does much more than merely provide the optical space in which a narrative unfolds. In terms of media studies, in optical arts such as the cinema and photography, light functions as both an informal and a formal medium of expression. In other words, for these arts, light is not only needed to make the work of art visible – something that also pertains to sculpture, painting or writing, except for braille – it is also, in terms of production, what marble, clay or wood are to the sculptor. With light as its ultimate medium, the cinema uses real objects and people, as well as material media such as celluloid, to allow light to incarnate itself and to allow luminous events to be stored. The result is situations that are made purely of light; in which light sculpts objects and people. Symptomatically, John Huston considered his films to be essays in light. In all of these contexts, the movement and the quality of the medium are important down to its smallest, most unconscious and imperceptible levels. The way a subtle shift in light can change a mood. The way a sound can bring a memory into consciousness. The way a shift in the electricity of the atmosphere can decide a long-standing historical conflict. The way a tiny point of hardness in the wood can create the specific expression of a face.

This, however, seems to contradict the fact that light, as an informal medium, has no quality. While this is true, there is a difference between structural and essential qualities. Although all media of perception are ideally formless, they have, like every medium, essential qualities, such as the quality of light to be luminous, that of sound to be sonorous, or that of wood to be of a specific hardness, grain and colour. Some events of light, for instance, are less luminous than others, some sounds are almost inaudible, and one block of wood is harder than another. When Heider talks about a loose coupling of elements, he is talking about a medium's ideal plasticity. And although the ratio of that plasticity is ontologically equal, it is empirically different with every medium. Pigment, for instance, is more plastic than marble, because it is more granular. When Heider talks about light as a medium without qualities, he is talking about this plasticity rather than about the specific medium's essential quality, which, in the case of light, is its luminosity. In terms of that luminosity, every luminous event or situation is assembled from what might be called pure events of light and luminosity.

Heider's proposition is to keep medium and form formally distinct. While Deleuze agrees, he also considers them to be, at the same time, ontologically identical. Media are invariably formed, and thus have specific qualities. At the same time, every form is invariably made up of a formless multiplicity. Light is a given plane of optical disparity that is given as given as the mode of the visibility of illuminated objects. The first aspect concerns a luminous ontology, the second a luminous phenomenology. When Rainer Werner Fassbinder notes that 'Sirk has said that one cannot make movies *about* something, one can only make movies *with* something, with people, with light, with flowers, with mirrors, with blood' (1992: 11), he is addressing both of these aspects. In Deleuzian terms, what Sirk maintains is that movies are not so much representative as they are expressive. Fassbinder goes on to note that Sirk also says that 'the light and the shot are the philosophy of the director' (11). If that is so, can one also say that the light and the shot are the aesthetics of the philosopher?

Cinema 1 and *Cinema 2* are fascinating books, but difficult to grasp. In fact, there is an almost surrealist beauty in how Deleuze superposes, in each text, several studies. The first concerns a cinematographic ontology that considers 'the universe as cinema in itself', as 'metacinema' (C1: 59). In that ontology, *Cinema 1*, which is modelled on Bergson's notion of the sensory-motor arc, covers the ontology of the actual world, while *Cinema 2*, which is modelled on Bergson's notion of the cone of memory, covers the ontology of the virtual world. This project is superposed onto a theory of subjectivation that treats real and cinematic subjectivation from within the same photonic registers. Centres of indetermination arise from the chaotic multiplicity of the photonic plane. A third project concerns a cinematographic epistemology that is ordered according to a luminous classification of cinematic images. The fourth project concerns a 'natural history' (N: 49) of the cinema, in which *Cinema 1* covers the time from its conception to the Second World War and *Cinema 2* the time from the post-war period up to 1985. No wonder that in this superposition, the books are difficult to navigate.

What the two cinema books do not provide is a ready-made scale by which to approach movies, or a fixed recipe for a Deleuzian reading of them, in the way that psychoanalysis or Marxism do. In this sense, they do not have a fixed cinematic programme. In fact, the books do not even answer the question of how a Deleuzian cinema might look, except in a very abstract sense. What they do provide, however, is a highly idiosyncratic conceptual field in which to position specific movies, scenes or even shots. In this field, the notion of genre can only be used as an attractor. 'A film is never made up of a single kind of image: thus we call the combination of the three varieties, montage. Montage (in one of its aspects) is the assemblage [*agencement*] of movement-images, hence the inter-assemblage of perception-images, affection-images and action-images. Nevertheless a film, at least in its most simple characteristics, always has one type of image which is dominant: one can speak of an active, perceptive or affective montage, depending on the predominant type' (C1: 70). As Deleuze notes about the difficulty of genre, 'neglecting differences of nature in favor of genres is like lying to philosophy' (DI: 34).

In *Matter and Memory* Bergson sets up the notion of matter that underlies Deleuze's cinematic ontology: 'Matter, in our view, is an aggregate of "images." And by "image" we mean a certain existence which is more than that which the idealist calls a *representation*, but less than that which the realist calls a *thing*; – an existence placed half-way between the "thing" and the "representation"' (1991: 9): *the Lucretian world of simulacra*.

From this in-between state of an ontological optics, Deleuze develops an ontological luminism according to which both the cinema and the world are equally made up of pure light and follow the same photonic logic. Deleuze's creation of a resonance between the logic of the world and the logic of the cinema is based on two complementary conceits that concern ontology and epistemology respectively. Images are electromagnetic formations within the photonic plane that humans experience as optical irritations and that they turn into images by way of the imagination. At the same time, humans are themselves nothing but photonic arrangements. Deleuze's question is about what follows, both philosophically and cinematographically, from these chiastic, complementary conceits: *the cinema as world* × *the world as cinema*.

In approaching the cinematic field defined as a conceptual set that designates the overall photonic field within which the production of movies is defined as a specific formation of the multiplicity of photons within the luminous world, Deleuze touches on something that film and media studies tend to ignore: the fact that the cinematic field not only comprehends the more or less clearly circumscribed space of the cinematographic representation of reality, but is also itself part of the overall photonic world, and as such part of the way this world expresses itself. Like philosophical sense, cinematic sensation is not about representation, but about an embodied expression. The cinema creates sensational compositions of figures of and in light.

The eclipse of the being-in-the-photonic-world of the cinema has been facilitated by the architecture of the classical movie theatre as a closed space that, like the second floor of the baroque house in *The Fold*, separates the projected movie as completely as possible from the world's overall optical multiplicity. It aims to exclude all optical irritations except those provided by the projected movie. While this optical closure stresses the projective character of both the cinema's and the spectators' psychic apparatus, which is why it has become a master trope for psychoanalysis, Deleuze's cinema is always conceptually open to the overall optical field around it. It is a desiring-machine rather than a dream-machine. Deleuze's cinematic analogy does not run between the technological and the psychic apparatus, but between the subject and the multiplicitous photonic field within which optical formations emerge. In other words, Deleuze's cinema is the philosophical version of a drive-in cinema, the challenge being to create both a drive-in philosophy and a drive-in life: *drive-in Deleuze*.

Deleuze's cinematic ontology and theory of subjectivation are conceptual *tours de force* that start, quite programmatically, with the image of a pure multiplicity: the universal, anonymous, white dance – what Bergson calls the 'undirected movement' – of photons in space. As the 'infinite set of all images' (C2: 59), this multiplicity constitutes the luminous plane of immanence; a field of 'universal variation, of universal undulation, universal rippling' (59). It is as such that Deleuze is asking the reader to imagine a world that is entirely made up of Light. As a '*machinic assemblage of movement-images*' (59), the cinematic world is a 'collection of lines or figures of light; a series of blocs of space-time' (61). In Bergsonian terms, the actualized photonic plane of immanence that in and of itself forms 'an indivisible continuity' (10), collapses into two aspects. The extensive aspect of particular photonic movements and their perturbations, and the intensive side of energetic waves and their patterns of interference: actual and virtual. In spatial parameters, the photonic plane is the plane of the world as 'any-location-whatever' (7); the given, anonymous space of the rainy sidewalk or the lonely hotel room in which Fred Astaire develops his dance routines, or the empty hotel lobby that is animated by Christopher Walken in Spike Jonze's 'Fatboy Slim' video 'Weapon of Choice'. In analogy, in temporal registers the photonic plane is the plane of 'any-instant-whatever', which 'can be regular *or* singular, ordinary *or* remarkable' (6). It is the plane of temporal bifurcations and of the creation of 'the new' (7). Optically, it is the open set of all images. 'The set of all these sets forms a homogeneous continuity, a universe or a plane . . . of genuinely unlimited content' (16). Ontologically, it is the overall field of optical disparity that is defined by a 'total, objective and diffuse perception' (64): *perception in Venus' diffuse light.*

An obstacle to a cinematic ontology is that Bergson differentiates between life and the movies. While the former is continuous and dynamic, the latter is discontinuous and static. Deleuze deals with this difference early on in *Cinema 1*. The Bergsonian logic is well-rehearsed. A movie consists of twenty-four equidistant stills that produce the perceptual illusion of movement when they are run through a projector with sufficient speed. In what Deleuze identifies as the first of Bergson's cinematographic theses, Bergson opposes this 'cinematographic illusion' of continuity – a 'false movement' (C1: 1) that is created from immobile sections or cut-out images, from optical stutterings one might say – to a truly continuous, living movement. Bergson maintains that while the quasi-movement of the cinema is based on the fast succession of discrete stills (*temps*), the movement of life is continuous (*durée*): 'movement is distinct from the space covered. Space covered is past, movement is present, the act of covering. The space covered is divisible, indeed infinitely divisible, whilst movement is indivisible' (1). Bergson's first thesis proposes a conceptual gap, and it entails a judgement between the two movements. Living movement is indivisible and continuous, while cinematic movement is falsely continuous because 'you cannot reconstitute movement with positions in space or instants in time: that is, with immobile sections' (1). At this point, Bergson argues on the background of the by now familiar recursive logic according to which true movement always takes place on what Deleuze calls a line of flight between two instantaneous stills. 'You can bring two instants or two positions together to infinity: but the movement will always occur in the interval between the two.' This operation is infinitely recursive because 'however much you divide and subdivide time, movement will always occur in a concrete duration' (1), in-between the stills. Philosophically, these stills figure chronic being and affections, while true movements figure aionic becoming and affects.

In a direct reference to the Dedekind cut, Bergson argues in *La pensée et le mouvant*, 'from movement, the intelligence only retains a series of positions: a point reached, another one, and then still another one. If one objects to reason that something is happening between these points, it immediately inserts new positions, and so on, up to infinity. He averts his gaze from the transition. If we insist it attempts to push mobility back into always smaller intervals, corresponding to an increasing larger number of inserted positions, until it retreats more and more, and finally seems to vanish in the infinitely small' (1969: 9).

In his first thesis, therefore, Bergson uses the cinema to differentiate between cinematic perception (*Momentaufnahmen*) and lived intuition, which captures 'the spirit, duration, pure change' (20). Cinema rests on perception and cognition posing as intuition. By way of its speed, film simulates intuition. This intuition, however, is fake. In the difference between cognition and intuition, Bergson situates not only that of *temps* and *durée* but also that of a simple cinematic unrolling, and of a lived evolution; a differentiation that also separates the inanimate and the animate. An artificial, fake and dead movement is staked against a natural, true, lived movement.

It would be difficult to develop a theory of the world as cinema from this thesis. It is, therefore, Bergson's second thesis on the cinema that Deleuze turns to, and that truly resonates with his philosophy. According to this second thesis, the cinematographic logic, with its freezing of a lived movement – it literally brings about 'a cooling down of the plane of immanence' (63) – is no longer set against the processes of natural perception and life. Rather, it is now seen as their recapitulation. If one looks closely, perception 'does the same' (2) as the cinema in that perceptual systems cut up continuous sets of irritations into discrete data. In other words, both natural perception and natural life are not at all natural in the sense that that would be in any way immediate or continuous. They are machinic in the same way nature is machinic rather than natural. Ultimately, perception and life create, like the cinema does, montages.

According to Bergson's second thesis, then, perception and life operate cinematically. The imagination covers the architecture of perceptual and biomaterial cuts with sheets of quasi-continuous images that are projected in a way similar to how the movie projector animates single stills into quasi-continuous movement. In fact, one might define schizophrenia, as well as the logic of Zen Buddhism, cinematically as a slowing down of the imagination until only the still body without organs remains. We 'lack in general a particle of the East, a grain of Zen' (DII: 90), Deleuze notes. Movement, then, 'is both: not only is the instant an immobile section of movement, but movement is a mobile section of duration, that is, of the Whole, or of a whole'

(C1: 8). Actual *temps* and virtual *durée* operate as two complementary registers: *crystal cinema; crystal life.*

In terms of the history of the cinema, Deleuze identifies the shift from Bergson's first thesis to his second thesis with the coming alive of the camera at the moment that it, and with it the cinematic world, begins itself to move. While the first thesis concerned the montage of still images within which figures move, the second concerns a montage in which figures move within images that are themselves moving. The static montage of in themselves static shots is taken over by the animated montage of inherently moving and moved shots. Griffith versus Welles, the cinematic collage of *The Birth of a Nation* versus the fluidity of the opening shots of *The Lady from Shanghai*. Historically, then, the difference between Bergson's two theses falls into the interval between a static camera as the time of the first thesis and of images in movement, and a moving camera, as the time of the second thesis and of movement-images. As Deleuze states, 'we can therefore define a primitive state of the cinema where the image is in movement rather than being movement-image. It was at this primitive state that Bergson's critique was directed' (24).

With a moving, a literally animated camera, the montage makes up a both locally and globally moving whole. It is only at this point that the cinema begins to truly resonate with the concept of a moving, animated world, of a living phylum within which perception and life operate, and to which they remain immanent. Both the camera, as the perceptual relay between the world and the image, as well as the material world, come alive: the camera gains an inherent *appetitus*: *As the cinema comes alive, life becomes cinematic.*

Deleuze's description of how planes of consistency emerge from the photonic plane of immanence is a loving, slow-motion account of how individual, actual movement-images and their virtual time-images emerge from the plane of pure light. From within cinematic registers, it recapitulates the genetic logic of the emergence of living beings from the plane of anonymous life. In cinematic terms, the question about the genesis of living beings concerns, in *Cinema 1*, the difference between an image in movement and a 'movement-image' (2). Centres of indetermination emerge within the multiplicity of the photonic plane of immanence. Mathematically, the photonic multiplicity – the cinema of the world – is the open set that contains all other sets. The identity of the cinema and of the world lies in that both cinematic and worldly entities result from cuts into that photonic plane. These cuts separate them from the allover milieu. Living beings separate themselves from their milieu through framings, such as, on the level of perception, those provided by the senses that register only reduced spectra of photonic intensity and fields of vision, or, on the level of cognition, those provided by specific decisions and cognitive bifurcations. On the biomaterial level, these framings concern the construction of borders and membranes; the creation of skins. On the background of the material modulations and of differentiations of and within this photonic multiplicity, *Cinema 1* describes the gradual composition of living beings as themselves nothing but aggregates made up of movement-images and their differen*t*/*c*iations.

It is not a simple organicism, therefore, when Deleuze notes that movies are assembled, like living beings, by way of the separation of a number of optical sets from an allover set of images. This is 'an operation which is exactly described as a framing: certain actions undergone are isolated by the frame . . . executed reactions are no longer immediately linked with the action which is undergone' (62). The cinematic shot 'relates movement [in a set] to a whole which changes' (22) on the cinematic plane of composition in the same way in which the movement of a local system is related to the overall plane of consistency. Because everything is connected to everything else within the overall set, 'each time there is a translation of parts in space, there is also a qualitative change in a whole' (8). In fact, no set is ever fully closed because it retains a direct structural relation to the out-of-field. This is shown, for instance, when an *acousmatic* voice enters the image from the off. 'A closed system is never absolutely closed; but on the one hand it is connected in space to other systems by a more or less "fine" thread, and on the other hand it is integrated or reintegrated into a whole which transmits a duration to it along this thread . . . a duration which is immanent to the whole universe' (17). In actual fact, 'sets are closed, and everything which is closed is artificially closed' (9). In terms of energy and resonance, 'each time there is a translation of parts in space, there is also a qualitative change in a whole' (8): *ecological cinema*.

Although each set is operationally closed off from the allover photonic milieu, and although 'the whole is neither given nor giveable' to either the movie or the living system because 'it is the Open, and because its nature is to change constantly' (9), all movement-images remain immanent to the allover photonic field as 'a pure ceaseless becoming' (10). For both Bergson and Deleuze, then, the open, photonic plane of immanence forms the conceptual ground for the conceit that living beings and movies are multiplicitous sets within a larger set of allover multiplicity. 'The model would be rather a state of things which would constantly change, a flowing-matter in which no point of anchorage nor centre of reference would be assignable. On the basis of this *state of things* it would be necessary to show how, at any point, centres can be formed which would impose fixed instantaneous views. It would therefore be a question of "deducing" conscious, natural *or* cinematographic perception' (57–8, emphasis added).

The given photonic multiplicity runs through any seemingly closed system at the speed of light. 'It is rather a gaseous state. Me, my body, are rather a set of molecules and atoms which are constantly renewed. Can I even speak of atoms? They are not distinct from worlds, from interatomic influences. It is a state of matter too hot for one to distinguish solid bodies in it. It is a world of universal variation, of universal undulation, universal rippling: there are neither axes, nor centre, nor left, nor right, nor high, nor low ... This infinite set of all images constitutes a kind of plane [*plan*] of immanence ... It is a set, but an infinite set. The plane of immanence is the movement ... which is established between the parts of each system and between one system and another, which crosses them all, stirs them all up together and subjects them all to the condition which prevents them from being absolutely closed' (59). This diverse, anonymous optical field is moving infinitely fast. Like the photon, it has no mass as it is never at rest. Both materially and perceptually, systems cut into this field, reducing its intensive multiplicity to the multiplicity of forms and data respectively. As he did in *Bergsonism* and in 'On Gilbert Simondon', Deleuze stresses that these reductions do not originate in the entity. Rather, the entities are themselves the result of their specific perceptual reductions and decelerations. In luminous and cinematic terms, this reduction involves a darkening. 'In short, it is not consciousness which is light, it is the set of images, or the light, which is consciousness, immanent to matter. As for *our* consciousness of fact, it will merely be the opacity without which light "is always propagated without its source ever having been revealed"' (C1: 61). To express light, we put ourselves into its path.

In this reversal of the position of the optical logic that defines the Enlightenment, human consciousness has to be subtracted from the ideal of pure light. If the photonic plane of immanence is defined by the dance of photons in constant, infinitely fast movement – pure light, like pure events – the cinema of the human world is an obscured and decelerated art. The vector goes from 'objective perception which is indistinguishable from the thing, to a subjective perception which is distinguished from it by simple elimination or subtraction' (64). In optical terms, living entities darken the plane of pure, white light – the total luminosity of the optical plane – by contracting elements of the overall optical set of intensities into singularized colour spectra; into individually perceived image architectures. Like the movie theatre, the living entity is a darkened space. As perceptually and cognitively clear images are subtractions from the pure intensity of white light, they are, as Deleuze noted in *The Fold*, in themselves obscure: *the clearer, the more obscure*. From the point of view of perception, the conceptual and the optical universes are always already imagined and thus obscured surfaces.

It is fitting for Deleuze's discussion, which covers the full spectrum from the purely material movement of things to the immaterial movement of thought, that the term *kinema* denotes both physical as well as affective movement, because within the plane of immanence, bodies are defined by both of these levels. 'On the plane of consistency, *a body is defined only by a longitude and a latitude*: in other words the sum total of the material elements belonging to it under given relations of movement and rest, speed and slowness (longitude); the sum total of the intensive affects it is capable of at a given power or degree of potential (latitude). Nothing but affects and local movements, differential speeds' (TP: 260). If the perceptual system is completely molecularized and deterritorialized, it literally dissolves into the photonic plane of movement-images. It becomes once more anonymous. 'In the final analysis, we would have to speak of a perception which was no longer liquid but gaseous. For, if we start from a solid state, where molecules are not free to move about (molar or human perception), we move next to a liquid state, where the molecules move about and merge into one another, but we finally reach a gaseous state, defined by the free movement of each molecule' (C1: 84). *Cinema 1* is about the actuality of corporeal movement and the actuality of physical change. Fittingly, its theoretical and philosophical reference within the Bergsonian frame is the actuality of the sensory-motor arc, whose conceptual registers are movement and space. In *Cinema 1*, time is part of the equation only as an attribute or an aspect of movement.

At some point in *Cinema 1*, Deleuze's account of the genesis of movement-images turns into an account of the Bergsonian sensory-motor arc that models the actual modes of their corporeal operations. Following that arc's vector from sensory irritation to motoric action – from impression to expression – *Cinema 1* provides an optical narrative of an entity's nervous conversion of irritations coming from the anonymous set of pure movement-images into corresponding actions. 'All things considered, *movement-images divide into three sorts of images when they are related to a centre of indetermination as to a special image*: perception-images, action-images and affection-images. And each one of us ... is nothing but an assemblage [*agencement*] of three images, a consolidate [*consolide*] of perception-images, action-images and affection-images' (66).

Within this vector, Deleuze identifies a number of conceptual stills that define particular moments within a general typology of cinematic images. Cinematic images are defined by the position they hold within the physical vector of the sensory-motor arc from irritation to action. Deleuze correlates a typology and history of the cinema and its images with the vector of perception, somewhat like Leibniz correlates mathematics and perception. It is doubtful that there has ever been a more daring thesis on the cinema. Corporeally, the vectorial movement of the sensory-motor arc starts when quantities of exterior stimuli impinge upon a system from the outside. It then charts the nervous perception of these stimuli, their corporeal affects, their relations to the drive and further to the qualities of cognitive processes. It ends in motor responses, which means in movements or actions. In general terms, the arc charts the vector from stimulus to response.

How does Deleuze transpose this arc into the cinema? If the photonic plane of immanence as pure light is defined by the white dance of photons in constant, infinitely fast movement, the pure movement-image designates the anonymous movements on this plane, while the perception-image designates the movement-image as related to 'a center of indetermination' (64); as an irritation of a living, perceptual entity. It denotes the moment when it is first perceived, as well as the logic of this perception. 'When it is related to a centre of indetermination, it becomes *perception-image*' (64). From this moment onwards, the conceptual ground is the plane of immanence as the plane of consistency.

Deleuze's next conceptual still on the arc is the affection-image, which designates the image as experienced on the inside of the perceptual system where it triggers 'a kind of motor tendency on a sensible nerve' (66). The action-image marks the end of the vector: 'the delayed reaction of the center of indetermination' to the initial stimulus. Within the arc, 'perception is . . . one side of the gap, and action is the other side' (64). The gap itself follows the logic of the affection-image. In conceptual slow-motion: if the pure movement-image denotes any modulation of the anonymous photonic plane of immanence whatever, the shift from the movement-image to the perception-image marks a first discontinuity; a first montage that cuts the world into two spaces and two times. 'What happens and what can happen in this acentered universe where everything reacts on everything else [pure causes]? . . . at any point whatever of the plane an *interval* appears – a gap between the action and the reaction.' Although 'this phenomenon of the interval is only possible in so far as the plane of matter includes time' (61), this temporality is a chronic one. It is a time of delay that is subordinated to the logic of nervous response. 'Executed reactions are no longer immediately linked with the action which is undergone. By virtue of the interval, these are delayed reactions, which have the time to select their elements, to organise them or to *integrate* them' (62, emphasis added). The world of nervous responses and both unconscious and conscious cognitions inscribes itself into this interval. 'By virtue of the interval, these are delayed reactions, which have the time to select their elements, to organise them or to integrate them into a new movement which is impossible to conclude by simply prolonging the received excitation' (62).

The logic of the sensory-motor arc is one of the reasons why Deleuze considers brains as nothing but intervals that cut into and slow down a both temporal and systemically immediate intensive relation. The logic of this operation follows once more the recursive logic of the Dedekind cut. 'And the brain is nothing but this – an interval, a gap between action and reaction . . . Even at the level of the most elementary living beings one would have to imagine micro-intervals. Smaller and smaller intervals between more and more rapid movements' (63): *smaller and smaller brains*.

Within the logic of the sensory-motor arc, the impulse-image and the affect-image are especially interesting because they lie in the interval between perception and action, and thus embody the milieu between unconscious, originary worlds (the plane of production and intensity) and conscious, derived milieus (the plane of reproduction, meaning and cognition). In terms of aesthetics, they are naturalist images. As Deleuze notes apropos Émile Zola, 'he had the idea of making real milieux run in parallel with originary worlds ... This is the essential point; the two will not let themselves be separated and do not take on distinct form' (124). The originary world 'only exists and operates in the depths of a real milieu, whose violence and cruelty it reveals. But at the same time the milieu only presents itself as real in its immanence in the originary world, it has the status of a "derived milieu", which receives a temporality as destiny from the originary world' (125). The originary world 'does not exist independently of the determinate milieux, but conversely makes them exist with characteristics and features which come from above, or rather, from a still more terrible depth ... Milieux constantly emerge from the originary world and retreat into it' (125–6). Almost always, in fact, realism contains, deep within it, a naturalist tendency, although it does not directly address the specific problematics that define naturalism, nor its cinematic equivalents, which, according to Deleuze's typology in *Cinema 1*, are the perception-image, the affect-image and the impulse-image.

On the surface, however, realism is mostly interested in the level of subjects, their culturally practised and programmed feelings and emotions, and with the actions that result from these. Its cinematic equivalent, therefore, is the action-image. 'Affects and impulses ... appear as embodied in behaviour, in the form of emotions or passions which order and disorder it. This is Realism' (141). Precisely because it excludes the anonymous, driven level of originary worlds, realism can easily include unrealistic spaces and elements, such as 'the fantastic, the extraordinary, the heroic and above all melodrama' (141), at least as long as the derived milieu remains undisturbed and unaffected by these intrusions. As long as they remain separated. 'What constitutes realism is simply this: milieux and modes of behaviour, milieux which actualise and modes of behaviour which embody' (193).

In terms of the sensory-motor arc, the aesthetics of naturalism are situated nearer to the perception-image than those of realism, which tends to follow the aesthetics of the action-image, which is situated at the end-point of the sensory-motor vector. In opposition to realist cinema, which portrays predominantly the complexity of derived milieus and which tends to repress the more driven, impulsive aspects of reality, naturalism evolves out of the feedback loops between the two worlds. It 'refers simultaneously to four co-ordinates: originary world/derived milieu; impulses/modes of behaviour. Let us imagine a work in which the derived milieu and the originary world are really distinct and well-separated. Although they may have all kinds of correspondences, it would not be a naturalist work' (125). Symptomatically, when realists such as Henry James become, at certain privileged moments in their work, naturalistic, they tend to do so under the shadow of the tropes of madness or death, according to the formula that naturalism can think a relation between the two milieus only from within the entropic dynamics of a general degradation.

In Lucretian registers, naturalist film evolves from within the shadow of the *clinamen*; showing, *en miniature* or metonymically, the inclination of a whole universe from birth to death. 'Naturalist time seems to be under an inescapable curse ... It is therefore inseparable from an entropy, a degradation' (126). Because of this inclination, naturalism can 'only grasp the negative effects of time; attrition, degradation, wastage, destruction, loss, or simply oblivion' (127). It is always within these inherently degraded registers that realism encounters the originary world. The inherent degradation is the reason for naturalism's inherent violence. It brings the subjects into closer and closer proximity to the drives and thus to the impulse-image. The fields of the driven and the impulsive form the reservoir of the energy or life-force that motivates naturalist plots and that bleeds into specific derived milieus, where they replace the cultural organization with the splendour and terror of an unbridled, excessive force; the terrifying and exhilarating beauty of degradation: the categorical monomania of the impulse. Naturalism implies a universal becoming-animal. 'The characters are like animals: the fashionable gentleman a bird of prey, the lover a goat, the poor man a hyena. This is not because they have their form or behaviour, but because their acts are prior to all differentiation between the human and the animal. These are human animals' (123–4).

Naturalist figures such as McTeague in Frank Norris's novel *McTeague*, which served as the model for Erich von Stroheim's movie *Greed*, embody, almost archetypically, these two characteristics, in charting 1. the 'originary violence' of an impulse that spreads over and 'gradually penetrates a given milieu, a derived milieu, which it literally exhausts in a long process of degradation' (C1: 136), and 2. the chronological degradation of this world. While McTeague's derived milieu, which functions as the 'medium' (124) for the movie's specific originary world, is the world of nineteenth-century capitalism, the originary world – which is permeated by 'energies which do not "organise"' (125) people and which follows the *'line of the steepest slope'* (136) that irrupts within the derived milieu and quite literally floods it – is that of pure greed and its mirror-image: avarice. 'The naturalist image, the impulse-image, has in fact two signs: symptoms, and idols or fetishes. Symptoms are the presence of impulses in the derived world, and idols and fetishes, the representation of the fragments' (125).

If one looks at the cinema books as complementary, *Cinema 1* is related to *temps*, in that it deals predominantly with the material aspect of the photonic plane, with actual individuation and with the actual passage from irritation to action. The overall focus of *Cinema 1* is the actual and processes of actualization: the actualization of perceptual systems through operations of contraction, resonance and rhythm.

Cinema 2 deals with the immaterial aspect of the photonic plane and the virtual ontology of the time-image. It sets the virtual passages in memory and duration against those of actual perception. Its theoretical and philosophical reference is no longer Bergson's sensory-motor arc but his cone of memory. More precisely: if *Cinema 1* positioned the typology and the history of the cinema before the Second World War within the sensory-motor arc, *Cinema 2* positions the post-war cinema within the sheets of memory that make up Bergson's cone of memory. *Cinema 2*, then, provides the complementary virtual ontology and epistemology to the actual ontology and epistemology of *Cinema 1: perceptual, chronic strobe; Cinema 2: mnemonic, virtual glow*.

The conceptual registers of the trajectory of time-images are movements in time. Now, movement enters the equation only as an attribute and an aspect of time. *Cinema 2* traces the virtual and processes of virtualization, the virtualization of the perceptual system, the virtuality of a-corporeal time and of temporal processes: the chronological, aionic world. In analogy to the anonymous movement of a spatial multiplicity of photonic particles that opens *Cinema 1*, *Cinema 2* opens with an image of the anonymous movement of a temporal multiplicity of images: the waves or sheets of virtual pasts that form the 'pre-existing in general' (C2: 98). If the action-driven 'classical narration' (26) of cinema gives time only indirectly as a measure of actions and movements, in *Cinema 2*, with the emancipation of time from movement, cinematic situations become important in themselves as sets of 'pure optical and sound images' (15). If before, actions favoured moments of bifurcation and change, 'the interval itself now plays the role of center' (40). From a succession of pulses of being, the perspective switches to intervals of becoming. Movies begin to slow down. Speech is no longer the rapid-fire speech of American comedies, it is now the insecure, fragile and stuttered speech of figures that are lost in memories or visions; both their own as well as those of the world at large. Action is no longer defined by chase-scenes, but by the aimless movements that define road movies with their slow pans of landscapes and their memories.

As in the actual series, the mnemonic vector goes from the anonymous to the individual level. As I noted, it goes from what Deleuze calls, in the conceptual footsteps of Bergson, 'pure recollection' (79) – an anonymous recollection in which the diversity of given images in time is recollected by time itself – to an individual recollection, in which differentiated images are given to a mnemonic system. In its assemblage, the overall, intensive set of anonymously differentiated images given in themselves to themselves is – in the process of their visual organization – contracted into and reduced to recollection-images.

The time-image has to do with the duration and intervals between actions; with beings in time and being in time. With filming time while figures are waiting or wavering; while they are contemplating or observing. The films of Vincent Gallo or Jim Jarmusch – *The Brown Bunny, Permanent Vacation* – are filled with such situations. In all of these contexts, time is no longer the carrier of movement, as it was in the movement-image, it is now a medium in and of itself. 'The movement-image of the so-called classical cinema gave way, in the post-war period, to a direct time-image' (xi). Unlike the 'classical narration' (26) of realist cinema, which is action-driven and gives time only indirectly as a measure of the action, after the war, situations become important in themselves, while action becomes less directed and slower.

It is probably because he aims to provide a history of cinema that Deleuze describes the shift from the actual to the virtual as the result of a general cultural change. 'What brings this cinema of action into question after the war is the very break-up of the sensory-motor schema. The rise of situations to which one can no longer react, of environments with which there are now only chance relations, of empty or disconnected any-space-whatevers replacing qualified extended space' (272). Space becomes indistinct and irreal. As Deleuze notes, 'the seer (*voyant*) has replaced the agent (*actant*)' (272). The slow images of Herzog's apocalyptic *Heart of Glass*, the empty moments of *Limits of Control*, which is an action movie that consists only of the times in-between the action.

The differentiation is not only into actual and virtual, but also into present and past. But what kind of past? Not only the individual past, which concerns the recollection-image, but also all of the pasts that designate the 'pre-existing in general' (98); the past of all chronological sheets that make up the virtual history of the present, in which all of the sheets are contracted onto the surface of now. The single moments of one's history that need to be brought into communication in an autobiography – 'We make use of transformations which take place between two sheets to constitute a sheet *of* transformation . . . which invents a kind of transverse continuity or communication between several sheets' (123) – but also the past of the world in general. In *Cinema 2*, Deleuze traces, again in loving slow-motion, the individuation of the time-image as the other aspect of living beings as photonic assemblages.

If *Cinema 1* describes an impulsive, actual world, *Cinema 2* describes a temporal, virtual one. If the spatial logic of terms in *Cinema 1* focuses on chronic time, the temporal logic of relations in *Cinema 2* focuses on aionic time. Against the movement-image and the material power of the truth of actual life, the time-image stakes the immaterial power of the false that defines virtual life. Against physical, actual matters-of-fact, *Cinema 2* sets metaphysical, virtual events. Against classical space, it sets topological space. Against being, it sets becoming. Finally, against the machineries of actualization in *Cinema 1*, *Cinema 2* sets the machineries of virtualization.

Luminous Topology

Cinema 1 X *Cinema 2 (1983, 1985)*, 'The Actual X the Virtual' *(1996, posthumous)*

Mind and body 'are one and the same individual thing, conceived now under the attribute of Thought and now under the attribute of Extension', Spinoza had noted (2002: 259). The sentence describes, quite literally, the logic that rules over the conceptual topology of *Cinema 1* and *Cinema 2*. In fact, a reversal of the order of Spinoza's sentence provides a perfect description of the project of the two books. *Cinema 1* and *Cinema 2* are about one and the same thing, conceived now under the attribute of material movement and space, now under the attribute of immaterial memory and time. Both implicitly and explicitly, Deleuze uses the projective plane as a conceptual plane in which to think specific philosophical concepts. The cinema books instantiate a moment at which his work becomes a concrete figure of the projective plane. Deleuze writes from within a tradition in which academic publications are content- rather than design-driven. In fact, the aesthetics of Deleuze's publishers Gallimard and Minuit are among the most formally austere and reduced. Even though Deleuze often deterritorializes the text's content in terms of its conceptual organization, such as setting the logic of series against that of chapters, the design of his books remains classic and subdued.

How is book-design related to the logic of the projective plane, and how can books become material figures of a conceptual complementarity? In the 1950s, pulp fiction novels, mostly science-fiction and detective novels, were often published in a *tête-bêche* format, which was a marketing device that gave the customer the feeling of getting two novels for the price of one. Although this mode of publishing had its heyday in the 1950s, even today some novels are still published this way, mostly in order to align either two authors or two works by the same author. Sometimes, however, the design becomes an inherent part of a specific work's poetics, as in Ted Nelson's book *Computer Lib* or in Mark Z. Danielewski's novel *Only Revolutions*, which aligns the book's actual materiality and its virtual poetics according to a logic of reciprocal presupposition or complementarity: *crystal literature*.

Although they are not published in a *tête-bêche* format, *Cinema 1* and *Cinema 2* are aligned in a similar fashion. The two books' projective alignment of the actual and the virtual is taken up in the books as material objects, making them a powerful figure of Deleuze's crystal philosophy. In 1983, which is the year *Cinema 1* is published and two years before the publication of *Cinema 2*, Deleuze notes in the interview 'Portrait of the Philosopher as a Moviegoer' that *Cinema 1* 'should have the feel of a complete work' (TRM: 220), which is a statement that implies, of course, that it is somehow not a complete book. Indeed, *Cinema 1* should 'leave the reader asking for more' (220). This inherent lack concerns both chronological and conceptual registers. *Cinema 2* adds modern cinema to its corpus, as well as the time-image. It is a 'sequel' rather than 'an opposition to the movement-image' (220). As Deleuze stresses, 'it would be pointless to claim that the modern cinema of the time-image is "better" than the classic cinema of the movement-image' (270), just as pointless as it would be to say that Bergson's notion of the cone of memory is better than his notion of the sensory-motor arc. Like these two Bergsonian concepts, the two books were conceived as complementary.

The projective topology of *Cinema 1* and *Cinema 2* is a figure of the alignment of Bergsonism's two logics: the epistemological logic of the formal difference between pure virtuals and pure actuals, and the ontological logic of their reciprocal presupposition as actualized virtuals and virtualized actuals. These logics provide the conceptual ground on which *Cinema 1* and *Cinema 2* can be thought of as being distributed on a projective plane. In designating the 'smallest internal circuit' (C2: 70) between the actual and the virtual, the crystal-image holds a privileged position within the projective topology, designating the point at which the actual and the virtual become identical at the impossible, infinitely receding point-at-infinity. At the point where the actual plane of the anonymous movement of movement-images folds over onto the virtual plane of the anonymous movement of time-images and vice versa. At this paradoxical point, actual perception (the sensory-motor arc) and virtual imagination (the cone of memory) are superposed. In his description of the crystal-image, Deleuze goes back to what Bergson had called 'pure recollection' (79). Deleuze describes the crystal-image almost as if he were talking about the production of a movie. It brings together 'life as spectacle, and yet in its spontaneity' (89): *life as moving images*.

Deleuze stresses that the conceptual space within which the crystal-image instantiates the meeting of the actual and the virtual – of actual perception and virtual memory – is a literally projective space. The crystal-image measures out 'a place and its obverse which are totally reversible' (69). In extracting the virtual from the actual and simultaneously incarnating the virtual in the actual, it is involved in 'the mutual search . . . of matter and spirit' (75). Temporally, it centres on 'the perpetual foundation of time' (81). Whether it is the fractured or the seedy crystal, every crystal-image shows 'the indiscernibility of the actual and the virtual' (87). The point-at-infinity of Deleuze's cinematographic projective plane lies in the crystal space between the two books; the point-at-infinity where its two sides meet in a conceptual *tête-bêche*. In the interview 'On the Movement-Image' from 1983, Deleuze defines this point as that where 'an actual image, cut off from its motor development, comes into relation with a virtual image . . . The actual image and its virtual image crystallize, so to speak. It's a crystal image' (N: 52). It is this unthinkable point that marks the ultimate crystal moment in Deleuze's philosophy. The ideal identification of the virtual and the actual at philosophy's point-at-infinity.

As two single volumes, the two books take up the topology of the 'smallest internal circuit' (C2: 70) between the actual and the virtual that is embodied in crystal-images, while their overall projective topology embodies 'the indiscernibility of the actual and the virtual' (87). In terms of unilateral space, these crystal-images, which refer back to the crystallization of the actual and the virtual Deleuze deals with in 'The Actual and the Virtual', designate the impossible moment-at-infinity at which the two formally distinct volumes are superposed on the unilateral projective plane; the moment at which the gap between the two series is reduced to zero. At that point-at-infinity, which is philosophy's point-at-infinity, the actual and the virtual become identical. *Cinema 1*: the actual, *Cinema 2:* the virtual; *Cinema 1* and *Cinema 2* as identical: *crystal, luminous convergence.*

Let me return, at this point, to 'The Actual and the Virtual'. At the end of his life, Deleuze uses, quite explicitly, the photonic complementarity of the actual and the virtual to describe how 'every actual surrounds itself with a cloud of virtuals' (DII: 148). These virtuals, according to Deleuze, are waves that 'vary in kind as well as in their degree of proximity from the actual *particles* by which they are both emitted and absorbed' (148, emphasis added). At this point, the actual and the virtual are as particle and as wave. Bringing a conceptual memory of his text on Lucretius into the present, Deleuze notes that these luminous exchanges happen 'in a period of time shorter than the shortest period imaginable' (148). Like Deleuze's description of lightning in *Gilles Deleuze from A to Z* – the zigzag of lightning is 'perhaps the elementary movement that presided at the creation of the world' – 'The Actual and the Virtual' describes the moment of a first luminous complementarity: *the luminous dawn of the world.*

Deleuze transposes this abstract complementarity as a figure of thought to the parameters of a cognitive complementarity when he notes that each corporeal perception is surrounded by a mist of a-corporeal, temporal (mnemonic) events: 'an actual perception has its own memory as a sort of immediate, consecutive or even simultaneous double' (150). Again, it is a matter of particles and waves. The complementarity lies in the luminosity of the photonic moment at which the sensible and the intelligible – matter and memory, the Bergsonian relation between the frameworks that had defined the logic of *Cinema 1* and *Cinema 2*: the actual sensory-motor arc and virtual memory – form luminous crystals. The aim of my text was to show that this term is not a poetic metaphor but a very concise philosophical concept.

Deleuze never stops maintaining that the two series need to be thought of as separate up until infinity. At the same time, the topology of the projective plane and the logic of complementarity allow the separate series to be aligned on two monist planes; spatially: the photonic plane of immanence; conceptually: the logic of complementarity. If Deleuze's crystal philosophy has to do with the mode in which to think the relation of the two series and if, throughout his work, Deleuze argues that, even in the infinitesimally small and the infinitesimally large, the two series remain radically separated, it is, with all of its ramifications, into this argument that Deleuze brings to bear the global topology of the projective plane, according to which the two series should be thought of as ultimately identical.

The two logics are reconciled only at the point-at-infinity on the projective plane, because this is the one point on the projective plane where the two series become truly identical; where all opposites are erased. At this impossible, monist point-at-infinity, all differences and oppositions are identical. It is the logical point-at-infinity at which particle and wave are one. The ultimate Deleuzian irony is that it is only at this unthinkable and ideal point that monism and schizophrenia are reconciled. Conceptually, it is the most important and the most paradoxical point for Deleuze: *the luminous point that marks the infinite vertigo of philosophy.*

Conclusion: White Light, White Life

'Immanence: A Life' (1995), *Gilles Deleuze from A to Z* (1996, posthumous)

AT THE END of his life, Deleuze maintains that only philosophy is truly in touch with the virtuality of the plane of immanence because it operates with concepts, which are made up of immaterial, pure events. If the plane of immanence is photonic, and as such both actual and virtual (the plane of immanence as the plane of consistency and vice versa), only philosophy can be witness to, or adequate to, the virtual aspect of the plane of immanence. Thought at the point-at-infinity: *the virtual wave of thought*. Philosophy at the moment of a-philosophy; the moment it creates diagrams of the plane of immanence in its aspect of pure, anonymous life and pure, anonymous consciousness. The moment a differentiating philosophy is born from indifference, but that trails this indifference behind. In 1995, two months before his death, Deleuze writes a short text, 'Immanence: A Life', which is published on 1 September. Deleuze dies on 4 November. Like 'The Actual and the Virtual', the text has the feel of both a testament and a legacy. Symptomatically, in the text Deleuze refers to two other late philosophies; those of Johann Gottlieb Fichte and Maine de Biran. (See also Kerslake 2009: 257–64.) The text shares with 'The Actual and the Virtual' the stress on the notion of two anonymous multiplicities made up of actual and virtual elements respectively. While 'The Actual and the Virtual' stresses the creation of crystals, however, 'Immanence: A Life' stresses the complementary process of de-crystallization.

The text opens with a question that at first seems very uncommon for Deleuze: 'What is a transcendental field?' (PI: 25). Deleuze's answer involves a final philosophical reversal; perhaps his most radical one. The transcendental, Deleuze states 'doesn't refer to an object or belong to a subject' (25). Rather, it is 'a pure stream of a-subjective consciousness, a pre-reflexive impersonal consciousness, a qualitative duration of consciousness without a self' (25). In Franz Reichle's documentary about Francisco Varela's life and death, *Monte Grande, What is Life?* (2004) Varela, shortly before his death, evokes something like Deleuze's anonymous transcendental field by way of the Buddhist idea of 'another level of consciousness'; a 'subtle consciousness that in fact is the foundation for the other types of consciousness'. The light of this anonymous consciousness sometimes shines into consciousness in 'very special dreams or very intense moments of special meditation practices or the moment when you die'. The time after death is the time of the becoming of the transmigration of souls. Varela describes this anonymous consciousness as 'a flow of consciousness which has moments in which it manifests as in a more layered consciousness including mental phenomena, cognition; and then after death it continues like a flow and it comes up again'. This notion of '*a* consciousness, in other words, an awareness that is aware of itself, without brain', Varela notes, with subtle irony, is hard to imagine for a scientist. He suspends judgement, he says, smiling. How can there be consciousness without an embodied mind that is conscious? How to conceptualize a non-subjective field without perception and without observers that is nevertheless conscious? If one might conceive of chaos as matter without form, how to conceive of mind without self? Precisely this, however, is Deleuze's wager. 'We will speak of a transcendental empiricism in contrast to everything that makes up the world of the subject and the object' (PI: 25). An anonymous consciousness in and for itself?: *Hegel-at-infinity.*

The purely virtual makes up the transcendental field, while sensation, which is always the sensation of and by someone, makes up the empirical field. 'There is something wild and powerful in this transcendental empiricism', Deleuze notes, in a loop back to his book on Hume. A virtual, 'absolute consciousness' is cut by actual sensations, each of which functions as 'a break within the flow' (25). The waves of pure virtuals and the particulars of pure actuals. This purely virtual consciousness might be seen as lying before the self as a not-yet-embodied virtual, like a pure sheet of light that travels at an infinite speed and that is completely spread out in space because it is not yet reflected by an actual surface. Deleuze stresses the luminosity of this purely virtual time when he notes that consciousness is purely virtual as long as it 'traverses the transcendental field as an infinite speed everywhere diffused' (26). From this angle, the purely virtual plane is a photonic wave, a storm of light made up of unobstructed and unreflected light; pure medium, the pure glow of white light: *pre-philosophical white-out.*

The transcendental photonic plane of immanence is without centres of indetermination. It cannot be revealed because there is nothing which it could be revealed to, and nothing that could reveal it, reflection being dependent on forms and subjects or objects. Stressing once more the chronological position of this consciousness, Deleuze states that 'as long as consciousness traverses the transcendental field at an infinite speed everywhere diffused, nothing is able to reveal it' (26). At this point, the virtual is purely 'in itself' (26); the attribute of nothing and nobody. 'It is only when immanence is no longer immanence to anything other than itself that we can speak of a plane of immanence' (27). It is literally ideal. Deleuze defines the white immanence of this anonymous consciousness as 'a life' (27). 'We will say of pure immanence that it is A LIFE, and nothing else. It is not immanence to life, but the immanent that is in nothing is itself a life. A life is the immanence of immanence, absolute immanence: it is complete power, complete bliss' (27). Luminous life without form; a life that 'contains only virtuals' (31). While this purely virtual life is empirically actualized in a 'state of things', it is possible to conceptualize it as 'lacking in nothing' (31); not even in its actualization.

While this indefinite life can be seen as lying before the individual as yet-to-be-embodied, it can also, from another angle, be located, within the individual, as the virtual time and space that lies between actual perceptions; as 'the passage from one [sensation] to the other as becoming' (25). In both cases, to enter its whiteness implies losing the self. Pure, white transcendence: *virtual light*. To fall into this virtual whiteness, however, is not to fall into something empty and lacking but to become part of the photonic plane of immanence in its purely virtual aspect. Ultimately, to enter the moment of infinity, where actual perception is, quite literally and paradoxically, identical to purely anonymous consciousness. At such a moment, every part of the living world contemplates itself in a communal, anonymous meditation. As Deleuze noted in *Difference and Repetition*, 'Ideas contain all the varieties of differential relations and all the distributions of singular points coexisting in diverse orders "perplicated" in one another' (206). This is why 'the Idea of colour, for example, is like white light which perplicates in itself the genetic elements and relations of all the colours, but is actualized in the diverse colours with their respective spaces; or the Idea of sound, which is also like white noise. There is even a white society and a white language, the latter being that which contains in its virtuality all the phonemes and relations destined to be actualised in diverse languages and in the distinctive parts of a given language' (206): *white light; white life*.

Deleuze illustrates the process of such a purification, singularization and de-crystallization in reference to the novel *Our Mutual Friend* by Charles Dickens, in which a 'disreputable man, a rogue' (PI: 28) becomes ill to the point of dying. When his individual character dissolves into a singular life at the brink of death, 'this wicked man himself senses something soft and sweet penetrating him' (28). At this moment, 'the life of the individual gives way to an impersonal and yet singular life that releases a pure event freed from the accidents of internal and external life, that is, from the subjectivity and objectivity of what happens: a "Homo tantum" . . . who attains a sort of beatitude. It is a haecceity no longer of individuation but of singularization: a life of pure immanence, neutral, beyond good or evil, for it was only the subject that incarnated it . . . A singular essence, a life . . .' (29). The individual becomes indefinite.

A life. 'There are no more forms but cinematic relations between unformed elements' (DII: 93). Again, however, it is not this life that is dying. What dies is the self. At this moment, the anonymous, virtual life is released from the shackles of its actualization and its specific form of embodiment. If the materiality of empiricism lies in the coloured materiality of subjects and selves, the virtuality of the transcendental lies in the fullness of white, virtual light.

Every form of embodiment is assembled from and thus based on these modules of pure life, which is why 'transcendence is always a product of immanence' (PI: 31). At the core of every assembly, there are infinitely fine singularities. Crystals. 'One is always the index of a multiplicity' (30). At the point-at-infinity, monism and schizophrenia become one.

The real challenge of Deleuzian philosophy, however, lies in becoming anonymous in every moment of one's life, because '*a* life is everywhere, in all the moments that a given living subject goes through' (29). To think the plane of immanent life is to think a presence in the world that is without observer, a pure resonance. 'Small children, through all their sufferings and weaknesses, are infused with an immanent life that is pure power and even bliss' (30). Still, in Deleuze's final sentence, the fundamental gap on which his philosophy rests remains operative. 'There is a big difference between the virtuals that define the immanence of the transcendental field and the possible forms that actualize them and transform them into something transcendent' (32): *the paradox of white light.*

If the genesis of a complicated entity is one of entrainment, composition, molarization and the creation of an eigenfrequency, its death defines a double, both extensive and intensive, dissolution, decomposition and molecularization. 'Each death is double, and represents the cancellation of large differences in extension as well as the liberation and swarming of little differences in intensity' (DR: 259). In the affirmative positivity of Deleuzian philosophy, each death gives rise to 'swarming possibilities' (260). It frees another plane of immanence. 'And death occurs when the body's characteristic or dominant relation is determined to be destroyed' (S: 32). As Spinoza had noted, 'I understand the body to die when its parts are so disposed that they acquire *a different relation* of motion and rest' (quoted in S: 32): *white death.*

There is a necessary non-correspondence between death as an empirical event and death as an '"instinct" or transcendental instance ... Suicide is an attempt to make the two incommensurable faces coincide or correspond. However, the two sides do not meet, and every death remains double. On the one hand, it is a "de-differenciation" which compensates for the differenciations of the I and the Self in an overall system which renders these uniform; on the other hand, it is a matter of individuation, a protest by the individual which has never recognised itself within the limits of the Self and the I, even where these are universal' (DR: 259). Thank you all for your kindness, Deleuze tells the film crew and Claire Parnet at the end of *Gilles Deleuze from A to Z*, after he has told Parnet that the video should be published posthumously. Already in *The Logic of Sense* Deleuze had envisioned 'the point at which death turns against death; where dying is the negation of death, and the impersonality of dying no longer indicates the moment when I disappear outside of myself, but rather the moment when death loses itself in itself, and also the figure which the most singular life takes on in order to substitute itself for me' (LS: 153): *step into the light.*

Bibliography

Abbott, Edwin A. (2013), *Flatland: A Romance of Many Dimensions*, New York: Sheba Blake Publishing.
Adams, Henry (1961), *The Education of Henry Adams. An Autobiography*, Boston: Houghton Mifflin.
Ansell-Pearson, Keith (1999), *Germinal Life: The Difference and Repetition of Deleuze*, London: Routledge.
Badiou, Alain (2000), *Deleuze: The Clamour of Being*, trans. Louise Burchill, Minneapolis: University of Minnesota Press.
Badiou, Alain (2017), *Black: The Brilliance of a Non-Color*, trans. Susan Spitzer, Cambridge: Polity Press.
Barad, Karen (2015), 'TransMaterialities: Trans*/Matter/Realities and Queer Political Imaginings', *GLQ: A Journal of Lesbian and Gay Studies* 21:2–3, pp. 387–422.
Bateson, Gregory (1979), *Mind and Nature: A Necessary Unity*, London: Wildwood House.
Beckett, Samuel (1956), *Waiting for Godot*, London: Faber & Faber.
Beistegui, Miguel de (2004), *Truth and Genesis: Philosophy as Differential Ontology*, Bloomington: Indiana University Press.
Beistegui, Miguel de (2010), *Immanence: Deleuze and Philosophy*, Edinburgh: Edinburgh University Press.
Bell, Jeffrey A. (2008), *Deleuze's Hume: Philosophy, Culture and the Scottish Enlightenment*, Edinburgh: Edinburgh University Press.
Berardi, Franco (2008), *Félix Guattari: Thought, Friendship, and Visionary Cartography*, trans. and ed. Giuseppina Mecchia and Charles J. Stivale, Basingstoke: Palgrave Macmillan.

Bergson, Henri (1911), *Creative Evolution*, trans. Arthur Mitchell, New York: Henry Holt and Company.
Bergson, Henri (1969), *La pensée et le mouvant*. Paris: Les Presses Universitaires de France.
Bergson, Henri (1991), *Matter and Memory*, trans. Nancy Margaret Paul and W. Scott Palmer, New York: Zone Books.
Bergson, Henri (2002), *Key Writings*, ed. Keith Ansell Pearson and John Mullarkey, New York: Continuum.
Berressem, Hanjo (2005), '"Is it Possible Not to Love Žižek?" on Slavoj Žižek's Missed Encounter with Deleuze', *Electronic Book Review*, www.uni-koeln.de/phil-fak/englisch/abteilungen/berressem/zizek/zizek.html.
Berressem, Hanjo (2006), 'Fluchtlinien. Deleuze liest Gombrowicz', in *Gombrowicz in Europa: Deutsch-polnische Versuche einer kulturellen Verortung*, ed. Andreas Lawaty and Marek Zybura, Wiesbaden: Harrassowitz Verlag, pp. 224–52.
Berressem, Hanjo (2008), 'Unsichtbar werden: Die Mathematik des Verschwindens bei Gilles Deleuze', in *Rhetoriken des Verschwindens*, ed. Tina-Karen Pusse, Würzburg: Königshausen & Neumann, pp. 61–71.
Berressem, Hanjo (2012a), 'Crystal History: "You Pick Up the Pieces. You Connect the Dots"', in *Time and History in Deleuze and Serres*, ed. Bernd Herzogenrath, London: Continuum, pp. 225–54.
Berressem, Hanjo (2012b), 'Light, Camera, Action! The Luminous Worlds of Jacques Lacan and Gilles Deleuze', in *Psychoanalyzing Cinema: A Productive Encounter with Lacan, Deleuze, and Žižek*, ed. Jan Jagodzinski, Basingstoke: Palgrave Macmillan, pp. 45–69.
Berressem, Hanjo (2018), *Eigenvalue: On the Gradual Contraction of Media in Movement*, London: Bloomsbury.
Borges, Jorge Luis (1962), 'The Library of Babel', in *Ficciones*, New York: Grove Press, pp. 79–88.
Bryant, Levi R. (2008), *Difference and Givenness: Deleuze's Transcendental Empiricism and the Ontology of Immanence*, Chicago: Northwestern University Press.
Bryant, Levi R. (2011), *The Democracy of Objects*, Ann Arbor: Open Humanities Press.
Busche, Hubertus (2009), 'Monade und Licht – Die geheime Verbindung von Physik und Metaphysik bei Leibniz', in *Lichtgefüge des 17. Jahrhunderts: Rembrandt und Vermeer – Leibnitz und Spinoza*, ed. Carolin Bohlmann, Thomas Fink and Philipp Weiss, Munich: Wilhelm Fink Verlag, pp. 125–62.
Cache, Bernard (1995), *Earth Moves: The Furnishing of Territories*, ed. Michael Speaks, trans. Anne Boyman, Cambridge, MA: MIT Press.
Capra, Fritjof (1982), *The Tao of Physics: An Exploration of the Parallels between Modern Physics and Eastern Mysticism*, London: Flamingo.

Carroll, Lewis (1939), *Sylvie and Bruno Concluded*, in *The Complete Works of Lewis Carroll*, London: Nonesuch Press, pp. 461–674.

Carroll, Lewis (1998), *Alice's Adventures in Wonderland, With Forty-Two Illustrations by John Tenniel, Volume One*, Illinois Publishing: Chicago.

Cramer, Friedrich (1998), *Symphonie des Lebendigen: Versuch einer allgemeinen Resonanztheorie*, Frankfurt am Main: Insel Verlag.

Crosby, Harry (1931), 'Chariot of the Sun', in *Collected Poems of Harry Crosby, Vol. 1*, Paris: Black Sun Press.

Culp, Andrew (2016), *Dark Deleuze*, Minneapolis: University of Minnesota Press.

Danielewski, Mark Z. (2006), *Only Revolutions*, New York: Pantheon.

DeLanda, Manuel (2002), *Intensive Science and Virtual Philosophy*, London: Bloomsbury.

Deleuze, Gilles (1946), 'Du Christ à la bourgeoisie', *Espace*, June 1946, pp. 93–106.

Deleuze, Gilles (1962), 'Sens et valeurs' (on Nietzsche), *Arguments* 15 (1959), pp. 20–8. Reprinted, in revised form, in *Nietzsche et la philosophie* (Paris: Presses Universitaires de France).

Deleuze, Gilles (1968), *Différence et repetition*, Paris: Presses Universitaires de France.

Deleuze, Gilles (1972), *Proust and Signs*, trans. Richard Howard, New York: George Braziller.

Deleuze, Gilles (1978, 1981), '*Les Cours de Gilles Deleuze: Spinoza*', www.webdeleuze.com/cours/spinoza.

Deleuze, Gilles (1983a), 'Image Mouvement Image Temps', 'Les Cours de Gilles Deleuze, Cours Vincennes – St. Denis', 7 June 1983, https://www.webdeleuze.com/textes/71.

Deleuze, Gilles (1983b), *Nietzsche and Philosophy*, trans. Hugh Tomlinson, London: Continuum.

Deleuze, Gilles (1984), *Kant's Critical Philosophy: The Doctrine of the Faculties*, trans. Hugh Tomlinson and Barbara Habberjam, London: The Athlone Press.

Deleuze, Gilles (1986), *Cinema 1: The Movement-Image*, trans. Hugh Tomlinson and Barbara Habberjam, Minneapolis: University of Minnesota Press.

Deleuze, Gilles (1988), *Spinoza: Practical Philosophy*, trans. Robert Hurley, San Francisco: City Lights Books.

Deleuze, Gilles (1989a), *Cinema 2: The Time-Image*, trans. Hugh Tomlinson and Robert Galeta, Minneapolis: University of Minnesota Press.

Deleuze, Gilles (1989b), 'Coldness and Cruelty', in *Masochism*, trans. Jean McNeil, New York: Zone Books, pp. 7–138.

Deleuze, Gilles (1990a), *Bergsonism*, trans. Hugh Tomlinson and Barbara Habberjam, New York: Zone Books.

Deleuze, Gilles (1990b), *The Logic of Sense*, ed. Constantin V. Boundas, trans. Mark Lester and Charles Stivale, New York: Columbia University Press.

Deleuze, Gilles (1990c), 'Lucretius and the Simulacrum', in *The Logic of Sense*, ed. Constantin V. Boundas, trans. Mark Lester and Charles Stivale, New York: Columbia University Press, pp. 266–79.

Deleuze, Gilles (1990d), 'Plato and the Simulacrum', in *The Logic of Sense*, ed. Constantin V. Boundas, trans. Mark Lester and Charles Stivale, New York: Columbia University Press, pp. 253–66.

Deleuze, Gilles (1991), *Empiricism and Subjectivity: An Essay on Hume's Theory of Human Nature*, trans. Constantin V. Boundas. New York: Columbia University Press.

Deleuze, Gilles (1992a), 'Ethology: Spinoza and Us', in *Incorporations*, ed. Jonathan Crary and Sanford Kwinter, New York: Zone Books, pp. 625–33.

Deleuze, Gilles (1992b), *Expressionism in Philosophy: Spinoza*, trans. Martin Joughin, New York: Zone Books.

Deleuze, Gilles (1994), *Difference and Repetition*, trans. Paul Patton, New York: Columbia University Press.

Deleuze, Gilles (1995a), 'Letter to a Harsh Critic', in *Negotiations, 1972–1990*, trans. Martin Joughin, New York: Columbia University Press, pp. 3–12.

Deleuze, Gilles (1995b), 'On *The Movement-Image*', *Negotiations, 1972–1990*, trans. Martin Joughin, New York: Columbia University Press, pp. 46–56.

Deleuze, Gilles (1997), 'What Children Say', in *Essays Critical and Clinical*, trans. Michael A. Greco and Daniel W. Smith, Minneapolis: University of Minnesota Press, pp. 61–7.

Deleuze, Gilles (2001), 'Immanence: A Life', in *Pure Immanence: Essays on a Life*, trans. Anne Boyman, New York: Zone Books, pp. 25–33.

Deleuze, Gilles (2004a), 'Bergson, 1859–1941' in *Desert Islands: and Other Texts, 1953–1974*, ed. David Lapoujade, trans. Mike Taormina, New York: Semiotext(e), pp. 22–31.

Deleuze, Gilles (2004b), 'Bergson's Conception of Difference', in *Desert Islands and Other Texts, 1953–1974*, ed. David Lapoujade, trans. Mike Taormina, New York: Semiotext(e), pp. 32–51.

Deleuze, Gilles (2004c), *Desert Islands and Other Texts 1953–1974*, ed. David Lapoujade, trans. Mike Taomina, New York: Semiotext(e).

Deleuze, Gilles (2004d), 'The Method of Dramatization', in *Desert Islands and Other Texts, 1953–1974*, ed. David Lapoujade, trans. Mike Taomina, New York: Semiotext(e), pp. 94–116.

Deleuze, Gilles (2004e), 'On Gilbert Simondon', in *Desert Islands and Other Texts, 1953–1974*, ed. David Lapoujade, trans. Mike Taormina, New York: Semiotext(e), pp. 86–9.

Deleuze, Gilles (2006a), *The Fold: Leibniz and the Baroque*, trans. Tom Conley, London: Continuum.

Deleuze, Gilles (2006b), *Foucault*, ed. and trans. Seán Hand, London: Continuum.
Deleuze, Gilles (2006c), 'Letter to Uno on Language', in *Two Regimes of Madness: Texts and Interviews 1975–1995*, ed. David Lapoujade, trans. Ames Hodges and Mike Taormina, New York: Semiotext(e), pp. 238–9.
Deleuze, Gilles (2006d), *Two Regimes of Madness: Texts and Interviews 1975–1995*, ed. David Lapoujade, trans. Ames Hodges and Mike Taormina, New York: Semiotext(e).
Deleuze, Gilles (2006e), 'Zones of Immanence', in *Two Regimes of Madness: Texts and Interviews 1975–1995*, ed. David Lapoujade, trans. Ames Hodges and Mike Taormina, New York: Semiotext(e), pp. 261–8.
Deleuze, Gilles and Claire Parnet (2002a), 'The Actual and the Virtual', in *Dialogues II*, trans. Barbara Habberjam, Eliot Ross Albert and Hugh Tomlinson, New York: Columbia University Press, pp. 148–52.
Deleuze, Gilles and Claire Parnet (2002b), *Dialogues II*, trans. Barbara Habberjam, Eliot Ross Albert and Hugh Tomlinson, New York: Columbia University Press.
Deleuze, Gilles and Claire Parnet (2002c), *Gilles Deleuze from A to Z*, trans. Charles J. Stivale, Los Angeles: Semiotext(e) (DVD). *L'Abécédaire de Gilles Deleuze*, Paris: Editions Montparnasse, 1997.
Deleuze, Gilles and Claire Parnet (2002d), 'On the Superiority of Anglo-American Literature', in *Dialogues II*, trans. Barbara Habberjam, Eliot Ross Albert and Hugh Tomlinson, New York: Columbia University Press, pp. 36–76.
Deleuze, Gilles and Félix Guattari (1977), *Anti-Oedipus: Capitalism and Schizophrenia 1*, trans. Robert Hurley, Mark Seem and Helen R. Lane, New York: Viking.
Deleuze, Gilles and Félix Guattari (1994), *What is Philosophy?*, trans. Hugh Tomlinson and Graham Burchell, New York: Columbia University Press.
Deleuze, Gilles and Félix Guattari (2005), *A Thousand Plateaus: Capitalism and Schizophrenia 2*, trans. Brian Massumi, Minneapolis: University of Minnesota Press.
Derrida, Jacques (1982), 'Différance', in *Margins of Philosophy*, trans. Alan Bass, Brighton: The Harvester Press, pp. 1–27.
Dillard, Annie (1976), *Pilgrim at Tinker Creek*, London: Picador.
Dosse, François (2011), *Gilles Deleuze and Félix Guattari: Intersecting Lives*, trans. Deborah Glassman, New York: Columbia University Press.
Emerson, Ralph Waldo (1850), 'Swedenborg; or, the Mystic', in *Representative Men: Seven Lectures*, Boston: Phillips, Sampson and Company, pp. 95–145.
Emerson, Ralph Waldo (1950a), 'Nature', in *The Complete Essays and other Writings of Ralph Waldo Emerson*, ed. Brooks Atkinson, New York: The Modern Library, pp. 1–42.
Emerson, Ralph Waldo (1950b), 'Love', in *The Complete Essays and other Writings of Ralph Waldo Emerson*, ed. Brooks Atkinson, New York: The Modern Library, pp. 210–21.

Fassbinder, Rainer Werner (1992), 'Imitation of Life. Über die Filme von Douglas Sirk', in *Rainer Werner Fassbinder. Filme befreien den Kopf. Essays und Arbeitsnotizen*, ed. Michael Töteberg, Frankfurt am Main: Fischer 1992, pp. 11–24.

Faulkner, William (1957), Interview, Faulkner at Virginia, http://faulkner.lib.virginia.edu/display/wfaudio06_1.

Foerster, Heinz von (1993), *Wissen und Gewissen: Versuch einer Brücke*, ed. Siegried J. Schmidt, Frankfurt a.M.: Suhrkamp.

Foerster, Heinz von (2003), *Understanding Understanding: Essays on Cybernetics and Cognition*, New York: Springer.

Foucault, Michel (1970), 'Theatrum Philosophicum', *Critique* 282, pp. 885–908.

Foucault, Michel (1972), *The Archaeology of Knowledge* and *The Discourse on Language*, trans. A. M. Sheridan Smith, New York: Pantheon Books.

Foucault, Michel (1989), *The Order of Things: An Archaeology of the Human Sciences*, London: Routledge.

Genosko, Gary (2002), *Félix Guattari: An Aberrant Introduction*, New York: Continuum.

Goethe, Johann Wolfgang von (1978), *Elective Affinities*, trans. R. J. Hollingdale, London: Penguin Books.

Gombrowicz, Witold (1966), *Pornografia*, New York: Grove.

Guattari, Félix (1995), *Chaosmosis: An Ethico-Aesthetic Paradigm*, trans. P. Bains and J. Pefanis, Bloomington: Indiana University Press.

Guattari, Félix (2006), *The Anti-Oedipus Papers*, ed. Stéphane Nadaud, trans. Kélina Gotman, New York: Semiotext(e).

Guattari, Félix (2011), *The Machinic Unconscious: Essays in Schizoanalysis*, trans. Taylor Adkins, Los Angeles: Semiotext(e).

Guattari, Félix (2013), *Schizoanalytic Cartographies*, trans. Andrew Goffey, London: Bloomsbury.

Hardt, Michael and Antonio Negri (2005), *Multitude: War and Democracy in the Age of Empire*, New York: Penguin.

Hawthorne, Nathaniel (1852), *The Blithedale Romance*, Boston: Ticknor, Reed, and Fields.

Hegel, G. W. F. (1894), *Philosophy of Mind*, trans. William Wallace and A. V. Miller, Oxford: Clarendon Press.

Heider, Fritz (1959), 'Thing and Medium', *On Perception, Event Structure, and Psychological Environment: Selected Papers. Psychological Issues 1:3*. Monograph, pp. 1–35.

Heider, Fritz (2008), 'Ding und Medium', in *Kursbuch Medienkultur*, ed. Claus Pias, Munich: Random House, pp. 319–33.

Heisenberg, Werner (1959), *Physics and Philosophy: The Revolution in Modern Science*, trans. A. J. Pomerans, London: Allen & Unwin.

Helmholtz, Hermann von (1896), 'Über das Sehen im Menschen', in *Vorträge und Reden Bd 1*, Braunschweig, 1896, 86–117.
Hilbert, David and Stephan Cohn-Vassen (1996), *Anschauliche Geometrie*, Berlin: Springer Verlag.
Hume, David (2007), *Enquiry Concerning Human Understanding*, ed. Peter Millican, Oxford: Oxford University Press.
Hurley Robert (1988), 'Preface', in Gilles Deleuze, *Spinoza: Practical Philosophy*, trans. Robert Hurley, San Francisco: City Lights Books, pp. i–iii.
The Incredible Shrinking Man, film, dir. Jack Arnold. Los Angeles: Universal Pictures, 1957.
James, William (1984), *The Works of William James. Psychology: Briefer Course*, ed. Frederick H. Burkhardt, Fredson Bowers and Ignas K. Skrupskelis, Cambridge, MA: Harvard University Press.
Johnson, Ryan J. (2017), *The Deleuze-Lucretius Encounter*, Edinburgh: Edinburgh University Press.
Kauffman, Stuart A. (2000), *Investigations*, Oxford: Oxford University Press.
Kaufman, Eleanor (2012), *Deleuze, The Dark Precursor: Dialectic, Structure, Being*, Baltimore: Johns Hopkins University Press.
Kerslake, Christian (2009), *Immanence and the Vertigo of Philosophy: From Kant to Deleuze*, Edinburgh: Edinburgh University Press.
Klein, Felix (1928), *Vorlesungen über Nicht-Euklidische Geometrie*, Berlin: Springer Verlag.
Kleinherenbrink, Arjen (2019), *Against Continuity: Gilles Deleuze's Speculative Realism*, Edinburgh: Edinburgh University Press.
Kleist, Heinrich von (1972), 'On the Marionette Theatre', *The Drama Review: TDR* 16:3, *The 'Puppet' Issue* (September), pp. 22–6.
Lacan, Jacques (1988), *Radiophonie Television*, Berlin: Quadriga.
Lacan, Jacques (2004), *Ecrits: A Selection*, trans. Bruce Fink, London: Routledge.
Lambert, Gregg (2002), *The Non-Philosophy of Gilles Deleuze*, New York: Continuum.
Lampert, Jay (2011), *Deleuze and Guattari's Philosophy of History*, New York: Continuum.
Lawrence, D. H. (1990), *Studies in Classic American Literature*, ed. Ezra Greenspan, Lidneth Vasey and John Worthen, London: Penguin Books.
Lawrence, D. H. (1998), 'Poetry of the Present', in *Selected Critical Writings*, Oxford: Oxford University Press, pp. 75–9.
Lawrence, D. H. (2005 [1931]), '"Chaos in Poetry": Introduction to Harry Crosby's Chariot of the Sun', in Harry Crosby, *Chariot of the Sun*, Paris: The Black Sun Press, pp. 1–18. Reprinted in: *The Works of D.H. Lawrence: Introductions and Reviews*, ed. N. H. Reeve and J. Worthen, Cambridge, Cambridge University Press.

Leibniz, Gottfried Wilhelm (1923), *Sämtliche Schriften und Briefe*, ed. Preussische (later: Deutsche) Akademie der Wissenschaften zu Berlin. Darmstadt/Leipzig/Berlin: Akademie-Verlag, 1923.

Leibniz, Gottfried Wilhelm (1998), 'Monadology', in *G. W. Leibniz: Philosophical Texts*, ed. Roger S. Woolhouse and Richard Franks, Oxford: Oxford University Press, pp. 215–77.

Lord, Beth (2010), *Kant and Spinozism: Transcendental Idealism and Immanence from Jacobi to Deleuze*, Basingstoke: Palgrave.

Lucretius (1973), *About Reality (De Rerum Natura)*, trans. Philip F. Wooby. New York: Philosophical Library.

Lucretius (2008), *De Rerum Natura: The Latin Text of Lucretius*, ed. William Ellery Leonard & Stanley Barney Smith, Madison: University of Wisconsin Press.

Lynch, David (2000), *Catching the Big Fish: Meditation, Consciousness, and Creativity*, New York: Penguin.

Margulis, Lynn and Dorion Sagan (1995), *What is Life?*, New York: Simon & Schuster.

Marvell, Andrew (2007), 'The Definition of Love', in *The Poems of Andrew Marvell*, ed. Nigel Smith, Harlow: Pearson Education Limited, pp. 109–11.

Marx, Karl (1958), *Differenz der demokritischen und epikureischen Naturphilosophie*, in *Karl Marx Friedrich Engels Gesamtausgabe, Band 1*, Berlin: Karl Dietz Verlag, pp. 7–92.

Marx, Karl and Friedrich Engels (1983), *The German Ideology Parts I & III*, ed. R. Pascal, London: Lawrence & Wishart.

Massumi, Brian (2002), *Parables for the Virtual: Movement, Affect, Sensation*, Durham, NC: Duke University Press.

Matheson, Richard (1969), *The Shrinking Man*, London: Corgi Books.

Merleau-Ponty, Maurice (1968), *The Visible and the Invisible*, Evanston: Northwestern University Press.

Möbius, August Ferdinand (1886), *Gesammelte Werke Vol. 2*, ed. Felix Klein, Leipzig: S. Hirzel Verlag.

Monte Grande: What is Life, film, dir. Franz Reichle, 2004.

Nail, Thomas (2018a), *Lucretius I: An Ontology of Motion*, Edinburgh: Edinburgh University Press.

Nail, Thomas (2018b), *Being and Motion*, Oxford: Oxford University Press.

Nietzsche, Friedrich (1989), 'On Truth and Lying in an Extra-Moral Sense' (1837), in *Friedrich Nietzsche on Rhetoric and Language*, ed. and trans. Sander L. Gilman, Carole Blair and David J. Parent, Oxford: Oxford University Press, 246–56.

Olkowski, Dorothea (1999), *Gilles Deleuze and the Ruin of Representation*, Berkeley: University Press California.

Peirce, Charles Sanders (1965a), 'A Survey of Pragmaticism', in *Collected Papers of Charles Sanders Peirce, Vol. V: Pragmatism and Pragmaticism*, ed. Charles Hartshorne and Paul Weiss, Cambridge: Belknap Press, pp. 317–45.
Peirce, Charles Sanders (1965b), 'Issues of Pragmaticism', in *Charles S. Peirce: Selected Writings (Values in a Universe of Chance)*, ed. Philip P. Wiener, New York: Dover Publications, pp. 203–26.
Peirce, Charles Sanders (1965c), 'Lowell Lectures on Some Topics of Logic Bearing on Questions Now Vexed. Eighth Lecture, Abduction', in *Collected Papers of Charles Sanders Peirce, Vol. V: Pragmatism and Pragmaticism*, ed. Charles Hartshorne and Paul Weiss, Cambridge: Belknap Press, pp. 590–604.
Peirce, Charles Sanders (1965d), 'Pragmatism and Abduction', in *Collected Papers of Charles Sanders Peirce, Vol. V: Pragmatism and Pragmaticism*, ed. Charles Hartshorne and Paul Weiss, Cambridge: Belknap Press, pp. 180–212.
Plotnitsky, Arkady (2010), 'The Image of Thought and the Sciences of the Brain after *What Is Philosophy?*', in *The Force of the Virtual: Deleuze, Science, and Philosophy*, ed. Peter Gaffney, Minneapolis: University of Minnesota Press, pp. 255–69.
Plotnitsky, Arkady (2012), 'From Resonance to Interference: The Architecture of Concepts and the Relationships among Philosophy, Art and Science in Deleuze and Deleuze and Guattari', *Parallax* 18:1, pp. 19–32.
Pound, Ezra (1975), *The Cantos of Ezra Pound* London: Faber and Faber.
Pynchon, Thomas (1990), *Vineland*, London: Secker & Warburg.
Pynchon, Thomas (2006), *Against the Day*, New York: Penguin.
Rutherford, Donald (1995), *Leibniz and the Rational Order of Nature*, Cambridge: Cambridge University Press.
Ruyer, Raymond (1952), *Neo-Finalisme*, Paris: Presses Universitaires de France.
Sambursky, Samuel (1959), *Physics of the Stoics*, Princeton: Princeton University Press.
Schneider, Christina (2001), *Leibniz Metaphysik: ein Formaler Zugang*, Munich: Philosophia Verlag.
Schrödinger, Erwin (1967), *What is Life?* With *Mind and Matter* and *Autobiographical Sketches*, Cambridge: Cambridge University Press.
Seferis, Giorgos (1995), 'On a Ray of Winter Light', in *George Seferis: Collected Poems*, ed. Edmund Keeley and Philip Sherrard, London: Anvil Press.
Serres, Michel (1982), *Hermes: Literature, Science, Philosophy*, ed. Josué V. Harari and David F. Bell, Baltimore: Johns Hopkins University Press.
Serres, Michel (1993), *Hermes IV: Verteilung*, trans. Michael Bischoff, Berlin: Merve.
Serres, Michel (1994), *Hermes V: Die Nordwest-Passage*, trans. Michael Bischoff, Berlin: Merve.

Serres, Michel (1995), *Genesis*, trans. G. James and J. Nielson, Ann Arbor: University of Michigan Press.

Serres, Michel (2000), *The Birth of Physics*, ed. David Webb, trans. Jack Hawkes, Manchester: Clinamen Press.

Serres, Michel (2003), *The System of Leibniz*, Manchester: Clinamen Press.

Simondon, Gilbert (1992), 'The Genesis of the Individual', in *Incorporations*, ed. Jonathan Crary and Sanford Kwinter, trans. Mark Cohen and Sanford Kwinter, New York: Zone Books, pp. 297–319.

Simondon, Gilbert (2005), *L'individuation à la lumière des notions de forme et d'information*, Grenoble: Jérôme Millon.

Spinoza, Baruch (2002), *Spinoza Complete Works*, ed. Michael L. Morgan Hackett, trans. Samuel Shirley, Cambridge: Hackett Publishing Company.

Spinoza, Baruch (2006), *Ethics* in *The Essential Spinoza: Ethics and Related Works*, Indianapolis: Hackett Publishing Company.

Stevenson, Frank (2009), 'On the Horizon: Nietzsche's Lady Dawn and Deleuze's Sky-Chance', *Concentric: Literary and Cultural Studies* 35:2 (September), pp. 355–78.

Stewart, Ian (1989), *Game, Set and Math: Enigmas and Conundrums*, Oxford: Basil Blackwell.

The Text of Light, film, dir. Stan Brakhage, New York: New York Filmmakers Cooperative/Canyon: Canyon Cinema, 1974.

Thoreau, David Henry (1906), *Walden, Or Life in The Woods*, London: Oxford University Press.

Tödliche Doris, Die (2019), quoted in *Mutant Sounds*, http://mutant-sounds.blogspot.com/2007/02/die-toedliche-doris-same1982sechs1986lp.html.

Toros, Yvonne (2009), 'Spinozistische Perspektiven: Die Ethik im Lichte der arguesianischen Geometrie betrachtet', in *Lichtgefüge des 17. Jahrhunderts: Rembrandt und Vermeer – Leibnitz und Spinoza*, ed. Carolin Bohlmann, Thomas Fink and Philipp Weiss, Munich: Wilhelm Fink Verlag, pp. 177–90.

Toscano, Alberto (2000), 'To Have Done With the End of Philosophy', *Pli: The Warwick Journal of Philosophy* 9, pp. 220–38.

Toscano, Alberto (2006), *Theatre of Production: Philosophy and Individuation between Kant and Deleuze*, New York: Palgrave.

Varela, Francisco, Eleanor Rosch and Evan Thompson (1991), *The Embodied Mind: Cognitive Science and Human Experience*, Cambridge, MA: MIT Press.

Vellodi, Kamini (2014), 'Diagrammatic Thought: Two forms of Constructivism in C. S. Peirce and Gilles Deleuze', *Parrhesio* 19, pp. 79–95.

Weeks, Jeffrey R. (1985), *The Shape of Space: How to Visualize Surfaces and Three-Dimensional Manifolds*, New York: Marcel Dekker Inc.

Wees, William C. (1992), *Light Moving in Time: Studies in the Visual Aesthetics of Avant-Garde Film*, Berkeley: University of California Press.
Williams, James (2011), *Gilles Deleuze's Philosophy of Time: A Critical Introduction and Guide*, Edinburgh: Edinburgh University Press.
Žižek, Slavoj (2004), *Organs without Bodies: Deleuze and Consequences*, New York: Routledge.

Index

abduction
    habit, 62
    perceptual judgement, 7
    see also Peirce, Charles Sanders
acousmatic, acousmêtre, 204
Adams, Henry, 102
aerosol
    atomism, 31
    continuity, 134
    Fold, 138
    immanence, 172
    integration, 139
    Leibniz' first matter, 149
    liquid crystals and states of matter, 38
    virtual, 45
æther, æthereal
    energy and light, 172
    Leibniz, 148–9
affect, affective, 111, 132
    affectation, 96–7
    aion, 202
    body and mind, 89, 206
    cinema books, 69
    clinamen, 41
    concept, 165
    Deleuze's philosophy, 1
    habit, 102
    image, 207–8
    individuation, 164
    intensity, 206
    light, Spinoza, 90–2, 94–5, 178–88
    lightning, 3
    multiplicity, 110–11
    percepts, 94
    physical cinema, 10
    Proust, 97
    surface of sensation, 161
    unconscious, 130, 141

affection, 52, 111
    affect, 96
    body, 158
    chronos, 202
    fold, 143
    image, 199, 206–7
    joy, 87
    light, 178–82, 185–6, 191–2
    mind, 85
    passive and active, 85
    perceptions, 104
affirmation
    anonymous life, 144
    Deleuze, 1–2, 30
    ethics of, 40
    false, the, 123–4
    intensity, 66
    joy, 38
    Lacan, 89
    light, 186
    naturalism, 42
    plane of immanence, 163
    Spinoza, 84
aggregate state
    aerosol, 139
    crystal, 13, 28
    fluid, 31
Aion
    Chronos, 64, 73, 103, 111, 113, 116–24
    cinema, 210–11
    duration, 44
    light and affect, 147, 179–81, 202
ambiance, 110
amor fati, 42
analog, analogicity
    affect, 180
    digital, 4, 67, 140
    diversity, 68, 108

informal diagram, 108–9
light, 180
matters-of-fact, 111
modulation, 193
painting, 191–2
quasi-analog, 128
unconscious, 130
see also digital
apperception, 63, 77, 136–7, 147–8
Arnold, Jack, *The Shrinking Man*, 126
art informel, 107, 109
Astair, Fred, 201
atom, atomic
 activity, 32
 clinamen, 37, 40
 crystal, 14, 51
 Deleuze, 31, 69
 events, 99, 101
 fold, 147
 girl, 20
 Heisenberg on, 172
 Hume, 55
 Leibniz, 150
 light, 173
 mind, 50
 molecules, molecular, photonic, 22, 49, 61, 125, 130–1
 monad, 146
 number of, 38–9
 perception, 9, 120
 plane of immanence, 167, 170–1
 rain of, 29, 67–8
 Schrödinger, 27
 simulacra, 124
 speed of, 204
 see also corpora; res
atomism
 actual and virtual, 171
 aerosol, 31
 Descartes, 32, 138
 Heider, 173
 Hume, 51
 Lucretius, 30, 32
attribute, to attribute
 active and passive syntheses, soul and heart, 65
 actual and virtual, 166, 179, 218
 actual and virtual history, 110–13, 179
 Chronos and Aion, 121–3
 darkness and light, 182
 differentiation and differenciation, 71
 effect and cause, 54
 event and matter-of-fact, 42, 101, 162
 mind and body, 212
 physicalism and perceptualism, 50
 Spinoza, 78–85, 89–90, 101, 186
 thought and habit, nature and culture, 53
 thought and life, 11, 55
 time and movement, 206, 210

aureole (corona, nimbus, halo), 8
autopoiesis, autopoietic
 allopoietic, 28
 concepts and philosophy, 84
 nature, 151

Bacon, Francis
 Faulkner, 193
 informal diagram, 106–8, 192
 painting and aesthetics, 188–90, 192
Badiou, Alain
 Deleuze as crystal, 13
 Deleuze's handwriting, 14
 Deleuze's philosophy, 91
 Deleuzian events, 99, 110
 misunderstanding with Deleuze, 99–100
 Outrenoir, 190
Bateson, Gregory
 difference, 67, 137
 plateau, 90
Baumgarten, Alexander Gottlieb, *aisthesis*, 194
beach
 Deleuze on, 22, 182
 Lawrence, D. H., 183, 185–6
 light, 178
 Spinoza, 177
 within the paving stones, 31
Beckett, Samuel
 Deleuze and Badiou, 99
 Waiting for Godot, 52
Bergson, Henri, 43–5
 cinema, 47, 126, 199, 201, 202–6, 210, 213–14
 Dedekind, Richard, 180, 202
 genesis, 51
 habit, 52
 light, 182, 197
 Lucretius, 31
 Proust, 97
 universal vibration, 171, 200
Biran, Maine de, 217
black box, blackboxing
 Serres' definition of the unconscious, 140
 simplification, 4
body without organs
 girls, 20
 Leibniz, 149
 luminous, 172
 plane of immanence, 89–90, 130, 165
 schizophrenia, 120, 202
Bohr, Niels, *contraria sunt complementa*, 4
Brecht, Berthold, Lucretius, 42
Broglie, de, Louis, hypothesis, 171

Cage, John, *frottage*, 112
camera obscura, Vermeer, Leibniz, 146
capitalism
 greed, 209
 Integrated World Capitalism, 92
 psychoanalysis, 35, 88

Carroll, Lewis
　Cheshire cat, 101, 126
　projective topology, 160–2
celluloid
　capture of light, 193–5
　cinematic perception, 12
　crystals, 2
　medium, 198
centre of indetermination, *Cinema 1*, 206–7
chaos
　informal diagram, 106–7, 109
　Lawrence, D. H., 'Chaos in Poetry', 183–4
　light and colour, 106
　Lucretius, 164
　multiplicity, 37
　Nietzsche, 105
　philosophy, science, art, 95
　plane of consistency, 141
　Simondon, vs. form, crystallization, 23–4, 27, 29, 76, 218
chiaroscuro
　Bacon, 190
　baroque, 176
　cinematic, 196
　ideational, 60
　Leibniz', 133
　life, 181
　light and colour, 190–1
　ontological, 190
　optical and chemical, 194
　perceptual, 136–7
　philosophical, 7, 60, 147–8
　spatial, 124–5
　van Gogh, 192
　Venus, 33
　virtual, 181
chiasm
　Irigaray and Merleau-Ponty, 159
　logic of, 9, 101
　spatial, 136
chromatism
　bodies, 189
　colour, 191
Chronos
　affection, 179
　Aion, 64, 124
　body, 113, 116–17
　depth, 119
　present, 111
　virtual and actual, 122–4
　see also Aion
cinema, drive-in, Deleuze's philosophy, 200
clinamen (swerve)
　Bacon, 106–7
　cinema, 209
　diversity, 37–8
　germ of Deleuzian philosophy, 42
　light, 34–5
　Lucretius, 29, 31
　simulacrum, 39–40

co-evolution, co-adaptation, 86
cohesion
　Leibniz' first and second matter, 149
　parts and folds, 32, 138
colorism, pictorial, 191–2
concrete universal
　concepts, 105
　intensive philosophy, 77
　light, 175, 197
cone of memory, cinema, 44–5, 199, 210, 213; *see also* sensory-motor arc
consistencies, 17
　dark, 182
　emergence, 51, 91
　Guattari, 17
　plane of, 2, 46
　plane of consistency, 83
contemplation
　body and soul, 143
　contraction, 45, 61–2, 64–5, 144
　event, 99, 111
　habit, 57, 61–3, 102
　history, 110
　Kleist, 19
　lightning, 9
　molecular, 61
　synthesis of memory, 116
　see also contraction
contingency
　historiography, 110
　multiplicity, 37
　necessity, 38
　philosophy and cinema, 195
contraction
　cinema, 209
　and contemplation, 45, 61–2, 64–5, 144
　crystallization, 75
　habit, 51, 63
　history, 102, 111
　ontology, 143
　plane of immanence, 165
　Spinoza, 82
　time, 116
　see also contemplation
control societies, 91–2
corpora
　atoms, 29–30, 32, 35
　res, 37
　see also atom; *res*
counter-actualization, 91, 105, 123, 184; *see also* dramatization
Crosby, Harry, 'Chariot of the Sun', 183

Dali, Salvador
　perspective, 153
　Voyage du Haute Mongolie, 112
Danielewski, Mark Z., *Only Revolutions*, 212
dark precursor
　Bacon, 106, 108
　Deleuzian philosophy, 2

differentiation and differenciation, 128
events, 100
ideas, 60
lightning, 5–6, 9, 35, 61
non-philosophy, 148
obscure perceptions, 137
perceptual judgement, 8
thought, 37, 75
De Chirico, Giorgio, 153
Dedekind, Richard
    Bergson, 180, 202
    mathematical continuity, 118, 127
    perception, 120
    quantity and quality, 72–3
    recursion, fractality, 130, 207
Delaunay, 187
Derrida, Jacques, Deleuze, 68
Desargues, Girard, Spinoza, 84
Descartes, René, Cartesian
    Cartesian space, 152–3, 163
    fluidity, 32, 138
    light, 171
    Margulis, Lynn, 12
    natural light, 7, 34, 136, 145, 147
deterritorialization
    collaboration with Guattari, 87
    crystal, 13
    molecularization, 118, 170
    plane of immanence, 165
    schizophrenia, 21
    singularization, 16
    smooth space, 50
Dickens, Charles, *Our Mutual Friend*, 219
differenciation, differentiation
    actual and virtual, 70–2
    cinema, 204
    conscious and unconscious, 128
    de-differenciation, 220
    given and given as given, 69
    Leibniz, 135–6
    perception, 135, 137, 148
    quality and quantity, 76, 82–3
    terminological pairs, 66–7
diffraction
    atomic waves, 171
    faculties, 59–60
    light, 8, 34
diffuse
    aionic glow, 118
    ecology of psychic fields, 6
    electric tensions, 3
    light, 173, 176, 192
    light of philosophy, 8
    luminous perception, 71
    perception, 201
    sunlight, 33
    virtual, the, 218
digital
    affection, light, 180
    analog, 67, 108–9, 111, 128
    blackboxing, 4
    cinema, 193
    code, 108, 191
    continuity, 135
    Dedekind cut, 127
    Leibniz, 137
    unconscious, 140
    see also analog
Dillard, Annie, *Pilgrim at Tinker Creek*, 131
disparity
    difference of intensity, 68
    lightning, 6
    Lucretius, 36
    ontic, 74
    optical, 176, 198, 201
    singularity, 72
    style, 60
diverse (the), diversity
    clinamen, 37
    difference, 5, 24, 28, 44, 66–8, 70, 76, 134, 136, 180
    differentiation and differenciation, 71
    events, 100
    ideas, 219
    joy, 38, 42
    Kant's a priori, 110
    Leibniz, 152
    light, 8, 34, 205
    modes, 83
    multiplicity, 30
    non opposita sed diversa, 84
    philosophy, 78, 87–8
    recollection, 210
    variety, 36
    world, 40
dramatization
    intensity, 74
    time of, 124
    see also counter-actualization
Duns Scotus, 20
durée
    Aion, 73
    cinema, 201–3
    temps, 179
    see also temps

ecology, ecologies, ecological
    cinema, 204
    contemporary, 90
    darkness and light, 194
    Deleuzian philosophy, 52
    elemental, 59
    ethics, 87
    global and local, 70–1
    living, the, 10
    Lucretius, 36
    mental milieu, 6
    mimicry, 125
    non-human, 78

of thought, 88
pigment, 108
site- and time specific, 85
Spinoza, 84, 86
eigenform, 173, 197
eigenfrequency, 173, 220
eigenhood, 173
eigenphilosophy, x, 58
eigenpulse, 117
eigenspace, 64
eigenstate, 31
eigentheory, x, 58
eigenvalue, 23
Einstein, Albert
intuition, 6
theory of light, 171
theory of relativity, 44
elective affinity
Deleuze and Foucault, 167
Deleuze and Serres, 31
see also sympathy
elements
Aristotle, æther, 172
Deleuze's books, 90
light as, 176
luminist painting, 176
Lucretius, 33–4, 36
emanation, emanate
cause and effect, 83
divine, 8
light, 34, 54, 83–4, 147, 60
simulacra, 39, 124–5
thought, 10
Emerson, Ralph Waldo, 14–15
Enlightenment
Badiou, 190
light, 12, 147, 205
Epicurus, Epicureans
divination, 3
Lucretius, 41
Marx, Karl, 42
simulacra, 124
Ernst, Max, *frottage*, 112
ethology
Spinoza, 84
thought, 87
evolution
Bergson, 202, 47
co-evolution, 86
genetic couplings, 76
Hume, 57
informal diagram, 109
processes of, 61
expressionism
abstract, 109, 189
colour, 190
immanent logic, 84
luminist, 195
patination of light, 194
projective logic, 83

representation and production, 162, 188
Spinoza, 81, 83
vital, 65
false, the
affirmation of, 123
fiction, 56, 75
life, philosophy, 124
movement, 201
myths, 40
philosophy, 36
power of, 39, 97, 100, 146, 148, 211
truth, 53–4, 148
virtual, the, 104, 191
Fassbinder, Rainer Werner, Douglas Sirk, 198
Faulkner, William
Bacon, 193
Foucault, 195
luminist, 187
Fichte, Johann Gottlieb, 217
Fontana, Luigi, *Attese*, 183
Foucault, Michel
Faulkner, 195
incorporeal materialism, 98
informal diagram, 109
light, 187
repressive societies, 91
topology, 167, 187
transcendental empiricism, 93
fluidity
camera, 203
Descartes, 32, 138
ontological, 31
fractal space
chiaroscuro, 147
continuity, 138
plane of immanence, 166
surface and depth, 124
frottage, history, 112–13; see also Ernst, Max

Gallo, Vincent, *The Brown Bunny*, 211
germ, germinal
Anti-Oedipus and *A Thousand Plateaus*, 87
crystal, 12, 23–5, 27, 30, 51
Deleuze's philosophy, 38, 42, 81
informal diagram, Bacon, 107
glow
Aion, 117–19, 124, 147
celluloid, 193
cinema, 123
virtual, 210
white light, 218
see also strobe
Goethe, Johann Wolfgang von
Elective Affinities, 15
light, 175
Gogh, Vincent van, 192
Gombrowicz, Witold
Pornografia, 15
The Possessed, 141

grace
    clear and obscure perceptions, 139
    inherent, philosophy, Kleist, 18–19
    Lawrence, D. H., 184
    Venus, 29–30
Griffith, D. W., *The Birth of a Nation*, 203
Guattari, Félix
    chaos, 164
    consistencies and consistency, 17, 65
    crystallization, 13
    philosophy, 87–8
    projective topology, 157
    Schizoanalytic Cartographies, 92

habit
    Deleuzian thought, 58
    history, 102, 111
    Hume, 50–3, 55–7
    individuation, 77
    intensity, 66
    Lawrence, D. H., 183
    Lucretius, 49
    self-organization, 152
    spatial orientation, 28
    thought, 11, 153
    time, 116
    unconscious and conscious, 59–65
habitat
    habit, 65
    inhabitants, 76, 146
    light, 172, 177
haecceity, haecceities
    A life, 219
    actual history, 111
    informal diagram, 105
    intensive, 131
    philosophy, 20
    plane of immanence, 165
Halwachs, Pierre, 182
Hawthorne, Nathaniel, girls and grace, 19
Haynes, Todd, melodrama and light, 196
Hegel, Georg Wilhelm Friedrich, Hegelian
    anonymous consciousness, 218
    arbitrariness of language, 9
    Deleuze, 88
    immanence of the notion, 10
    Nietzsche, 123
    sublation, 6
    synthesis, 62–3
Heider, Fritz, light, 172–4, 197–8
Heisenberg, Werner, complementarity, 171–2
Helmholtz, Hermann von, æther, 149
Herzog, Werner, *Heart of Glass*, crystal, 13, 211
heterogeneity
    actual and virtual, 166
    control societies, 92
    disparity, 6
    Leibniz, 142
    Lucretius, 30, 36

multiplicity, 43
Spinoza, 79
time, 117
Hitchcock, Alfred, vertigo of life and philosophy, 69
Huston, John, 198

idealism
    affection and affect, 179
    bilateral space, 165
    Kleist, Heinrich von, 18
    Lawrence, D. H., 184
    materialism, 10–11, 19, 32, 144, 158
    negativity of, 66
image
    action-image, 199, 206–8
    affect image, 207–8
    affection and affect, 180
    affection-image, 199
    Bergson, 199
    camera obscura, 146–7
    celluloid, 194
    cinema, 39, 126–7, 143, 199–200, 203, 205–9
    crystal, 13
    crystal-image, 14, 45, 213–14
    Deleuzian philosophy, 1
    expressive, 193
    frottage, 112
    Hume, 55–7
    imagination, 200
    impulse-image, 207–9
    Leibniz, 139
    light, 178, 187, 205
    lightning, 3, 5–6, 59
    matters-of-fact, 93
    memory, 116
    naturalism, 208
    optical stimulation, 11
    perception, 75, 140–1
    perception-image, 199, 206–8
    recollection-image, 210–11
    simulacra, 40–1
    Spinoza, 87
    thought, 14, 81
    virtual and actual, 12, 123, 157, 213
    see also movement-image; time-image
imagination
    cinema, 202, 213
    Hume, 54–6
    integration, 135
    optical irritation, 200
    projective geometry, 153
    Proust, 97
    spontaneous, 115
    time-image, 39
imperceptibility
    Deleuzian virtues, 125
    history, 111
    intensity, 74
    plane of consistency, 141

indeterminacy, 38
individuation
    actual and virtual, 14
    cinema, 209, 211
    crystal, 13–14, 27, 43
    death, suicide, 220
    Deleuze's philosophy, 50
    Difference and Repetition, 59
    event, 13, 100
    infinity, 38
    intensity, 66–7, 70–3, 75, 77
    phases of, 94
    plane of, 166
    pre-individual singularities, 65
    primary habits, 61
    resonance, 62
    Simondon, 12, 22–6, 46, 75–7, 134
    singularization, crystallization, 16, 141, 219
    Spinoza, 78, 82–4
    thought, 9
    topology of, 158, 160
infinity
    affect, 181
    Bergson, 201–2
    cuts, Dedekind cut, 73, 127
    folds, 32, 137–8
    formally distinct, ontologically one, 80
    fractality, 164
    Hegel, 218
    infinitesimal, 133–4
    Lucretius' multiplicity, 38
    luminous nuances, 197
    naturalist philosophy, 41
    negativity, 40
    parts, 185
    philosophy, science and art, 94–5
    plane of immanence, 90, 217
    plateaus, 125, 140
    real projective plane, 154–6, 215
    reduction of, 70
    Spinoza, 78, 81–2, 84
    time, 119, 123
    virtual and actual, 89, 130, 143, 146–7, 165, 179, 219
    worlds, 139
    see also point-at-infinity
informal diagram
    Bacon, 188–9, 192–3
    definition, 105–9, 109
    frottage, 112
    history, 105
integration
    actual and virtual history, 105
    conscious, 99
    differenciation, 71–2
    informal diagram, 109
    Leibniz, 127, 135, 137–41, 143, 146–8
    science, 95
    time, 117, 122

intelligent materialism, 11, 63
intelligent matter, 151
intuition
    Bergson, cinema, 202
    lightning, 6
    Peirce, C. S., 7, 120

James, Henry, realism and naturalism, 208
James, William
    habit, 64
    pragmatism, 51
Jarman, Derek, *Blue*, 196
Jarmusch, Jim, *The Limits of Control*, 196, 211
jouissance
    birth of the world, 38
    intuition, 6
    thought, 58

Klein, Felix, real projective plane, 154–6, 161
Kleist, Heinrich von
    'On the Marionette Theatre', 18–19
    D. H. Lawrence, 184
koan
    difference and diversity, 5
    lightning, 4
    point-at-infinity, 179

Lacan, Jacques, Lacanian
    Badiou, 99, 190
    crystal, 13
    Guattari, 87
    semiotics, 94
    style, 97
    syntheses of time, 116
    thought of, 58
    topology, real-projective-plane, 156–60, 167
    unconscious, 61, 89, 128
Lawrence, D. H.
    crystallization, 13
    Spinoza, 178, 183–4, 186
    spirit of place, 85
Leonardo da Vinci, *frottage*, 112
light of Thought, 8
lightning
    clinamen, 31–6
    concept, 3–19, 35, 59, 214
    dark precursor, 61, 75–6
    Leibniz, 145
    Nietzsche, 42
line-at-infinity, real projective plane, 154
local colour, and local light, 176–7
Lucretius, 3, 29–43, 49–51, 53, 55, 59, 66–9, 71, 74, 78–9, 87, 112, 123, 124, 137–8, 142, 149, 161, 167, 170, 173, 176, 186, 214
lumen naturale, il lume naturale, naturae lumen
    extensive philosophy, 86
    history of, 8
    immanent light, 84
    Kant's faculties, 13
    Leibniz, 136, 145–6

Lucretius, 34
metaphysics, 15
Peirce, C. S., 7
  propria, 81
luminism
  cinema, 196, 199
  Delaunay, 187
  Deleuze, 1–2, 12, 33, 54, 173
  Desargue, 84
  Lucretius, 59
  painting, 176–8, 188, 191
Lynch, David, light, 196

Margulis, Lynn
  Descartes, 12
  integration, 143
  Schrödinger, 27
  solar energy, 182
Mars, Venus, 35–6
Marvell, Andrew, 'The Definition of Love', 153
Marx, Karl, Marxism
  cinema, 199
  consciousness and life, 20
  Epicure, 42
Matheson, Richard
  Deleuze on, 132
  The Shrinking Man, 126
media studies
  Heider, 172, 174
  light, 197, 200
medium, media
  actual and virtual, 96–8, 112, 118, 125, 197
  æther, 148, 172
  anonymous, 144, 184
  becoming-medium, 130
  biophysical, 10
  cinema, 209, 211
  colour, 192
  crystal, 12, 14, 26
  gelatin, celluloid, 194–5, 198
  history, 111
  language, 193
  light, 35, 173–7, 196–8, 218
  light and sound, 187
  luminous, 149
  memory, 98
  modes, 79
  molecular, 61
  obscure, unconscious, 140
  painting, 188
  perception, 137, 139
  photonic plane, 170
  pigment, 195
  plane of immanence, 90, 130
  time, 120
melodrama
  light, 196
  realism, 208
metastability, metastable, Simondon, 23–4
Mettrie, Offray de la, 65

Möbius, August Ferdinand, Möbius strip, 155–6, 161
monism
  Bryant, 74
  dualism, 43
  multiplicity, 24
  schizophrenia, 50, 215, 220
  Spinoza, 82
  vitalist, 21
morphogenetic, 33, 57, 76
Morrison, Bill, *Light is Calling*, 194
movement-image
  actual, 43
  affection, 179
  assemblage, 200, 204
  camera, 203
  crystal image, 45
  medium, 211
  montage, 199
  perception-image, 207
  photonic plane, 206
  time-image, 213
  truth, 39
  see also time-image
Musil, Robert, *The Man Without Qualities*, 31, 173

$n-1$
  diversity, 30
  passive synthesis, 63
  plane of immanence, 163
  probe-heads, 104
  survey (*survol*), 151
  see also $n+1$
$n+1$
  overview, 151
  plane of transcendence, 63, 83, 163
  see also $n-1$
Necker cube, 82
Nelson, Ted, *Computer Lib*, 212
Newton, Isaac
  fluxions, 142
  light, 171, 175
noise, 31, 61, 97, 125, 129
  analog, 109
  Leibniz, 148
  optical and chemical, 194
  white and pink, 37, 219
Norris, Frank, *McTeague*, 209
noumenon
  language, 77
  phenomenon, 9, 61, 70
  see also phenomenon

orientation, crystals, 23, 25, 28, 65

parallelism
  Deleuze and Peirce, 8
  Lucretius, 39
  Schrödinger, 178
  Spinoza, 18, 78–81, 84, 181

Peirce, Charles Sanders
  abduction and natural light, 7–8, 34
  discontinuity, 138
  habit, 51–2, 62
  informal diagram, 107–8
  intuition, 120
  pre-established harmony, 57
perceptual judgement, Peirce, C. S., 7–8, 62
phase-space, mathematics, 23, 140
phenomenon
  colour, 178
  dark precursor, 75
  difference, 9
  interval, 207
  life, 182
  light, 177
  lightning, 5, 8–9
  Lucretius, 3
  noumenon, 62, 70
  optical, 175
  see also noumenon
photon, photonic
  cinema, 194, 196–7, 199–201
  complementarity, 2, 179, 185, 214
  definition, 170–3
  imagination, 135
  intensity, 203
  medium, 170
  milieu, 204
  monad, 134, 148, 150
  movement-image, 206
  multiplicity, 22, 143, 196, 203–6, 210
  optical field, 205
  time-image, 211
  wave, 218
photonic plane of immanence
  cinema, 196, 200–1, 203–7, 209–10
  complementarity, 2, 215
  luminosity, 170, 172, 181, 183
  multiplicity, 199
  transcendental, 218
  virtual, 219
pigment
  actual, painting, 192–5
  colour, 188–90
  frottage, 112
  informal diagram, 106–8
  luminism, 176–7
  medium, 174, 198
Plato, Platonic
  Darwin, 52
  essences and events, 101
  ideas and multiplicities, 103
  light, 34
  Lucretius, *simulacra*, 36
point-at-infinity (line-at-infinity)
  complementarity, 134
  crystal, 180
  crystal image, 213–15
  Kleist, 19
  line-at-infinity, 154
  perception, 141
  philosophy at, 101, 214
  projective topology, 15–17, 127, 133, 147–8, 153
  schizophrenia and monism, 21, 24, 220
  thought, 217
  see also infinity
pointillism, philosophical, 31
polarization, crystal, 23–4
positivity
  Deleuzian philosophy, 2, 30, 35, 220
  Lucretius, 29, 38
  naturalism, 41
  Nietzsche, 123
  Spinoza, 86
potentiality
  actual and virtual, 28, 39
  dark precursors, 6
  history, 109
  individuation, 16
  lighting, 3
  plane of consistency, 166
  plane of immanence, 172, 193
  Simondon, 24–5
  surplus of, 107
probe-head, history, 104
projective plane, real projective plane
  actual and virtual, 214
  affect and affection, 179
  cinema, 212–13
  frottage, 112
  infinity, 164
  Kleist, 19
  light, 170
  plane of immanence, 150
  Spinoza, 80
  topology, 2, 152–62, 165–7, 215
Proust, Marcel
  poetics, 55, 74, 95–8
  virtual and actual, 46
psychoanalysis
  A Thousand Plateaus, 88
  Anti-Oedipus, 89
  Badiou, 190
  capitalism, 35
  cinema, 200
  Deleuzian unconscious, 128
  Difference and Repetition, 59
  Guattari, 87
  literature, 92
  Marxism, 199
  topology, 156–9
Pynchon, Thomas, 196

quantum physics, Lucretius, 31, 74
quasi-cause
  event, 121–2, 153
  history, 110–13
  projective topology, 162

radiation
  light, 177, 182
  plane of immanence, 171–2
  science-fiction, 126
reciprocal presupposition
  actual and virtual, 32, 55, 80–1, 143, 152, 159, 213
  body and mind, 178
  chiasm, 18
  continuity and discontinuity, 137
  event and thing, 161
  given and given as given, 73
  nature and culture, 53
  tête-bêche, 212
refraction
  light, 8, 14, 24, 59, 84
  mathematics into aesthetics, 134
refrain (nomos)
  conceptual, 12
  crystal, 14–15
Reichle, Franz, *Monte Grande, What is Life?*, 217
res
  corpora, 37
  elements, 36
  see also atom; *corpora*
resonance
  body and mind, 81–2
  cinema, 204, 209
  cinema and philosophy, 195
  cinema and world, 200
  concepts, 58
  elective affinity, 15
  false, the, 148
  habit, 57, 61–3
  history, 102
  individuation, 25, 51, 76, 91, 118
  Leibniz, 146
  phenomenon and noumenon, 9
  plane of immanence, 220
  Proust, 95–8
  science, art and philosophy, 94, 134
  virtual and actual, 152
Riemann, Bernhard, multiplicity, 103

Saussure, Ferdinand de
  semiotics, 93
  topology of the sign, 158, 160
schizoanalytic
  becomings, 129
  Guattari, 92
Schrödinger, Erwin
  crystals, 27
  light, 177–9
sensory-motor arc
  brain, 207
  cinema, 44–5, 213–14
  Cinema 1, 199, 206, 208, 210
  see also cone of memory
sentience, 87, 100

Serres, Michel, 30–1, 33–4, 50, 103, 117, 119, 136, 139–41, 149, 152
Simondon, Gilbert, 12, 22–6, 28–9, 36, 38, 43, 46, 50–1, 53–4, 66–8, 71–2, 75–6, 83, 134, 160
simulacrum
  clinamen, 39
  frottage, 112
  ideas, 161
  Lawrence, D. H., 184
  Lucretius, 29–30, 40–1
Sirk, Douglas
  Fassbinder on, 198
  melodrama and light, 196
smooth and striated space
  Foucault, 73
  fractality, 164
  haecceity, 165
Soulages, Pierre, *Outrenoir*, 190
space of thought, topology of
  complementarity, 17, 152
  Hume, 55
  real projective plane, 2, 156–8, 167, 170
spatium
  continuity, 160
  topology, 74–6, 153
Spinoza, Baruch de, 1, 18, 38, 41, 53, 78–92, 142, 151, 162, 167, 170, 177–86, 212, 220
Stoics
  cause and effect, 41, 83, 110, 117, 157
  Lacan, 94
  Lucretius, 79
  Surface and depth, 42, 53
  Time, 119
  Topology, 162
strobe
  Chronos, 117–19, 147
  cinema, 123, 210
  glow, 124
  time, 115
Stroheim, Erich von, *Greed*, 209
survey [*survol*]
  informal diagram, 109
  Lucretius, 30
  monad, 143
  multiplicity, 103
  probe heads, 104
  Spinoza, 83
sympathy
  natural, 7
  symbiosis, 15
  see also elective affinity

temps
  complementarity, 179, 209
  discrete, 73, 201–3
  see also durée
tête-bêche, *Cinema 1* and *Cinema 2*, 212–13
thought, figure of
  Baroque, Leibniz, 134, 137, 139, 146, 149

cinema, 11
Deleuze, 14, 32, 52, 58, 71, 91, 214
Peirce, 8
Spinoza, 81, 90
Thoreau, Henri David, *Walden*, 14
time-image
   affect, 179
   Cinema 2, 43
   crystal image, 45
   medium, 211
   memory, 210
   movement-image, 39, 213
   plane of light, 203
   see also movement-image
torsion
   world, 152, 155
   world and soul, 165
transcendental empiricism
   cinema, 12
   complementarity, 179
   Deleuze, 69, 91, 93–4, 152, 218
   history, 111
   Hume, 52, 54, 58
   Lucretius, 34
   real projective plane, 159
trompe l'œil, Spinoza, 146

ultra white, pigment, 195–6

Varela, Francisco
   light, 178
   transcendental field, 217–18
Venus
   light, 84, 201
   Lucretius, 29–30, 33–6, 38
vertigo
   Badiou, 100
   immanence, 78
   intensity, 69–70
   philosophy, 8–9, 84, 215
   rationality, 86
vitalism, vitalist
   Deleuze, 17, 28, 73
   monism, 21
   pantheism of mothers, 36

Walken, Christopher, *Weapon of Choice*, 201
wave-function, ontology, 31
Welles, Orson, 12, 203
Whitehead, Alfred North, idealism, 32

Zola, Émile, naturalism, 208

EU representative:
Easy Access System Europe
Mustamäe tee 50, 10621 Tallinn, Estonia
Gpsr.requests@easproject.com